EDDY ARNOLD

EDDY ARNOLD

PIONEER OF THE
NASHVILLE SOUND

Michael Streissguth

Schirmer Books
An Imprint of Simon & Schuster Macmillan
New York

Prentice Hall International
London • Mexico City • New Delhi • Singapore • Sydney • Toronto

Copyright © 1997 by Michael Streissguth

Schirmer Books
An Imprint of Simon & Schuster Macmillan
1633 Broadway
New York, New York 10019

Library of Congress Catalog Number: 97-3009

Printed in the United States of America

Printing number
1   2   3   4   5   6   7   8   9   10

Library of Congress Cataloging-in-Publication Data

Streissguth, Michael.
    Eddy Arnold : pioneer of the Nashville sound / Michael Streissguth.
      p.   cm.
    Includes bibliographical references, discography, and index.
    ISBN 0-02-864719-X (alk. paper)
    1. Arnold, Eddy.   I. Title.
ML420.A77S77   1997
                                           97–3009
                                             CIP
                                           MN

This paper meets the requirements ANSI/NISO Z39.48-1992 (Permanence of Paper).

PREFACE

Like most fascinations people have with musicians, my interest in Eddy Arnold springs from my youth. Every day after school in my ninth-grade year at Damascus High School, I plopped down on the couch with a snack and the day's sports section and flipped on WXTR radio—a station from southern Maryland that reached my home in the distant suburbs of Washington, D.C. I listened because the station featured half of an Elvis album each afternoon. I loved Elvis.

For a few weeks, after Elvis and during the time I should have started my homework, the station placed Eddy Arnold's "Happy Everything" in heavy rotation. Eddy hooked me. His baritone, which seemed more agile perhaps than it should have been, breezed through the joyous lyrics, and for a while I forgot Elvis. But this was 1981, and Eddy had reached the end of his long line of hits. I can't recall hearing Eddy again on the radio after that spate of "Happy Everything" plays. Elvis regained my attention.

One day a few years later, while in college, I found myself killing time yet again—this time I was going through a shelf of "cut-out" records in Gaithersburg, Maryland. A solemn, carved face dotted with two blue eyes stopped me. Eddy Arnold. Could this album have "Happy Everything" on it? The song lingered in my memory. I turned the jacket over, and my wish came true. For $2.99, I went home with Eddy and "Happy Everything" under my arm. As the years passed, my album spun frequently, and as I read more about music, I realized just how important Eddy Arnold had been to popular music in the twentieth century. Elvis had recorded his stuff for goodness' sake, and he seemed to be on every country singer's list of influences.

This book can be tied directly to "Happy Everything." The voice that caught my ear and held it for many years put me on a journey to find out more about the work of Eddy Arnold. After all, his career had to be remarkable if at the age of sixty-two he had grabbed the attention of a fifteen-year-old. I wondered what preceded "Happy Everything." After college and throughout my stints in television and public relations, I always figured I would end up writing about Eddy Arnold.

Writing is learning, and I marveled at the degree of popularity Eddy Arnold had gained in the late 1940s and then again in the 1960s when he caught fire with a middle-of-the-road approach to music. I observed a man who, over the years, had set goals for himself and achieved them through a

v

potent mixture of focus, hard work, patience, and flexibility. And he had help. Before Elvis, Colonel Tom Parker had managed Eddy. And RCA producer Steve Sholes (again, before Elvis) had produced hit after hit with Eddy Arnold. Chet Atkins, the great guitarist, pushed Eddy along, too.

With the famous names also came a team of people from the background. Names like Charles Grean, Speedy McNatt, and Bill Westbrooks appeared in my research to claim a role in Eddy Arnold's career. Here, I decided, was a man who traveled roads pocked with challenges, but lined with interesting friends who helped him along. Certainly, Eddy Arnold's ideas about his career path landed him in ill-advised positions occasionally, but more often his ideas took him to circles that helped him grow.

Eddy Arnold likes to say that he is a simple man. He is. But this simple man built one of the most brilliant careers in twentieth-century popular music. In the pages of this book I hope to guide you along the route he followed to that stature.

Michael Streissguth
Columbia, Maryland
1997

ACKNOWLEDGMENTS

Biography is, at best, a flawed attempt to define the life and work of an individual. This biography reached a lesser degree of imperfection only with the assistance of people. I am indebted to many.

Ahead of all help, of course, was Eddy Arnold, who spent five days patiently reviewing his life with me. His candor, sharp memory, and willingness to engage my sometimes uncomfortable questions make this a better book. My special thanks are also due to Eddy's wife, Sally Arnold, daughter Jo Ann Pollard, manager Jerry Purcell, and assistant Roberta Edging.

A partial measure of a man, someone once said, is the people with whom he associates. Colleagues and friends of Eddy, some of whom go back to his Chester County childhood, displayed a graciousness to me befitting Eddy Arnold. Thanks to: Trigger Alpert, Chet Atkins, Odessia Austin, Brenton Banks, Gordon Bossin, Harold Bradley, Owen Bradley, Tauso Branch, Jack Burgess, Jerry Carrigan, Eva Clifford, Cy Coben, Carolina Cotton, Chick Crumpacker, Joe Csida, Bob Davie, Danny Davis, Don DeLacy, Dolly Denny, J. W. Denny, Danny Dill, Ann Dodelin, Ray Edenton, Bob Ferguson, Jim Foglesong, Joe Gallante, Marty Gold, Lou Grasmick, Charles Grean, George Hamilton IV, Johnny Hicks, Tommy Ivo, Betty Johnson, Moselle and Robert Jones, Anita Kerr, Millie Kirkham, Sheldon Kurland, Exie Latham, John Loudermilk, Jim Malloy, Bob McCluskey, Brad McCuen, Don McNatt, Lynn McNatt, Melton McNatt, Jeff Miller, Wayne Moss, Cam Mullins, Jamie Nash, Louis Nunley, Al Pachucki, Tom Pick, William Pursell, Tandy Rice, Hargus "Pig" Robbins, Chuck Seitz, Velma Williams Smith, Redd Stewart, Gordon Stoker, Henry Strzelecki, Rollin Sullivan, Gabe Tucker, Pete Wade, Bill Walker, Irving Waugh, David Weir, Tresaw Weir, Roy Wiggins, and Chuck Wright.

And there are more to thank—at Bertelsmann Music Group in New York, Dan Beeferman, Claudia Depkin, Mike Fitzell, Glenn Korman, and Paul Williams; at the Country Music Foundation, Kent Henderson, John Rumble, and Ronnie Pugh; at Polygram Records, Fernando Dos Santos; at the Broadcast Pioneers Library, Mike Mashon. Also: Earl Aldrich, Brian Clifford, Don Comer, Stephen F. Davis of *The Devil's Box*, Steve Hillse, James Hoppers, Beverly Jarrett, Kenneth Johnson, Don Mackin, Andy Marshall, Al Moss, Patsy Tervooran, and Dean B. Upson.

Special thanks to Richard Carlin at Schirmer Books, who believed in the potential of this project, and Steve Andreassi of the IUP Lodge and Convocation Center in Hoboken, New Jersey. And my sincerest appreciation to Leslie Bailey Streissguth, my wife, who indulged me in this project and steered me in better directions.

PROLOGUE

Eddy Arnold stepped off a passenger airliner in New York City during the summer of 1964. The metropolis was old territory to Arnold. The singer who had dwarfed any country performer to ever bend a note could remember passing through the city on a World War II tour of military bases; he had recorded there as far back as the mid-1940s, working with legendary producer Steve Sholes. As recently as ten years before, Arnold had tapped into the best New York City had to offer—top-notch management, the best musicians, popular television shows—hoping that it would mold his country fortunes into glistening popular fame. Springboarding from America's excitement over his 1948 hits "Bouquet of Roses" and "Anytime," he jumped into the nation's entertainment establishment, acting in Hollywood films, starring on television and radio, and employing sharp Northeast songwriters to compose material to suit his new popular image. But on that humid, summer day in 1964 that all seemed a long time ago.

By 1964, Eddy Arnold's fountain of hits had dried, and history's top-selling country artist slumped into the deepest valley of his career. Fifteen years ago, it seemed the country chart's number-one spot belonged to Arnold, but many years had passed since he last reached the top. Sure, his records sold in adequate numbers, but not in the millions as they had in the late 1940s and early 1950s. Even RCA Victor, his longtime record label, considered dropping him.

Arnold had hoped to be a great singer of songs, not just a great country singer. Professional New York management and the city's sophisticated producers and arrangers could help write his ticket, he thought. But his New York efforts never gelled, and he spent most of the late 1950s and early 1960s cutting country music in Nashville and struggling to keep his name current with a public that was forgetting Eddy Arnold. In 1964, nudged by an enterprising new manager, he had come again to New York, seeking the success the city had thus far denied him.

At RCA Victor's 24th Street headquarters, young producer Jim Foglesong and veteran arranger Marty Gold awaited him. With Eddy, the men sketched plans for an album of country hits recorded with light orchestral arrangements. Eddy would sing "Your Cheatin' Heart" and other country classics accompanied by seven vocalists, three violas, three cellos, and twelve violins: not exactly a surefire pop winner in the summer of the

British Invasion, but a strong possibility in the market of middle-aged Americans who might not know a mop-topped Beatle from a small German car.

With Foglesong at the helm, Gold's arrangements meshed with Eddy's vocals to create an easy-listening sound that appealed to older pop fans who rejected rock and roll and found solace in singers like Andy Williams and Frank Sinatra. The resulting album, *Pop Hits from the Country Side,* sold moderately but, more importantly, marked the first ripple of Eddy Arnold's splash in the 1960s pop market. The marriage of Arnold's relaxed country vocalizing with symphonic instruments and grand, formal arrangements would carry him to audiences in the 1960s that he had tried for years to reach. He would soon score smash pop hits with songs like "Make the World Go Away" and "Somebody Like Me," and earn a regular place in front of the nation's prime-time television audiences.

—————— • ——————

Before the New York session that unveiled *Pop Hits from the Country Side,* producer Jim Foglesong knew little about Arnold. Many around the RCA executive offices and studios, of course, knew about the star's legendary past and worried that he had sagged too low. "That certainly happens with artists who have been with the label for a long time," explained Foglesong. "Nobody can stay on the top of the charts forever, and anyone who's around for a long time will have some peaks and valleys. He was in the valley."

And while Foglesong wondered if Eddy's career could be revived, he worried that the Big Apple would swallow Eddy. "I'd been on dates when people came in from Nashville or similar areas—rural backgrounds—and they were just totally intimidated by the whole New York scene," recalled Foglesong. "It was very fast moving. Even the accents [frightened them]. They were scared to death." Foglesong was himself a respectful West Virginia boy, and knew how intimidating New York musicians and recording executives could be. How would Arnold, the very model of a modern Southern gentleman, react to Walter Fleischer, Foglesong's loud pianist who spoke in fluent New York-ese, Foglesong fretted. "Whadda ya meeen?" Fleischer spat when Eddy tried to explain what he wanted. "I mean this," replied Eddy with a chuckle. To the anxious producer's relief, Arnold took Fleischer's gruff attitude in stride.

Foglesong began to get the picture; Arnold breezed through New York. The man known in a different day as the "Tennessee Plowboy" fell right in step with the New York musicians and relaxed in the city's eateries and night spots. Eddy clicked in an environment that Foglesong assumed to be wholly foreign to a Nashville boy. But, if Foglesong had thought to learn more about Arnold's history before the session, he would have had to dig every bit as fervently in New York as in Nashville. And although Foglesong's search would take him through New York and Nashville and to such unlikely places as France Field in Panama and a sparse, second-story room on a St. Louis corner, it would begin in a small western Tennessee farming community.

1

ennessee's hills lose their blue, bulbous splendor as they roll west from the midstate Cumberland Plateau to the Mississippi River. Their decline marks the final chapter in the east-to-west descent of the terrain that tumbles from sharp, rugged ridges near North Carolina across the Tennessee River Valley and Appalachians to the lowlands of West Tennessee. After a strenuous journey through the state's eastern and middle highlands, a traveler finds haven in the gentler land of the west.

Prehistoric peoples, known in retrospect as the Early Mississippian Indians, found West Tennessee inviting, settling there around 1000 A.D. and raising corn, beans, potatoes, squash, and pumpkins from land enriched after centuries beneath the sea. The Mississippians planted their human roots throughout the wild land and, near present-day Henderson, Tennessee, erected a capital city that they protected with sprawling fortifications. Thousands of Indians dwelt within the walled city, and among their homes, they built clusters of mysterious temple mounds that rose from the earth and incited the imaginations of future inhabitants.

The precise chronology and movements of the Mississippians elude historians, but these native peoples remained in West Tennessee and birthed the Chickasaw Indians, who found the area as welcoming as their forebears. Centered primarily in today's northern Mississippi, the Chickasaw tribe claimed West Tennessee as hunting grounds, and every autumn fanned out through the wilderness searching for deer, bears, and turkeys. "Steeped in nature," as one historian described the Chickasaws, they dried and stored their game for winter use, made clothing, shoes, and blankets with animal skin, and fashioned weapons and fishing nets with animal bone and sinew. Chickasaw women even used deer brains to tan and soften animal skins. Like their native predecessors, the Chickasaws exploited the land for crops and roamed the countryside plucking grapes, plums, persimmons, strawberries, and other indigenous fruits.

The image of Chickasaws collecting fruit and living so close to nature suggests a peaceful existence, but in reality they were a warring people. They jealously guarded their land and raided nearby tribal nations for slaves

1

and other plunder. Spanish booty hunters led by Hernando de Soto battled these people when they crossed the Mississippi River into Chickasaw territory during the 1500s. As the Atlantic Coast boomed in subsequent centuries, other Europeans passed warily, and not always unscathed, through the region. The Chickasaw ferocity, however, ultimately proved little match to the growing numbers of white colonists from Europe, and by the 1700s, the Indians' hold on West Tennessee slipped.

Of course, before the state of Tennessee's entry into the Union, "West Tennessee" never existed in name. During America's infancy, North Carolina claimed "West Tennessee" as a western district; would-be settlers staked out land there but, fearing the Chickasaws, hesitated to move there. White pioneers and their black slaves could count on little protection there until 1790, when North Carolina ceded its claim to the western territory to the U.S. government. Six years later Tennessee became the sixteenth state. Tennessee's statehood sparked vigorous efforts on the part of the federal government to rid West Tennessee of the Chickasaws and consolidate control of the land. President Thomas Jefferson, especially, coveted the Chickasaw territory and devised plans to gain control of it. "The method by which we may advance towards our object," he proclaimed in 1802, "will be to establish among them a factory or factories for furnishing them with all necessaries and comforts they may wish . . . and encouraging these, and especially their leading men, to run in debt beyond their individual means of paying; and, whenever in that situation, they will always cede lands to rid themselves of debt." Jefferson's plan was apparently never carried out, and the territory remained in Indian hands.

In 1818, the fabled General Andrew Jackson and former Kentucky governor Isaac Shelby finally negotiated the purchase of West Tennessee from the Chickasaws. The West Tennessee door swung open, and hopeful Americans swarmed in from the Carolinas, Virginia, and middle Tennessee. Every year, by the 1820s, observers along the western way out of North Carolina counted thousands of wagons, carts, and carriages carrying people to the newly opened portion of Tennessee. "During the last four months," wrote a North Carolinian newspaper reporter in 1827, "the flow of emigration through Asheville has surpassed anything of the kind the writer has ever witnessed. It was not uncommon to see eight, ten, or fifteen wagons, and carts passing in a single day . . . wending their way to the more highly favored climes of the West."

The influx of land-hungry whites made it difficult for the Chickasaws to stay, and ultimately they were driven to barren territory more than 500 miles to the west.

— • —

In the following years, optimistic farmers, many of whom owned slaves, aimed to develop West Tennessee. They drained wetlands and cleared large primeval forests thick with hickory, elm, pine, white oak, and gum trees. Cotton dreams preoccupied the farmers, and, on the fertile soil of their new home, they set about supplying the exploding demand for the white, fluffy stuff. In the early years of the 1800s, Southern cotton production had skyrocketed in the wake of Eli Whitney's cotton gin, a device that easily separated the pesky seeds from cotton fiber, fueling the mushrooming textile industry at home and abroad.

Cotton drew legions of people to West Tennessee. In 1820, only two people per square mile occupied the region, but that number swelled to more than thirty by 1860. "The greater part of the mass," wrote historian Samuel Cole Williams in 1930, "were plain folk with little or no pretension of polish. A considerable element of the lowest stratum was illiterate, but few were ignorant. Many who were illiterate were fairly well informed and able to take care of themselves, in dealing or in conversation." The large towns of Memphis and Jackson buzzed with Williams's "mass," a conglomeration of farmers, businessmen, and the ever-arriving newcomers. Smaller towns popped up and bubbled, too.

In 1860, a few families from Henderson County in West Tennessee settled close to a stretch of railroad in nearby Madison County. They hammered together a few homes, established businesses, opened a hotel, and built a small Mobile and Ohio railroad depot. They named their town Dayton, but soon redubbed it Henderson after a nearby county of the same name. Henderson's modest growth, though, halted with the onslaught of America's war between the states.

＊

West Tennessee screamed for secession from the North. When Tennesseans voted on February 9, 1861, on whether to formally discuss following other Southern states fleeing from the Union, middle and eastern Tennessee balked; voters in the cotton-rich, slave-dependent west, however, overwhelmingly supported secession. West Tennesseans were outnumbered by pro-unionists to the east of them but were ultimately vindicated when in April 1861 fighting between Confederate and Union troops flared at Fort Sumter, South Carolina. The outbreak of hostilities turned lukewarm anti-secessionists in populous middle Tennessee into hot-blooded rebels. On June 8, 1861, just four months after rejecting a proposal to discuss secession, Tennessee voted to abandon President Lincoln and the Union.

Early in the Civil War, Union troops occupied Henderson and parked their supplies in the town's railroad depot. On a bluff nearby, the soldiers set up camp and appeared to be planning a long stay. But in an unguarded moment in 1862, a force of Southern cavalrymen led by A. B. Crook swept in, torched the depot, and captured a large share of the Union defense. The Confederates, laden with prisoners, dashed for safety that lay back east over the Tennessee River some two counties away. Union forces bit the heels of the Confederates all the way to the river, but failed to overcome heavy fire they met at the crossing. It's said that the embittered Union commander back in Henderson forced locals to pay for the incinerated supplies before he vacated town. Railroad business, hampered first by the Union occupation of the depot and then Crook's incineration of it, had to be conducted from a boxcar for the rest of the war.

In the end, Crook's small victory in Henderson was as useless as Confederate currency. The North hammered Southern forces, leaving West Tennessee, along with much of the South, short of food and manpower. But despite war-imposed hardship across the region, stuttering development resumed in Henderson after General Robert E. Lee's surrender, and eventually the town flourished to become a center for surrounding farms. Along the railroad tracks, Front Street bustled with farmers who had cotton to sell and corn to mill, and shoppers who had come in from the country to purchase supplies. Schools and churches in and outside the city prospered, and in 1882 Henderson became the seat of Chester County, a new jurisdiction that absorbed parts of various surrounding counties.

Robert M. Arnold, a veteran Confederate fighter whose brother had fought for the North, returned home from war to reap cotton and other crops from the generous land outside Henderson. Born in 1837, he married Tabatha Hendrix, who bore five children: William, Nannie, Molly, Milton, and George.

William, the oldest, grew to be a large man. Towering above many at six feet, three inches, William, or Will as he was known, could rattle a room with his powerful laugh. He wed Mary Etta Lane, a neighbor girl, and established a farm about five miles outside Henderson on land that Mary inherited from her father. The couple had eight children and together carved a prosperous farming life. But Mary Etta met an early death. On April 7, 1905, according to recollections of family, she died of milk leg—a condition associated with childbirth that clots veins in the lower portion of the body and can cause swelling, burning, and, as perhaps in Mary Etta's case, death.

Shortly after Mary Etta's demise, Will chose another bride.

Georgia Wright's family came from Saltillo, a dot along the Tennessee River just north of where 25,000 troops died in the Battle of Shiloh. After the war, the Wrights had cast their lot with the burgeoning town of Henderson. In 1871, Georgia was born there. The child grew to be an attractive, dark-haired woman with a sweet disposition; in 1892, she took the hand of a Henderson man named J. D. Ingle. They had two sons, Robert and David, but, like the tragedy of Will Arnold's wife, Georgia's spouse met death at a young age. With her two children, Georgia moved back to her father's house.

But marriage beckoned Georgia a second time. At the age of thirty-four, she accepted the proposal of a man more than ten years her senior. Will Arnold was forty-six in 1905 when he married Georgia in the New Friendship Baptist Church. Pragmatism, as much as love, likely guided Will to Georgia. Mary Etta's death earlier in the year had left him without a wife to oversee the household while he ran the farm. Georgia too probably saw marriage as a practical course: she found a father for her boys and a home on one of the most envied farms in the area. Georgia happily moved into Will's five-room house. The young ones from the newlyweds' first families would stay on until they were grown, and about two years after their marriage, Georgia and Will began working on their own family. First came Patty in 1908, then W. D. a year later; John Arnold followed in 1912, and a fourth child died after only eighteen months. On May 15, 1918, Richard Edward Arnold arrived. Folks around the Arnolds' farm knew Richard as Ed, but America would call him Eddy.

2

$\mathcal{W}$hen Ed Arnold unleashed his first chorus on May 15, 1918, America's first war with Germany was little more than a year old. Newspapers on that Wednesday in May traced the inch-by-inch advances against the Germans in Hailles, France, where French troops pushed the enemy back toward their homeland in a nighttime shower of bombardments. The press also hailed the tenuous inauguration of airplane mail delivery. Letters on that first day of air mail moved unfettered between New York and Washington, D.C., but a Washington-to-Philadelphia plane made a forced landing in Maryland just minutes after President and Mrs. Woodrow Wilson watched the carrier take to the sky; a car took the mail on to Philly.

Closer to Henderson, state of Tennessee officials announced war-induced sugar rationing, and the United Daughters of the Confederacy prepared to unveil a monument at the nearby Shiloh National Military Park. And for those lucky enough to have a wind-up record player, the Victor Talking Machine Company advertised the latest recording by tenor Giovanni Martinelli: on a ten-inch record selling for only a dollar, the tenor sang "Welcome Love."

The Arnolds had no such automated entertainment. Fate delivered Ed to a family that worked. Nestled in an area pocked with swamps, the Arnold farm had spread since the death of Will Arnold's first wife, and that meant a large workload for the family. In 1908, to add to his more than 100 acres, Will bought thirty-five acres of adjoining land from the Roberts family, and he came into possession of an additional thirty-five acres willed to him and his sister after his father Robert Arnold died in 1909, which also connected to his first wife's original tract. So, with more than 200 acres to his name, Will owned a fair-sized piece of land by community standards. The fertile soil rarely failed him, and several acres of wet bottom land thick with timber—perfect for axing and selling—provided another source of income.

The family boasted the best in farm accouterments: two mules, a two-horse cultivator, a sawmill, and a wheat binder for gathering and bundling grain at harvest. Few Chester County farmers could say they owned a

Little Ed Arnold with his parents on the Chester County farm. (Eddy Arnold collection)

wheat binder and still fewer had a grist mill and cotton gin on their property. Will Arnold ground his own corn, separated his raw cotton, and charged other farmers to use his mill and gin. Not a man to shun diversification of income, Will also operated a kiln on his property and sold bricks to area builders.

When Ed turned two, the Arnolds moved to a larger home. The five-room house that Will and Georgia had occupied when they first married was really a two-room cabin that Will had improved. Using timber from his land, Will built a new home that had a second-story loft and a front porch perfect for lolling about after the evening meal and a long day's work. The new house fronted a spread of land impressive enough to make any man proud. Will could look out back and see five other structures: a hen house, barn, tool shop, corn crib, and the all-important outhouse. On the south side of the farm passed the route to town—Needmore Road—and to the east, Needmore Creek carried water for the steam that drove Will's cotton gin. In the middle of all this lay the prize, the land that rendered cotton and corn. West of the house, fields climbed and fell in gentle waves until they reached the woods to the north. Will Arnold cut a gigantic sight as he criss-crossed this land behind two mules; tall, large, bespectacled, and musta-chioed, Will looked for all the world like the nation's former "Bull Moose" president, Theodore Roosevelt. A man of great vigor and stature, Will suit-ed this productive and ancient land.

Young Ed Arnold sensed the strength of his dad, but he felt warmth also. The two explored the farm together on quiet walks, and often Will hoisted his excited son onto a mule named Tobe so he could ride. "He was the lazi-est mule I ever saw in my life," Eddy explained. "He didn't want to carry his load. When you had two mules hooked to an implement and you said, 'Get up!' he'd let the other mule pull the majority of the load. My father loved that mule; I never did figure out why he loved that mule so much."

Will regaled his blue-eyed boy with stories about earlier times. He devoured history books and passed what he learned on to his family and other local farmers. Georgia and her children often sat through lengthy historical and political debates between Will and his sister Nannie, who taught school for many years. Nannie engaged Will in a way few could, and although the exchanges made little sense to Ed, he listened anyway. "When I got older I realized they were talking about politics," Eddy Arnold recalled. "It's quite obvious that my aunt was a Republican and my father was a Democrat. They'd really get going." After a while, Ed absorbed the Democratic line and innocently volleyed parroted criticisms of Herbert Hoover to Aunt Nannie.

Storytelling reached new heights on the Arnold farm when Georgia's father, Dick Wright, moved into the house. Cataracts riddled Grandfather Wright's eyes, and he did little more than sit on the porch all day, but he welcomed conversation and a chance to tell yarns of his Civil War days. In service to the Confederacy, Grandfather Wright had guarded a wealthy

Mississippian's plantation on a nightly basis—a wearying task in the sleepy eyes of Wright and a comrade. One morning at dawn, they approached the house for breakfast. The men had never asked for breakfast before, and on this morning the owner predictably refused them. Infuriated and fed up, Wright and the partner dragged the planter from his house, whipped him hard, and left him writhing on the ground. They dashed to the kitchen and made their own morning meal, and when their relief arrived, Wright and his friend burped in satisfaction.

Such tales guaranteed plenty of visits from his grandchildren's friends. Ed stayed close to his grandfather, too: "I became his pet, really his pet. He was blind, and I was his eyes. I led him everywhere he went. We had outside plumbing in the rural area, and I led him to the toilet. I led him wherever he went. He was the jolliest man." The young guide also tricked his blind grandfather a time or two: "I'd get out of the back part of the house and go down the road that went up to the main road, and then I'd walk to our house. He'd be sitting on the front porch, and I'd change my voice. (Of course, he was looking for somebody to come in and sit down and talk to him.) I'd say, 'Hello, Mr. Wright.' He'd say, 'Hello, there. Come on in and sit down. Talk to me.' Then I'd go in, and he'd realize that it was me. He'd grab me, put me across his lap, and play spank. I'm sure I entertained him a lot by doing that. I played tricks on him, but he thought the world of me."

The young Ed Arnold had little care in the world. Shielded by his youth from strenuous farmwork, he concentrated on his little chores and play. When summer's heat and humidity descended on West Tennessee, the area boys stripped their clothes and dived into Needmore Creek. No more than two-tenths of a mile down Needmore Road from the Arnolds, the creek bottom cackled with the shrieks of little boys splashing away. They kept one eye on the bridge that spanned the creek, always ready to hide on the banks should a wagon with women aboard pass. Throughout Ed's childhood, he always found time for the creek. The boys there roughhoused, talked, and taught little ones to swim.

When not in Needmore Creek, Ed sometimes wandered up the road to the curious mounds that loomed over land once occupied by the Mississippians but now owned by his Sunday school teacher. Awed by the sight of these arbitrary eruptions in otherwise flat land and unaware of their historical significance, Ed mingled with the remnants of an ancient culture, playing and resting on religious constructions where the Mississippian Indians once worshiped. Closer to home, the farm kids competed in the wetlands to see whose fists could knock the most bark off small trees and—in less rambunctious moments—built projects in the Arnold's tool shop. Ed played baseball and basketball and even took up musical instruments as a youngster, banging on a board with soda pop tops for piano keys and thumping overturned molasses buckets.

As calendars in Chester County flipped into the 1920s, the community, like many rural areas across the nation, seemed more at home in the late 1800s. Those who lived around the Arnolds would not mark the decade of the 1920s in the fashion of their city counterparts. Chester County yawned while urbanites celebrated the Jazz Age, flouted anti-drinking laws, adapted to new technological innovations like electricity, and frolicked in newfound individual freedoms. The Arnolds still relied on coal-oil lamps for light. Centralized heat also bypassed them; in winters, which occasionally turned icy, the family relied on the warmth of a wood heater. Every night before bed during cold spells, Will, Georgia, or one of the children banked the heater's fire so it could easily re-ignite in the morning. And, although Chester County had eight miles of concrete and ten miles of gravel road by the mid-'20s, Ed's family and their neighbors still either jumped in a horse-drawn wagon or walked if they had business far afield.

While a tide of secularism rose in the 1920s, Chester County clung to a spirit of community and strict principles advocated by churches. Ed attended two churches: Big Springs Methodist Church, Georgia's preference; and his father's favorite, New Friendship Baptist Church. If illness prevented a fellow farmer from harvesting his crops, neighbors stepped forward and finished the job. Friends also likely helped nurse that sick farmer back to his feet, and, when somebody died, neighbors dug the grave and sometimes made the casket.

Farming families found their entertainment in the community, too. They gathered at local homes for dances, barbecues, and candy breakings. These occasions allowed folks to catch up on the week's activities and gave young, single people a chance to get to know one another. At candy breakings, a boy and girl who were sweet on each other might share a stick of confection, drawing from either end of it; together, they snapped the candy and stole a kiss.

Food and candy were more likely than booze to be at the center of these gatherings, although a few men sneaked a nip outside the house. Not free from sin by any means, the community shared foibles with its fellow Americans. Chester County moonshiners tended stills in deep hollows under canopies of pine trees. Neighbors gossiped, and others condemned foreign ideas and peoples. This was young Ed Arnold's rustic world: idyllic in many ways, but limiting, too. Chester County exposed him to the importance of hard work, the joys of community, and the insularity of rural life.

— • —

When Ed reached school age, he had only to walk a half mile up Needmore Road to County Line School, a whitewashed, one-room affair. Kids had long before dubbed the building "Possum Trot," and the name stuck. Ed spent grades one through eight there.

Minnie Roberts, a stern, robust woman with black hair and glasses, presided over Possum Trot school when Eddy arrived there. Every morning, Mr. Roberts drove Mrs. Roberts to work and lit a fire for her in the school's tubby, cast-iron wood stove. The children arrived shortly after, placing their lunch pails on a shelf in the back and hanging their hats and caps on racks along the wall. They sat in double desks and watched Mrs. Roberts step up on a stage in front to lead the day's first event: the Lord's Prayer. Naturally, the kids looked past their lessons to lunch and scattered out of the building when midday arrived. The boys organized ball games and played marbles while, behind the school, the girls picked wild muscadine grapes and entered imaginary playhouses carpeted with moss. The games ceased with the tinkling of Mrs. Roberts's tiny clapper bell, and Ed and his mates formed a line at the foot of the school's stairs. One by one, and always in silence, the students filed back into the dim school room. Mary Brady succeeded Minnie Roberts and carried the chalk at Possum Trot for the bulk of Eddy's time there. Ms. Brady tolerated little tomfoolery and even spanked Ed three times one day. "I deserved all three of them," Eddy recalled.

Any wise guy who stepped out of line at Possum Trot might find his mouth washed out with lye or his nose in a circle on the chalkboard. Ed sometimes landed in such predicaments after a fight or firing an eraser at another kid. Years later, at a Possum Trot party, Ed sneaked away with a few other guys, jacked up a car parked outside the school, and slid a Coke case under it so the wheels hovered just above the ground. Old friends also remembered him slipping behind the wheel of a car that belonged to a friend's father—which he apparently had no business doing—and running the vehicle off the road. These shenanigans notwithstanding, Ed generally shunned trouble. As he grew older, the farm consumed more time, and while Ed kept one eye on his teacher's lessons, he discovered another discipline.

— • —

Chester County hopped with music. Fiddlers, banjo players, and guitarists dotted the land, and Ed heard them at church, candy breakings, community picnics, and other local gatherings. These amateur musicians lived next door, up the road, and around the corner. Boys from the Latham, Griffin, and Vestal families all played music, and Will Arnold was known to pick up a fiddle every now and then; his wife, Georgia, strummed the guitar a little.

The music that drifted across the fields was the Chester County adaptation of folk music and songs from Tin Pan Alley. Musicians learned the folk music from their fathers, preachers, and schoolteachers and the Tin Pan Alley songs from sheet music or 78-rpm records. With their untrained string accompaniment, Ed's neighbors sang popular standards like "Let Me

Call You Sweetheart," "Missouri Waltz," and "By the Light of the Silvery Moon" next to traditional favorites such as "John Henry," "Old Joe Clark," and "Turkey in the Straw." The fiddlers and guitarists also heard the music of emerging hillbilly artists, particularly Vernon Dalhart and Carson Robison, both of whom sold millions of records in the '20s by blending a cosmopolitan singing voice with lyrics appealing to rural audiences. Dalhart, a Texan who once performed light opera, especially captured imaginations with macabre ballads like "The Death of Floyd Collins," "The Wreck of the Old 97," and "The Letter Edged in Black." All of this, along with traditional hymns and the back-country sounds of recording artists Jimmie Rodgers and the Carter Family, filtered down to the musical experience of Chester Countians.

Ed absorbed the performances he saw as well as what he heard on the few neighborhood Victrolas. He played a harmonica early in his childhood, but the guitar ultimately gained his attention. Ed's cousin Susie Seaton loaned him her Sears Roebuck Silvertone guitar when he was seven, and Georgia taught her boy a few chords and his first song, "My Darling, Nelly Gray":

> When the moon had climbed the mountain
> And the stars were shining too,
> Then I'd take my darling Nelly Gray
> And we'd float down the river in my little red canoe
> While my banjo, I would sweetly play.

Ed rarely drifted far from the guitar, and he steadily compiled a repertoire of simple tunes like "Way Out on the Mountain," "The Lady in Red," and "Casey Jones," which told about the brave engineer who wrecked his train in Vaughn, Mississippi (at the time, Jones's widow lived up the road from Henderson in Jackson). Later, Ed took a few lessons for 75 cents apiece from a traveling musician. At a school in the nearby Friendship community, the musician diagrammed some chord positions on the chalkboard for Ed.

Ed hung the guitar on a nail in his room, and friends noticed that when Ed showed up, more often than not, he showed up with his guitar. "Wherever you saw Eddy, which was always walking," boyhood chum Willard Latham told an interviewer, "he had a rope tied around his guitar and had it hanging over his shoulder or around his neck. If you stopped to talk to him . . . he would start playing the guitar and singing." Another friend remembered seeing the boy on the way to a market with the guitar around his neck and two chickens under his arm.

When not encumbered with chickens or picking for pals, Ed would search out a quiet dell or patch of woods to practice. At home, Grandfather

Wright encouraged the dedicated boy, but Ed strummed only a rare chord there, because the noise bothered his father. Will Arnold was ailing.

— • —

Suffering from what doctors called dropsy—a condition often connected with heart and kidney disease that prevents the body from flushing bacteria and fat, causing swelling of the legs, digestive problems, and anemia—Will Arnold had slowed by his sixty-sixth birthday. The man who once walked tall over a small empire and commanded any number of weighty, unwieldy farm instruments could do little more in the late 1920s than stroll around the place. High blood pressure hampered Will, and doctors treated the dropsy by periodically draining fluid from his swelled body.

Will deteriorated as the '20s marched on. Even walking drained him. Mostly, he stayed in bed, laying quietly while his family tried to fill his large shoes. John and W. D. tackled the farmwork, and Ed pitched in, although, at the age of only nine or ten, little heavy work could be expected of him. Productivity plummeted, and a threat more treacherous to a farm than any flood, frost, or drought circled the Arnolds: debt.

In April 1924, before Will fell ill, he borrowed almost $2,000 from a money lender named D. S. Parker, offering the entire farm as collateral. A son from Will's first marriage had failed in business, and Will took the one-year loan to bail him out. Two thousand dollars was a grand sum indeed, but Will had his health, and the farm's bounty seemed endless. However, a year later, he had yet to make a payment on the note. The family managed a $90 payment in December and $475 in April of 1925, but mustered no more. In debt and increasingly infirm, Will grasped for solutions. He found one in November 1926, when he deeded his land to Millard Arnold—another son from his marriage to Mary Etta—in exchange for $1,000 and Millard's promise to settle the debt. With a simple mark of the pen, Will, in effect, yanked his second family's inheritance from under their feet. Ed's family remained on Millard's land, but could be evicted at any time. Millard paid almost $400 toward the debt in 1927 and '28, and then stopped altogether. By 1929, Millard's debt threatened to leave the Arnolds homeless.

Caught in the eye of this storm, Ed tried his best to stay out of the way. The sight of his deteriorating father unsettled him, and Will needed silence anyway. "I'm sure he worried a lot about his debts," Eddy Arnold said in retrospect. "That may have hastened his [demise]." At the time, Ed knew little of his family's financial entanglements and went about his chores and school lessons. He found solace in the guitar, while Georgia, Grandfather Wright, and his older brothers filled the gaps an ailing father left. Being with friends helped, too. Ed passed many an afternoon with the Latham boys at their home. He was playing with the boys on his eleventh birthday in 1929 when the Arnold's clanging dinner bell ominously tolled. The bell never sounded so late in the afternoon; usually it drew the family to their dinner at noon, not 5:00 P.M., but Ed instantly recognized the message. "I got to go," Ed told the boys. "My daddy's dead." Ed flew from the yard and sprinted the mile and a half back home to find his family awash in tears. Ed knew his dad had little time, but the death stung nonetheless.

The next day, outside the New Friendship Church, atop a hill overlooking a country road, Will's friends and large family buried him. Between his sobs, Ed wondered what lay ahead.

— • —

What began in 1924 as Will's simple effort to help his struggling son had snowballed into catastrophe for Georgia and her children. Faced with ongoing delinquency on the debt, the creditor, D. S. Parker, scheduled an auction for the farm on September 21, 1929. Parker planned to sell the entire tract of Will Arnold's old land to satisfy the debt, but two days before the auction Millard's brother Allan went to court to block the sale.

Because the main tract of Will's land—some 167 acres—came down through Allan's mother, Allan claimed, Will had no right to offer the deed for collateral in 1924. Will really only owned a half-interest (which he had purchased from his first wife, Mary Etta's sister Cornelia, in 1897). The other half-interest, Allan argued, actually belonged to Will and Mary Etta's heirs. As far as Allan was concerned, Will's second family had no rights to the Mary Etta Lane land whatsoever, and he named them in his complaint to illustrate his point. Allan argued that proceeds from the creditor's sale should be split between Will and Mary Etta's heirs and D. S. Parker. The next day—one day before the scheduled auction—the Chancery Court of Chester County agreed to hear Allan's case and issued a temporary injunction to halt the sale. The case would drag on for almost a year, frustrating Ed's family, but also buying them more time on the farm. In the proceedings, Millard surrendered claim to the deed that his father had signed over to him, and Georgia attempted to assert homestead rights to the land and suggested that D. S. Parker was asking for more than was due him, but her statements did little but illustrate her panicked state.

On September 11, 1930, chancellor Thomas C. Nye stepped forward with his ruling that Will Arnold's first set of heirs could in fact claim a half-interest in the Lane tract. Nye also set aside Millard's deed to the Arnold land and diverted the other half-interest to Georgia Arnold and Will's second heirs. All of the land, though, would have to go up for auction to settle the debt to D. S. Parker, and if any proceeds from the sale remained, the court ruled they would go to the children and grandchildren of Will's first family. Nye ordered the clerk and master of the court to post handbills around Chester County to announce the auction of Will Arnold's land. For purposes of the sale, the court divided the land into three sections—the Lane tract, the Nannie Arnold tract (where Ed's Aunt Nannie lived), and the Warren Roberts tract—and sold them separately on October 25. D. S. Parker entered the highest bid for each parcel of land. The creditor, it seemed, would pay himself.

For the moment, Ed's family faced certain eviction. Only guardian angels could save them—and three happened to live near the farm. On December 1, 1930, Obe and M. B. Latham and Mrs. E. L. Smith successfully pleaded with the court to reopen bidding on the three tracts of land. The court allowed further bidding until noon on Thursday, December 11. Parker had won bidding in October with a $1,950 total offer for the three tracts of land, but together Smith and the Lathams produced a check for $2,366 to reopen bidding. By noon on the eleventh, the Lathams had successfully bid for the Lane and Roberts tracts, while Enloe Burress won the Nannie Arnold tract. Eight days later, the Lathams approached the court again, this time seeking to transfer their successful bid for the two tracts to Allan Arnold. After Allan assured the court that he could pay for the land, the chancellor approved the Lathams' request.

Ed's family could stay, Allan determined, but they had to settle for tenant status on land they once owned: a bitter pill to swallow, but sweeter than the taste of eviction. The legal wrangling, though, chilled relations between Ed's family and Allan, and there would be other disputes over Will's estate. But, in the end, Allan's actions in 1929 probably saved the Arnolds from a bleaker existence during the years of the Great Depression. After Will's long decline and nineteen months of awful limbo since his death, the Arnolds limped into the 1930s.

—•—

Although the stock market had crashed just two months before, the *Chester County (Tenn.) Independent* of January 2, 1930, predicted a prosperous new year for the area. Local banks held deposits of $1 million, and improved roads made increased winter business likely. In addition, most farmers had plenty of feed for their livestock and would soon take to market thousands of dollars' worth of poultry and unsold cotton. The *Independent* trumpeted that 1930 would mirror 1929, which, despite the Arnolds' fortunes, boomed with prosperity. In '29, Chester County refurbished its schools, Tennessee Power and Light Company expanded service in the area, more homes poked up on the horizon, and the city of Henderson spent $7,000 on an American La France fire truck. Farmers also fared pretty well in 1929, shipping out by rail more than 15,000 bales of cotton, seventy-five cars of cottonseed, thirty-three cars of cattle, and sixty cars of poultry.

Optimism blanketed the *Independent*'s pages in January of 1930, but summer told a sadder story. By August, soaring temperatures shattered heat records, and drought shriveled the land. The summer's corn and hay harvest dropped, prompting government officials to urge farmers to conserve feed and give work animals first dibs at feeding time. Egg production fell, and later in the year, the cotton harvest shrank. "It was drier than dry," remembered a Chester County resident who lived through it. The drought burned on, and by 1931 the Depression had greatly driven down crop prices. Hitting Chester County in the heart, cotton prices sank like a stone: from a 1919 high of about 40 cents a pound, cotton prices floundered at a sickly 4 cents a pound in 1932.

On Needmore Road, the Depression only exacerbated the Arnolds' obvious difficulties. Georgia boiled the printed text off of feed bags to make shirts out of them, and most of the family's farming tools, livestock, and machinery had been sold to satisfy debts. W. D. and John, both around the age of twenty, carried most of the burden, but—in the midst of the land fracas—Patty had left the farm seeking better opportunities in St. Louis. She stayed in St. Louis with her half-brother Mitchum Arnold and, whenever possible, sent home money and gifts. The situation demanded contributions from Ed, too. He spent more time in the fields, and struck a deal with a neighbor to procure a cultivator, a contraption that the Arnolds once owned, but had lost at auction. "Mr. Joe Stovall had an extra two-horse cultivator," recalled Eddy. "I bought it from him and paid him in labor for it so we could cultivate a crop. In those days a two-horse cultivator was worth something to a farmer. I used to go help him work when I wasn't working at home: Whatever he had to do—if he was hauling hay or if he was cutting firewood or fixing a fence, anything."

Arnold also helped at the Dwight Nash farmstead, where he received a sex education of sorts. "He had a jackass, and farmers would bring the mares over and breed them to the jackass and get mules," said Eddy. "Mr. Nash had to keep that jackass separate from the other animals, and farmers would bring their female horses and breed them. I'd go over and watch them, and if they needed some help, I'd help. A jackass makes a lot of noise!"

When the Arnolds became tenant farmers in 1930, they joined the majority of farmers in the South. Tenancy, just a step above sharecropping, meant the farmers paid rent, not a portion of the crop, to the landowner. For those who fell from ownership to renting in the Depression—and hundreds of thousands did—tenancy was a blow to the will. Without their own roots in the soil, many farmers lost their motivation. Ed Arnold, who had entered his teens in 1931, figured that he would never own land himself and that wage work would be the means of his future. So, when not engrossed in farmwork, Ed sought any opportunity to earn hard cash that he could funnel back into the household. He sold hockey puck–sized tins of Cloverine salve, and trimmed the hair of country boys who had never really paid to have their hair cut. W. D., who would make barbering a career, showed his teenage brother the rudiments of the trade, and on weekends Ed sat boys down on crates outside a nearby general store and clipped away; a hand-

The Arnolds' tool shed, the only structure left from Ed's days on the farm. (Photo by Michael Streissguth)

Pinson High School, vacant in 1995. (Photo by Michael Streissguth)

made barber chair teetered on the Arnolds' front porch for those who missed Ed at the store.

In the summers, after the Arnolds had cultivated or plowed their crops for the last time, letting the crops grow unassisted until harvest (farmers called this "laying the crops by"), part-time work beckoned. Ed dropped the plow and tackled the timber trade. "I remember very well, I worked for a fellow that was cutting 'piling,' which was cypress timber. They made telephone poles out of it. It was cut off the place we lived on, which was [now] owned by my half-brother Allan. It was in the swamps, and they would dry up in the summer. Otherwise, you'd be in mud and water up to [your waist]. You'd cut it, throw it, skin it, and snake it out (which means drag it out). I did a lot of things like that. Anything to make a dime. It was just hard to get something to do."

In between work and school, Ed clung to his guitar. The young teenager picked a note or two at Georgia's quilting parties and often brought the guitar to school. On a woodpile outside Possum Trot, Ed's friends reclined and volleyed song requests at the handsome, well-groomed teenager. One day he would leave the farm, Ed told those friends on the woodpile, and he'd make a lot of money doing something other than plowing a field.

Such talk, such music, and such good looks wooed many of the girls around Ed. They sent anonymous love notes and watched him closely, but he hardly bit. "I was embarrassed to date a girl. I didn't have any money to buy an ice cream cone. That's what you did back then, go to Henderson to the drugstore and get an ice cream cone." A moonlit walk along Needmore Road would have satisfied the girls, but they rarely got the chance.

"He never did date nobody," one frustrated admirer quipped. "He dated that guitar."

Possum Trot kept students through the eighth grade, and if children could go further—meaning if they weren't needed on the farm and had a speck of intelligence—they went across the Chester County line to the nearest high school in Pinson. Every morning, Ed walked across the fields and through the woods to the crossroads of Five Points, where he caught the bus for Pinson, which was actually a flatbed truck with canvas draped over the back. The schoolchildren stepped onto the bus from the back and took a seat, either on one of the benches that lined the truck's bed or on the one that ran down the middle. Shaken by gravel roads and much singing and cutting up, the bus rattled all the way to Pinson. The Pinson School's brick construction, sprawling ranch style, and multiple classrooms made Possum Trot seem a hundred miles away; Pinson even had electricity! This twentieth-century school introduced Ed to new kids and to a new mass medium that captivated America.

Radio station WTJS in nearby Jackson often asked local teachers to send talented students for one-shot appearances on the air, and, as a result of Ed's singing and strumming at Pinson's morning chapel sessions, he was sent there to perform. He grabbed the opportunity, although his family had never owned a radio and he rarely listened. Ed did listen to radio during his night visits to Dwight Nash, the farmer who owned the jackass. Nash had a set wired to a large battery, and on clear nights Ed listened with him and his sons to Pete Cassell—a blind singer with a silken voice—on WSB in Atlanta. The signals of WSM's "Grand Ole Opry" from Nashville and the "National Barn Dance" from WLS in Chicago also crisscrossed the quiet darkness above Chester County, and these were among their favorite shows.

For his first broadcast performance in a string of broadcast performances that would last more than sixty years, Ed chose to sing "If You'll Let Me Be Your Little Sweetheart," a ditty he heard on a Gene Autry record.* Ed found the chance to perform on WTJS, however, less remarkable than the station itself. The smooth, thick glass separating Ed from the control room, the sleek microphones, and the sight of the engineer turning the knobs on the control board mesmerized him. Ed had his first glimpse of fame's scenery. "What if I could just earn me a living doing this?" Ed thought. "Wouldn't that be something."

In the fall of 1934, Ed decided against returning for the tenth grade at Pinson. The farm could use the strong arms of a sixteen-year-old, and nobody accused Ed of having a love affair with schoolwork anyway. His love affair with music, though, continued unabated.

Ed and his guitar were common sights at the local Saturday night house parties, where folks shoved the furniture from their kitchen or parlor to make room for dancers. "I began to learn the latest songs," Arnold told a radio interviewer years later. "When I was getting in my early teens, I started trying to sing a little bit and couldn't go too fast because my voice started changing. I'd play at these little parties. Then I'd play little square dances and little barbecues. They have all these kind of little things out in the country, and that's what you go to." In the summer, he dressed up and joined the other area musicians to play for the local picnics and church suppers. With every performance, Ed's singing and picking improved as well as his ability to play in step with other band members.

Arnold's repertoire grew also, due in large measure to a new Victor Talking Machine Company Victrola that arrived in the home, thanks to sister Patty. She worked in a St. Louis department store, and one Christmas

---

* Not to be confused with the old standard "Let Me Call You Sweetheart," "If You'll Let Me Be Your Little Sweetheart" was written by Gene Autry and Slim Bryant and recorded by Gene on June 22, 1933.

sent the cabinet-style record player to her family back home. The music machine revealed a new world to Ed. With extra nickels from his jobs, he ordered the records of America's singing sensations from the famous Sears Roebuck catalog. Soon 78-rpm records bearing the names of Bing Crosby, Kate Smith, Gene Austin, Jimmie Rodgers, the Carter Family, and Gene Autry arrived on the Arnolds' front porch. Ed had learned his radio debut song—"If You'll Let Me Be Your Little Sweetheart"—from an Autry record, and with the Victrola, he could learn more.

Gene Autry, a regular on the "National Barn Dance" in the early '30s, found a home on American Victrolas in 1933 with "The Last Round Up," and a year later hitched his horse in Hollywood, where he made the first of more than 100 films. Although Ed seldom found money to date, he managed to find 15 cents to see "Oklahoma's Singing Cowboy" in films like *Tumbling Tumbleweeds, The Sagebrush Troubadour,* and *The Singing Vagabond.* Anticipating the Saturday afternoon Autry showing, Ed and his friends spent weekdays planning their trip down the narrow Garland Road and over low bridges spanning wet bottom land to the high school in Henderson where the films were shown. Hollywood cast Autry as a cosmopolitan cowboy. In the turmoil of the Wild West, Autry acted straightforward and urbane, and his gentle, enunciated singing style matched the acting. Autry's rendition of "That Silver-Haired Daddy of Mine" was one of Ed's favorite songs. If Gene Autry was a sophisticated cowboy, then Bing Crosby was sophisticated, period. With 1930s' hits like "Love in Bloom," "June in January," and "Soon," Bing defined the word "crooner." Bing, a graduate of the popular Paul Whiteman Orchestra, drew Ed in as he did millions of young Americans.

Ed's attraction to these performers was logical considering that few other musical performers even neared the popularity of these men in the 1930s. Crosby's romantic ballads and Autry's vision of the American frontier brightened the Great Depression for many, and ensured millions of record sales despite such hard times. How could Ed not have added their records to his collection? The men's sophisticated vocals piqued Ed's attention. When Ed sang a song, he sang it straight, eschewing the more nasal sound of the Carter Family or Jimmie Rodgers. Although Ed's guitar playing and the playing of those around him was fairly traditional, his vocals were truer to Bing and Gene's sound and would continue to be for as long as he sang.

—•—

Like many rural musicians in the South—black and white—Ed's first professional gig was with traveling salesfolk, but Ed's vendors hawked flour, not patent medicine as was usually the case. A husband-and-wife team who represented the flour company hitched a trailer to their car every Saturday and roamed the small towns around Henderson. They would park, cook biscuits in the trailer, and give away free samples in hopes of selling the flour.

They hired Ed to sing for 50 cents, hoping to attract people to the trailer (if the aroma of baking biscuits didn't entice them).

Little-paying gigs like this came Ed's way more frequently, but he doubted music could be a full-time job. After all, the musicians around the farm generally played for laughs and small change. But what would *he* do with his life? In the fields, behind a plow, he entertained his destiny. "A boy that works on a farm and does labor, he does a lot of daydreaming," Eddy told an interviewer. "If you have any imagination at all, you do a lot of day-dreaming about what you're going to do. I didn't know what I was going to do." Would he marry a nice Chester County girl and drive a truck for the rest of his life? A fine education was out of the question for a high school dropout. Like many teens approaching adulthood, the future perplexed him. He watched boys in Chester County grow up, marry, and dig into farmwork, but Ed detested chopping cotton, especially on rented land; he resolved to follow a path away from farming.

3

$\mathcal{T}$he future, Ed decided, dwelt up U.S. Route 45 in Jackson, Tennessee. Georgia, John, and W. D. could keep the farm going, and he would send money home. So, like his sister Patty before him, Ed—guitar in hand—blazed a path away from the farm. He told friends around the area that he could make a living with his voice. Many encouraged him, but some in the community scoffed, branding him crazy for wanting to sing and do as well as Gene Autry. "So many rural people have problems seeing past their nose," countered Arnold. "They don't know what's out there. I thought I knew what was out there. I went and seldom ever went back. I just went."

Jackson is about twenty miles northwest of Henderson, and for anybody from Chester County, it defined the notion of "big city." Although Memphis and Nashville dwarfed Jackson, people in Chester County rarely had occasion to visit them. Hotels, movie houses, crowded department stores, and classically styled government buildings lined Jackson's broad avenues. The seat of Madison County, Jackson was also the region's seat of railroads and agricultural trade. Farmers poured into town with their harvested crops, and thousands of residents worked on the five railroads that ran through town. In early 1937, Jackson added another person to its population of 22,000: an eighteen-year-old from down south in Chester County.

When Ed hit Jackson, he headed for the corner of Market and Baltimore, home of WTJS radio. The owners of the *Jackson (Tenn.) Sun* newspaper opened WTJS (for West Tennessee Jackson Sun) in 1930, and outside of Memphis it was among the oldest stations in the region. Eddy had represented his school on the station some years before, but a recent and impromptu audition led him once again to the station's door. "In the rural area, you always sit on the front porch, and I did," Eddy said. "And there was a man that came by selling subscriptions to the newspaper . . . which owned the radio station. The fella came by there selling, and I strummed him a little song. He invited me to come down and take an audition, and I did."

The Bill Westbrooks outfit at radio station WTJS in Jackson (1937). *Left to right:* Ed, Albert "Happy Jack" Goebel, Jimmy Allen, Speedy McNatt, Val Morse, Bill Westbrooks, Arizona Lou (Mrs. Bill Westbrooks), Buddy Tucker, Angelina Palazola. (Gabe Tucker collection)

A Jackson musician named Bill Westbrooks* who had a show on WTJS heard about Ed's audition, and invited the young man to join his band. A vocalist who strummed guitar might just add some spice to his line-up, which included Westbrooks's wife (known on stage as "Arizona Lou"), Jimmy Allen (a WTJS staffer), guitarist Buddy Tucker, accordionists Albert "Happy Jack" Goebel and Angelina Palazola, and Val Morse (a steel-guitar player dubbed "The Happy Hawaiian" and a WTJS engineer). Of all the members of Westbrooks's group, Morse helped Ed the most, teaching him new chord progressions and other guitar techniques. "He was a good musician," Eddy recalled. "He was nice to me. He could of just fluffed me off and said, 'I don't want to fool with you' because he was a fine player. I wasn't. But I learned a whole lot from him." Westbrooks's outfit played every day at noon on the radio station for next to no pay. But paltry pay could be tolerated, because WTJS offered a valuable forum for bands like Westbrooks's to promote their local appearances and solicit offers for future shows.

---

* Employing the nickname "Cousin Wilbur," Westbrooks worked as a sideman for Bill Monroe in the 1940s.

Musicians with a radio base to amplify their talent could easily find work in a station's listening area. Those who did in the 1930s include such country performers as Roy Acuff, who fiddled on WROL in Knoxville; Hank Williams on WSFA in Montgomery, Alabama; and Little Jimmy Dickens, who camped at WJLS in Beckley, West Virginia. Just about every other early country act to reach stardom boasted a radio base. Radio stations in the South even opened their doors to black performers, who were typically barred from white institutions (although blacks and whites rarely took to the air together). Carl Martin, a black man and master of many stringed instruments, worked on WROL, and black blues guitarist Calvin Frazier appeared on KLCN in Blytheville, Arkansas, at roughly the same time in the 1930s as the Southern Melodiers, a white gospel quartet. From Bristol in eastern Tennessee to Memphis and across the mid-South, live, local music—black and white—filled the airwaves. In 1937, Ed Arnold joined the radio ranks. With the small yet potent range of a 250-watt station behind him, Ed's performances drifted over Jackson and a few miles beyond, helping to attract business for Bill Westbrooks's services.

But Ed had to eat. Live performances paid slightly more than radio work—a minimal amount—so he needed a steady job. Not long after his arrival in Jackson, he found part-time work on East Main Street at the George A. Smith funeral home and ambulance service. Ed got a room in the funeral home in exchange for pallbearing and assisting in funerals, and, at night, made 25 cents for each run he made with Smith's ambulance service. Ed practiced the guitar in his room, often joking about the tough funeral-home audience.

On the ambulance runs, Ed escorted his share of women in labor to the hospital and brought them home after delivery. Helping mothers, however, was an easy task compared to the bloody scenes the ambulance often came upon. He grew accustomed to corpses and mangled bodies, but one ambulance run, he would often tell people, spooked him. A boy, not much younger than Ed, had shot himself, and the Smith ambulance rushed to the gruesome event to pick him up. On the way to the hospital, Ed cradled the boy and watched life leave his body. He died in Ed's arms. "I'll never forget that. . . . That shook me."

Equally unforgettable for Ed was the chore of seeing to the corpse of a man who died alone and impoverished. "[George Smith] and I one day buried [the] man—just the two of us," said Eddy. "A bum had died. We didn't know who he was. We had no name. There was no funeral—just Mr. Smith and I. . . . If you don't think that'll shake you up . . . oh man . . . I'll tell you, it will make you think."

—▬ • ▬—

Not long after joining Bill Westbrooks, Ed learned that his boss needed a fiddler. He knew just the man for the job—a recent Henderson High School graduate named Howard McNatt—and mentioned his name to Westbrooks. Howard grew up in Luray, about twelve miles from the Arnold farm, and knew Ed from the various community gatherings where the two boys often played together. Around Chester County, people who knew anything about music respected Howard's abilities. He had classical training, often won local fiddle contests, and came from a musical family. Howard's mother gave piano lessons, and his three brothers played various instruments: Lynn mastered the trumpet, Melton tinkled the piano, and Tom blew the clarinet and saxophone.

In Luray, the McNatts owned a general store, and, during the Depression, took the job of cleaning the town train station when the railroad company could no longer staff it. The arrangement allowed the McNatts to ride the train for nothing, which meant that Howard could take the two-hour train ride to Memphis every week for classical violin lessons from his uncle, Noel Gilbert. But there was little use for a classical violinist around Chester County, so when Howard graduated from high school in 1937, he went to Jackson as a fiddler and joined Ed and Bill Westbrooks at WTJS. After Howard's arrival in Jackson, Ed moved from the funeral home and took a room with Howard in a boardinghouse.

Every day, as the noon hour approached, the two fresh-faced boys climbed to the *Sun* building's third floor to broadcast for the citizens of Jackson and surrounding areas. There was nothing grand about the "Biggest Little Station in the South," as WTJS was known, only a small office, control room, and studio. A piano and sofa furnished the sparse studio, and for acoustics, management had carpeted the floor and nailed fiberboard to the walls. In this space, the Bill Westbrooks band warbled their hillbilly songs while letters trickled in requesting their services around Jackson. They performed at church picnics, in taverns, and at coal–lamp-lit schoolhouses.

Clutching a homemade guitar he had purchased in Jackson, Ed held a pleasant appeal for those who came to see the band. He piled his wavy hair atop his sculpturesque head and peeled his eyes wide when he sang, flashing blue eyes that dazzled some women. Ed's take-him-home-to-mother looks were a perfect fit for the gentle, reflective voice he used to put across a song. And while Ed's plaintive touch and wide smile wooed the audiences, the new band member from Luray wowed them with fiddling on songs like "Boil Them Cabbage Down," "Red Wing," and "Four String Boogie"—numbers that really cooked the joint. In a display of high showmanship, Howard often loosened the horse hair strings on his bow, inserted the fiddle between the hair and the bow stick, and ran it across the strings. Howard also drew the bow across all four strings at once to produce full-sounding chords and bounced the bow off the fiddle strings to give a rapid-fire staccato quality to a melody. Audiences loved the one-two punch of Ed and Howard: ballad and boogie.

Ed and Howard's friendship warmed as they spent more time together, and each admired the other's talent. Howard taught Ed to read music, and, with Ed humming and Howard writing the notes, they even wrote some songs together. The duo complemented one another, Ed opening doors for Howard with his singing and good looks, and Howard helping Ed in the technical aspects of music. But Ed had one major problem with Howard. In the morning, Howard's bed held a mystical sway over him. He habitually arrived late for radio shows and evening personal appearances, irking the punctual Ed. Ed tacked the ironic sobriquet "Speedy" on his pal, and it stuck. Audiences assumed the nickname referred to Howard's lightning-fast fiddling, but they were only partly right.

Despite Ed's objections, Speedy probably had a perfectly good reason to lie in bed, because, by the fall of 1937, Westbrooks and the band seldom had a night off. The band played small communities around Jackson like Chapel Hill, Union Cross, and Center Hill, where Ed made as much as $2.50 a night or as little as 33 cents. According to records Speedy kept, the band played better than an average of every other night between November 6 and December 11. New Hope, Moor's Hill, Palestine, Mt. Carmel, and a number of other hamlets called the Westbrooks band to their stages, and after little more than a month of speeding through the late autumn darkness to meet these dates, Speedy calculated his cut of the concert earnings to be a total of $45; Ed probably took home about the same amount.

Meanwhile, at the funeral home, George Smith asked Ed to come on fulltime to replace an employee who had joined the Jackson police force. Ed needed the money, and had decided to accept Smith's offer, when a Memphis radio station called. A few months before, Westbrooks and the band had auditioned for WMPS (a 1,000-watt station operated by the Scripps-Howard newspapers), and now the station wanted to put them on the air. Ed weighed his options and, with little pause, headed west toward the Bluff City after less than a year in Jackson.

Memphis, known more for its contributions to blues than country music, would be little more than a footnote in Arnold's early career. Ed, Speedy, and the rest landed in Memphis just after Christmas, and WMPS slated their radio debut for January 3, 1938. For New Year's Eve, they copped a gig at the King's Court on Summer Avenue. They wrapped up their performance at 2:00 on Saturday morning. Each took the $3.50 cut, killed Sunday at the movies, and landed in the lobby of WMPS at noon on Monday; Speedy, however, confirming Ed's criticisms, arrived an hour and a half later.

WMPS (located in the downtown Columbian Tower) plugged the Jackson troupe into their format and paid each member about $10 a week. On their first day, the station manager, George Engleton, told the band that they would appear twice daily—at 6:00 A.M. and noon—and once on a weekly show, "The Family Program" on Friday evening. Speedy noted in his diary that during the morning slot the band played mostly "hoedowns" and set aside ten minutes for reading jokes submitted by listeners (the listener with the best joke won a buck).

In his daily recording of events, Speedy also bragged that after only a few days on the air they had begun to receive fan mail. But management seemed less enthralled with Westbrooks and company, and by January 15, George Engleton pulled the plug. "We were just not that good," Arnold told an interviewer thirty years later. "It was a larger job and they demanded their talent to be a little better, but in a nutshell, we were not ready."

The initial sign of trouble appeared on January 8, according to Speedy. "Engleton said . . . that the rhythm was ragged, and he wanted to get with us next week and see if he couldn't straighten us out. If you ask me, Bill [Westbrooks] messes up as well as Buddy Tucker." As he promised, Engleton corralled a few of the band members—including Ed, Speedy, and Buddy—and played a few records for them. "He wanted us to play just like the records," Speedy lamented that day. "'Red River Valley' and 'Birmingham Jail' is the type." Although the band tried to meet their radio boss's expectations, they failed. On the Thursday of their second week on WMPS, Engleton told them that the next day would be it. "I was not surprised," Speedy wrote. "Bill was quite down in the dumps and said it was the dirtiest he had ever been treated."

It's unclear how Ed reacted to the abrupt firing, but on Saturday morning—the day after their swan song on WMPS—Ed and Speedy (without Westbrooks) hit the pavement in search of new radio work. If they struck out, the duo figured they might go up to St. Louis for work. They took the street car downtown to the Hotel Gayoso, where WMC blasted forth with 5,000 watts. The program director welcomed the boys, auditioned them, and enjoyed what he heard. Their stuff sounded good, the program director told the boys, but unfortunately he was chockablock with talent. He asked Ed and Speedy to put their tunes on record for his future reference, and they complied. In short order, Ed and Speedy performed "Nighttime in Nevada," "Four or Five Times," "St. Louis Blues," and "Merry-Go-Round Broke Down" (a pop hit for five different acts in 1937). They left the Hotel Gayoso with little hope for a job at WMC, but Ed Arnold's voice had just been recorded for the first time.

———— • ————

"Ed and I are catching the 7:30 bus tonite for St. Louis, Mo. to see what we can do there," Speedy wrote in his diary a few hours after the audition. And why not? Ed's sister Patty shared a place with her and Ed's half-brother Mitchum there, and they certainly would take the young musicians in. Ed and Speedy jumped on the evening bus and arrived in St. Louis just before 6:00 on Sunday morning, January 16, 1938.

"First in booze, first in shoes, and last in the American League," folks joked about St. Louis, referring to its reputation for alcohol distillation, a massive shoe industry, and the hapless St. Louis Browns baseball team. But late in the 1930s—despite the Browns—St. Louis fared slightly better than most other cities in the South and Midwest, and, in the midst of the Great Depression, promised more to two struggling musicians than Memphis could.

When Ed and Speedy pulled into St. Louis, they saw a city like they had never seen before. Legal booze, flowing again after the repeal of Prohibition, loosened up drinkers (and the brewing industry) and was condoned in a way unthinkable in conservative Chester County. Italians, Russians, Poles, and other immigrants clogged the city's streets and neighborhoods, and soot from the furnaces and stoves of homes and businesses choked the air. Roughly three times the size of Memphis, the city exuded a more cosmopolitan atmosphere, boasting more radio stations and infinitely more small-time music venues. Disappointed by the Browns baseball team, St. Louis could bask in the perennial success of the St. Louis Cardinals and its top pitcher, the zany Dizzy Dean, who averaged twenty-four wins a season between 1932 and 1936. Another member of the Cardinals' so-called Gashouse Gang, Pepper Martin, led a band that added to a St. Louis musical calliope that already wheezed and whistled with a combustion of blues, jazz, polka, and country. Remnants of the heady 1920s still lingered in St. Louis, but, undeniably, few could afford to pay to see Pepper Martin's band or watch the Cardinals play. The Depression sapped St. Louis, too. Ed and Speedy saw poverty almost everywhere, in ramshackle neighborhoods and along the Mississippi River, where the unlucky huddled in their Hooverville shacks and sifted through garbage for food.

A perception of prosperity created by the city's diversified employment market lured legions of people to the "Gateway of the West" during the Depression. Jobs associated with the city's appliance manufacturing, retail outlets, hard machinery production, and breweries attracted hopeful workers like Patty Arnold. Many who came found only disappointment, but still others found work and, with their meager pay, sought cheap entertainment.

— · —

Ed and Speedy landed at 4001 Russell Boulevard, Patty and Mitchum's front door, as planned. On Monday morning, they boldly set out for KMOX, the "Voice of St. Louis," a station that dominated the Midwest. A slot on this 50,000-watt broadcasting behemoth would be a real coup, and they saw a glimpse of encouragement when management agreed to audition them on Tuesday. They returned and performed, but as they had heard from WMC, KMOX had no place for them. A welcoming hand, however, met the undaunted duo at KWK radio, where the program director hired them (after an audition) to work as "Mac and Ed, The Tennessee Harmony Lads." They started on Friday, January 21. "Up at five o'clock this morning," wrote Speedy on the big day. "We almost froze waiting for the Russell

"Mac and Ed, The Tennessee Harmony Lads," on radio station KWK in St. Louis (1938). (Eddy Arnold collection)

bus and also the Kings Highway bus. The expense is rather heavy with 2 car fares . . . each day. We got through the first program fine. . . . We did 'Ding Dong Daddy,' 'Home on the Range,' and 'Riding Down the Canyon.'"

KWK, a 5,000-watt station broadcasting from the Hotel Chase, proved to be a powerful break for the boys. The station tied into the Mutual and NBC networks, ran an artists' bureau, and employed a large staff of professionals. Initially, KWK paid little, but the fallout of club work more than motivated the partners to show up for their early-morning radio gigs. In addition, by March, KWK arranged for Ed and Speedy to make fifty 15-minute transcriptions that would be distributed to Australia and New Zealand as well as throughout the United States. Each time a show sold—*if* the shows sold— Ed and Speedy would make $18 each. Throughout March, the boys often cut five records a day. "This afternoon," explained Speedy to his diary on March 10, "we made 6 records which took us until almost six o'clock. This makes a total of 16 records . . . we've made for the last three days. We were all tired out so we listened to 'Bing' Crosby on the radio while in bed then went to sleep."

With the radio transcription pay and the stepped-up club work, "Mac and Ed" saved enough money to move out of Patty's place. Above a drug-store on Laclede Avenue, they found a $4-a-week room that had to be paid for by Mondays at noon or else. The "or else" option never befell the boys, but feeding themselves on what money (if any) was left strained their creativity. Except for an occasional meal with Patty, the boys survived (literally) on peanuts, nickel hamburgers, and day-old Chinese food from an eatery across the street from their room. When money was particularly scarce, they ordered hot water from a restaurant and concocted soup using the ketchup, salt, and pepper on the table.

Adjusting to life and performing in the big city was difficult for the two musicians. In cramped taverns such as the 2 Mile House, Russo's, the Bottle Inn, and Dick's Place, a distracted owner might introduce them to patrons who, intent on drinking, conversation, and finding a date, drowned the duo's songs. One night a drunk called Ed over and poured a glass of St. Louis's finest straight into his guitar's sound box. He seethed, wanting to crush the man, but, remembering his dollar-a-night job, refrained. "They were really just joints, smoke-filled places," he told a reporter in 1980. "I hated 'em. Sometimes people would come up and tell me point-blank how much they hated my singing." After all matter of indignities and late nights, Ed and Speedy often trudged straight to the radio station and napped in the lobby before the 6:00 A.M. sign-on. If they went back to their room, they feared oversleeping and losing the radio gig.

While still at KWK, "Mac and Ed" widened their St. Louis radio audience in June of 1939 when they hopped on KXOK radio to perform as a

The musically equipped Speedy and Ed posing in St. Louis for the Newell Music Company (1939). (Eddy Arnold collection)

duo for the Newell Music Company, as well as with two other male musicians as the "Golden Lager Boys." KXOK was a new venture of the *St. Louis Star-Times*—it was dwarfed by KWK and needed talent desperately.

The second radio job sometimes delivered more than $30 a week, and with that extra cash Speedy studied classical violin and Ed took a few voice lessons to improve his breathing. Ed's career turned in St. Louis. Faced with unappreciative club audiences, he tried to entertain, not just play. To be acceptable on two of only six stations in a city of almost a million persons, his singing and playing had to shine, so he practiced and practiced. He blackened his teeth and learned to clown for KXOK's studio audience. An old station photo captured Ed the comedian dressed in a hideous plaid suit, wearing a weird wig, and holding his left foot as if he was picking corns. However embarrassing, the comedy helped round out Ed's stage presence and enliven his audience rapport.

Ed also broadened his repertoire of songs. He devoured the song folios of Gene Autry and Jimmie Rodgers to please his radio audiences and the bar patrons, finding his version of Gene Autry's "That Silver-Haired Daddy of Mine" to be among the most requested. Speedy told an interviewer that the two played hillbilly and popular tunes. "We did numbers where I played hot fiddle. Eddy would sing the current songs, as well as some of the country music—more or less a variety." A list of repertoire Speedy kept at the time reveals just how diverse the boys' performances were. Mainstream pop numbers like "In the Mood" or "The Woodpecker Song" fell on the audience alongside popular western ones such as "Rose of the Rio Grande" and "Leaning on the Old Top Rail."

After more than a year in St. Louis, life had brightened for Ed and Speedy. A dollar or two for a night's work had multiplied to $4 or $5, and their Golden Lager beer radio spots often paid as much as $30 a week. In contrast to their empty-pocketed arrival in the winter of 1938, the two boys now had cars of their own—ten-year-old flivvers, but nonetheless, cars. Although they dated girls and saw an occasional movie, their world was practice, practice and perform, perform.

When they had no other engagements, Ed and Speedy often hung around the studios of KXOK or KWK, chatting with the staff and absorbing the on-air performances. It was on one such winter's afternoon at KWK that the two heard a beer with the unlikely name of "Greasy Dick" get an incongruous plug. Pope Pius XII had just assumed the papacy, and was about to address the world from the Vatican. KWK's chief announcer, Allan C. Anthony, was on the air in one studio, and Bill Edwards, another announcer, sat daydreaming or distracted in the other one. In any event, Edwards wasn't listening as Anthony, with great reverence, introduced the new pontiff. Edwards assumed he had to read a commercial when Anthony finished whatever he was saying.

"And now friends," Anthony announced like a priest at mass, "I hope you will stay with us because the next voice you will hear will be the voice of Pope Pius the Twelfth."

But Edwards usurped the Pope and spat the next words. "I'll take Greasy Dick Brothers beer!"

The ill-timed ad shattered Anthony's respectful atmosphere and hurled Ed and Speedy into convulsions of laughter. "The station manager, the program manager, secretaries, and everyone fell out of their offices," said Arnold, "because they were getting ready to hear the Pope!"

Ed and Speedy laughed a lot in St. Louis. They chased girls and shared the life of friends, each knowing the other's thoughts and sharing his dreams. Ed's dreams told him that better things lay ahead. "I always had a quiet confidence. I was always aggressive in a quiet way. I knew where I wanted to go because I couldn't go back. There wasn't anything to go back to." Speedy, though, had tired of the St. Louis grind and yearned for home. Ed refused to go, so Speedy returned to Jackson, where he joined the

Musical Ramblers, a group fronted by a Pierce, Kentucky, boy named Gabe Tucker. "Speedy came down and wanted to meet us," said Tucker. "He had heard us on the air. So, I talked him into staying because our fiddle player, Henry Sullivan, had left to go in the service."

Speedy's departure left a hole in Ed's life: "I missed him because we were good first friends." But Ed kept to it, playing radio shows and live gigs with other guys. Ed still got together with Speedy when he drove home in his rickety automobile to visit his family on the farm. Around his old stomping grounds—at the little schools and dances—Ed sat in with Speedy and Gabe Tucker's Musical Ramblers. "He liked what we were doing," explained Tucker. "We played a little bit of everything . . . and Eddy came up and introduced himself. He got to going out on dates with us. He wasn't getting paid for it. We'd introduce him, and he'd play. Eddy had acquired quite a bit of showmanship."

On one such journey home in 1939, Ed flipped the dial to WSM to hear cowboy accordionist Pee Wee King. Ed had tuned to King many times, but on this morning he noticed the absence of King's lead vocalist, Jack Skaggs. Pee Wee just might need a new lead singer, Ed thought.

"When I went back to St. Louis I wrote him a letter and told him that I sang, and I played the guitar. If he was interested in what I could do, I'd send him a transcription." Ed added that he could sing harmony if somebody taught him. King's father-in-law and manager, J. L. Frank, replied and asked Ed to send a transcription. With a few musicians, Ed performed some selections at KXOK, and Blaine Cornwell, the program director, cut the transcription. Ed mailed the disc to Frank and King, and a few weeks later Frank invited him to join Pee Wee King and His Golden West Cowboys at a salary of $3 a performance with a guarantee of at least $15 a week. In the dawning days of 1940, Ed went back east to Nashville.

*F*rank Julius Anthony Kuczynski died in the early 1930s, and Pee Wee King rose from his remains. As Frankie King, a name he took in tribute to his favorite bandleader, Wayne King, Kuczynski led the King's Jesters, a Wisconsin-based band that toured the Dairy State dishing out polkas and western music. Kuczynski's fortunes rose when a car carrying Gene Autry's Range Riders crashed in Wisconsin, injuring some of the band members. Autry, who had yet to gallop to Hollywood fame, needed more men fast and called Kuczynski when, sitting in a gas station, he heard the Jesters on the radio. Autry sang in front of the Jesters that night and asked Kuczynski, sans the Jesters, to join the Range Riders on a tour of Minnesota. Kuczynski played the Minnesota tour and later joined Autry on the "National Barn Dance" radio show out of Chicago, and then on WHAS in Louisville. Referring to Kuczynski's height, Autry's manager suggested that he use the name "Pee Wee." The name stuck, and Kuczynski later made the name change legal.

When Ed sent his letter and transcription to Nashville in 1939, Pee Wee King and His Golden West Cowboys had fashioned a following on the country-and-western circuit. Joseph Lee Frank, or J. L. as he was better known, helped pave Pee Wee's way. Through Frank (who was managing Gene Autry at the time of his car wreck), the band had served stints at WROL and WNOX in Knoxville, and in 1937 they debuted on WSM's "Grand Ole Opry" in Nashville. The band also played fish fries, county fairs, schools, and dance halls throughout the upper South and Midwest. When the crowds emerged from the gullies and fields for Pee Wee King and His Golden West Cowboys, they saw a spectacle, a real show. Pee Wee and the band did more than plod through some traditional standards. With a fiddle, bass, banjo, guitar, the vocals of Texas Daisy Rhodes, and Pee Wee's accordion, the band sizzled. They gleamed in flashy cowboy attire and always played upbeat, tight sets. Pee Wee's band didn't dawdle, they came to entertain and give the audience good music, a few chuckles, and a feast for the eyes. When the handsome Ed Arnold arrived, he embellished the feast and, with his knack for a ballad, broadened the group's repertoire.

The Golden West Cowboys had settled in Nashville when Ed joined them in early January of 1940. But they soon moved on to Louisville, Kentucky, for an extended stint on WHAS, the radio home of the "Renfro Valley Barn Dance," a major competitor to both the "Opry" and "National Barn Dance" shows; the Golden West Cowboys had their own show on the station and used the outlet to break in their new boy. J. L. Frank and Pee Wee stuck the billing "Smilin' Eddy Arnold" on a reluctant Ed. "I don't know what that meant. I don't know how that helped," he said. If not "Smilin'," Ed would at least be known as Eddy from that point on.

Pee Wee turned the new colt into his workhorse. Eddy sang lead for the band on songs like "Old Fashioned Mother," "Temple on the Hill," and "You Go Your Way Darling, and I'll Go Mine," and when the Golden West Cowboys broke out into a trio or quartet during a show, "Smilin' Eddy" sang lead, too. The deluge of work helped Eddy improve his voice and learn the art of delivery. "I used to watch the audiences when Eddy was a Golden West Cowboy," Pee Wee told researcher Douglas Green in 1974. "He would sing a 'mother' song, and he had that audience in tears. And the next time he came back, he'd sing an up-tempo tune and yodel, and he'd have them standing on their seats applauding. So when you can get that mixed reaction from people in the audience, you've won them over. You got them in the palm of your hand."

Eddy also learned about the rigors of the road with the Pee Wee King organization. After broadcasting their daily, early morning shows on WHAS, the band often set out for a live evening concert—sometimes more than 100 miles away. Motoring along in giant Chevrolets that read "J. L. Frank Presents Pee Wee King And His Original Golden West Cowboys" on the side and rear, they would return home in time to catch a few hours of sleep before the morning's radio gig. When not encamped at a radio station, the band met date after date on the road where, from his perch on the stage, Eddy observed all manner of human behavior. "I was standing in the center of the stage singing," Arnold said to an interviewer about an especially humorous night in the limelight, "and this lady was sitting in the front row with a baby in her arms, and the baby was nursing (the lady was a full-grown lady!). All at once, she leaned over to say something. Of course, the baby lost hold. It began to climb, trying to get back. I had to stop singing. It was necessary for me to laugh a little." At intermission, Eddy sold Pee Wee King songbooks and, after the show, swept the auditorium for extra money. Later, in addition to his chores on vocals and rhythm guitar, Eddy acted as master of ceremonies for the band.

But more than extra duties and fatigue, rigors of the road often meant car accidents. Eddy and J. L. Frank, driving in one of the cars that moved the band and its instruments, wrecked on a rainy trip through the mountains from Knoxville to Asheville, North Carolina. A truck pulling a trailer swerved out of control on the slick road and slapped their car, inflicting con-

Eddy (*far right*) picks with the Cowboys on a tour through Florida. The neck of Speedy's fiddle partially obscures Pee Wee King's face. (Don McNatt collection)

The Caravan gang takes five in Hollywood, Florida. (Dolly Denny collection)

siderable damage, but spared Eddy and Frank. Luck sat next to Eddy again on a drive back to Louisville from a gig in Vincennes, Indiana. "We were doing early programs [on WHAS] and then working out at night, which means we didn't get enough sleep. Wherever we stopped, you had to rest, or I did. We were going down the highway, and I heard somebody say, 'Let's make the singer drive.' Well, the singer started driving, and I went to sleep and went off the road. I didn't damage the car luckily and didn't hurt any of us, but I went off the road." The car careened off the blacktop into a field, plowing up a few rows of corn before stopping just shy of the farmhouse. When the farm family realized who their unexpected guests were, they fixed a breakfast of ham and eggs for Pee Wee and the boys. "When we straightened up again," Eddy continued, "I said to Pee Wee, 'I guess that'll teach you to make me drive at night when I'm worn out.'"

The sleepy singer's bandleader also had problems on the road. For Pee Wee, the main highway was never the quickest way. "I know a shortcut," Pee Wee would tell his driver. "There's a little state road that cuts across . . ." Unfortunately, that little state road often led the Golden West Cowboys to a town called "confusion." After too many wrong turns, Pee Wee learned to like the main highways.

Although the constant travel and work tired Eddy, he viewed the Pee Wee King experience as an education in all aspects of the music business. He observed the value of quality musicianship, good management, professionalism, preparedness, and promotion. When the band rolled into town, for example, instead of hanging around the motel, Eddy accompanied Pee Wee to the local radio station, where they promoted that evening's performance. "I wanted to learn all I could," Arnold recalled. "I wanted to learn my craft, and I learned a lot from Pee Wee. He was a good little showman. He was lively . . . and he was fun. Oh . . . I liked Pee Wee."

Eddy really began to feel at home soon after joining Pee Wee when his old friend Speedy McNatt joined the group. Once again, Speedy found work at Eddy's recommendation after Pee Wee's regular fiddler was drafted. According to Speedy's records, he joined Eddy and Pee Wee on January 31, 1940, in time for a radio appearance on WSM and a two-week jaunt through the Carolinas.

━ • ━

Like Speedy's predecessor in the Pee Wee King outfit, thousands of young Americans poured into training camps as the nation prepared for war. (Eddy said he was classified 4-F because of flat feet; his brother John would die a member of the 101st Airborne.) Adolph Hitler's swift aggression in the spring of 1940 had subdued Denmark, Norway, Belgium, and the Netherlands and brought a rain of Blitzkrieg fire on Great Britain. By June, France had bowed to Germany. The United States, anticipating involvement in what would be known as World War II, launched its first peacetime conscription in October 1940, requiring men between the ages of twenty-one and thirty-five to serve one year in the military.

The military's rapid growth presented several problems for the War Department. Foremost among them, at least from the enlistees' point of view, was entertainment. But, like a wave of invading Marines, show promoters around the nation proudly emerged to serve their country and capture some of the millions Uncle Sam earmarked for entertainment. Vaudeville, a medium crippled by Hollywood and radio by 1940, received a temporary shot in the arm from the sudden demand for performers. Troupes with names like Harry Howard's Beachcomber Revue, Benny Meroff's Funzafire, Harlem on Parade, Rhythm Revels, and Swing Along Revue revived the days of vaudeville theater on the khaki circuit. Big bands and hillbilly bands also signed on for the march through military camps, and, in 1941, Pee Wee King and His Golden West Cowboys enlisted, too.

J. L. Frank and WSM struck a deal with R. J. Reynolds Tobacco Company to put a traveling country-music show on the road using "Grand Ole Opry" talent at no cost to the military; they dubbed it the "Camel Caravan." Reynolds financed the shows, correctly predicting that the Camel Caravan would generate goodwill and name recognition for their Camel brand cigarette. A gang of performers hopped on the Caravan—Pee Wee's band, comedienne Minnie Pearl, dancer Dolly Dearman (who later married music publisher Jim Denny), singer Kay Carlisle, master of ceremonies Ford Rush, and a trio of girl singers that included Evelyn Wilson, Mary Dinwiddie, and Alcyone Bate Beasley (the daughter of early "Grand Ole Opry" performer Dr. Humphrey Bate). Four girls—dubbed "the Camelettes"—dressed in short skirts and gave out free Camel cigarettes to the soldiers.

Chaperoning the Camelettes, Minnie Pearl would recall, was next to impossible. Eddy, on the other hand, kept his own counsel on the Caravan's outings. "He was quiet, and I guess you would call him shy," said Dolly Denny. "He was never a smart aleck. He would do what he was supposed to do. I never heard him say or do anything that was ugly. We had a good group, and Eddy just fit right in."

The Caravan left Nashville for the first time in the summer of 1941 on their way to Louisville. A parade of four cars—one pulling a house trailer—and a truck carried the WSM stars and their gear (they later traveled by bus). If a military camp had a theater or access to one, the Caravan set up there; if not, the side planks on the Caravan's truck unhinged to make a stage. Virtually a self-contained unit, the troupe also lugged lighting and a sound system ready to go if the situation required. The tour would reach many corners of America, bringing Eddy to places that Pee Wee's band never hit. When distance permitted, Pee Wee's band and Minnie Pearl rushed back to Nashville for the Saturday night "Grand Ole Opry" show.

Dolly Denny remembered the Caravan arriving in Louisville that first night on the road. There was no show that evening. "Mr. Frank got us all out of the car and [we] went in this horrible, beat-up place to stay. Mrs. Pearl said, 'Nooo way! Miss Dinkle [Pearl's pet name for Dolly] and I are going up the street.' We left them. They got straightened up the next day. They said we had to stay in the best places."

In late 1941, the show snaked through installations like Camp Grant in Illinois (September 25), Camp Shelby in Mississippi (November 1), and, in the days immediately following the Pearl Harbor invasion, Fort Sam Houston in Texas, where the band performed for 8,000 enlistees and garnered an excited review despite the ominous world events. "Mr. Ford Rush, master of ceremonies, presented his rhythmical traveling troubadours in a blazing fantasy of the legendary Tennessee hillbilly," the camp paper gushed.

On a typical performance, Ford Rush introduced Pee Wee King and His Golden West Cowboys, and then dancer Dolly Dearman, whose vibrant red hair curled down her back. With Pee Wee and the band playing the music, Kay Carlisle followed with a few pop selections for the boys, and the girl trio added others. The show was nearing an end but peaking when comedy hit the stage. Joe Zinkan, Pee Wee's bassist, cracked some jokes as "Cicero Sneedweed," but the real laughs showered down on Sarah Ophelia Colley, a.k.a. "Minnie Pearl." Her tales of the fictional hamlet of Grinder's Switch brought down the house. The excitement continued when the Camel Caravan performers showered cigarettes on the soldiers. Alcyone Bate Beasley lobbed cigarettes with a sling shot, and the Camelettes weaved through the crowd, handing out smokes while the men inhaled the girls' good looks. "The soldiers were hungry for entertainment," Arnold recalled, ". . . hungry for it."

Before their evening performance, the traveling musicians often visited injured servicemen in the hospital, walking from bed to bed to make conversation and offering an impromptu song or two. Otherwise, the men and women of the Camel Caravan read and played cards to while away time during the day. "It was like a big family really," said Dolly of those days. "We had good people. Everybody was young and this was something new. Everybody worked hard and gave the boys the best they could."

The Camel Caravan reached first gear in early 1942, speeding from Nashville to bases in the Northeast. During the first two weeks of February, they played New York's Camp Upton, Fort Slocom, and Fort Ontario and Fort Dix in New Jersey before landing back in Nashville for the Valentine's Day broadcast of the "Grand Ole Opry." On Saturday nights in 1942, the NBC network fed thirty minutes of the "Opry" to a regional network of stations under the sponsorship of R. J. Reynolds's Prince Albert Tobacco. The expanded coverage opened new doors for country music and the people who played it. On this Valentine's Day, Pee Wee and the boys took their turn in the spotlight.

Eddy kicks up his boot with the Camel Caravaners. He's between fiddler Redd
Stewart and dancer Dolly Dearman. (Dolly Denny collection)

Foreground, left to right: Minnie Pearl, WSM announcer Ford Rush, Eddy, and singer-
guitarist San Antonio Rose (Eva Nichols), with the Caravan. (Dolly Denny collection)

"Howdy all you friends and neighbors. Join us in our Prince Albert show," welcomed the announcer who segued into the house band's rendition of the "Opry" theme song.

> *Tune up your five-string banjo.*
> *Take down your fiddle and your bow.*
> *Throw back the rug on the floor.*
> *Light up your old cob pipe.*
> *Everyone will have some fun*
> *At the Grand Ole Opry tonight.*

Judge George D. Hay—the "Opry's" founder and protector from modernism—took the show from there and introduced the Camel Caravan headliners. "This is Pee Wee King with His Golden West Cowboys coming over to take another layer of bark off your heart. And the gent who's singing is the only fellow in the world that dang cupid himself walks up to and says, 'Who's next, boss?' 'Smilin'' Eddy Arnold singing 'Darling How Can You Forget So Soon.'"

Eddy's mellow interpretation of the song personified the hurt Valentine's Day can bring to the lonesome, and Pee Wee's up-tempo swaying salved the wound. Together, they added a piece of sophistication to the proceedings. But when Pee Wee and Eddy's notes faded, Roy Acuff and Minnie Pearl returned the show to the farm with his nasal singing and her rural humor. "How-deeee! I'm just so glad to be here," Minnie screeched. "I'm just so proud I could come!"

Soon after the Valentine's Day performance on the Opry, the military's demand for entertainment carried Eddy and the other Caravan performers farther afield than usual. In March, they embarked for bases in Central America from the port of New Orleans. The Pearl Harbor invasion had drawn America into war three months before, and to avoid potential enemy attacks, the Camel Caravan's ship, the Veragua, clipped through the night with every light dimmed or hidden, zigzagging away from its normal path through the Gulf of Mexico and Caribbean Sea. The United Fruit Company owned the fancy Veragua, but the government had commandeered the liner and converted it to a troop ship. The Veragua's luxury, though, remained intact, and as the Camel Caravan players cruised toward Panama they enjoyed the free food and nighttime party atmosphere that prevailed behind blackout curtains. After five days and nights of high living, the Veragua docked in Panama.

The Southerners on the Camel Caravan thought they knew heat, but the tropical temperatures near the equator added an extra steamy touch to at least one show. In her autobiography, Minnie Pearl wrote that the heat and humidity at France Field in Panama so drenched Kay Carlisle's flesh-colored dress that it clung tightly to her fetching figure—a figure Kay never bothered to restrict with a brassiere. The boys loved the pretty Kay anyway, but braless and in a wet dress, she received an even more enthusiastic reception. "If she'd been out there topless those boys wouldn't have seen a bit more," wrote Minnie. "None of us backstage knew what was going on, and neither did Pee Wee and the boys in the band because her back was to them. All we knew was that Kay was getting an incredible response from that audience." Minnie adjusted her angle and saw that Kay looked nude from the waist up. Minnie summoned the singer from the stage and frantically stuffed handkerchiefs and paper down the front of her dress to hide the excitement. Kay returned to perform for more subdued soldiers.

Other unexpected circumstances confronted the Caravan as they wound up their stay in Panama. The military could furnish neither boat nor plane to transport them out of the country. "We began to wonder if we were ever going to get home from Panama," said Eddy. "Finally, they had a plane. One of the generals down there arranged for us to fly to Guatemala." But home would have to wait. The Caravan performed one show in Guatemala, but spent more than a week idling there. Dolly Dearman fell ill from something she ate, and boredom lulled Eddy and the rest. "It was the dullest thing I'd ever done in my life," Eddy moaned. "There wasn't anything for us to do. We'd stay in the hotel, get up in the morning and get breakfast, and get out on the street and stand around." Eddy studied the directing techniques of traffic police and marveled at men who moved furniture by balancing couches and chairs on their head. Finally, a plane heading for Brownsville, Texas, collected the tired vagabonds. The Caravan's equipment truck met them in Texas, and Eddy and a few others who found no other way home rode to Nashville in the back of the truck.

No sooner had the Camel performers collected themselves than they set out again. By late June, they had passed through Cleveland and were heading to Buffalo for an Independence Day show. Speeding northeast again, the troupe performed at nine New England camps in seven consecutive days. Starting with Fort Revere in Hull, Massachusetts, on July 22, they continued on to Fort Church in Fall River, Massachusetts, then to five installations in Newport, Rhode Island, before concluding at Fort Rodman in New Bedford, Massachusetts, on July 29.

When Pee Wee's contract with the Caravan expired in December 1942, Eddy and the band probably celebrated by collapsing in a heap. "We went to seems like every military camp that existed," said Eddy. The dizzying schedule and long, hurried drives back to Nashville for the Saturday night "Opry" show took their toll on a Golden West Cowboy. Besides, the war's gasoline rationing and rubber shortages restricted travel. "Opry" talent would continue to entertain military personnel throughout the war, but only on weekends at nearby camps.

Although Eddy knew Pee Wee and the Camel Caravan were training him for greater stops ahead, he had every reason to hail the Caravan's demise. A

year earlier, he had married a pretty brown-haired woman named Sally
Gayhart.

— • —

Tennessee folklore esteems a man with a dimpled chin as steady and
trustworthy. So perhaps Eddy's rock-solid, indented chin drew Sally
Gayhart's attention, or maybe it was his quiet confidence and outright
good looks. Whatever the source of her attraction, the sight of Eddy
Arnold stirred Sally on a Friday night in 1940, not too long after Ed joined
Pee Wee King.

The band was broadcasting on WHAS in Louisville, and, while the new
vocalist serenaded the radio audience, he scanned the faces that had gathered to hear them. Eddy's eyes met Sally's. "Pretty girl," he thought. "Kind
of small . . . sort of fragile looking." After the show, he rushed to the lobby
to find her. As he searched for the dark-haired girl who looked a bit like
actress Olivia de Havilland, another girl stopped him for an autograph. He
obliged, and when he looked up from his signature, Sally stood next to her.

"I'd like an autograph, too," Sally said. "But I don't have any paper, I'm
afraid." She had no pen either, and frankly, was uninterested in Eddy's
autograph. She just wanted to meet this young troubadour dressed in a cowboy hat and boots who had gazed at her with his blue, floating eyes. They
mumbled some pleasantries before Sally stepped out into the Kentucky
darkness. She left neither a phone number nor an address, but Eddy soon
discovered—through a friend of Sally's who frequented WHAS—that she
worked nearby at the F. W. Woolworth soda fountain. Eddy, belying the
quiet confidence he projected, phoned Sally's friend and asked if she and
Sally would go for a Sunday drive with him and a buddy. The friend
arranged everything, making sure that Sally sat in the backseat with Eddy on
the drive. "I asked him later, 'How did you know which girl was going to get
in the backseat?'" recalled Sally Arnold. "He said, 'I already knew which girl
was going to get in the backseat!'" Soon Eddy began to frequent the drug-
store counter, chatting with Sally and mustering the nerve to ask her out by
himself. A courtship evolved.

Sally Gayhart was born in 1920 in Owenton, Kentucky, not too far from
the Bluegrass State's border with Ohio. One of Jasper Pendleton Gayhart
and the former Lula Belle Kunitz's ten children, Sally moved with her teem-
ing family to Le Grange, just outside Louisville, when she was three years
old. The Gayharts owned and operated a dairy farm in Le Grange, where
each child was expected to take up chores commensurate with their age.
Jasper and Lula Belle—second-generation Americans of German heritage—
imposed an order and discipline on their family that would remain with their
daughter Sally throughout her life.

Eddy traveled a lot, and in the last six months of 1941 the Camel
Caravan's schedule led to even longer trips. Eddy still dreamed of Sally,

though, visiting her when possible and envisioning marriage. On the road in Charlotte, North Carolina, he made up his mind. He called Sally from a pay telephone and announced his intentions to marry her, promising to have a token of his intentions once he returned to Louisville. Sally spent time with other young men and never really thought about marriage until Eddy called. She lay awake all night pondering his call, and made up her mind, too. When Eddy reached Louisville, she accepted.

They married in Nashville on November 28, 1941, and Sally moved into Eddy's apartment on Pinnock Avenue, where his mother, Georgia Arnold, also resided. What followed seemed to Sally to be a pale interpretation of wedded bliss. "When we were first married," recalled Sally, "he was on the Camel Caravan, and we hadn't been married a few days and he left to go down in Texas. And, due to the war, he was gone six weeks. There were times that I'd wonder if he just married me to stay there with his mother! That really gets boring, but I accepted it because it was part of his work."

Marriage to Eddy made Sally a music widow, and she would have to tolerate her husband's frequent and extended absences as his career prospered. But Sally adapted to her new life, slipping away whenever women crowded Eddy for autographs and pitching in with his efforts to better himself. When Eddy told Sally he could make more money singing solo on WSM than traveling with Pee Wee, for instance, she pushed him ahead. "See, he was just wondering about it and afraid to leave [and] of what would happen," said Sally. "I already knew that he could get a radio show on WSM, and I also knew that he would bring in more than he could with [Pee Wee's] salary and staying gone all the time."

With a new wife and his mother in the house, Eddy needed more than Pee Wee's salary to support the family. He hated to leave Pee Wee, and although his salary had edged up to $20 a week, he had to look ahead. Melton McNatt—Speedy's brother—remembered Eddy agonizing over the decision when Pee Wee King played Turner Field in Albany, Georgia, where Melton was stationed. If he went solo, he told Melton, he'd like to hire Speedy, who had left Pee Wee for a regular and more lucrative job on WHAS before the Camel Caravan embarked on their jaunt through America's military camps.

With Sally prodding him, Eddy finally knocked on the door of WSM's manager, Harry Stone. "I knew Harry Stone really liked what I was doing," explained Eddy. "He told me two or three times when I was out on the Caravan." Stone had run the station since 1930 and particularly understood the selling power of country music over the radio. He knew if the "Opry" pushed a product on Saturday night, the client felt it move on Monday, Tuesday, and Wednesday. Stone also knew that the "Grand Ole Opry" had to change its style of entertainment to reflect the urbanizing America of the 1930s and '40s. He had helped open the "Opry" door to Pee Wee King's more progressive sounds and admired Eddy's work with the band. A lean, practical man, Stone invited Eddy into his office and listened to his propos-

al. "I am going to quit what I'm doing," Eddy explained. "I'm working for
Pee Wee and I love him . . . great man. But I'm not getting anywhere. I'd
like to go to work for you."

Stone was an easy sell. His dour face blossomed. "I don't see any reason why
you can't work for me. You got a job," he said. Stone offered to start Eddy
on WSM's early morning broadcasts when the station nursed its new talent.

— • —

Anyone who ever worked for Pee Wee King and J. L. Frank knew they
were free to follow better opportunities should they call. Eddy heard his
calling, and in May of 1943, while Pee Wee and the gang were playing the
City Auditorium in Montgomery, Alabama, he told J. L. that he planned to
trade in his Golden West Cowboy duds. "We always had an understanding,"
remembered J. L. Frank in 1950, "[that] we would have at least two weeks
notice with each other in case I terminated his services or he was going to
leave the organization. . . . I talked it over with him, and he said he had an
opportunity of getting a solo spot on WSM radio station and could better
himself, which I was mighty glad to know."

With that, Eddy put another stage of his career development behind him.
Through his experiences with the band, Eddy—unwittingly perhaps—had
seen clearly the intricacies of a traveling musician's life and the critical balance of business acumen, promotion, good management, and entertainment
that helped a performing act excel. Although he knew that stepping right
into the forefront of a group as polished and professional as Pee Wee King's
was unrealistic, he figured a similar ensemble could grow up around him,
someday. So he acted.

— • —

WSM, before switching to NBC network programming at 9:00 A.M.,
aired four hours of live music. It was on the early side of those four hours
that Eddy Arnold's songs and strumming soothed many a morning listener,
including a sleepyheaded teenager, Danny Dill, who later worked for Eddy.
"I would hear Eddy come on in the morning, and I thought he was the
greatest singer I ever heard," Danny recalled. "It was one of those cases
where your mama's waking you up, and the radio is already on. Of course
that was like eating fish [on the bank]. It had a kind of aura about it that is
different from anything else. That singing sounded prettier to me than anything I ever heard. He was singing 'Mommy Please Stay Home with Me,'
'Molly Darling,' and all that stuff."

Three to five mornings a week Eddy appeared on WSM alongside such
fellow early risers as Paul Howard's Arkansas Cotton Pickers and the John
Daniel Quartet. "Then there was a magazine called the *Southern Agricul-*

turist," said Eddy. "They wanted to advertise on the station, so they put me on somewhere around noon. So that's what ran my salary up. . . . All at once, I was up to $35 a week." Letters praising Eddy poured into the station, and the WSM shows, like the radio spots in Jackson, led to live work in churches and schoolhouses around Nashville. His radio tether sometimes allowed him to venture as far as 125 miles away from home for a one-night stand, and, in the summer of '43, he went out on the tent-show circuit with the John Daniel Quartet for $10 a night. One date brought him to a theater in Dothan, Alabama, where the expectations were a little bit greater than he anticipated. "When I went there," Eddy told *Billboard* magazine more than twenty years later, "I found they had me doing twelve shows a day. There was nothing in the contract about it; I was just expected to grind away like a team of mules in a sorghum mill. Now I needed the money, but pride was worthwhile. I finally went out and saw the manager and said, 'Friend, I ain't doing any more shows.'"

The head of the WSM Artists' Service Bureau, Dean Upson, also helped place Eddy with his old boss Pee Wee King and WSM staff musician Owen Bradley on a syndicated radio program sponsored by the Chattanooga Medicine Company's Black Draught laxative. ("It's about as bad as it sounds," groaned Bradley.) They recorded about three or four shows a day on to large, unwieldy discs and stockpiled them for distribution to radio stations. According to Bradley, they each made $24 a show: $18 plus an $18 leader fee that Eddy, Owen, and Pee Wee shared.

Seeing the force of Eddy's potential, Harry Stone made room for him on the "Opry," where he debuted singing "Sinner's Prayer." Judge Hay dubbed him the "Tennessee Plowboy," and the "Grand Ole Opry" fraternity embraced Eddy. He accompanied his colleagues on weekend jaunts to military bases and performed for WSM client dinners whenever Harry Stone asked. Between the radio spots and personal appearances, Eddy brought home about $100 a week—a dramatic improvement over Pee Wee's salary. Sally loved Eddy's improved fortunes: Her husband was around more often and had extra cash to buy such luxuries as a used two-door Ford sedan. "I was staying home—wasn't traveling, didn't have to pay a hotel or eat out. I ate at home," Eddy recalled.

━ • ━

Up to this point, Eddy accompanied himself on the WSM shows, and, if he needed backing on the "Opry," the Georgia Peach Pickers took care of him. But a rising solo artist needs his own band, so, in the summer of 1943, Eddy assembled one. Ivan Leroy Wiggins, a sixteen-year-old steel guitarist, joined Eddy first. Known as "Little Roy" because of his youth and stature, Wiggins served briefly with Pee Wee King earlier in 1943 before King's full-time steel guitarist, Clell Summey, returned from the war to claim his job. King, Eddy

An early publicity shot. (Gabe Tucker collection)

remembered, persuaded him to hire Roy, who cried like the child he practically was when Pee Wee released him. Eddy also remembered that the neck on Roy's steel guitar was crooked. "If you tuned it in one key, it wasn't in tune for another key. It was a terrible guitar. So I helped Roy get him a good guitar."

Born in Nashville on June 27, 1926, Roy first heard Burt Hutcherson, an early "Opry" musician, play a Martin guitar with raised strings using a metal slide to fret it. The singing sound that Hutcherson conjured from his instrument inspired Roy, and he picked up the Hawaiian steel guitar at the age of six when his mother bought one from a traveling salesman. He quickly mastered the ability to run a steel bar across the strings, and, before his fifteenth birthday, earned a spot with Paul Howard's Arkansas Cotton Pickers.

Speedy McNatt and Gabe Tucker came down from WHAS to round out the band that Eddy would call the "Tennessee Plowboys." Gabe Tucker, the bassist and comedian who played with Eddy in Jackson during the late 1930s, urged Speedy to hook them up with Eddy. Both were living in Louisville and, with the armed forces taking more musicians every day, they strained to keep a band together. Eddy, Gabe supposed, might offer something more permanent. He was right. Eddy welcomed the two on a percentage deal, taking 55 percent and dividing the remaining 45 percent equally among Roy, Gabe, and Speedy. Beyond their musical responsibilities, Gabe helped promote the shows, and Speedy kept the books for a while before Sally took over the job.

Eddy and the band eschewed the Pee Wee King cowboy motif and cultivated a plowboy image, in keeping with their new name. However, their costumes more closely resembled the garb of gentleman farmers than boys behind a team of horses. On stage and in WSM promotional material, Eddy wore the Stetson hat of a country gentleman, a plaid or dress shirt, a striped ascot, slacks, and street shoes. The band dressed similarly yet not as nattily. "Eddy Arnold and His Tennessee Plowboys," a WSM advertisement read, "Currently on the air singing and playing folk song hits with the WSM Grand Ole Opry."

For a time, the Tennessee Plowboy's morning appearances followed Ernest Tubb's, and Eddy often ate breakfast with Tubb's guitarist on the show, Harold Bradley (Owen's brother). After bacon and eggs, Eddy and Harold headed home (they lived near each other along Dickerson Road in north Nashville). "Eddy and I would catch the street car together and ride to the end of the line, which was North 1st Street," said Harold Bradley. For two and a half blocks, the men walked abreast as far as Harold's house. Eddy lived a few blocks ahead. "I remember the last time that we took that little walk. I told Eddy good-bye. I remember seeing the back of him walking away in a brown summer suit—that was the end [of the summer] of 1943." Bradley was a student and went back to college for the fall semester; by the time he graduated in the spring of 1944, his old walking partner had accelerated his pace.

The Tennessee Plowboys atop the National Life Building (home of the WSM studios) in Nashville (1943). *Left to right:* "Little" Roy Wiggins, Speedy McNatt, Eddy, Gabe Tucker. (Gabe Tucker collection)

With the Jamup and Honey tent show in Mobile, Alabama (1944). Surrounding Eddy and Minnie Pearl (*left to right, from the top*) are Roy, Speedy, Gabe, Honey Wiles, Jamup (Bunny Biggs), and Uncle Dave Macon. (Gabe Tucker collection)

In 1944, the "Grand Ole Opry" gave Eddy his own segment. Sponsored by *Southern Agriculturist* magazine—known familiarly as the "Southern Aggie"—Eddy and the boys usually took the stage at 10:45 P.M. central time, right after Roy Acuff's fifteen minutes. In addition, Eddy frequently helped kick off the main "Opry" broadcast after hosting a fifteen-minute WSM show that aired just before it. Eddy's typical *Southern Agriculturist* set opened with a number like "That Little Kid Sister of Mine" or "My Star of Blue Has Turned to Gold," and featured "Opry" groups like the Poe Sisters or Gully Jumpers. Typically, Speedy or Roy performed an instrumental— Speedy on "McNatt's Reel" or "Whistling Rufus" and Roy on something like "Blue Bonnet Rag" or "Steel Guitar Rag." Eddy, of course, usually closed the segment. Eddy appears to have made his solo debut on the NBC segment of the "Opry" in late 1944 singing "The Cattle Call," a Tex Owens–composed ode to the lonely cowboy that would become Eddy's theme song. Eddy christened "The Cattle Call" with a soaring yodel, one of the few songs in which he featured this vocal effect: *"Where spurs are a jingling, the cowboy is singing this lonesome cattle call."*

During the war years, thousands of Americans tuned into the "Opry" on Saturday nights, either over WSM's 50,000-watt clear channel that reached most U.S. states or for a half hour over the NBC network. For the international audience, a transcribed version of the "Opry" went out over the Armed Forces Radio Network. The show had already helped to make national stars of Bill Monroe, Ernest Tubb, and Roy Acuff and had the potential to do the same for Eddy by beaming his name and talent to America's living rooms, helping to build a national base of Eddy Arnold fans. His western songs ("The Cattle Call"), morbid ditties ("I Don't Want to Be Buried at the Bottom of the Sea"), and weepers ("I Wouldn't Trade the Silver in My Mother's Hair") appealed to various audience segments. Eddy's straight, nasal-free delivery stood out among the "Opry" performers and attracted those looking for a smoother sound. On the other hand, his tragic, rustic themes and rural instrumentation (bass, fiddle, guitar, and steel guitar) rang true for the audience members who preferred a traditional flavor.

WSM, however, probably cared less about the demographics of Eddy's audience than for the sheer numbers he reached. Irving Waugh, a sales manager in the mid-'40s and later president of WSM, said the station considered Eddy hot property. "We thought he had a great future. We even thought he'd make a good host. He never really learned to use his hands as well as he might of. I always felt like we should hang a flowerpot on one of them or something. But there wasn't any question that he had a very rare voice and a most pleasing, charming, boyish personality."

To capitalize on his rising star, Eddy went out on his second tent show, this one in the summer of 1944. A sort of "'Opry' on the road" venture, the tents brought WSM regulars like Bill Monroe, Minnie Pearl, and banjo player Uncle Dave Macon to rural areas around the South. Jamup and

Honey—a blackface comic duo portrayed by Bunny Biggs and Honey Wiles—owned and headlined Eddy's first tent show that started in May at Meridian, Mississippi, and continued until the fall. According to Roy Wiggins, most of the tent talent came off the road for the Saturday night "Opry" broadcast and promptly beat it back to the tent the next day. "We'd leave every Sunday night at 10:30," Wiggins said. "I don't care where we were going, thirty miles or three hundred miles. Minnie Pearl, Eddy, and myself were in [Eddy's] car. Everybody else was in another car. Sometimes we'd get home sometime during the day on Saturday, play the 'Opry' Saturday night, and leave again Sunday night."

The hectic dash for Nashville and back to wherever the tent was ensconced had to be done. Contracts aside, there were masses of potential fans to be won on the road and on the radio, not to mention the decent money to be made. Standing in vacant lots on the back sides of towns, the tent could shade more than 3,000 people and, more times than not, reached its capacity. The locals, many of whom had lined up hours before show time for a seat, finally had a chance to see in person the stars that they had only heard previously through their radio sets. "It was always packed because it was something new," said Rollin Sullivan, who, as "Oscar" of the comedy duo "Lonzo and Oscar," played the tents with Eddy. "You would see them selling Eddy Arnold songbooks and pictures. . . . The tent concessionaires would sell candy with prizes and little ole things like that. They'd do that plumb on up until it was time to start the show. Most of the time we didn't even take an intermission. We just went right on through." The troupe went right on through during a rainy, weeklong stay in Mobile, Alabama, where the ground under the tent turned so soggy that the band kicked off their shoes and played barefoot.

When Eddy scanned the assembled tent patrons in front of him, he saw elderly and youthful folks dressed often in their Sunday best: a tie or buttoned collar for the men and flowered frocks for the women. Shoulder to shoulder, divided into four sections by rows of slender poles, they sat gazing at him. Their faces stretched far into the back, as far as the dangling light-bulbs allowed Eddy to see.

The WSM Artists' Service Bureau also found live gigs for Eddy and, for 15 percent of his gross, allowed him to bill himself as a "Grand Ole Opry" star. "Fifteen percent" translated to "theft" for many WSM stars, who also detested the station's demand that they return from the road every Saturday to play the "Opry." Even when the entertainer booked his own gig or went through another agency, he still owed 15 percent if he plugged his personal appearance on the "Opry" or billed himself as a "Grand Ole Opry" artist. Doubly frustrating was WSM's additional clause that no "Opry" performer could play a town either thirty days before or after another "Opry" member appeared there.

For Eddy, though, the 15 percent fee and the other WSM-imposed inconveniences were small prices to pay in light of the radio station's benefits. WSM put him out in front of the eyes and ears of the growing country audience, and station manager Harry Stone helped make that happen. Another WSM executive, Artists' Service Bureau chief Dean Upson, stopped Eddy in the halls of the radio station in the fall of 1943 and offered to be Eddy's personal manager. Upson, who also handled the Delmore Brothers and the Bond Sisters, offered Eddy a five-year personal management contract, but Eddy hesitated and on October 5, 1943, only agreed to a one-year deal with the option to renew for one more year.

Dean Upson came to Nashville for the first time in 1931 via St. Louis, where he appeared on KMOX radio with a vocal trio known as the Vagabonds, just one of the group's many radio stints around the nation. The son of a Protestant minister, Upson first assembled a singing group in Ohio during 1926 with his brother Paul and college chum Curt Poulton. He then traveled alone to Chicago for a stint on WLS, where he appeared as a member of the Y.M.C.A. National Quartet with folk singer Bradley Kincaid. Upson worked in another group called Tom, Dick and Harry before forming the Vagabonds in Chicago. They moved to St. Louis and on to WSM in 1931, where they rose to the top of the "Opry" cast. They thrived on the "Opry" despite a smooth, Tin Pan Alley–influenced sound that stood out from the show's usual fare and hinted at the mellower style that Eddy Arnold would popularize. Acquiring a dedicated following at WSM, they sold records on their own label, Cabin Hill, and later waxed for Gennett, Brunswick, and RCA Victor's Bluebird label. Forever bouncing around as radio journeymen sometimes do, Upson took the Vagabonds to radio station WGY in Schenectady, New York, but disbanded the group shortly after to become the program director of WMBD in Peoria, Illinois. However, WSM wanted the Vagabonds back, so around 1938 Upson reincarnated the group only to promptly break it up again when Nashville's WSIX radio offered him the program director slot there. A similar job carried him to WGRC in Louisville, but Upson turned up again at WSM in June of 1943, when he became head of the Artists' Service Bureau.

⎯ • ⎯

In the middle of his Upson contract, Eddy met the man who would later be his manager on a more long-term basis, Thomas A. Parker. Parker was a transplanted Floridian and onetime carnival worker who promoted "Opry" talent like Ernest Tubb and Roy Acuff, as well as one of Eddy's idols, the fading Gene Austin, when they passed through the Sunshine State. In the early 1940s, he worked for the Tampa Humane Society but really wanted to promote more shows. J. L. Frank and the WSM Artists' Service Bureau employed him when they sent acts to south Florida, but Parker guessed he'd be busier if he hung around Nashville more often.

Eddy Arnold's name had caught Tom Parker's eye in 1943 when *Radio Mirror* magazine ran a story on the singer. "Although Eddy is a comparative

Dean Upson.
(Patsy Tervooran collection)

The crowd lines up for the Jamup and Honey tent show in Mobile. (Gabe Tucker collection)

newcomer to the nationally famous Grand Ole Opry," the magazine noted, "he is an experienced entertainer. Already, at 25, he has been in radio for seven years. For many of those years he played in a well known folk music and cowboy group. Lately he has branched out on his own with a solo act that is increasing in popularity with every appearance."

Parker met Eddy in the Ryman Auditorium, the home of the "Opry." "It was on a Saturday night," Eddy recalled, "and I was there getting ready to do an early evening show before the 'Opry,' and he introduced himself to me." They finally worked together when Jamup and Honey hired Parker to book and do advance promotion for their 1944 tent show.

Parker slapped up posters in the tent show's next town, driving ahead of the troupe in a lumbering yellow truck that served as home and office. "It smelled like hell because he put them posters up with . . . a sticky stuff [made] out of flour and water," declared Gabe Tucker. "God damn! It was sour and smelled like hell. I don't know how he slept in it." During the winter of 1944–45, Parker, working on behalf of freelance promoter and soon-to-be record man Jim Bulleit, booked Eddy for two weeks in Florida. The two struck a formal association in the fall of 1945 when Eddy's contract with Dean Upson lapsed.

5

"*Hillbilly* music," the term music journalists tended to use at the time to describe country-flavored music of all styles, exploded commercially in the early 1940s. "Thar's gold in them thar hillbilly and other American folk tunes," *Billboard* magazine declared in 1942. Sales of country sheet music and records reached an all-time high in 1943, and, in response, *Billboard* debuted a chart to track the popularity of hillbilly records on jukeboxes. The entertainment trade magazine even put Roy Acuff on its cover one week, an honor typically reserved for big band leaders and vocalists. Radio stations in the Northeast joined the square dance, too. In New York alone, at least three stations aired live hillbilly acts.

Major record labels relentlessly signed country talent. Decca grabbed Ernest Tubb, Floyd Tillman, Jimmy Wakely, and Red Foley, and Columbia lured Roy Acuff, Bill Monroe, and western swing king Bob Wills. Gene Autry, the late Jimmie Rodgers, and a few other western and country artists had sold well for years, but by the early '40s a swell of new artists flooded the field. Who could deny that country music had arrived when the field produced pop smashes like Elton Britt's "There's A Star-Spangled Banner Waving Somewhere" (1942), Al Dexter's "Pistol Packin' Mama" (1943), and Ernest Tubb's "Soldier's Last Letter" (1944)? The themes of war in Britt and Tubb's hits suited country verse and fed off of the emotional insecurities of American people who watched hoards of their young go to war each day.

One recording label struggled to join the country craze: Victor Records, a subsidiary of the huge Radio Corporation of America (RCA). Twenty years before, the company dominated the white traditional music scene. Many of the artists popular all around rural America recorded for Victor. Vernon Dalhart, Carson Robison, Carl "Doc" Sprague, Jules Allen, the Carter Family, and Jimmie Rodgers helped Victor lead the way, but, except for the deceased Rodgers, whose catalog continued to sell, the popularity of these artists had waned by the early 1940s. And although Victor released Elton Britt's "There's A Star-Spangled Banner Waving Somewhere" in '42, the label generally lagged behind in the hillbilly market. In addition to Britt,

Victor had Zeke Manners and Texas Jim Robertson under contract. They each notched a hit every now and then (like Robertson's "I'll Be Back in A Year Little Darlin'" in 1941). But Britt, Manners, and Robertson mostly worked out of New York, and their popularity dated back to the early '30s. The hot, new artists were based in the South and Midwest.

Frank B. Walker, a Victor vice president, oversaw RCA's recording operations and tried to shake Victor from the doldrums. A onetime stockbroker and agent-manager associated with Enrico Caruso, Walker joined Columbia Records in the 1920s and set about combing rural America for talent. With other record men like Ralph Peer and Art Satherly, Walker helped bring Cajun, blues, Southern country, and other forms of American music into homes across the nation by way of the major recording labels. Walker joined Victor in the 1930s and, by the 1940s, saw the need to diversify the division's talent roster.

Walker had told his friends in the allied areas of the music industry to keep their eyes open for new talent. Chicago music publisher Fred Forster was one of Walker's friends and also one of Harry Stone's down at WSM. In 1943, Forster lunched with Stone when Stone was in the Windy City for a National Association of Broadcasters (NAB) meeting. The subject of "Opry" talent came up, and Eddy's name sprang to Stone's lips.

"There's a young boy down on my station doing pretty well," Stone said. "He's young and he sings well. I think he has a lot of promise."

"Well . . . I'll tell you what. When you think he's ready I'll make a pitch for him at Victor," the music publisher replied. "Maybe we can get him a recording contract."

"He's ready now," Stone said.

Forster, whose company owned chestnuts such as "Down by the Old Mill Stream" and "Missouri Waltz," put in a call to Walker in New York and introduced the name Eddy Arnold to him. With little hesitation and on the word of Forster, Walker wired Eddy an offer to record for Victor; Eddy grabbed the opportunity. He had auditioned for Columbia, Capitol, Decca, and Majestic—every label he knew about—and each rejected him. "At that point in my life," Eddy has often said, "I would have crawled on my belly all the way to Louisville to get a record contract." When the contract arrived from Walker, Eddy sent a copy to Forster, who had his lawyer draft a letter under Eddy's name essentially asking RCA for clearer contract language. Forster sent the draft back to Nashville, and Eddy asked his manager, Dean Upson, to review it. At this point, Upson took over the responsibility of communicating with Forster on Eddy's behalf, though both deferred to Forster's recommendations.

On November 30, 1943, after Forster approved the contract for him, Eddy signed with Victor, initiating a relationship that would last for most of the next five decades. Although he had yet to make a national splash in any aspect of his career, Arnold now owned a coveted recording contract.

The excitement of a recording deal soon waned, however, as Eddy realized a rag might be more useful than this paper contract of Victor's. Eddy had a contract sure enough, but a man named James Caesar Petrillo barred him from the studio. No, Petrillo wasn't a hostile Victor executive. James Petrillo presided over the American Federation of Musicians (AFM), and on August 1, 1942, he officially banned union musicians from America's recording studios. He feared that the proliferation of jukeboxes in the bars and restaurants across America and radio's increasing fascination with records would kill live music and put musicians on the unemployment lines.

The federal government, radio broadcasters, and recording companies vilified Petrillo. To the recording companies, Petrillo was Hitler, and although Petrillo didn't know Eddy Arnold from a 78-rpm disc, Eddy felt Petrillo directed the ban solely at him. Without records on the market, Eddy worried that his career would stall. He took welding classes to hedge his bets on a career in music and wondered when the strike would end.

The government brought antitrust suits against the AFM, and record companies chewed their nails as they watched potential earnings dissipate. Petrillo's enemies, for propaganda purposes, claimed the ban was hampering the war effort. "No soldier risking his life on a lonely post of danger has heard a freshly recorded phonograph record," wrote Neville Miller, president of the National Association of Broadcasters (NAB). "No band leader has achieved success; no patriotic music, hailing the achievements of our forces, has been generally available to the public."

The new country records doing so well in 1943 and 1944 were waxed before the ban, but the record companies' stockpiles soon dwindled. In impotent attempts to circumnavigate Petrillo, the companies released all-vocal performances and sent representatives abroad to record foreign musicians. Victor dispatched a team to Havana, where they hoped Cuban musicians could simulate the down-home sounds of American music, but the vocalists Victor hired hardly knew English; the company mercifully buried the master tapes in some obscure nook of their vault.

Petrillo knew that he had to release his musicians to the recording studios sooner or later, but he also saw his actions paralyze the industry. Grasping this power, he demanded that the recording companies deposit all payments to musicians directly into the AFM's treasury and contribute to a performance trust fund for unemployed musicians. Despite pleas from as high as the White House and an order of the federal War Labor Board to end the strike, Petrillo persisted. Ultimately, the federal government refused to enforce the War Labor Board's order, prompting the record companies to cave in to Petrillo. In September 1943, Decca conceded defeat to Petrillo, and on November 11, 1944—Armistice Day—Columbia and Victor followed suit. In a statement to record distributors and dealers, Victor general manager James W. Murray hailed the return to work.

"Prepare for some of the most outstanding recordings of popular hits and musical masterpieces in Victor's history," he boasted. Eddy Arnold, guitar in hand, stood poised to help Murray fulfill his promise.

New recording began almost immediately at Columbia and Victor. Columbia recorded trumpeter Harry James on November 13, but Victor beat its rival to the mark, sending Vaughn Monroe and his orchestra to work on the twelfth. A few weeks later, on December 4, Eddy Arnold entered the studios of WSM for his first session.

As far as the major labels were concerned, Nashville was still a frontier outpost in the recording business. Victor had recorded harmonica player DeFord Bailey and a few of Bailey's fellow "Opry" artists there in the late '20s, but, except for periodic field trips in the South, the company confined its work to New York and Chicago. For Eddy's session, Victor opted to pay WSM $5 a song to record their man instead of hauling equipment or sending any A&R men to Nashville.

During the strike, at Frank Walker's urging, Eddy and Dean Upson had cleared the use of WSM's studios for Eddy's session and zeroed in on the selections to be put to wax. Eddy also selected musicians for the date, initially asking a few of the guys from Pee Wee's band to back him. But Pee Wee had an engagement, so Eddy assembled the Tennessee Plowboys in WSM's familiar studios on 7th and Union. "I just got my guys and got around the microphone. The engineer and I kind of worked it out. I was singing the songs—I'd done all of them dozens of times."

Eddy cut four sides on that day: "Mother's Prayer," "Mommy Please Stay Home with Me," "The Cattle Call," and "Each Minute Seems A Million Years." Along with the Plowboys, Herbert "Butterball" Paige, who would also back Ernest Tubb, joined in on guitar and relieved Gabe Tucker on bass fiddle when Gabe blew a trumpet on "Mother's Prayer," a war-oriented weeper. "I would have been happy at that point just to have made one record then gone home," Arnold declared. "That's what I was thinking about when I made my first record, not dreaming of where it would lead to—whether it would sell one record or five records."

As Eddy said, he knew these songs cold, especially "The Cattle Call" and "Mommy Please Stay Home With Me," after performing them for months on the road and on the radio. Of "Mommy Please Stay Home with Me," Tucker complained, "I played that thing until I got sick and tired of it." But Tucker would have to bite his lip, because, in January 1945, Victor released "Mommy Please Stay Home With Me" on its budget Bluebird subsidiary.

At the time, Victor sealed their wax records with shellac imported from India via Great Britain, but government rationing during the war drastically reduced Victor's shipment to only 5,000 bags per month. Because the supply of shellac dwindled, Victor only pressed 85,000 copies of Eddy's first release, saving the raw material for major artists like Perry Como and Vaughn Monroe. But Victor should have pressed more. Eddy Arnold fans depleted the record company's supply of "Mommy Please Stay Home with Me."

The Tennessee Plowboys serenade a downtown Nashville gathering. (Gabe Tucker collection)

Signing autographs in Mobile, Alabama, with Minnie Pearl. (Gabe Tucker collection)

Eddy later called the Wally Fowler composition a morbid effort, the story of a woman who leaves her ailing son for a party only to find the grim reaper hovering nearby when she returns: *"She hurried home to find her baby in raging pain and nearing death."* However, the disc's sales proved that macabre meant money. Country fans liked the themes and the Eddy Arnold sound. True to his style, Eddy delivered the song with little embellishment, only the plaintive vibrato that dramatized the tragic lyrics. "Mother's Prayer," a tale of a mother's devotion to her soldier son, and "Each Minute Seems A Million Years" wept also, yet both proved hugely profitable.

In June of 1945, "Each Minute Seems A Million Years" (released with "The Cattle Call" on the flip side) entered *Billboard*'s "Most Played Juke Box Folk Records" chart in the stellar company of Gene Autry's "At Mail Call Today," Red Foley's "Hang Your Head in Shame," and Carson Robison's "Hitler's Last Letter to Hirohito." "'Each Minute Seems A Million Years,'" wrote *Billboard*, "is taken at a lively pace, with Arnold crying out his heart in song as he awaits to hear from his lady love gone away. Both sides stack up swell for juke box spinning." "Each Minute Seems A Million Years" reached number five on the five-song chart, selling over 125,000 copies. However, the yodel-laden "The Cattle Call" failed to pull its weight on the platter, so Eddy subsequently steered away from this style on his records. "I'd been yodeling a long time," Eddy said, "but the yodeling thing sort of went out with Jimmie Rodgers. People would yodel, but it wouldn't sell records for some reason."

Still, "Each Minute Seems A Million Years" proved Eddy's mettle to Victor. He could compete with the giants and deserved better than the radio station session Victor sponsored from hundreds of miles away. By August of 1945—after less than eight months of having discs on the market—Eddy had earned $1,284.09 from sales of his Bluebird Records. Eddy gleaned one penny from each record sale, which meant that he had sold 128,409 units, and, at a retail price of approximately 35 cents, that left more than $43,000 for the writers, publishers, and Victor. For Eddy, the thousand or so dollars dropped in his pocket none too soon: Sally and Eddy's first child, daughter Jo Ann, was due in December.

The WSM session, in addition to paying off for the star and his record company, helped satisfy a debt of gratitude to Fred Forster for his overtures to Victor on Eddy's behalf. Three of the four numbers Eddy recorded on his first time out belonged to Forster's publishing concerns: Forster Music and Adams, Vea and Abbott. It was apparent that Forster's introduction of Eddy to Victor exceeded mere altruism on Forster's part because, shortly after, Forster unabashedly peddled his songs to Eddy. In a letter to Dean Upson just a few weeks before the first session, Forster plugged "The Cattle Call" and hinted that Eddy's fortunes would rely on selecting songs from Forster's catalog: "My interest in Eddie [sic] Arnold is beyond just getting a couple of recordings—what I want to try to do is build him up and I think it can be done. The main thing for any guy who records is to get the right tunes. Without question RCA will pick some for him to do. However, he should insist on making 'I WALK ALONE,' 'SMOKE ON THE WATER' and if possible 'I'M SENDING YOU RED ROSES.'" In the same correspondence, Forster also scoffed at an unidentified tune that Eddy apparently wanted to record. "There is something else for Eddie to think about and it's this—that it's the push behind things that are published that counts and helps to sell records," Forster beseeched Upson. "I know that he is interested in the number that you mentioned but from an earning standpoint and helping to make himself, he should get on what is being plugged."

The tone of Forster's urgings indicated the sway publishers had over performers (although Eddy only recorded one of the songs Forster pushed in the letter: "I Walk Alone"). Not only had a music publisher found Eddy a record label, the publisher appeared to have a strong say in what he recorded—namely, as Forster wrote, "things that are published." In the early 1940s, the publishing industry's promotion efforts still influenced record sales to a large degree, so if a Frank Walker at Victor knew that a powerful music publisher would be pushing an artist's songs, he might be inclined to sign that artist. Such an understanding probably helped Eddy get a contract with Walker, but priorities and powers were rearranging themselves as Eddy experimented with recording for the first time. Radio stations and their ability to entrance legions of listeners were changing the rules of the music business. Mass media appearances, rather than the publishers' marketing efforts, could ignite record sales for a young artist like Eddy Arnold. As a result, Forster's patronage and the influence of other publishers held less and less control over the careers of Eddy and others. As his records sold, Eddy Arnold's name and image, fueled by jukebox and radio exposure, became the motor of his advancement. The gravity of his good fortunes drew publishers into his orbit, so never again would a publisher—even a friend such as Fred Forster—suggest that Eddy "should get on what is being plugged."

Most of Eddy's appeal, of course, dwelt in his voice. Although his band, good looks (for those who saw him), and song selection helped sell his music, Eddy's voice stirred the drink. He sang with absolute sincerity, whether conjuring tragedy or painting the lonely West in "The Cattle Call." But the seriousness and sincerity couldn't hide Eddy's deficits. He lacked savvy. He was too serious, almost stiff. A Bing Crosby or Red Foley winked at their audiences when they sang, but Eddy seemed to put on blinders. He projected warmth, grief, and any number of emotions, but failed to communicate worldliness or a bond with the audience that suggested, "We're in this mess together." So, although Eddy articulated his lyrics and even crooned like his heroes Bing and Gene, he'd yet to conquer the art of putting a song across to the audience. Eddy also battled flatness. During rehearsals, his voice occasionally lapsed to monotone—a flaw that later found its way onto a record or two—but the band usually alerted Eddy to the problem during rehearsals, allowing him time to correct it. Eddy was unpolished, uncertain, and unworldly, but growth would come. Besides, who could argue with success? In his very first session, Eddy had kicked a song through the goalposts and onto the national charts.

That first session in Nashville also revealed traces of the brilliance in Eddy's band. Speedy McNatt burned brightest, his familiarity with Eddy showing through on record as clear as in life. Speedy's fiddle flirts with Eddy's vocals, flitting in and out of earshot and teasing the lyrics from his mouth. On "Each Minute Seems A Million Years," Speedy's fiddle break cried the longing tears that Eddy cried, and all the while, he carpeted the song with a soft and easy cushion on which broken hearts could fall. Speedy's fiddle exploits seemed effortless, but recording scared him, and he had to work up to his excellence, sometimes with a little help from Gabe Tucker. "I'd irritate him a little, and that would get him going like gangbusters," Tucker recalled.

Steel guitarist "Little" Roy Wiggins, too, left a ringing mark on the first sessions, and for many sessions to come—without Gabe's provocation. If somewhat timid off-stage, Roy was gregarious on. What Roy calls his "ting-a-ling" sound—a high-pitched vibrating effect—kept pace with Eddy's singing at every turn, underscoring Eddy's points and sometimes springing up to drown the singer. Although the first session allowed a liberal helping of Roy's work, the steel guitar's role would burgeon on Eddy's subsequent recordings.

Wiggins played an electric steel guitar without pedals, and one night after an "Opry" performance, he persuaded Eddy to let him try the "ting-a-ling" sound. "That's what Oswald [Beecher Kirby, a.k.a. Bashful Brother Oswald of Roy Acuff's band] does with his dobro except it will be on the electric guitar, which will make it sound different," he told Eddy. "I'll try to keep it an octave higher."

The ting-a-ling, or tremolo sound, actually emerged in the days before electrification of musical instruments. Acoustic guitar players often added vibrato to a note to sustain it. Roy was one of the first to bring the sound to the electric steel guitar, and the result possibly attracted some fans who might otherwise be repelled by Eddy's choirboy vocals. Roy took pride in his playing and practiced until the new style came easily.

The teenage Roy Wiggins became a fixture on Eddy Arnold's show and stayed long after Gabe and Speedy left. In fact, Eddy continued to pay Roy years after they stopped playing together. "It was part of a promise he made to me in 1945," Roy told researcher Douglas Green in 1974, "that if I stayed with him, and I didn't cause any trouble or embarrass him in any way, that it would be a lifetime proposition." He recorded with his boss through the early '60s, and although Roy and Eddy never developed a brotherly bond, Roy looked to Eddy as he would a father.

The young star. (Eddy Arnold collection)

With a national hit, a tight band, and the expansive "Grand Ole Opry" radio platform to his credit, Eddy needed to capitalize on his recent successes. And no better capitalist lived than Tom Parker. As time would tell, Parker never excelled at grooming unknowns, but he worked wonders with rising stars like Eddy. So when Eddy's deal with Dean Upson expired, the Tennessee Plowboy cast his fate with Parker. Parker still worked out of Tampa, and he promptly put Eddy and the boys to work all over Florida. Parker had a comfortable sphere of influence in the Sunshine State, but the band could do without the Nashville-to-Florida trek, which, at the time, included an hours-long crawl through Atlanta.

"He and I didn't hit it off too hot," complained Roy Wiggins of Tom Parker. "First thing he did was take the songbook sales away from us. He took it himself. I probably made $100 a night selling songbooks." Gabe, Speedy, and Roy hawked the songbooks to eager fans at intermission and after shows, and every Saturday night after the "Opry," Eddy advertised them on his own WSM show. The orders poured into Eddy's house, and Sally filled them with a little help from Speedy's brother Lynn, who was studying trumpet in Nashville. Day after day, Sally mailed the songbooks, often needing three or four days to fill seven days' worth of incoming orders. For many of the major "Opry" stars, songbook revenues equaled performance revenues (Roy Acuff's made him a rich man); with Tom Parker and Sally engineering the distribution of the Tennessee Plowboy's, songbook sales proved to be a major component of Eddy's total income.

Parker stepped up the band's pace in 1945, adding dates as far north as Pennsylvania, where Eddy and the boys appeared on their own without other "Opry" stars. "[Parker] was queer for that white line in the highway," recalled Wiggins. "He wanted to work every show he could." Like in the Pee Wee King days, the whirlwind pace exhausted the band and made driving hazardous. Traffic lights, mountainous climbs, hairpin curves, and livestock set a course of road obstacles that made it difficult to maintain high levels of speed. They pushed to sustain sixty miles per hour as often as possible. "I did a lot of driving," said Wiggins, "and I started to pass a car. When I got out there in the other lane, here comes a vehicle right at me. Fortunately, there was one of those old-fashioned truck stops that had the great big parking lots, and I ran up in there." Initially Eddy, the band, and their instruments traveled in a 1941 Ford car and a 1941 Ford station wagon before graduating to a bulky stretch limousine with "Eddy Arnold and His Tennessee Plowboys: WSM" emblazoned on the side.

Flat tires, broken axles, and other inconveniences hampered the band's travels, but they found humor in it all. "We stopped to get some gasoline back when they serviced your car," Wiggins continued. "Whoever [serviced the car] left the radiator cap sitting on the battery. When we gassed up again after 250 or 300 miles, there sat that cap on that battery! We all told Eddy if that had been [our car], that thing would have went through the border block, out through the exhaust pipe, and killed the people behind us." Eddy earned the nickname "Goldie" because of such luck and what the band saw as his ability to turn anything to gold.

Car problems never seemed to bother Eddy. They were the snags of the road and had to be tolerated. One night, "Butterball" Paige, who sometimes played guitar with Eddy on the road, fell asleep at the wheel and slammed into another car. "Eddy didn't say a word," Speedy McNatt told a radio interviewer in the early 1970s. "It didn't look like it even bothered him."

It seemingly took lesser events to ruffle the boss's feathers. "About a week later," Speedy went on, "we were all riding in the car and somebody else was driving. Eddy had this hat that he wore at that time. He wore kind of a country gentleman, Texas style hat and he was particular about the hat. He didn't want any dust on it. He didn't want any wrinkles in it. He didn't want anything on it. He wouldn't put it in the trunk for fear it would get mashed up. He left it on the back of the seat. So it fell down the seat, and 'Butterball' sat down on that hat, and Eddy almost fired him on the spot. That really shook him."

Gabe Tucker left the Tennessee Plowboys in 1945 to perform comedy on the Jamup and Honey tent show. His departure opened the door for bassist Lloyd George, mandolin player Rollin Sullivan, and Rollin's brother Johnny Sullivan, a guitarist, to join Roy and Speedy behind Eddy. Lloyd George hailed from Alabama and the Sullivans were from south-central Kentucky. Rollin, who, like Eddy, came to Nashville via WTJS and Bill Westbrooks, had worked up a comedy routine with Lloyd, and Eddy used them to open his road show, initially dubbing the duo "Cicero and Oscar."

Rollin was "Oscar" and Lloyd was "Cicero," but Eddy wasn't quite comfortable with the name "Cicero." He was inspired to change Lloyd's stage name, according to Rollin, one evening when the troupe stopped for a night's rest. "While we was checking in, this black man, a porter, was coming down the steps just covered with dirty linen. The desk clerk looked up and said, 'Lonzo! Don't you ever come down those front steps with dirty linen anymore.' Well, Eddy reared back and slapped them hands together and pointed at Lloyd George and said, 'You are Lonzo!'"

Lonzo and Oscar would survive in name—with various Lonzos—for thirty years; from 1945 to 1947, they opened virtually every Eddy Arnold concert. "We'd go out on the stage," Rollin remembered. "And, boy, we'd wang-bang them, get them all laughing and having a good time. Then we introduced Eddy. Eddy came out on the stage, and he would sing 'Mommy Please Stay Home with Me,' and they'd all start bawling." It was for that reason Eddy hired Lonzo and Oscar to do comedy. He knew his songs often leaned toward the teary side and didn't want his audience weighted with trouble in mind or a heavy heart when he took the stage. Lonzo and Oscar gladly met Eddy's need, delivering a twenty-minute barrage of nutty jokes and crazy musical numbers. Before every Eddy Arnold performance, they

Eddy on the "Opry." With him, *left to right*, are: Roy, Speedy, Dempsey Watts, "Butterball" Paige. (Eddy Arnold collection)

One long limo prepares for another string of shows. *Left to right*: Eddy, Rollin Sullivan, Lloyd George, "girl singer" Lillie Belle, Speedy, Johnny Sullivan, Roy Wiggins. (Eddy Arnold collection)

trotted on the stage in ill-fitting suspenders, straw hats, and tattered shirts (the standard country-bumpkin uniform), and Oscar announced, "Welcome to the Eddy Arnold show. He's Lonzo, and I'm Oscar."

"You know what, Lonzo?" Oscar said without losing a beat. "I suuure do think a lot of you."

"I like you too, Oscar," Lonzo answered.

"Lonzo, there ain't nothing I wouldn't do for you."

"Well, Oscar, there ain't nothing I wouldn't do for *you.*"

"That's the way we go through life," Oscar cracked to the audience, "doing nothing for each other!"

Lloyd soon left Eddy to go out on his own as "Ken Marvin," and Johnny Sullivan became "Lonzo." "Lonzo and Oscar" stuck with Eddy until 1947, opening his live appearances with comedy and providing musical accompaniment on radio shows and recording sessions.

One evening, Eddy's "Mommy Please Stay Home with Me" absolutely broke down the audience, an amazing sight to Johnny Sullivan, who happened to be backing Eddy on guitar. Johnny became so amazed that he lost time. Eddy slid his foot back toward Johnny and tapped it hard on the wooden stage to bring his straying guitarist back on the beat. When the show ended, Eddy approached Johnny. "Johhnnn," Eddy drawled, "where were you in my song?"

"Well, Eddy, I'm going to confess to you, you really had them people going on 'Please, Mommy, Please.' You really had them going. I got to watching them and everything, and I got off time."

"Johhnnn," Eddy admonished, "stay on beat and I'll handle the audience."

Guitar players who wandered off beat were the least of the periodic indignities Eddy grappled with on the road. While playing a mill town somewhere in the nation's heartland, virtually an entire audience cleared the hall smack in the middle of an Eddy Arnold hit song. Dumbfounded and disconcerted, Eddy's voice trailed off as he watched the people vacate row by row. Later, Eddy learned that at 9:00 P.M. it was time for a shift of mill workers to start their eight hours. Another round of fans, just off the previous shift, trickled in for a second show. "Another time, we played Harlen, Kentucky, where the mean folks are," said Roy Wiggins. "We were playing this schoolhouse, and the kids were making so much noise. Eddy was begging them to be quiet . . . and the principal came out and said, 'Mr. Arnold, I'll have to do this. They don't understand what you say.'" Eddy stepped aside while the principal took the microphone and unleashed a torrent of threats and curses at the little devils. "They cut our tires," Roy lamented.

—▬ ∙ ▬—

While Eddy perfected his live appearances and battled road weariness in 1945, changes were afoot at Victor. Frank Walker informed Eddy that he was leaving to start MGM Records and Steve Sholes, an RCA veteran, would replace him in the hillbilly department (which Walker had directly overseen despite his senior executive level). "That scared me to death," Eddy recalled. "I didn't know Mr. Walker much less know Steven H. Sholes. Being young and green, the first thing I said to myself was, 'What in the heck will happen to me?'" Eddy fretted that Sholes would fire him, but Sholes harbored no such intentions. He was eager to meet Eddy and squeezed two Victor dates into the Tennessee Plowboy's hectic 1945 schedule. "It wasn't very long after he got there that I became a good seller. He found good songs for me."

Steve Sholes's history with Victor coincided with RCA's. In 1929, the same year RCA took over the company, Sholes joined Victor as a part-time messenger while he pursued a degree at Rutgers University. Born in Washington, D.C., Sholes moved with his family to New Jersey when his father took a job at the Victor Talking Machine Company in Camden. While Eddy Arnold practiced his guitar in Chester County, young Steve dabbled with the clarinet and saxophone across the river from Philadelphia in Camden.

After his 1933 graduation from Rutgers, Steve filled a full-time slot in the factory storeroom of RCA's radio department. In 1936, he jumped to a clerk's job in the record department and, trading on his music experience, soon wriggled his way into the recording operations. Victor's pop A&R chief, Eli "Obie" Oberstein—another great leader of recording expeditions into America's hinterlands—started Steve out on a jazz track. The man who would build Victor's country preeminence initially recorded jazz greats Jelly Roll Morton, Sidney Bechet, and Mezz Mezzrow. He kept his finger in jazz and years later worked with Earl Hines, Coleman Hawkins, and Dizzy Gillespie, who recorded his 1948 hit "Manteca" with Sholes at the helm.

Sholes tasted a new musical flavor in 1939 when Frank Walker, Victor's new vice president, asked him to coordinate field sessions in Atlanta. Sholes knew little about country music when he and his engineer, Frank Lynch, set up portable recording equipment in an Atlanta hotel, but he adapted to the task as, one by one, hopeful artists filed in the room in search of the $20 Steve paid for each song he waxed. Steve sweated through the whole experience, because every time he opened the mike, he had to shut the windows to muffle street noise.

During World War II, Steve refined his recording skills in the military, recording bandleader Hal Kemp, pianist Fats Waller, and other pop and classical artists for distribution to America's fighting forces. Originally, Steve expected to be fighting overseas, but when his commander ordered his company to dig ditches shortly after processing at Fort Dix, New Jersey, the corpulent record man scrambled for an alternative to manual labor. He sought out Fort Dix's head of music, Jack Leonard (bandleader Tommy Dorsey's vocalist), and pleaded for a chance to play sax or clarinet in the base's band. But he never blew a note and instead snagged an assignment as the military's first enlistee in the V-disk ("V" for Victory) program that distributed recorded entertainment to fighting forces throughout the world.

At just a few years over the age of thirty, Steve had already contributed volumes to America's recording history, but that was just a prelude. His most significant work lay ahead of him. Sholes's career turned when Frank Walker left for MGM and placed the folk and race (the name recording companies gave for recordings made by black artists) division in his hands. To shore up the hole Walker left in Victor's musical expertise, the company rehired Eli Oberstein, who had left Victor in 1939 to form the U.S. Record Company. Sholes reported to "Obie," who had assumed the title of director of artists and repertoire, and the two made an effective team in Victor's efforts to solidify the label's presence in the country market.

"Obie" could rattle cages and make sure country got respect within the Victor organization. He was as blustery and controversial as Sholes was mild-mannered and diplomatic. Sholes could gently embrace Southern artists who mistrusted Yankees, especially Oberstein's overbearing variety of Yankee. Those who knew Sholes remembered a man who laughed like Santa Claus and defused tension in the studio with acutely relevant jokes. From behind the control room glass, he let the musicians be themselves as long as they stayed within the realm of commercial potential, and he never made scenes when things went awry. "Steve, as record producers go, was unaggressive," according to one associate. "He knew what he was after, and if it wasn't happening, in a gentle way he would change what needed to be changed. Instead of talking over the mike from the control room, he would come out and speak with somebody quietly and privately." That style endeared musicians to Steve, especially young apprehensive performers from the South like Eddy Arnold.

And Sholes labored for Victor, so much so that many who worked with him throughout the years thought him a workaholic. When other Victor executives were schmoozing and downing drinks at restaurants around New York, Steve was combing publishers for songs or scheduling sessions. "Steve was a very dedicated man," recalled a colleague. "He didn't have really any outside interests. His whole life centered around RCA and those country artists. I don't know if he ever did anything else." One summer's day, Sholes called an RCA producer, complaining that the producer had improperly recorded the playing time of a few songs. This was during an era when disc jockeys ignored songs longer than three minutes, and producers shaved a few seconds off the song on paper if their songs went over. "We shouldn't mislead these guys," Sholes complained to the producer. Sholes had called from a "vacation" home in Cape Cod, where he sat with a turntable and records while his family played outside on the beach.

Sholes's work converted Victor's struggling status in mid-'40s country to superiority status by decade's end. In 1946, Victor claimed only three of the year's top twenty songs in the hillbilly category, but that number grew to

Steve Sholes (*with finger raised*)
makes a point on a Victor session.
(Cy Coben collection)

nine in 1948—more than any other label. Sholes diversified his roster to
include Roy Rogers, Pee Wee King, and Hank Snow, easing his reliance on
the aging Carson Robison and Elton Britt. Sholes probably would have
accomplished little without Eddy Arnold, who was responsible for the
label's biggest country hits from 1946 to 1949. Sholes capitalized on the
increased revenue that Eddy created to strengthen Victor's overall position
in the hillbilly market. From these roots, RCA Victor grew to be the top
label in country music history.

However, this success was very much in the future when Sholes first
arranged to produce Eddy. Sholes booked Brown Brothers studio—a radio
transcription service in Nashville—for July 9 and personally supervised the
session. Two newcomers, Dempsey Watts on guitar and Golden Stewart on
bass, joined Speedy, Roy, and "Butterball" as Eddy's studio accompanists,
and together they cut four more songs in the melancholy mold, including
another war weeper, "Did You See My Daddy Over There?" Eddy also
recorded "Many Tears Ago," the first of many fine songs Jenny Lou Carson
sent his way. Carson, a sometime hillbilly singer herself, had written hits for
Tex Ritter and Red Foley, but throughout the 1940s, Eddy was her most frequent interpreter.

The Nashville session did not produce any hits, but Sholes's first contact
with Eddy intensified his interest. In November, he brought Eddy and the
band to Chicago for the young star's first session in a legitimate RCA Victor
studio. Again, Eddy failed to replicate the success of "Each Minute Seems
A Million Years" or significantly compete with late 1945–early 1946 hits like
Bob Wills's "Silver Dew on the Blue Grass Tonight" or Tex Ritter's "You
Will Have to Pay." But Sholes held fast and signed Eddy to a new one-year

contract at the end of '45. Eddy's Bluebird sides sold well enough, Sholes decided, and his voice grew bolder and his band tighter with every outing. "There wasn't much arranging for what I was doing," Eddy explained. "I usually had learned the song before I went there. It was me singing a chorus, the steel guitar would play a chorus, and me sing another chorus. It was about over then, but they were selling." With a few tweaks and Steve's support, Eddy could sell much more.

Not until Steve's third session with Eddy did the young singer show his true muscle. Eddy brought six musicians to Chicago in March 1946, including a young WSM staff pianist named Owen Bradley (who worked the "Black Draught" radio shows with Eddy). Standing out from among the six tracks Eddy recorded was "That's How Much I Love You," a playful tribute to a woman. In that it was playful, it was different. Up to that session, Eddy Arnold songs scolded women for their unfaithfulness and moaned over death and broken hearts. "That's How Much I Love You" revealed another dimension: A sense of humor came with that innocent voice.

In the song, Eddy was "an old gray mare" and his girl, a "horsefly." This was just what America seemed to be waiting for from Eddy. The gloom that burdened Eddy's songs had dissipated along with worries of World War II. He seemed more relaxed and even giggled at one point. A perfect foil to Eddy's silly lyrics on "That's How Much I Love You," Speedy's masterful, determined fiddle breaks gave the song an edge, and Roy's steel guitar chimed only sparingly, not battling Eddy's vocals.

Owen Bradley was really along to help keep the band in time, and his piano is overshadowed by the other instruments. ("You don't hear it," Owen said of his playing. "You just kind of felt it. That was the idea.") Lloyd George played bass, Johnny Sullivan strummed rhythm guitar, and Rollin Sullivan picked the electric mandolin. "They hadn't been using a piano," Owen Bradley remembered. "Eddy told the bass player, 'Watch Owen's left hand. When he hits a note, you hit a note.' He told the guitar player, 'Watch his right hand. When he hits a chord with his right hand . . .' All of the sudden, all three of us were so tense. Hell, I didn't dare make a mistake. I tried to be like a mechanical man, and they're staring at me [thinking] I might do something tricky. Eddy didn't have a lot of confidence in what was going on."

Eddy actually had less confidence in "That's How Much I Love You" when songwriter Wallace ("Wally") Fowler introduced it to him. The father of the Oak Ridge Quartet, which later became the Oak Ridge Boys, Fowler had sung with the John Daniel Quartet when Eddy and the quartet appeared together on the early-morning WSM lineup in 1943 and '44. In those days, Fowler had pitched "Mommy Please Stay Home with Me" and a couple of other songs to Eddy (and evidently believed, like many of his writing peers, that song titles should be at least five words long!). When Eddy chose to record one of his numbers, Fowler often voluntarily gave Eddy partial writing credit to show his appreciation; in keeping with that practice,

Wallace "Wally" Fowler,
who wrote "That's How
Much I Love You" and all
of those other Eddy Arnold
hits with long titles. (Dolly
Denny collection)

Eddy had one-third of the writing on "That's How Much I Love You." (It
was common practice at the time for songwriters to give artists—and sometimes deejays, managers, or producers—partial writing credits on songs to
encourage them to record a song.) But mere writing credit couldn't warm
Eddy to the song, and on that March day in Chicago, as he pulled the wrin-
kled lyric sheet from his guitar case and handed it to Owen to write an
arrangement, he seemed reluctant to record it. The song would not win
Eddy's respect until it blasted up the charts for him and spawned cover versions from Frank Sinatra and Eddy's hero Bing Crosby. "Just in a few weeks
it was a hit," remembered Eddy. "Jukeboxes meant a lot then. It was on
every jukebox . . . everywhere."

   "That's How Much I Love You" and another song from the March session, "Chained to A Memory," entered the charts the same week in early
October 1946. Victor had scrapped the Bluebird label, and these songs were
Eddy's first releases under the Victor name. "Chained to A Memory" sput-
tered, but "That's How Much I Love You" seemed certain to knock
"Divorce Me C.O.D.," by the great guitarist Merle Travis, from the number-
one spot on *Billboard*'s chart. In the second week of October, Eddy skipped
from number five to three as Al Dexter's "Wine, Women and Song" kicked
Merle Travis from the top. Surely, Eddy would be next, but one week later
Travis regained the throne, and Eddy remained at number three. Eddy
dropped to number four, but edged back to third place in time for
Halloween. With Travis still atop the chart, Eddy moved to number two,

where he camped for three of November's four weeks. That damned Merle Travis! When November turned to December, Travis still sat at number one while Eddy celebrated his tenth week on the charts at number four. The Tennessee Plowboy stalled in the top five, and bounced high only to be repelled by "Divorce Me C.O.D." In January, "That's How Much I Love You" lost its grip and fell off the charts completely. Ernest Tubb's "Drivin' Nails in My Coffin"—a chart entry two weeks after "That's How Much I Love You" tumbled—summed up Eddy's chances for number one. But during the last week of January, he rallied. Eddy re-entered for two weeks, but couldn't muster the steam to press on. "That's How Much I Love You" dropped off the charts for good in February while his nemesis Merle Travis licked his paws with another number one: "So Round, So Firm, So Fully Packed."

Eddy finally struck back in May when "What Is Life Without Love," also from the March 1946 session, crawled over "So Round, So Firm, So Fully Packed" and checked into number one. "What Is Life Without Love" spent twenty-two weeks in the charts, more than a month longer than "That's How Much I Love You." But the earlier song deserved the credit for opening the door for Eddy's first number one and steering him to new lyrical themes. Not to say that heartbreak and temptation vanished from his music, but against the quickening current of cheating and misery in country music, he began to celebrate love and life's pleasures more often. Not only would Eddy's lucid delivery separate him from most of the pack, his subject matter now would, too.

On their way home from the "That's How Much I Love You" session in Chicago, Eddy turned to Owen Bradley with good news. Steve Sholes, Eddy said to Owen, believed he had star potential and had promised to throw Victor's full strength behind him.

6

*E*ddy probably could do little but laugh as "Divorce Me C.O.D." pummeled "That's How Much I Love You" on the charts and, if he did laugh, he laughed heartily because Eddy Arnold never titters. Even the word "laughter" inadequately describes Eddy's eruption when he finds humor in life; "guffawing" seems more appropriate. Jokes and one-liners fly freely over the tedium of a musician's life, and Eddy welcomes the diversions with unrestricted expulsions. Humor has lightened his long, tiring drives and the "hurry-up-and-wait" regimen of recording and live performances.

On a Chicago session subsequent to the "That's How Much I Love You" date, Lonzo and Oscar cooked up a good one. All the boys had flown to Chicago except for harmonica player Bronson Reynolds, a.k.a. "Barefoot Brownie," who was slated to play on one Lonzo and Oscar song (they too had a Victor contract) after the duo finished with Eddy. Flying horrified Brownie, so he took the overnight train from Nashville while Eddy and the boys landed in Chicago on Saturday evening and showed up Sunday morning fresh and ready to play. Brownie, though, spent Saturday night on a train full of crying babies and arrived at the studio bleary-eyed and unshaven. Worse than that, the poor man had to wait through Eddy's nine recordings until Lonzo and Oscar were free to work. When Brownie's appointed time finally came, either Lonzo or Oscar slipped into the control room and whispered to Steve Sholes, "Tell Brownie that you don't think the harmonica fits this song." Steve went along and broke the bad news to Brownie. Everyone in the studio watched what life was left drain from the weary harmonica player. He was dumbfounded, crestfallen until everybody broke out in laughter, led by Eddy's guffaw. Steve, incidentally, let Brownie play his riffs.

To those around Eddy, his guffaw became one of his most memorable traits. Owen Bradley observed during a Bob Hope–Bing Crosby Road movie that Eddy continued laughing about five seconds after the rest of the audience stopped. So when the crowd settled down, Eddy's bellowing rang out. Joe Csida, who ran RCA's pop division in 1949 and later managed Eddy, observed the same thing when he and Eddy attended a performance of Andy Griffith's *No Time for Sergeants* in the 1950s. "Eddy was so absolutely outgoing and irrepressible that when something funny happened on stage, he would let out this loud and incredible guffaw. It would shake the theater and everybody within five rows of you would look around and say, 'Who the hell is that?' If you were going to go where something funny was going to happen and you didn't want to be noticed, you wouldn't want to have Eddy with you. If he thought something was funny, he was going to let you know it was funny."

In 1946 and '47, Eddy increasingly had reason to laugh.

With Tom Parker's help, Eddy widened his national exposure every day. In addition to the furious schedule of live appearances, Tom multiplied Eddy's radio presence in 1946 by arranging a weekly segment on the Mutual network. Every Saturday, with sponsorship from Purina, Eddy sang and led a cast that included Lonzo and Oscar and the Cackle Sisters (Carolyn and Mary Jane DeZurik, a yodeling duo from Minnesota). The "Checkerboard Matinee" went over so well that in January of 1947, Purina extended its sponsorship to Mutual's "Checkerboard Jamboree," a weekday show that originated live from radio station WMAK in Nashville's Maxwell House Hotel at 12:15 P.M. "I sold a lot of merchandise," recollected Eddy. "I used to do their commercials. When I started that program they had an announcer who would billboard the show, put it on the air ['Here's Eddy Arnold!'] and then do the commercials. One day, I went to rehearsal, and one fellow from the agency said, 'I want to hear you read a commercial.' I read him a commercial and he says, 'You do them from now on.' So from there on, all the announcer did was billboard the show." When Eddy left Nashville to meet live engagements, he transcribed several editions of the "Checkerboard Jamboree" or, if the technology was available, aired the show live from the road.

Eddy and Tom saw even greater radio opportunity beyond the "Jamboree" and contracted with the Brown Advertising Company (owners of the Brown Brothers Studios) to produce the transcribed "Eddy Arnold Show." Whenever Eddy and the band had spare time in Nashville, they mass-produced fifteen-minute segments to send to stations nationwide. "One night we were cutting away," said bassist Chuck Wright, who played on many of the transcriptions, "and everything was going pretty good. All at once, the door opened and 'Clang! Bang! Bang!' The night watchman came in making his rounds, and here we were right in the middle of a song. We kept right on going. You let things go by." The transcriptions featured gaps for local radio stations to fill with their own advertising. By the end of 1947, more than 300 stations subscribed.

The "Grand Ole Opry," though still an important radio affiliation for Eddy, was now just one channel in his ever-unfolding national distribution system. Eddy was able to drop the "Grand Ole Opry Star" billing to avoid paying WSM 15 percent of his concert gross. "I didn't need to use the name

Late '40s fan and publicity shot. (Dolly Denny collection)

of the 'Opry,'" Eddy said. "People knew me who didn't know anything about the 'Opry.'"

RCA Victor, Tom Parker's crafty management, and songs from the best writers in Nashville helped fuel that national distribution effort. When Steve Sholes told Eddy that Victor was ready to flex its muscles for him, he meant business. Sholes sent Victor advertising dollars in Eddy's direction and made sure he had the full support of the company's massive distribution system.

For sales and marketing purposes in the mid-1940s, Victor divided the country into several regions and placed its own distributors and field representatives in each area. Most of the major record companies owned distribution outlets that supplied product to jukebox operators and record dealers, but independent distributors, which stocked records from all the majors and smaller independent labels and offered easier credit terms, had begun to mushroom. Called "one-stops" because jukebox operators and record store owners could replenish their inventories in one place without visiting each label's distribution outlet, these independent distributors grew in stature. Victor relied on these operators to push their records, and Victor's field representatives, like Jack Burgess in the Midwest, made sure the one-stops did just that. Burgess met constantly with one-stop owners north to south from Minnesota to Missouri and east to west from Indiana to Iowa. He kept watch to ensure the one-stops had proper inventories, relationships with the right dealers, and meetings with the Eddy Arnolds of Victor when these stars visited town.

The one-stops, however, didn't deal with disc jockeys, and record companies were just realizing that stroking disc jockeys was a critical component to an integrated marketing strategy. Records and record spinners, as musicians' union chief James Petrillo predicted, slowly crept across radio, replacing live music. With Eddy Arnold discs in hand, Burgess focused on Randy Blake, an announcer who bought time from WJJD in Chicago and either sold it to someone else (a practice known as "brokering") or kept the time for himself, making money from advertisers he attracted. "I remember one time he was selling ballpoint pens when people couldn't give them away, but he was moving them," recalled Burgess. "On top of that, I remember walking into the studio, and he was selling tombstones by mail!" Like WSM, WJJD was a 50,000-watt station whose signal carried far beyond Chicago's city limits. Blake hosted a program, "Suppertime Frolics," that reached Midwest farmers and featured a heavy dose of Eddy Arnold. "He was a fan of Eddy's, no doubt about that," said Burgess. "I could take a record of Eddy's in there and say 'hey put it on,' and he never heard it. He'd put it on when I told him to. Randy Blake could say this is the first time [Eddy's new record was played] in the Midwest."

Victor's efforts in placing Eddy's records on the radio, as well as on jukeboxes, helped pave the way for the monstrous record sales that still awaited him.

—·—

Steve Sholes scheduled what would be Eddy's most prosperous session up to that date for September 24, 1946, in New York City. Roy Wiggins, though, wouldn't be with the gang. He had fled to Red Foley's outfit. "After Speedy and Gabe, he had some more guys," Wiggins complained, "and I made about $10 a week more than they made. He raised them up to my salary, but he didn't raise me, and that was the straw that broke the camel's back. I quit."

In 1945, Eddy and Tom Parker had put all the band members on salary, which disgruntled Roy and partly prompted Gabe Tucker and Speedy McNatt to leave. Speedy went to work in a string ensemble in Memphis, but the meager pay brought him back to Eddy. In early '46, though, Speedy finally tired of the traveling musician's life and left the road for good. Speedy agreed to rejoin Eddy one more time for the September 24th New York session—his swan song as a Tennessee Plowboy.

Eddy and the band left Nashville for New York on an overnight train, and after about 300 miles, they stopped in Cincinnati to let on passengers and connect with other eastbound cars. Once the train lurched from the station, Eddy sauntered to the dining car for his evening meal, ate, and returned to his compartment, where he read for a while. Restlessness, though, got the best of him. Eddy left his seat and made his way through the chain of cars to the club area, where a familiar face startled him. The hero of Eddy's youth, Gene Autry, actually sat there in front of him, in the flesh, talking to somebody—a Columbia Records executive, Eddy later learned. "I didn't interrupt," said the fan who now had fans of his own. "They were talking, and I waited until they were finished their conversation. At this point, I had a hit on the jukeboxes. 'That's How Much I Love You' was a hit already. Now, I'll give Gene credit. He already knew about it. When the Columbia man left, Gene was still sitting there, and I walked over and introduced myself to him. He was very, very nice to me."

Meeting Gene Autry was truly one of the perquisites of show business. "It was something to me to meet somebody that I really admired and knew something about," he said. They talked for a spell and Gene, who was just out of the U.S. Army Air Corps and heading to New York for a rodeo, let Eddy go with good luck wishes. "I've never forgotten Gene for that. I was a young, new artist. He was already a big, big name at this point. . . . He could have fluffed me off, but he treated me very nice. I always remembered it." The romantic might say that with his good wishes, Gene passed a torch to Eddy. For more than ten years, Autry, with his hits and Hollywood success, embodied the standard for cowboy performers, but as the late 1940s approached, Eddy Arnold was fast becoming all a newcomer could hope to be.

When Eddy and the band finally entered the studio on 24th Street in Manhattan, Speedy seemed ready to leave his last mark on Eddy. On "Easy Rockin' Chair," his fiddle reached combustion temperature. Speedy opened the song with a joyous energy that challenged Eddy to convince listeners that nirvana truly dwelt in an old rocking chair. The song and Eddy hopped like never before: *"Rockin' free and easy, times a passin' by. Hand me that evenin' paper 'til I swat this pesty fly."*

Because Roy Wiggins was with Red Foley, steel guitarist Eddie McMullen stepped in and complemented Eddy. However, listeners associated Roy's "ting-a-ling" sound with Eddy, and McMullen couldn't mimic this effect. When Steve and Eddy turned to "It's A Sin," the biggest hit to emerge from the session, Rollin "Oscar" Sullivan stepped forward to take the lead with his electric mandolin where Roy usually would have with his steel guitar. Rollin had never played lead before, he mostly played harmony or rhythm and kept the beat with the crisp, snare drum sound his electric mandolin produced. But Rollin stepped to the foreground on "It's A Sin" and played the middle turnaround note for note with zero embellishment. "I recorded that thing, and I played the mandolin," declared Rollin, "and everybody says, 'It won't sell thirty records.'" "It's A Sin" spent five weeks at number one in 1947. Another hit from the same session, "To My Sorrow," reached number two.

In May of 1947, Sholes brought Eddy back into the studio, this time in Chicago. The Chicago session and a two-day follow-up in New York during August yielded the songs that would crown Eddy king of what many people now began to call country music.

Well before the May session in Chicago, Roy Wiggins had wandered home to Eddy. His two months with Red Foley left him missing his old boss. "I wasn't enjoying playing with Red," Wiggins said to Douglas Green in 1974, "'cause all I did was play the last four bars, and I had been playing the introduction, the turnarounds, the choruses, and everything else. I really wasn't pleased, and the money difference wasn't that much."

Roy caught Eddy backstage at the "Opry" one Saturday. "How much would it be worth to you to have a good steel guitar player?" he ventured.

Eddy looked at him. "How much would it be worth to you to have a good job?"

Later that night, the two met again as they made their way out of Ryman Auditorium. "I'm not telling you this to get you to come back," Roy remembered Eddy saying, "but if you do come back, it will just be me and you. I'm going to let the other guys go."

By the other guys, Eddy meant Lonzo and Oscar, and, at the end of 1947, he let them go with golden parachutes on their backs. Eddy had persuaded Steve Sholes to give them an RCA Victor contract, hired Johnny "Lonzo" Sullivan to manage a record store he owned in Murfreesboro, Tennessee, and secured a spot for the Lonzo and Oscar act on the "Grand Ole Opry." The future treated Lonzo and Oscar kindly. They had a smash hit in 1948 with the novelty "I'm My Own Grandpa" and became one of the most loved comedic duos in "Grand Ole Opry" history.

Despite his impending departure, Rollin made the May and August sessions. Fiddler Adrian McDowell filled Speedy's shoes in May, and Ben "Buck" Lambert took up the fiddling chores in August. In May, Eddy record-

The much-loved Lonzo and Oscar. (Dolly Denny collection)

ed the hits "I'll Hold You in My Heart (Till I Can Hold You in My Arms)," "Bouquet of Roses," and "What A Fool I Was." He followed up in August with "Molly Darling," "Texarkana Baby," "My Daddy Is Only A Picture," "Then I Turned and Walked Slowly Away," and "Anytime" (which Eddie Fisher later appropriated for a theme song).

Sholes wanted to squeeze Eddy dry because James Petrillo was rattling his sabers, threatening another recording ban in 1948. Sholes added one final 1947 session in New York that would ultimately produce the chart toppers "A Heart Full of Love (For A Handful of Kisses)" and "Just A Little Lovin' (Will Go A Long, Long Way)." These three 1947 sessions produced an incredible line of hits for Eddy that would last from August 1947, when "I'll Hold You in My Heart (Till I Can Hold You in My Arms)" ran up the charts, to well into 1949. "I'll Hold You in My Heart" hit number one during the week of November 8, 1947, and by the following week, Eddy held the top three spots on *Billboard*'s "Most Played Juke Box Folk Records" chart: "It's A Sin" sat in the second slot and "To My Sorrow" earned the third. "I'll Hold You in My Heart" took up residence at number one for an unprecedented twenty-one weeks (in the fifty years since, only Hank Snow and Webb Pierce have equaled the feat).

Petrillo went forward with his strike, but this time Eddy held the upper hand. When the recording ban took effect on January 1, 1948, Victor sat on enough Eddy Arnold masters to sate his fans for many months to come. RCA also revamped its operations to concentrate on moving the stockpiled music.

Eli "Obie" Oberstein had left Victor to start another record company, and Victor named Jack Burgess to oversee the pop-music division. "That was not by choice," said Burgess, who had left Chicago to work in the national sales department. "It was by assignment. I said, 'Hey, I'm not a musician in any sense of the word.' I was placed there for a very different reason. I knew something about the marketing of the product and what the market would take. A lot of advance recording had been made in anticipation of the strike. Everybody expected Petrillo to walk out and take everybody with him. Not knowing how long it would last, they had recorded a lot of material up front. So the question was trying to schedule it, time it, and figure out where it fit and what artists you could promote. . . . You didn't want to waste it and throw out too much at one time."

Burgess, according to RCA Victor's restructuring, would work with an eight-man committee to schedule releases. Among those eight men was Charles Randolph Grean, a former copyist for the Glenn Miller band and, more recently, Steve Sholes's assistant. Grean helped Sholes procure songs and hire musicians for Victor's folk and race sessions. On Eddy's August 1947 sessions, Grean also played bass. Grean would be the bassist and arranger on most of Eddy's sessions for the next ten years and, under the direction of Steve Sholes, help him to move in new musical directions.

In 1947, Sholes hired Grean away from Russ Case, a conductor-arranger on many of Victor's pop discs. Grean wrote out music for Case and helped him do arrangements when Sholes noticed him. "I think he gave me a job for about $100 a week, which was pretty good money then," recalled Grean. "I remember one of the first things he did was give me a pile of acetates . . . and told me to take them home and listen and evaluate them. I listened to them, and some of them were very corny hillbilly songs. But there was one song in there that struck me as being a great idea. It was called 'That's How Much I Love You.' It had a couple of extra bars and extra beats—which a lot of country songs do—and at that time it annoyed me because being a musician I wanted it even. So I came back to [Sholes] and said, 'There's one song in here that's a great idea, but we should change it. We should eliminate those extra beats.' And he said, 'Well, let me show you something.' And he took out the sales charts, and that week it was [Victor's] number one seller of country music. From then on, I never doubted an extra measure or an extra beat because country singers would sing along, and if they wanted to take a breath, they'd just add a bar. It didn't have to come out even."

—— • ——

While RCA Victor thought of ways to record and sell Eddy Arnold, Eddy logged thousands of miles on the road between 1946 and 1948. Tom Parker had struck up relationships with booking agents around the nation who helped Eddy maintain a continuous string of work. Jolly Joyce, an influential Philadelphia agent, offered Eddy up to the burgeoning Pennsylvania ranch scene.

Ranches and music parks had sprung up throughout the South, East, and Midwest and comprised the bulk of Eddy's venues in the late '40s. The ranches offered national country-and-western acts to rural people who flocked to see their favorites in the flesh. Typically the parks opened on Sunday morning during the summers and featured live talent until late in the evening. From June to September, Eddy and his troupe roamed through Pennsylvania parks like Musselman's Grove in Claysburg, Himmelreich's Grove in Reading, Columbia Park in Nanticoke, New Holland Park in New Holland, Sunset Park in Oxford, and Sleepy Hollow Ranch in Quakertown (where performances were often picked up by WFIL radio in Philadelphia). He played three straight Sundays at Sleepy Hollow Ranch in August of 1947 and returned for another date in September. "That area was good for me," said Eddy of his Pennsylvania excursions. He was consolidating his popularity outside the South.

When Eddy looked out over the ranch crowds, he saw grannies and toddlers, married couples and adoring teens—all sitting attentively on wooden benches and packed into a clearing in the woods. Skinny trees sprouted in arbitrary spots among the crowd, shading the pilgrims from the summer sun.

"When the intro would start," Rollin Sullivan recalled, "Eddy would go into the song, and if somebody dropped a pin on the floor, you could have heard it. [The fans] were real respectful. When Roy Wiggins took a chorus, then you would have a light applause. When the song was over, a lot of times Eddy got a standing ovation, but the whole thing was sophisticated. . . . Everybody kept their seat and was civil."

Between acts, though, the ranch fans deluged Eddy and the band, making small talk, seeking autographs, and often inviting the musicians to share their picnic lunches. The fans enjoyed unrestricted access to the acts, according to Danny Dill, who had joined the Eddy Arnold package show in Lonzo and Oscar's wake. "I always had a saying that I hated to play those [ranches] because people had a chance to 'handle' you all day. You were at their mercy all day long. You'd get there early in the morning and play about four or five shows during the day. But during the day, they could talk to you, and they could come in the dressing room, and you would have no privacy. They just wore you out."

More respectful were the Mennonites, who soaked in the music but kept their distance from the musicians. "For a long time, they didn't say anything," said Dill. "They would kind of stay off by themselves and listen. They finally got to where they would talk to us. I guess there was something simple about country music that fit into their way of life."

Ranches were rustic venues for rustic music, but Eddy played indoors, too. With a contingent of "Grand Ole Opry" talent like Minnie Pearl and her fellow comedian Rod Brasfield, Eddy played two shows on Halloween night, 1947 at Constitution Hall in Washington, D.C. Organized by Washington's country-music entrepreneur, Connie B. Gay, the shows sold out, grossing a total of $18,000. "We are not going to tell any jokes about Congress tonight," Judge Hay opened the shows. "Congress has a much better show than we have."

From the nation's capital, Eddy and the band journeyed as far west as Los Angeles for KHL radio's "Sagebrush Western Theatre" and, by December, came back east for a show in Trenton, New Jersey, before heading to New York for their last pre-recording ban session. Eddy and the Tennessee Plowboys ended 1947 with a New Year's Eve performance in Amarillo, Texas.

The year of 1947 had treated Eddy well. Since New Year's Eve, 1946, when he played the Ball and Watch Party at Nashville's Hippodrome Theater, he had scored three number-one hits and enlarged his audience through increased radio exposure and live dates. The road, though, offered little time for reflection on the past year. On the first day of 1948, he appeared in Tulsa, Oklahoma, and in March, Tom Parker dispatched Eddy down the eastern seaboard on the strength of "What A Fool I Was" and "Anytime." The Jaffa Mosque in Altoona, Pennsylvania, the Philadelphia Arena, the Rajah Theater in Reading, Pennsylvania, the Norfolk Armory, the Richmond Armory, the Baltimore Coliseum, and the Roanoke Theater

Eddy performs a radio broadcast before a live audience. At least one little girl is mesmerized. (Don Mackin collection)

shimmered in the twenty-nine-year-old's rearview mirror. "I got tired of it even though I was young," Eddy said of the traveling. "I was hot at the moment, and we were taking advantage of it . . . [but] I treasured the time I could come home and sleep in my own bed."

In the absence of Lonzo and Oscar, Eddy and Tom Parker assembled a new traveling package from a list of "Opry" talent just dying to go with him. Peripheral talent only made about $15 a night on the "Opry," forcing such performers to ride the country-music circuit with bigger stars. Eddy and Tom brought on a solid lineup including comedian Whitey Ford (better known on stage as the Duke of Paducah), the musical duo Annie Lou and Danny (Danny Dill and his wife), and the Oklahoma Wranglers (composed of Vic, Skeeter, and Guy Willis, along with the only non-Willis, Chuck Wright). Under the terms of Tom and Eddy's partnership, Eddy gave Tom about half his revenues, which Tom used to pay himself and the other members of the troupe. Only Roy Wiggins received his pay directly from Eddy. The Duke of Paducah and the rest of the troupe traveled free of charge, but paid for their lodging and food.

Danny Dill emceed Eddy's personal appearances, introducing the Oklahoma Wranglers first, then following with himself and Annie Lou. The Duke of Paducah or, if the Duke wasn't available, comedian Rod Brasfield warmed up the audience just before Eddy took the stage.

The Oklahoma Wranglers (later renamed the Willis Brothers after Eddy suggested the old name was too limiting) pumped the audience's blood with their souped up, hot western music. "The Willis Brothers was one of the greatest acts going," said Dill. "They were really a great opening act, although we didn't call it 'opening' back then. You just started." Skeeter, the group's ham, amazed fans with his fiddle acrobatics, jerking the instrument around his head, behind him, and between his legs with rarely a note missed. To great laughs, Skeeter wedged the bow between his abdomen and Vic's backside, running the fiddle across the bow, or he simply laid the bow on the ground, crouched, and mashed the fiddle to and fro while the brothers sat on his back.

"I'm going to play 'Listen to the Mockingbird,'" Skeeter would announce. "My dad played it, and my grandfather played it, and I'm going to play it for you now. But I'm pretty sick and tired of hearing it!" Skeeter and the rest also clowned and cavorted to songs like "I'd Love to Be a Cowboy but I'm Afraid of Cows," "Old Indians Never Die," and "Cimarron."

Annie Lou and Danny played hymns and folk selections for the old-timers in the audience and worked in comedy at appropriate moments. For laughs, they often sang a novelty or created a routine around Annie Lou forgetting her lyrics. "Annie and I built an entire act on mistakes," Danny said. "If we ever did anything that was funny—that people laughed at—we just kept it in. It was not a comedy routine as such."

The Duke of Paducah, however, made no such claims to accidental comedy. Decked out in a bowler hat, buckled shoes, and a button-bursting plaid suit, he came to make people laugh, joking about his big fat wife and life on his fictional farm. "I got a wonderful mule out there on my farm," he would tease. "That mule is really intelligent. Anytime anybody yells, 'Hey there— you jackass!' both of us turn around." On and on, he worked the audience with humor until he closed by singing "Ding Dong Daddy" and quipped in conclusion, "I'm going to the wagon, boys, these shoes are killing me."

When the stitches of laughter subsided, Danny Dill reappeared and introduced Eddy. With his country gentleman hat pushed back on his head and wearing a smile as big as the gait that carried him on the stage, Eddy greeted the faithful. "Hello, folks. I just happen to have a few songs I'd like to sing for you. Some of them have been on the radio, and some didn't make it." At six feet in height and cut like a football linebacker, Eddy dominated the vision of his fans. He gleamed in a crisp, white shirt, pressed slacks, and street shoes; no fancy rhinestones or elaborately embroidered jackets on this idol. Eddy Arnold let his singing and reputation shine for him while he ran through his hits for an audience that sat in virtual rapt silence.

In one of those hushed audiences of the late 1940s sat a young John D. Loudermilk who, with his father, had driven twenty-seven miles from Durham, North Carolina, to Raleigh for the event. The boy would later write and play session guitar for his hero. "We saw Eddy sing and he was with Roy Wiggins and a bass player. Eddy was in a white suit and white hat and had a big Gibson guitar. . . . They put one blue spotlight on him, and he

Pushing Purina in Alabama. *Front row, left to right:* Danny Dill, Roy, Eddy, Rod Brasfield, Annie Lou Dill. *Back row:* Skeeter Willis, Vic Willis, Chuck Wright, Guy Willis. (Danny Dill collection)

sang those things, and it was out of sight. I sat up there in the balcony, right over the stage, and just cried."

As one might imagine, the handsome Eddy's gentle approach touched women especially, though they never screamed like bobby-soxers. Women in the audience seemed to respect him, and if they longed, they did so quietly. One November night in 1948, however, a Houston woman broke her silence. "I was sitting on the stage singing 'Anytime' when I saw a lady get up out of the audience and come down front," Eddy explained to a reporter in the 1950s. "I didn't pay any mind to her. But I'm plunking away on my guitar when, all of a sudden this woman was standing by me on the stage reaching for my arm."

Danny Dill emceed the show that night and watched the scene unfold. "I thought she was going to the bathroom or something," explained Dill. "She just came around to the edge of the stage and proceeded to come up on stage. She had her arms out. She was just transfixed. She was mesmerized. I don't know what she was going to do if she got him. It was like a dog chasing a car. I was standing there talking to a policeman and said, 'Look at that woman!' And she was coming to hug Eddy. I don't think she meant to harm him, but she just had to come and touch him, I guess."

"That's my boy. He sings my songs. I've got to take him home with me," she chanted.

The cop ran from the wings and walked her outside. "I figured he sort of saved my life," Eddy continued, "because I was about to die of fright."

"He affected women like that," Dill concluded. "He affected all people, men, women, children alike, in that they recognized that they were hearing a great artist."

—— • ——

The motor that kept this great artist in front of the people stayed humming under the nimble fingers of Tom Parker. He basked in Eddy's complete loyalty, and, in return, Parker gave all. He was Eddy Arnold's shadow, always scheming, always on the hunt for new opportunities to exploit his boy's popularity. With Eddy, Parker honed the skills that later served him so well with Elvis Presley.

Sometime during his tenure with Eddy, Parker finagled the unofficial title of "Colonel" from part-time singer, part-time governor of Louisiana Jimmie Davis. Pretty soon, Parker had everyone calling him Colonel— everybody, that is, except Eddy. He would always be "Tom" to Eddy. In Eddy's employ, the Colonel revealed himself to be an unabashed self-promoter and addicted deal maker. Magazine advertisements designed to plug Eddy often plugged Parker, too. "Under Exclusive Management of Thomas A. Parker," ads screamed in bold lettering, rivaling the size of Eddy's name. "Plowing a Million Acres of Thanks, Eddy Arnold and Tom Parker," another ad read. News items that Parker sent to the press rarely omitted his name: "Jolly Joyce, Philadelphia agent, in conjunction with Tom Parker, Tampa, personal manager, is routing Eddy Arnold thru the East"; "Tom Parker, manager of Eddy Arnold, reports that the singer has just concluded a tour of Alabama, Tennessee, and Georgia." "I believe that anyone in show business," declared Parker once, "in our field especially, would know that the minute they think of Eddy Arnold, they would think of me as his manager; there is no way they could get around that."

Little of Parker's self-elevation affected Eddy professionally, and it was probably useful that people knew where to go if they wished to deal with Arnold. As far as Eddy was concerned, his manager earned every dime he paid him. Nobody can deny, whatever their opinion of Parker, that he—with the help of RCA Victor—kept Eddy Arnold's name in front of America. Parker even maintained a small staff to help him do it. "Tom Parker had 'Bevo' . . . a little runabout for the Colonel," said Oklahoma Wrangler Chuck Wright. "We would be sitting in the lounge of the hotel, and everything would get a little quiet. Tom would say, 'Bevo! Go have Mr. Arnold paged.' . . . He was keeping [Eddy's] name out there."

Nothing stopped the Colonel. He plastered Eddy's name to anything that stood still for more than five minutes and liberally employed police escorts to hype the show's arrival in town as if it were the circus coming. "We'd get to town and sirens were blowing," recalled Roy Wiggins. "I remember one time, we were in the hotel, and all of the sudden you heard eight sirens just screaming. All of us were coming down in the hotel lobby, and the bellboy said, 'Where are you all going?' We said, 'To go out to get a hamburger.' That's all we were going to do . . . eat lunch!"

Country music lore bursts with stories of the Colonel, some fact and others merely fantastic products of people who figured they knew what Tom was capable of doing. Few "Tom tales" bear close scrutiny. What does stand up, however, is Eddy's embarrassment in the face of Tom's antics. The serious, mild-mannered boy raised in the practicality of farm life made a strange bedfellow to the blustery, flamboyant Tom Parker who served him. "The sky was the limit for him," said Eddy. "A lot of things he'd do would kind of embarrass me." Sometimes it seemed Tom was in it for the game, the obsession with the art of the deal, getting the most from giving little.

"Tom's greatest thrill on this earth," said Danny Dill, "was conning somebody out of a free lunch for all the troops. He'd come to us and tell us how great it was to work for him because he got us free lunch. He had conned somebody out of it—a radio station or something. It was not the money. It was just that he had conned them out of it."

"It was a game," Dill ventured. "He was a carny. He was raised a carny, and he was still a carny."

Eddy trusted this carny, looking the other way when it came to his antics because Tom's determination, however unbecoming, produced results. "Tom was absolutely ruthless in his approach to booking Eddy Arnold," Dill remembered. "He lived, breathed, and promoted, and his every waking-moment thought was Eddy Arnold. He'd get all the record stores and the Victor promoter in that area in on [the show], and he threatened them. He said, 'Look, if you don't get in on this and help us out on this, the next time it comes signing time, he won't sign.' He had Victor people buying ads in the paper."

"He would many times quote figures to other promoters that were absolutely outrageous," Dill observed. "You know what? Eddy was already booked. . . . He was raising his prices when he knew Eddy couldn't work anyway." When the promoters approached Tom the next year, Eddy's manager would quote a lower fee for his boy. The promoters jumped on the better price. "They never would suspect it," said Dill.

Most RCA Victor officials tried to avoid Parker. They found his style obnoxious, a weight around Eddy's neck, and soon tired of him. Jack Burgess's limited exposure to Parker soured him, and he happily let Steve Sholes and the label's head of country-and-western sales, Ed Dodelin, deal with him. "There were other people who were managers who were much more pleasant—that you preferred to work with," Burgess said. "Parker had a lot of people baffled. If things weren't going right, in other words, if a particular tour didn't work as well as he thought it would, Parker would start reaching out to blame everybody and anybody. It was never Parker, of course! That was just Parker's nature, always point the finger if somebody else didn't do something. When things went right, he had to take front and center."

Eddy's success, however, made it easy for Victor to forget Tom's prickliness. Tom was one of the hazards of the entertainment racket, and Eddy's sales more than made up for him. Standing orders for Eddy's records (advance orders on yet-to-be-released product) eclipsed those of his peers, and Victor's profit margin on them exceeded all other Victor artists. Vaughn Monroe or Perry Como might have up to thirty musicians on a session. Eddy rarely had more than seven, including himself, and he often knocked out eight songs in one day. In short, Eddy was cheap to produce and, with record sales numbering in the hundreds of thousands, RCA didn't get hot and bothered about a manager with a big front.

On one of Eddy's recording visits to New York in the late '40s, Victor's vice president, Jim Murray, decided he wanted to spend a little time with this golden calf from Tennessee. Steve Sholes called Eddy in his hotel room.

"Mr. Murray wants to meet you," said Steve.

"Okay," Eddy hesitated. "What does he want to meet me for?" Eddy reacted to Murray like he had the first time he heard Sholes's name three years earlier. "What's he going to do to me?" Eddy wondered to himself. "He's a big shot. He'll cancel my contract!"

"He just wants to meet you," Steve assured him. "Come a little early."

Eddy arrived at 24th Street before his scheduled time in the studio, and Steve brought him to Murray's office. "Be seated, young man," Murray offered. "I've been wanting to meet you. I see the sales figures come across my desk every Monday morning, and I want to know what you look like."

Eddy smiled. "Well fiiine sir . . ." His apprehension melted as Murray fawned over Eddy's profit margins. Realization replaced apprehension. For the first time, it hit him that he was one of the top sellers, if not the top seller, at RCA Victor. In Eddy's mind, big sellers meant Perry Como, Vaughn Monroe, Mindy Carson, or Spike Jones, not the "Tennessee Plowboy." Sure, he knew he made money for Victor, but not this much. With Steve in tow, Eddy floated out of Murray's office that morning.

"I was selling so many records at that point and had no idea why," Eddy said. "I really didn't. I thought everybody was selling records."

7

*D*uring 1948, only six songs reached number one on *Billboard*'s country chart; incredibly, five of those songs belonged to Eddy Arnold. For eleven weeks in '48, Jimmy Wakely's "One Has My Name (The Other Has My Heart)" claimed the top spot, but every other week belonged to an Eddy Arnold song. Wakely, who also had a Hollywood career and sang pop-appeal duets with Margaret Whiting, seemed to be Eddy's only serious competition for country preeminence in 1948. "Jimmy sang good, very good," said Eddy. "I'd see him, and he'd say, 'You son of a gun.' He was talking about the charts."

Eddy actually had a sixth song in the number-one spot in 1948, "I'll Hold You in My Heart (Till I Can Hold You in My Arms)," but it first hit the chart's top in November 1947 and carried over into 1948. Never, before or since, has an artist so dominated his genre's chart listings. Bing Crosby, Elvis Presley, and the Beatles outpaced their peers in their time, but never did they dwarf their field as Eddy did his in 1948.

"Anytime" was the first of the new batch of 1948 hits for Eddy. Two writers, Zeke Clements and Carl Weber, claimed to have created "Anytime" and cut Eddy in on the song when he agreed to record it. They registered the song with the publishing company Hill and Range, who discovered something fishy. While conducting a title search at the Library of Congress, Hill and Range found the song credited to Herbert "Happy" Lawson, an old vaudevillian who had apparently penned "Anytime" years before. Eddy still wanted to record the song, however, so Hill and Range set out to sign "Happy" Lawson to a publishing deal. Lawson was playing piano in a little bar in Daytona Beach, Florida, when Hill and Range found him. He probably never had to work again.

In addition to scaling the country charts, "Anytime" made the pop charts for one week. The song had pop appeal. Steve muted Eddy's combo, draining them of any country sound. Roy's steel guitar and Buck Lambert's fiddle tiptoed in and out of earshot as Eddy's baritone warmed the rather half-baked lyrics: *"Anytime you're thinking 'bout me, that's the time I'll think of you."*

Noting the success of "Anytime," Victor rushed out another simple love song, "Bouquet of Roses." Eddy had recorded it a few months before "Anytime," and it featured more overt country instrumentation, which might have threatened its chances for pop prosperity. There was no reason to worry, though. The song sailed to number thirteen on the pop charts and a nineteen-week stay at number one on the country side, delivering Eddy his first gold record ever. "Texarkana Baby," "Just A Little Lovin'," and "A Heart Full of Love" followed "Bouquet of Roses" in the top position during 1948, and each crossed over to the pop charts—even "Texarkana Baby," which celebrated a girl whose name is *sweet as sorghum syrup and good ole Blue Ribbon cane.*

When *Billboard* magazine sat down to tally record popularity at the end of 1948, they reserved the four highest country slots for Eddy. With "Bouquet of Roses," "Anytime," "Just A Little Lovin'," and "Texarkana Baby," Eddy owned the country field. "When I was head of A&R at RCA [in 1949]," recalled Joe Csida, "the big problem with Eddy was that he'd have four or five records in the top ten of the country charts. You'd have another session done, and you'd be afraid to put out another record because the market would be glutted."

The Victor corporate offices in Camden, New Jersey, buzzed with excitement when "Anytime" and "Bouquet of Roses" crossed over. Eddy had reached a whole new market, and Victor was only too happy to help him exploit it. Two people especially stood in Eddy's corner to make sure Victor supported him: Steve Sholes, of course, and the label's director of folk and race sales, Ed Dodelin. Eddy had grown close to Steve, and Tom Parker, although he irritated many Victor staffers, got on sportingly with Ed Dodelin. A Camden-area native who, like Sholes, worked his way up the Victor ladder, Dodelin centered his sales strategy around his breadwinner and consequently spent much time with Parker. They befriended one another and plotted strategy often, while Tom's wife, Marie, and Ed's wife, Ann, shopped together.

In coordination with Dodelin, Brad McCuen also labored behind Eddy to make sure his records moved. As the link between Victor and independent distributors, McCuen roamed Virginia, the Carolinas, part of Kentucky, and most of Tennessee starting in January of 1949. McCuen was to this slice of the South what Jack Burgess had been to the Midwest in the mid-1940s.

McCuen first met Eddy in the Hotel Charlotte's coffee shop in Charlotte, North Carolina. The broad-shouldered, confident singer immediately struck him as someone he could believe in as he traversed the South promoting his records. "In the infantry," said McCuen, "he would have made a sensational line company captain. His men would have gone to their death if he so ordered it. . . . He inspired confidence."

McCuen filed a weekly report with Camden, and he constantly communicated that the distributors clamored for more Eddy Arnold records. "We lived at the distributor level for the new releases. Eddy was a bit of a problem for the distributors because he sold so well that he might only have three or four new singles a year," McCuen explained. "Of course, they were doing a land-office business on the singles that were out."

McCuen's observations soon confirmed what the charts indicated: Eddy's songs seemed to be reaching new listeners, an audience beyond the conventional country fan. City slickers, McCuen reported, were curious about Eddy. "I remember in Charlotte . . . being in a record shop and a distinguished gentleman came in, and the clerk excused himself and went and got two or three records and put them in a shopping bag." The man took the bag and quickly left the store. This mysterious man, the clerk told Brad, was one of Charlotte's leading surgeons. "He came to buy Eddy Arnold," remembered McCuen, "and he didn't want anybody to know that he bought those kinds of records."

The prospect of gaining a whole new audience in addition to the country fans inspired everybody involved with Eddy to think about new directions. The most radical new direction, though, took Eddy away from the "Grand Ole Opry." "I thought I had done about as much as I could do there," explained Eddy to interviewer Ralph Emery in 1991. "I had two [network] radio programs outside the 'Opry.' I had the daily program on the Mutual network—everyday for fifteen minutes—and I had a [transcribed] Saturday night show for the Ralston Purina Company, which was on a regional network." Eddy outgrew the "Opry." To continue on the Ryman stage when larger opportunities (that didn't require him to share the spotlight) beckoned was unrealistic and unacceptable. So Eddy left.

In the weeks leading up to Eddy's departure, Parker, according to the recollections of former WSM sales director Irving Waugh, approached the station and demanded a piece of the "Grand Ole Opry" gate, an absurd request he must have known would be rejected. Although Eddy dwarfed the other "Opry" stars in almost every respect, acquiescence to the Colonel would spark similar demands from Ernest Tubb and Roy Acuff. WSM would never concede part of the gate to anybody or admit that Eddy was bigger than the "Opry." "It never occurred to us that we couldn't do it," exclaimed Waugh, "it just never occurred to us to do it!"

Correctly predicting WSM's reaction, Parker prepared to throw a bone to management that would help keep Eddy's name in front of the "Opry's" large Saturday night audience, but not chain him to the Ryman Auditorium stage. At Parker's instigation, Gardner Advertising Agency, which handled Eddy's transcribed half hour for Purina, offered Irving Waugh Eddy's transcribed show to use on Saturday night.

Waugh shot back: "We don't accept transcribed programs on Saturday night." WSM was legendary for its flat rejection of any prerecorded material. ("We were very difficult to get along with, without realizing it," Waugh said in retrospect.) The Gardner official then threatened to sell the show to WLAC in Nashville—another 50,000-watt powerhouse and WSM's most significant competition in town.

"You're not going to put it against [the 'Opry'], are you?" Waugh asked.

"No," the agency representative replied. "We'll put it on Friday night."

"If you put it on Friday," Waugh warned, "I'll put a live show before you and a live show after you. And I'm not trying to be ugly. I just can't afford to have someone else start a country show in Nashville."

The advertising executives at Ralston-Purina resented Waugh's bullying, and Waugh flew to St. Louis to try to reach a compromise. After extended haggling, Waugh agreed to take the show for use on Friday night, but he lived up to his threat and put live music before and after Eddy's canned performance—thus, the birth of WSM's "Friday Night Frolic" (later known as "Friday Night Opry").

Eddy's last night on the "Opry"—in September 1948—left unforgettable impressions in the minds of those who were there and those who heard his departure on radio. Eddy finished his set and, for one final time as an "Opry" member, looked over the old Ryman Auditorium with its arched, stained-glass windows and jam-packed rafters. Five years after Harry Stone took him on, he bade farewell to the audience. Eddy thanked Harry Stone, WSM, and the "Opry" fans and then turned to walk away from the microphone that helped him catch fire. Eddy's old breakfast partner, Harold Bradley, backed Eddy on guitar that last night. "We went around the curtain," Bradley recalled, "and he and Minnie Pearl hugged and both of them cried like babies because he was leaving."

Tears flowed out in radioland, too. In the darkness of the teenage John D. Loudermilk's bedroom—lit only by the glow of the radio dial light—the young boy cried and cried after Eddy's good-bye. "My mother came in and assured me that he would be back on the 'Opry.' I remember her combing my hair with her fingers and assuring me that he was going to come back on." Mrs. Loudermilk was wrong; Eddy would never come back.

"There was great controversy and much talk about it around the station," recalled one WSM staffer. "Who would leave the 'Grand Ole Opry'? The 'Grand Ole Opry' was it."

Somebody even challenged Eddy to his face. "The Opry made you!"

"If it made me, why hasn't it made the Fruit Jar Drinkers?" Eddy answered, referring to an old-time band that never rose above the "Opry."

"One thing nobody remembers or is conscious of," Eddy said years later, "beginning in '47 I was on the Mutual network five days a week for the Ralston-Purina people. People always want to give the 'Opry' credit, and the 'Opry' was important. But I was on the network five days a week. . . . I introduced lots of records on there."

Irving Waugh took a cavalier attitude toward the star's departure from the 'Opry.' "We hated to see Eddy leave. But, as I recall, it didn't make that much difference to the 'Opry.' . . . At that stage, people were lined up all the way around the block [to get in]. New people, including Hank, were coming all the time."

When Irving Waugh referred to "Hank," he meant Hank Williams. Williams leaped up to rival Eddy's country dominance in 1949 and ultimately came to define what people thought of when they thought of country music. Williams was the most exciting new face in Nashville since Eddy emerged in 1946. In 1949, Hank's "Lovesick Blues" and "Wedding Bells" streamed out of record stores, and his "Opry" debut set so many tongues fluttering that he more than filled Eddy's void.

Hank rose up to claim the spirit of country music with hits that dealt with desperation and cheating—just the kind of themes Eddy had abandoned. A goosed-up rhythm and constant beat also infected Hank's music, suggesting the coming of rock and roll, in marked contrast to Eddy Arnold's style that soothed and swayed. More influential, though, than Hank's sound and compositions on country music's image was Hank's lifestyle. His incessant boozing, raucous bouts with wife Audrey, and drifting ways settled into country music's landscape and became its themes for decades to come.

Hard living finally caught up with Hank on New Year's Day, 1953. At the age of twenty-nine, he expired in the back seat of a car on his way to a Canton, Ohio, performance. America would never know an old Hank Williams, so it lionized the young. His short, tragic life inspired generations of country singers and writers to romanticize his foibles and canonize him. Hank's life and songs came to measure authenticity in mainstream country music.

Eddy Arnold's phenomenal success in the country category notwithstanding, to many of country music's songwriters, singers, and historians, Eddy never had the soul of Hank Williams or his disciples. Eddy generally sang love songs while Hank coughed up gritty, hurting songs. Hank's life, at least as it's interpreted, resembled a gothic tragedy; no such mystery or desolation pervaded Eddy's. Hank and his equally legendary wife, Audrey, feuded in public while the Arnolds lived quietly in suburban Madison, where they moved shortly after their daughter Jo Ann's birth in 1945. Ernest Tubb shot up WSM's lobby; Eddy fired guns on hunting trips. Other "Opry" stars drank too much; Eddy drank prune juice for breakfast and sipped an occasional Scotch. Hank Williams died young; Eddy endured, his image and legacy molded by the encounters of an aging legend. "Eddy was always a decent man," said Danny Dill, who traveled with Eddy for many years. "I've seen him irritated, and I've seen him peeved, but I never saw him in any situation where he wasn't a gentleman and tried to be fair about everything." For the most part, Eddy's themes, both in song and life, strayed from those of country music throughout the rise and demise of Hank Williams and the subsequent rise of Hank's followers.

—•—

Increasingly, Steve Sholes gave Eddy material from New York writers Steve Nelson (of "Bouquet of Roses") and Cy Coben (who penned 1951's "There's Been A Change In Me"), who composed for a broader audience. With the "Opry" out of Eddy's way, the Colonel moved the Tennessee Plowboy's mass media base out of Nashville.

Parker had another insurance policy against losing Eddy's "Opry" spot, in addition to the Purina half hour. The Columbia Broadcasting System (CBS) wanted Eddy as an alternative to NBC's "Grand Ole Opry" segment. Every Saturday night for about a year beginning in late 1948, Eddy's "Hometown Reunion" emanated from various cities around the country over the CBS radio network. Eddy and his road cast, the Duke of Paducah, the Willis Brothers, and Annie Lou and Danny, performed their first two shows in front of a studio audience at WLAC—the CBS affiliate in Nashville—before moving out to other cities. "'Reunion' is a rapidly paced and talent-laden collection that will provide a full measure of entertainment to devotees of this type of show," *Variety* magazine wrote in a lukewarm, mildly patronizing tone. "Participants are experienced hands in this kind of shindig, with name value contained in Eddy Arnold . . . and the Duke of Paducah, whose maizey observations at least bring studio laughs."

Eddy's touring routes followed the "Hometown Reunion" programs. The producers, Charles and Bill Brown of Brown Brothers fame, hired Owen Bradley to travel ahead of the troupe to arrange the music and assemble any extra musical accompaniment that might be needed. The Browns also organized barbershop quartet competitions in advance of Eddy's arrival, the victors winning a chance to sing on the "Reunion."

On March 27, 1949, the "Hometown Reunion" stopped at Constitution Hall in Washington, D.C., to play two benefits for the U.S. Coast Guard Memorial Chapel Fund. A *Washington Star* headline proclaimed, "Eddy Arnold to Get 3 Awards On Coast Guard Show Tonight. . . . Mr. Arnold will receive a citation from the Music Guild of Washington labeling him as its outstanding artist for Western and folk tunes on a Nationwide survey of juke boxes. Another award will be a certificate of appreciation from the commandant of the Coast Guard [and] the third will be a gold record from the RCA Victor Co." A swank affair indeed, many in the audience dressed in tuxedoes and ermine, and attendees included former heavyweight champ Jack Dempsey (who playfully socked Roy Wiggins on the cheek), Steve Sholes and Ed Dodelin from RCA, Rear Admiral Ellis Reed-Hill, and Jean Aberbach of Hill and Range Songs (a New York publishing company that fed many songs to Steve Sholes for Eddy's use). Rumors also flew around the hall that President Harry Truman might show up, so the Colonel rented a tux for emcee Danny Dill, who had to change back to a plaid shirt for his Annie Lou and Danny routine. Eddy occasionally peeked from behind the curtains, incredulous that so many people would pay $6 for floor seats. Truman never showed, but after the show, as promised, Ed Dodelin presented Eddy with a gold record for "Bouquet of Roses." Shortly after, the Colonel dutifully told *Billboard* that the shows netted $8,500 for the chapel that would be erected in New London, Connecticut.

In the wake of Constitution Hall, Eddy's appearances took on a higher tone. Tom kept Danny in the fine apparel, and Gabe Tucker—who had returned in '48 to do comedy after stints with Red Foley, the "Hoxie Tucker

Fresh from his departure from the 'Opry,' the Eddy Arnold voice beams out over CBS, with the Duke of Paducah waiting in the wings. (Eddy Arnold collection)

Eddy and Roy with the recently returned Gabe Tucker on bass. (Gabe Tucker collection)

Girl Show" in Miami, and the "Renfro Valley Barn Dance" in Louisville—donned a tie and tails. Tucker's new look was suggested by Colonel Parker in a moment of inspiration.

"I think I got it figured out," Tom blurted to Gabe one day in the car.

"What you got figured out? What you've been figuring on?" asked Gabe.

"Your part of the show," said Tom. "I figured out what me and Re's [Tom's wife, Marie] going to give you for Christmas. I'm going to buy you a complete outfit, white tie and tails, for Christmas."

"What can I do with white tie and tails? I don't even know how to put them on!"

"Well . . . we can take care of that," replied the undeterred manager of Eddy Arnold.

So Gabe Tucker acquired a tasteful look to go with his comedic routine. Before Eddy came out, Vic Willis attracted the audience's attention by announcing, "We are very fortunate to have a very great classical artist with us today. We've asked him to come out and play a tune for you." Classical music? The fans scratched their heads. They came to hear Eddy Arnold and "rube" comedy, not classical music! "Here he is, ladies and gentlemen," Willis told the skeptical audience, "Professor Gabe Tucker."

Gabe, whose distinctive face suggested a distinguished European conductor, waltzed on to the stage in his sophisticated garb with his trumpet tucked underneath his arm. The people laughed, but the solemn Gabe stared them down, commanding silence. Could this be a classical artist? Professor Gabe Tucker turned to address the assembled.

"Good evening, ladies and gentlemen, monsieurs and madams, señors and señoritas. My first selection will be Rachmaninoff's 'Prelude in C Sharp Minor' or 'Get Up Son and Light the Lamp I Think I Knocked One of Your Ma's Eyeballs Out.'" The place collapsed in laughter, and Gabe launched into the same old corny jokes he'd been telling for years.

Now that Gabe and Danny Dill had gone uptown in their dress, Eddy asked Danny to polish his emcee spiel. "Most country emcees would tell who [the star] recorded for, all his big songs, where he was born and raised, his wife and his kids, and if Santa Claus came to him," explained Dill. "It was a thing where you just went on and on telling what a great guy the star of the show was. So Eddy went to New York [and saw a pop crooner's show], and all the emcee said was, 'And now, ladies and gentlemen, here is . . .' Eddy picked up on that."

Eddy told Danny to simply tell the fans, "And now, here he is, Eddy Arnold."

"From that day on," Dill noted, "I never said any more than that. There was no use to. They came to see Eddy Arnold. They didn't come to see Annie Lou and Danny. They didn't come to see the Willis Brothers. They didn't even come to see the Duke of Paducah. They came to see Eddy Arnold."

— · —

Eddy performing over WLAC, a CBS affiliate; Harold Bradley (turned away) is accompanying him on second guitar. (Eddy Arnold collection)

They came indeed, and they bought records and listened on the radio. *Newsweek* magazine reported in 1949 that all the interest in Eddy Arnold translated to a $250,000 gross annual income for the Tennessee Plowboy. But *Newsweek* came in short on their estimate. Eddy Arnold actually pulled in more than $500,000 annually and was well on track to being, if he wasn't already, a millionaire. Sally had given birth to their second child, Richard (or "Dickey" as everyone called him), on January 2, 1949, and the family prepared to move to a farm in Brentwood, just south of Nashville.

Prospects continued to rise for Eddy. He was unquestionably a national star and anticipated the new opportunities this stature engendered. In conjunction with Tom Parker, the powerful William Morris Agency placed Eddy in new mass-media outlets. Starting a fourty-year, on-and-off love affair with the medium, he tapped into the thriving world of television for the first time in 1949.

Television's niche in the entertainment field began to boom in the late '40s, and a performer who ignored the new tube with grainy reception risked certain obscurity. In 1948, only 850,000 TV sets were manufactured in the United States, contrasting with the 2.2 million sets the industry produced in the first eight months alone of 1949. Over the same time period, sales of radios dropped by 750,000, and, from 1948 to '49, the number of hours Americans spent listening to radio dropped along with national radio network advertising revenues. Perhaps the most telling sign of television's emergence was the shrinkage of radio's nighttime audience. In homes that had both radio and television, 73.1 percent of the homes had their televisions switched on at 8:00 P.M., compared to 4.8 percent of the homes that remained faithful to radio at that time of the evening. It was high time for Eddy to introduce himself to television, and he did so on Milton Berle's "Texaco Star Theater." A string of appearances followed on other fledgling TV programs like the "$64 Question," and Tallulah Bankhead's and Arthur Godfrey's shows.

The Berle television show would be unforgettable for Eddy, not so much for his appearance but for the meeting Tom Parker had with Berle's other guest star, Boris Karloff. Karloff, of course, terrorized America via the silver screen as Frankenstein's monster, but even without makeup he could deliver a fright, as Eddy's manager discovered when he met Karloff in Milton Berle's dim, empty studio. "Tom is a stickler for being on time for an appointment," explained Eddy. "Tom is always early. He'll never keep you waiting if he has an appointment with you. Boris Karloff was early, and he was booked on the same show, which we didn't know. Boris Karloff was already at the studio, and he was the only person in there. . . . The sun was coming through this window [and projecting an eerie glow on Karloff]. . . . Well, Tom walked in there, and Boris Karloff was standing up there. . . . Tom stood there, and he looked at him. Nothing was said. They didn't say hello. Tom turned around and left 'cause he saw that face. That was funny!"

The William Morris Agency also opened the door to Hollywood for Eddy. In April of 1949, the Colonel announced Columbia's plans to film two Eddy Arnold motion pictures in the summer. The first film, the Colonel told the trade press, would be shown in conjunction with Eddy's live performances in theaters across the nation.

Before the Hollywood excursion, however, Eddy had to tie up some loose strings. After the Coast Guard benefit at Constitution Hall, he swung south for dates in Norfolk and Richmond and backtracked to New York for a session on April 5. The recording ban had ended in 1948, and, on December 20, Eddy did a session of "mother" songs for his first album of original material, a collection of 78-rpm records dubbed *To Mother*. As Charles Grean recalled, it was the first session in which RCA Victor recorded Eddy's voice with an echo effect. On December 21 and 22, Eddy laid down a string of songs that kept him atop the charts: "Many Tears Ago" (a re-recording of a 1946 release), "One Kiss Too Many," and "Don't Rob Another Man's Castle," which was an unusual cheating song (but one with a moral!): *"I robbed another man's castle. Now someone just stole her from me."* "Don't Rob Another Man's Castle" scaled the country charts and remained at number one for twelve weeks in 1949, finishing the year second in overall popularity to Hank Williams's "Lovesick Blues." The April 5 session produced the third biggest hit of the year, "I'm Throwing Rice (At the Girl that I Love)."

Before shooting on his films was to begin in California, the Colonel committed Eddy to a two-week stretch of shows at the El Rancho Hotel in Las Vegas. Eddy never played Vegas before, much less a club. He played theaters and ranches—venues that were officially free of liquor and certainly gambling. Chuck Wright, bass player for the Willis Brothers, remembered his boss agonizing about the possibility of alienating his fans when they discovered he played "Sin City." In the end, small spurts of critical letters came to Eddy. "I answered with the fact that I had nothing to do with the gambling side of the hotel. I sang in the entertainment room," he said.

Eddy really feared the El Rancho management expected him to gamble away his days in the desert. "I kept hearing stories about artists appearing out there and gambling away all their money before they left—the money they were paid to perform. I'm not really a gambler. I might play two dollars at the slot machine. . . . I thought maybe the hotel management might expect me to gamble. So I got a hold of Tom Parker and I asked him, 'Tom, they may be expecting me to gamble out there in Vegas.' He said, 'I'll check it out.' He got a hold of the William Morris Agency who booked me in there. In a few days the word came back and Tom said, 'Don't worry. They're not expecting you to gamble.'"

Eddy drew decent crowds for his two weeks, and tasted a bit of what the glitter of Hollywood had in store. In Vegas, the occasionally starstruck singer met actor Robert Mitchum, matinee star Clara Bow, and her husband, Rex Bell.

Roy Wiggins and the Willis Brothers accompanied Eddy to Hollywood, and as on their first visit to New York, none of them had any idea of what to expect. "I wasn't ready . . .," Eddy said. "I couldn't act." The films bear witness to Eddy's statement. He had matinee-idol looks, but the stiffness he had successfully shed on records crept back on film. Columbia marketed the two movies, *Feudin' Rhythm* and *Hoedown,* as Eddy Arnold vehicles, but sadly they failed to accomplish even that. The company splashed Eddy's name and photographs on the movie posters and newspaper advertisements, but Eddy hardly appeared in the flicks.

It was as if the studio and director Ray Nazarro (a Boston-born director of B-westerns) lacked confidence in the new actor. They unimaginatively cast Eddy as himself and, instead of grooming him, built the plot around other talent. *Feudin' Rhythm,* in which a cowboy combo struggles to get a TV show on the air, really features veteran bandleader and western movie star Kirby Grant as well as child star Tommy Ivo, who plays Eddy's obnoxious son. The corny comedy of vaudevillian Fuzzy Knight and endearing chirpiness of the leading lady, sixteen-year-old Carolina Cotton, almost made the movie bearable. Eddy's tender interpretations of "You Know How Talk Gets Around" and "The Nearest Thing to Heaven" helped, too: *"And just like his mommy, he's everything divine. Nearest thing to heaven is that little guy of mine."*

"He was much more talented than they gave him lines for on the screen," said Carolina Cotton of her costar. "[Even though] he came across not as a comic, . . . he actually kept the set rolling all the time in jokes. Of course, I was too young to hear them. They all shut up when I came by, but I know they were funny."

Feudin' Rhythm reached theaters in 1950, and its partner *Hoedown* followed later in the year. Clearly, Columbia hadn't reconsidered its "star's" abilities when production began on the second film. The company cast Eddy as a ranch owner and mere prop to Jock Mahoney, who played hapless cowboy star "Stoney Rhodes." Mahoney, who came to Hollywood as a stunt man and later played the heavy in many westerns, got a few laughs and Carolina Cotton charmed the audiences again, but the two couldn't save the film from Columbia's haphazard attention. Designed as a spoof of western movies, a *Variety* review thought the concept backfired: "It's a tossup as to who is kidding whom in 'Hoedown.' Opening scenes of this low-budget programmer unreel as a satire on oatuners. Later, however, the cast does it straight." *Variety* did however praise Eddy for his performance: "Name of the film's star, Eddy Arnold, will help draw trade to the wicket to some extent. One of the top cowboy crooners, his platters sell big. It's unfortunate that he's spotted in a story that's so feeble and embarrassing for he's photogenic and his songs register nicely."

"I went out there and did two and then came home," Eddy said of his silver screen career. "I was glad to get home." *Hoedown* and *Feudin' Rhythm* never pretended to be high art, and the Colonel really only aimed to put

Child star Tommy Ivo implores Eddy to stay in *Feudin' Rhythm.* Actor Dick Eliot looks on. (Eddy Arnold collection)

Eddy's name in front of even more Americans than he already had. But contrary to what the films' quality might suggest, the lackluster efforts fueled Eddy's success. They made money, and, more importantly, left a flickering 1940s document of a thirty-one-year-old Eddy Arnold and his musicians, Roy Wiggins and the Willis Brothers.

8

Over the years—between traveling, recording, Hollywood, and radio—Eddy has squeezed in time for a favorite hobby, reading the history of remarkable Americans like Andrew Jackson, Sam Houston, and Abraham Lincoln. A story from his casual studies that Eddy has often told has a simple, honest man from Springfield, Illinois, visiting Lincoln, who recently assumed the presidency. Unannounced, the man met the White House receptionist, and Lincoln, starved for news from his hometown, asked that the visitor be immediately ushered in. "Stay for dinner!" the President told his guest, and, after dinner that night, Lincoln asked the man why he came. Did he want a postmaster job or some other patronage position? No. The man had simply come to say hello and sought no favors. Lincoln was incredulous. Nobody stopped at the White House to merely say hello. Since he had assumed the office of the presidency in 1861, everybody wanted something from him.

Eddy could relate to Lincoln's burden of celebrity and power. If a huckster or investment counselor wasn't trying to take Eddy's money, somebody was asking him to endorse a product or a writer was calling to arrange an interview. Zealous autograph hounds never rested, and crazed fans who bought one-way tickets from their faraway homes showed up at his doorstep. An obsessive woman from Hobbs, New Mexico, appeared backstage one night and asked her idol if he remembered all the letters she had sent him over the years. "A warning bell rang in my brain," Eddy told a reporter in the 1950s. "And I thought, 'Oh, no, not Hobbs, New Mexico.' I was sweating by that time and my hands were clammy against the guitar. She said she'd driven 100 miles just to see me. I thanked her politely and, about that time, her sister called to her from the wings to come on if she was going with her. The woman answered, 'I don't know whether I'll go back with you or not.' I began saying 'Good night' real quick and backed all the way across the stage as fast as I could."

It didn't take long for Eddy to acclimate to the people that fame draws. He viewed his ardent fans as part of the music world's toll and came to detect the dollar signs in the eyes of questionable businessmen. But fame and increasing wealth held another pitfall. In April 1949, his former manager, Dean Upson, dragged him into court and demanded a piece of his recording and radio transcription earnings from the previous five years.

In November 1946, Dean Upson vacated the WSM Artists' Service Bureau to join KWKH in Shreveport, Louisiana, where he helped start the "Opry"-inspired "Louisiana Hayride." But by September of '48 he had returned to Nashville to start an advertising venture. Since leaving Nashville for KWKH, he had watched his former client accumulate more popularity and money each year. The Tennessee Plowboy's acclaim grew with such abandon that Upson decided that a portion of the Eddy Arnold dividend belonged to him. Claiming that his management contract with Arnold remained fully viable, Upson filed suit against his old WSM colleague in the Chancery Court of Davidson County, Tennessee.

Eddy, of course, considered Tom Parker his personal manager in all aspects of his work, but in 1949 he was faced with paying back commissions to another manager who claimed to have a valid contract with him. In his complaint, Upson produced a contract with Eddy dated October 5, 1943, that was written to coincide with the length of Eddy's RCA Victor contract. "It is mutually understood and agreed that the party of the first part [Dean Upson]," the contract read, "shall have the right or option to renew this contract upon the same terms and conditions for a period of [the] RCA Victor contract and options. . . ." Soon after signing this contract with Upson, Eddy signed his first one-year RCA Victor deal, which renewed at one-year intervals over the next few years. The key phrase in the contract, if Upson were to prove that he still had a valid deal with Eddy, addressed Upson's right to renew his contract with Eddy. Upson, for the purposes of the suit, interpreted his contract to mean that as long as RCA Victor had Eddy Arnold under contract, he had Eddy under contract and could claim part of the singer's earnings. Upson asked the court to order a full accounting of what Eddy allegedly owed him, but estimated that amount to be $35,000. Upson, who claimed to have negotiated his client's RCA Victor contract in October and November of 1943, suggested that Eddy had earned some $300,000 in recording royalties from 1945 to 1949, and $50,000 from his radio transcription series; he demanded his 10 percent.

Eddy secured the services of Nashville's Goodpasture, Carpenter and Dale law firm to defend him against the warring Upson. A partner in the firm, William F. Carpenter, had become a good friend and valuable adviser to Eddy, and Eddy often visited his offices, where they exchanged jokes before getting down to business. "He became almost a father to me," recalled Eddy. "He was a good man. He advised me a lot. I was very green, and there was a lot I didn't know about business—about dealing with people. Without him, a lot of people would have taken advantage of me . . . but he would always give me good advice."

Carpenter filed an answer with the court, denying that Upson had any commission coming to him and blasting Upson's claim that he negotiated the RCA contract; Eddy always gave that credit to Fred Forster and Harry Stone. In fact, despite Eddy's claim, Upson did have a role in the contract negotiations, as documentation in the case would reveal. But the question of who did or didn't negotiate Eddy's contract really was a peripheral issue. Eddy and his lawyers had to establish that Upson's contract had languished four years before. Upson had received everything due him under the contract, Eddy asserted in his rebuttal, and, furthermore, the contract had expired in late 1945 without peep or protest from Upson.

Upson appeared at his lawyer's office to give a deposition on November 7, 1949, where he painstakingly outlined his qualifications to look out for Eddy's interests and how he worked through Fred Forster to secure a recording contract for Eddy. Upson even went as far as to imply that his old singing group, the Vagabonds, influenced Eddy's style. "I feel that there is a great similarity in that Eddie [sic] Arnold interprets songs a great deal as the Vagabonds interpreted them," Upson claimed. "I don't mean by that copied, because he is definitely an individualist. However, the basic interpretation is much the same—in fact, in Arnold's early history in the singing profession, or radio profession, he sang a great many of the songs that the Vagabonds did, and, in fact, complimented me in singing many of the songs I wrote or helped write; namely, 'Little Shoes' [and] 'Little Mother of the Hills.'"

As far as the contract, Upson claimed that Eddy concurred when he suggested that the deal coincide with the RCA Victor contract. "When I first typed . . . this contract, it was in my mind that we had agreed upon a five-year term," said Upson, harking back some six years. "However, when Mr. Arnold came and sat down and read the contract, and we were ready to sign it, Eddie [sic] requested that that period be changed, and I suggested that it be for a period of the RCA Victor contract and options to which Eddie agreed and signed it." In other words, Upson claimed his contract with Eddy ran for one year, concurrent with the RCA Victor contract, and then automatically renewed if RCA Victor exercised its options to renew Eddy's recording contract. Upson further claimed in his testimony that he had written and called Eddy several times since 1946 to recoup his money, going as far as asking Roy Acuff to persuade Eddy to pay up, but Eddy had never responded.

Carpenter took his turn at questioning the complainant five days later and focused on the word "options" in the contract. What if, Carpenter mused, the word was singular? "In other words," Carpenter suggested to Upson, "if the artist had a contract with RCA Victor, say for a year, with an option for RCA Victor to renew it on the same terms for the same period, that would mean that the option was exercised and the contract would be for an additional year."

"It would," Upson replied.

Carpenter peppered Upson with alternately empty and meaningful questions before bearing down on a few handwritten additions and alterations to the contract. The contractual clause referring to "options" had been penciled in over Upson's original typewritten term of five years, an alteration, Upson correctly stated earlier, that came at Eddy's urging. But it appeared to Carpenter that the "s" on the end of "options" in Upson's copy of the contract was written in a different color ink than the rest of the letters. "When was that added?" Carpenter queried.

Upson's lawyer, Roy Miles, futilely objected.

"Answer the question," Carpenter pressed.

"You are implying that that was added," Upson retorted. "There was nothing added. That was written as is on the day it was written in there."

Carpenter startled Upson, and he proceeded to spit a line of questions at him that muddied his claims. When the day's questioning ended, Upson was bruised, but Carpenter still hadn't proved that the contract referred to an "option" rather than "options." If Carpenter could prove that Upson had altered the word, he could establish that the contract between Upson and Arnold had run only two years. Eddy's first contract with Victor had only stretched for one year, which meant that one option would extend Upson's contract for only one additional year.

Upson and his lawyer rallied, corralling J. L. Frank, Pee Wee King's manager, to establish the respect that Eddy had achieved in the industry and to confirm that Dean Upson attended Eddy's first RCA session in the WSM studios (Frank said he was at the session and remembered seeing Upson there). Frank helped build the case that Upson was important in Eddy's career, not just a manager in name only, as Eddy claimed. Next, the lawyers and their clients traveled to Chicago to take a deposition from the seventy-year-old music publisher Fred Forster, who had tipped off RCA Victor about the young talent in Nashville. In a series of responses, Forster discounted Upson's role in the negotiations with the record company. "No one had any connection with the negotiating of that contract except myself," Forster asserted. "I made all the contacts." Forster failed to recall any conversations with Upson about the contract, but Upson's lawyer refreshed his memory, dredging up a pile of letters from Forster's files that indicated significant dialog between Upson and Forster about the terms of the contract RCA Victor had proposed to Eddy. Still, Upson's lawyer was only succeeding in establishing Upson's influence on Eddy's work; doubts about Upson's alterations to his contract with Eddy lingered.

The case dragged on into April of 1951 without any real progress until Eddy himself entered his lawyers' offices and stood for a deposition. It was Eddy's first turn at answering questions in this case, and lawyer Carpenter promptly demonstrated why he called Eddy. He produced Eddy's copy of the Upson contract and passed it to his client. "I notice in both places there, Mr. Arnold, that the word 'contract' and the word 'option' are in the singular. Is that right?"

"Yes, sir," Eddy concurred.

The revelation appeared to stupefy Upson's counsel. "Let me see that, please," he demanded. Carpenter handed the contract to his opponent and then entered the damning piece of paper as evidence. Eddy's lawyer later recruited a handwriting expert to confirm that the "s" had been attached to "option" on Upson's copy of the contract. In May 1953, Chancellor Thomas A. Shriver disallowed Upson's claims to have a current deal with Eddy, judging that the complainant had, in fact, altered the contract without Eddy's knowledge. Shriver ruled that the Upson-Arnold contract ran from October 1943 to November 1945 and ordered the deputy clerk and master of the court to determine the amount due Upson, if any, under the correct terms.

In Upson's original complaint, he said Eddy had paid him only $175, but Carpenter shredded that claim. In a deposition taken before Chancellor Shriver's ruling, Eddy had produced canceled checks written to Dean Upson totaling some $350 and representing 10 percent of Eddy's RCA Victor royalties on his recordings made before the end of 1945. But Eddy was less certain—as a deposition taken after Shriver's decision revealed—of how much he made and paid Upson as a result of his radio transcriptions. Upson's attorney, Roy Miles, grilled him about income from the broadcast appearances for the Chattanooga Medicine Company, finding Eddy to be a poor record keeper.

"Do you have a record of your income from those transcriptions?" Miles queried.

"I do not," Eddy replied.

"Were they reported on your income tax returns?"

"I imagine they were."

"Do you have copies of your income tax returns?"

"I haven't found any, not in those years."

"You haven't found any what, Mr. Arnold?"

"Income tax returns, what you said."

"You mean you don't find any copies of returns for those years back there, 1943, 1944, and 1945?"

"No, sir."

"Do you have any idea where they are, what could have become of them?"

"No, sir, I do not."

Roy Miles seemed incredulous as he turned up the heat on Eddy. "Do you have any other source of information, Mr. Arnold, from which your income from those transcriptions might be determined?"

"No, sir, I haven't," Eddy answered, "because in those days I didn't keep accurate records so I don't have them."

Eddy's response rang alarm bells in his lawyer's head. "You mean permanent records instead of accurate records," Eddy's lawyer corrected his client.

Eddy couldn't understand his lawyer's admonition.

"You mean permanent records," his lawyer repeated.

"Yes, sir, permanent records," Eddy stated, picking up the cue.

Roy Miles protested. "I object to counsel answering for the witness. Let the record stand as it is."

Although Eddy claimed to have paid Upson his share from the transcription income, the record showed that, by not keeping "permanent" records, his assertion carried little validity. Eddy had probably recorded hundreds of "Black Draught" radio transcriptions for the Chattanooga Medicine Company before November 1945, and now the door opened wide for Upson to come in and take 10 percent, whether or not Eddy had paid him originally.

In addition to the transcription commission and the $350 Eddy had paid out a decade before, Upson wanted a piece of the royalties Eddy had made since November 1945 on records waxed before that month, eight songs in all, including "The Cattle Call" and "Each Minute Seems A Million Years" (his first *Billboard* hit). The court agreed that Upson had a claim to part of all royalties generated by the songs, but, unfortunately for Upson, RCA had removed most of the songs from its catalog and there was little money to be had. Also, in what was to become a common Eddy Arnold practice, Eddy had re-recorded "The Cattle Call," "Many Tears Ago," and "I Walk Alone" after the Upson contract had lapsed. Royalties from these re-recordings, the court determined, were off limits to Upson. Only "Each Minute Seems A Million Years"—which had sold more than 300,000 records since 1945— remained to put anything resembling a jingle in Upson's pocket. In 1954, the court finally decreed that Eddy owed Upson a total of $1,133.09 minus the $350.15 Eddy had already paid him. Before his lawyers took their share, Upson went home with $782.94. Luckily for Eddy, the court forgave his poor record keeping and ruled that Upson had already received his due from the radio transcription work.

A five-year ordeal had ended for Eddy, and not without a lesson. In years to come, he would tell up-and-coming performers not to latch on to a manager so early in their careers. "Every time a young artist comes to me and talks now, I warn them about getting managers and getting themselves tied up with managers . . . when early on in life they don't need a manager. Then when they get rolling, get a manager. But get a good manager, somebody you can trust." Eddy never saw Dean Upson again. Upson died in 1973.

—·—

Although the Dean Upson lawsuit often preoccupied Eddy's thoughts during the five years it inched along, Eddy's career thrived in spite of the wrangling. However, he was also trying to steady himself in a changing music world. A lot had happened for him between 1949 and 1954.

In 1950, Eddy placed eight songs on the charts, including four of the year's top twenty. Eddy, though, spent only one week at number one (with "Take Me in Your Arms and Hold Me"), overshadowed by Hank Williams and newcomer Hank Snow. Snow, who, like Williams, rejected Eddy's unadorned interpretations for a rougher, wailing country sound, dominated 1950 with "I'm Movin' On."

The crooning style of country singing claimed disciples, too—Red Foley and George Morgan among them—but the Hank Williams brand dominated country music's top shelf in the early 1950s. As each day passed, Eddy surrendered territory to Snow, Lefty Frizzell, Carl Smith, and Hank Thompson—singers closer to the Hank Williams tradition. But Eddy and Steve Sholes compromised nothing to the new sound despite its rising preeminence. They essentially stuck to a recipe of Eddy's easy vocals, optimistic songs, a pinch of tearjerkers, and Roy Wiggins's steel guitar.

Why change? The records sold, and Eddy's voice matured with every session. He had developed that talent to deliver a sage knowingness and a sense of humor in his songs. He could always project sadness or happiness, but now he winked at his listeners. The ability to laugh at himself, not to take himself so seriously, refreshed his recordings. Eddy seemed to have had the most fun yet on his 1950 sessions. In April, Eddy toyed with "Cuddle Buggin' Baby," a silly ditty that Eddy performed with good humor. With lazy bravado, he brags about his willing partner: *I can tell she'd rather cuddle bug than stay and see the show.*

Another whimsical tune, Jenny Lou Carson's "The Lovebug Itch," hit the charts for Eddy in 1950, peaking at number two—the same spot "Cuddle Buggin' Baby" reached. Eddy waxed "The Lovebug Itch" on August 20, 1950, in Nashville, his first session in the city since 1945. Besides being a homecoming for Eddy, the Nashville session is remarkable because Sholes hired Anita Kerr to play organ and a young Chet Atkins to pick the guitar. Both would have significant roles in Eddy's future, Kerr as an arranger and vocalist and Atkins as a producer.

Atkins joined Loren "Jack" Shook on guitar, resulting in three guitars—including Roy Wiggins's steel—on the session. When his fans bought a copy of "The Lovebug Itch" they saw their hero credited as the "Tennessee Plowboy and His Guitar." But, in fact, on the Nashville session Eddy had laid down the guitar, and as the 1950s wore on, he less frequently picked it up on record. (Eddy essentially strummed rhythm on his sessions, and considered himself a substandard player when compared to the studio guitarists' talents.)

RCA Victor had yet to set up permanent operations in Nashville, so Sholes often booked Brown Brothers Studio for Eddy's work there. Preparing a Nashville session was like readying for war. Steve first dispatched Victor's recording equipment to Nashville and then engineer Jeff Miller who set up the session (labor union rules barred Victor engineers from operating any equipment but Victor's). Steve followed, hopping the Cannonball Express from Pennsylvania Station in Manhattan and waking up in Nashville.

Sholes also carefully chose the venues, as Nashville was notorious for espionage. If a competing label heard that Eddy Arnold had recorded a

A portrait of Nashville royalty. *Left to right:* Hank Williams, Milton Estes, Red Foley, Minnie Pearl, George Rosen, Harry Stone, Eddy, Roy Acuff, Rod Brasfield, Lew Childre. *Front:* Wally Fowler. (Dolly Denny collection)

song, they might rush a cover version to the consumer—hoping to piggyback on Eddy's reputation and eat into his market share. Also, publishers tried to discover when their songs were recorded before artists and their A&R representatives approached them for permission to use the songs. An A&R man might tell the publisher that he was merely thinking about recording a particular song and demand a lower royalty rate. But if the publisher knew the song had already been recorded, he could stand firm on his rate. Castle Studios, according to RCA's Brad McCuen, was one Nashville studio fraught with leaks. "What we later found out was that Troy Martin, who was a representative for Peer Southern [publishing company], lived in the Tulane Hotel, which was where the Castle Studio was. . . . He had gotten a microphone into the ceiling. So when anybody recorded in there all Troy had to do was go up in his room and turn his mike on, and he could hear what was being recorded."

Steve avoided Castle Studios and opted for Brown Brothers Studio, a cramped space with boxes full of transcribed radio shows, including Eddy's, teetering on top of one another. (Brown Brothers became Thomas Studios when purchased by Cliff Thomas in the mid-'50s.) When air travel made more frequent visits to Nashville possible, Victor rented a garage to store its recording equipment and set up roomier facilities in a building on McGavock Street. "They put a big Nipper dog out front [made of] concrete, and everybody thought it was RCA's first studio," said McCuen, "but it wasn't really because it belonged to [the Methodist TV, Radio and Film Commission] that recorded an awful lot of Sunday school lessons for their churches." Sholes used the McGavock Street site from 1955 until Victor opened its own studios in 1957.

Sholes recorded Eddy only sporadically in Nashville, opting instead for New York, where his best equipment and personnel were available. Eddy was one of RCA Victor's biggest money makers, and naturally Steve wanted to record him with as few variables as possible. Engineer Jeff Miller was a frequent presence on the sessions, particularly those in New York. "Steve would see that I got Jeff Miller," remarked Eddy. "I liked working with him. He was a familiar face. . . . I knew what I was doing was pretty good; that's the reason I wanted the same engineer. He understood me, and I could talk to him."

While Steve Sholes adhered to the familiar in the studio, the Victor marketing and promotion people stuck to their old game plan, too. Whenever they could get on Eddy's schedule, they had him out with disc jockeys, jukebox owners, and one-stop operators. By the 1950s, disc jockeys had become the most important avenue for record promotion; the jukebox operators bought what the stations played. Both of the two sources, however, needed full attention, and RCA Victor nurtured them whenever possible. For years, Eddy pressed the flesh with jukebox people at the annual Music Operators of America conventions and made short regional tours of radio stations. Although not exactly relishing the rushed tours, Eddy performed his duty faithfully and seemed comfortable with the stream of new faces he met. "He never seemed to have a problem," said Bob McCluskey, RCA's head of country-and-western promotion in the late '40s and early '50s and Eddy's escort on the marketing tours. "He knew he was a country artist, and he laughed about it. He enjoyed what he was and who he was. He never seemed to have a problem with feeling out of place. . . . I explained who these people were, and he went along with it."

"He had a sense of his popularity," added McCluskey, who also had plugged Perry Como and other RCA pop stars before going country. "He had a sense of his worth. He knew who he was. He knew he had talent, and he had control of himself. He wasn't negative about anything."

Eddy could little afford to be negative about these junkets around the country. The radio stations, especially, helped promote his music across the country, and disc jockeys who attracted large numbers of listeners—like Nelson King in Cincinnati, Bob Neal in Memphis, Johnny Hicks in Dallas, and Randy Blake in Chicago—commanded attention. Nelson King, particularly, demanded respect because his country show on WCKY, propelled by 50,000 watts on clear channel, picked up listeners down in New Orleans and cut a swath in the ether to eastern cities like Washington, D.C., and New

York. "Nelson's program," McCluskey said, "really controlled that whole section of the country late at night. The people that listened to the station were very, very record conscious at that time because what was played, they bought. One of the things I did [when I visited King] with Eddy was I bought time on the station. In so doing, I involved Nelson [and his partner] Marty Roberts with a promise to play the records that I asked [them] to play."

McCluskey said he never paid disc jockeys cash to play RCA Victor country records—a practice known as "payola"—but in buying ad time on their stations and expecting increased play for Eddy Arnold, he came rather close. Rewarding stations and disc jockeys for promoting records was a common business tactic among major and independent record companies in the 1940s and '50s, and executives showered disc jockeys with perks ranging from dinner to writer's credit on songs. KLRD's Johnny Hicks, whose "Hillbilly Hit Parade" was heard from its Dallas home to Canada and west to Colorado and Wyoming, believed that a recording contract he had with Columbia Records came as a result of the company wanting him to spin more Columbia artists.

In light of Eddy's immense popularity, however, any rewards for disc jockeys probably were overkill and represented Victor's gratitude more than anything else. A country station or program that refused to play Eddy Arnold records in the late '40s and early '50s did so at the risk of inciting mobs of Eddy Arnold fans. "Eddy would sell 40, 50, 75, 100 thousand records every time he came out, and that was important to our company," said McCluskey. "That catalog kept [selling] over the years."

Still, Eddy—not arrogant about his popularity—pounded the pavement with McCluskey. "You got to Cincinnati. You got to Louisville. You got to Nashville. You got to Memphis. You got to a bunch of places that are reasonably close together," explained McCluskey. "You pile Eddy in the car and say, 'Hey, let's go.' Then you go see the people, and you go all day long and maybe you have dinner with them. Then [you] get in the car and drive to the next city that night and get some sleep." To bear the tedium of the road, Eddy and Bob rated their dinners and the looks of their waitresses, dreamed about breakfast, and traded stories. Once they traded their cars. "On one of the trips that Eddy and I took, I had my little Ford station wagon," said McCluskey. "We were driving around the country, and Eddy fell in love with the station wagon. He wanted it for the farm. I said, 'You oughta get one.' He said, 'I want this one. Incidentally, I'm turning in my Chrysler convertible.' I said, 'Why don't we swap?' I kept the Chrysler convertible for many years. . . . He gave me a dollar, and I gave him a dollar for his car."

On these promotional tours and on the concert circuit, Eddy often drifted off in solitude while his car sped across the highways. Staring out the window at the land he whizzed past or gazing ahead in the headlighted darkness, Eddy might not speak for hours. "I'd say something, and he wouldn't even answer me," explained Roy Wiggins. "Next day, he'd say, 'Roy, you started to say something to me yesterday. What was it?'" His traveling companions could only speculate on his thoughts. Was he pondering Sally and the kids, his next recording session, the Dean Upson suit, or the fields of Chester County? Only Eddy knew, though one might have made an educated guess that the future filled his mind. Eddy harbored definite feelings about his future.

9

In the light of his forays into the pop charts, Hollywood, and network broadcasting, Eddy yearned to shed the "country" label. With record sales totaling some 18 million by 1952, he had the luxury to make a few choices about his direction. Eddy already had amassed an audience of rural and urban admirers—the Philadelphians of Pennsylvania were just as familiar with "Bouquet of Roses" as the Philadelphians of Mississippi.

The trick for Eddy was using the widespread recognition to elude classification. The national press used terms like "corn" and "hillbilly" to refer to country music, which caused Eddy to shudder. He also disliked being clustered with purveyors of the coarser brand of country. Eddy's professional peer group tended to consist of people like Arthur Godfrey, not Arthur "Guitar Boogie" Smith, and he coveted the respect that the Arthur Godfreys commanded from Americans of all stations, not just certain segments of the population. On TV (and on occasional concert appearances), Eddy shared the stage with Perry Como, Bob Hope, zany bandleader Spike Jones, and other stars with broader appeal and no strong connections to a particular genre. "I never wanted to desert the country side," Eddy emphasized, "I just wanted to broaden my thing. I thought there was an audience out there that I could get if I just reached for them a little bit."

Reaching out, Eddy and Steve Sholes rearranged his studio accompaniment to formulate a more worldly sound, sparing Roy Wiggins but stripping the Willis Brothers, while adding Nashville guitar virtuoso Hank Garland. But Wiggins and Garland notwithstanding, a decidedly New York cast of instrumentalists dominated Eddy's sessions: Al Chernet on acoustic guitar and pop/jazz player George Barnes on electric guitar, along with Garland, Charles Grean (who also wrote arrangements) on bass, Marty Gold or Bob Davie on piano, Eddie Litvan on organ, and Phil Kraus on drums. Drummers had never appeared on Eddy's records, but in 1952 Sholes included Kraus. "Phil Kraus was an Eddy Arnold–type drummer," recalled pianist Bob Davie. "Phil was helpful—anything you wanted. Phil never got his back up when you changed his whole part around. . . . Charlie [Grean] would say, 'Phil, that stinks.' Phil was the type of guy who would say, 'Okay, what won't stink, Charlie?'"

121

Walter Louis Garland, though, proved to be the most exciting new addition to Eddy's sessions. A native of Cowpens, South Carolina, Garland had joined Eddy's road show in 1952 after serving stints with Paul Howard and Cowboy Copas, as well as lighting up several singers' records as a session guitarist. Years back, before his tenth birthday, Garland had shown a natural inclination toward the guitar, absorbing the licks of Piedmont guitarists Mother Maybelle Carter and Arthur "Guitar Boogie" Smith. While still a scruffy fifteen-year-old, Paul Howard invited the boy to Nashville after hearing him perform some pretty amazing stuff in a South Carolina record store. Surely, the young Garland's playing was frayed in spots, but as he waded deeper into the Nashville scene, it improved. When a few of his colleagues turned him on to jazz guitarists Charlie Christian and Django Reinhardt, heaven seemed just a pluck away. "Hank Garland, the most active guitarist in [Nashville]," Chet Atkins (no slouch as a guitarist himself) once said of his colleague, "plays faster than Tal Farlow [the nimble jazz guitarist who played with Artie Shaw, Red Norvo, and others] . . . and he's at home in more styles than anybody I ever saw." The versatile Garland reveled in playing jazz on his guitar, later rocked behind Elvis Presley, and even accompanied his own vocals on a few numbers released on the Decca label.

Garland's first session for Eddy in May of 1952 turned out to be the last session for the Willis Brothers. The session spun off a number-one hit, "A Full Time Job," and immediately demonstrated to listeners the wisdom of enlisting Garland. The familiar Roy Wiggins introduced the song with a flashy, steel-guitar riff to which Eddy slyly suggested, *I wanna full time job making love to you!*" In Eddy's wake, Wiggins took another solo, but Hank Garland commandeered the record shortly after. Like a rapid succession of bullets pinging off a metal surface, Garland's notes feverishly rang in step with the upbeat rhythm. Garland's performance on "A Full Time Job" was supercharged, yet each crisp note seemed individually nurtured, resonating on the vinyl as Garland glided up and down the scale.

Garland, indeed, proved to be an asset to his new employer, polishing Eddy's sound in the studio as well as on the road (where he was forever squeezing a rubber ball to keep his fingers spry), and exuding an easygoing disposition that mirrored Eddy Arnold's. "He was just a super, super nice guy and was a lot of fun," remembered Gordon Stoker, who, as a member of the Jordanaires vocal group, often appeared on the bill with Eddy. "He played jokes on people. He cut up a lot. . . . He was an intelligent guy, and he just had a lot going for him."

A mounting demand among other artists and producers for Garland lured him away from Eddy's full-time employ later in the '50s. "He didn't need to be with me anymore," said Eddy. "He could make more money [as a studio guitarist]." But Garland continued as an occasional session man for his old boss until a disastrous car accident took him from the Nashville scene in 1961.

A jazzy shuffle beat, stirred up by Garland and the New York guys, pervaded Eddy's studio background, and popular standards found their way

A new group of comrades. Eddy looks to the right to see Arthur Godfrey and then Bob Hope. (Eddy Arnold collection)

A more refined Tennessee Plowboy with Hank Garland and Roy Wiggins. (Eddy Arnold collection)

onto his records. "Moonlight and Roses," "I'm Gonna Sit Right Down and Write Myself A Letter," and "Angry" (an oldie revived in 1951 by Kay Starr) replaced songs with visible country appeal. Among the original non-country material to emerge from this period were "Free Home Demonstration" (a Coben-Grean composition) and "How's the World Treating You" (penned by Chet Atkins and Boudleaux Bryant). Both songs hit the top five of the country charts, indicating that Eddy's huge country audience could stomach his straying from their idea of the mainstream.

The William Morris Agency also supported Eddy's quest for new worlds. In June of '52, *Billboard* reported that Eddy would host his first TV show, a summer replacement for Perry Como's regular CBS spot. Eddy's fifteen minutes debuted in July and aired Monday, Wednesday, and Friday through August. Eddy moved his family to New York for the summer, and his guitarists, Roy Wiggins and Hank Garland, came, too. Milton Berle and other stars in the television world had nothing to fear from Eddy's first dip into hosting a television program, but he kept the time period afloat until Como returned. Over at NBC, programmers delighted in Eddy's performance for CBS and invited him to spell Dinah Shore during her 1953 vacation. At NBC, a degree of confusion reigned when Russ Case, the NBC orchestra leader, wrote out parts for Roy Wiggins, who reads little music. "I looked at the music and the ting-a-ling thing . . . you ought to see it written out on a piece of paper," recalled Roy. "If it's within the staff someplace, I can read it. But if it gets way above or way below, I get lost. This was way, way above the staff, and I went up to Mr. Case and said, '. . . pardon me, but what is this?' He said, 'Don't worry about it, Roy. That's what you played on the record. I just copied it off the record.' . . . It was like seeing a hoedown written on paper."

His first extended TV run under his belt, Eddy sailed south to the Carolina Theater in Greenville, South Carolina, which, according to press reports, had never featured a "rustic" act before. Then it was out to California for Eddy's first tour of the West Coast. He played Pasadena, San Diego, Long Beach, and other towns in the Golden State, giving a whole new region a taste of Eddy Arnold in person.

During January and February of 1953, "Eddy's Song" (another Coben-Grean collaboration) held the number-one country spot for three weeks. The song crossed the line to self-parody, opening and closing with an exaggerated Roy Wiggins ting-a-ling and stringing together the titles of twenty-two Eddy Arnold hits (less than half his total to that point!). The hit harked back to older days, but in 1953 Roy Wiggins rarely was prominently featured on his steel guitar, and Eddy generally dodged songs like "Chained to A Memory" or "Don't Rob Another Man's Castle" ("Eddy's Song" named both). Eddy was now reaching for the pop charts. In May 1953, Eddy sent wires through Victor to a host of pop disc jockeys, imploring them (vainly, as it turned out) to play his songs, particularly "You Always Hurt the One You Love," a lazy ballad caressed by a vibrating organ (a common instrumental embellishment on pop songs in the mid-'50s).

Charles Grean strikes up the band. (Betty Johnson collection)

One of the prime catalysts in Eddy's new sophistication was Charles Grean. Grean cast his lasting mark on popular music as a writer, producer, arranger, conductor, musician, and A&R man. He arranged and conducted the orchestra on hits such as Nat "King" Cole's 1950s version of "The Christmas Song (Merry Christmas to You)" and Vaughn Monroe's "Riders in the Sky." Born in 1913, Grean learned to play bass in college and soon found work playing clubs and society parties around New York City with various bands. For a brief period in the mid-1930s, he captained his own groups on cruise ships, but soon settled in New York again and won a spot playing bass in the NBC house band. Grean had also become a capable copyist—one who adapts an arrangement to each band instrument. Artie Shaw hired Grean as a copyist, as did Glenn Miller, who employed the young man for three years (1939–1942). Popular music history, however, will best remember Grean as the father of "The Thing." His story of a man who finds an indescribable "thing" on the beach scaled the charts for Phil Harris in 1950, and will probably be considered one of the most popular novelty songs of the twentieth century.

Grean was hired by Steve Sholes in 1947 and quickly moved up in the organization, sitting with Sholes and eight others on a committee that directed the A&R operations. The committee concept in Victor's A&R department fell apart after a year, and the company returned A&R power to one man: Jack Hallstrom. Hallstrom hired *Billboard* editor-in-chief Joe Csida for the pop A&R directorship in July of 1949, but by May of the following year Csida had returned to *Billboard*. Grean stepped in for Csida, remaining in the pop A&R job for almost two years until he left in 1952 to form his own label, the short-lived Comet Records. When Comet burned out, Grean went into partnership with Joe Csida, who had left *Billboard* again to start a publishing and artist-management firm.

All the while, through the upheaval of the record business and his job changes, Grean remained with Sholes in the studio. On the Eddy Arnold sessions, he left his imprint. Grean chose the session musicians (except for Wiggins and Garland, who came with Eddy), wrote the arrangements for each instrument, and penned, with and without Cy Coben, many of Eddy's numbers. Grean's jazzier, polished approach to music fit right in with what Eddy hoped to achieve.

One piece of the puzzle, though, seemed ill-formed to Eddy's evolving style: Colonel Tom Parker. Parker had certainly done his part, working with William Morris to land choice TV and personal appearances and looking out for his boy's interests at RCA. He even had finagled for Eddy the highest royalty rate of any RCA performer; additionally, should another artist negotiate a higher rate, RCA was obliged to raise Eddy to that level. Increasingly, though, it became apparent that you could take the man out of the carnival, but you couldn't take the carnival out of the man. The Colonel cooked up promotional advertisements that more resembled circus posters than plugs for an aspiring pop singer. One multi-page spread in the trade magazines touted Eddy with the tag line "Something About A Plowboy . . ." and featured a photo of the Tennessee Plowboy ankle-deep in dirt with a team of horses. Eddy went along, but he grew skeptical of the Colonel. Was he an asset or liability?

Parker often draped a cloth reading "Never Forget Eddy Arnold" over an elephant or caravan of ponies and led the animals through industry conventions. The Colonel always looked for ways to inflate Eddy's name and reputation. "Roy, which one of our planes did you bring when you came down here?" Parker would ask Roy Wiggins in a public place, knowing well that Eddy and the boys traveled by car, not private jet. The Colonel often brandished what he called his "snow plow" to exaggerate Eddy's reputation (even after the singer was well-established).

Joe Csida stumbled across Parker's wackiness in 1949 when Csida still worked at RCA. Eddy had come to New York to record, and Victor threw a press party for him. Csida asked the RCA Corporation's top executive, Frank Folsom, to stop by. Tom Parker attended, too, and brought gifts. "To everybody who showed up at the party, he was giving straw hats with very vivid checkered bands for Purina for whom Eddy at that point was doing a radio show," recalled Csida. "Poor old dignified Folsom walks in, and Parker goes over and slaps one of these terrible looking straw hats on his head. . . . I think that was a point at which Folsom said, 'I didn't know this went on in our company!'"

Eddy had placed tremendous trust in Parker, and Parker rarely let him down. But the Colonel's offbeat promotional tactics and frequent bickering with members of Eddy's road crew sealed his fate in Eddy's eyes. "Tom's a dear man, a good manager, but a completely different personality from me," Eddy told an interviewer years later. "I'm very laid back, very quiet, not flamboyant at all. Tom is. There was just two different personalities that clashed. That's what we were doing. We were clashing. So in 1953, I decided to make the move and not be associated with Tom. . . . He was distraught about it. I made a cash settlement with him, and we both went on our ways."

Eddy's patience with Parker snapped in the midst of Eddy's second Las Vegas run, a two-week stay in May 1953 at the Sahara Hotel. One afternoon during the engagement, Eddy picked up a telephone call meant for Tom. Tom had gone down to the hotel coffee shop with Tom Diskin, his assistant. The caller asked for Parker. "He's not here," Eddy answered. "Do you want me to have him call you?"

"No," said the voice on the other end. "Just tell him that the show we got together with Hank Snow is doing great."

The words fired a chill through Eddy's six-foot body. The Colonel managed Eddy exclusively! Or so Eddy thought. He found the Toms in the coffee shop, and when they saw him, they shoved some papers under the table. "There's no need to do that," Eddy said calmly. "You just got a phone call. I know what that's about. The caller said to tell you that the show you all got together with Hank Snow is doing great."

For the remainder of the Las Vegas engagement Eddy silently fumed. "I just ignored him for several days," Eddy explained. "I wouldn't talk to him. But then we came home, and he went away on a trip. . . . I sent him a wire—told him I wanted to end."

"I was displeased about the exclusivity," Eddy continued. "His take on me was for exclusivity. He was getting 25 percent of me—not 10—25." When Parker returned to Nashville, the two met with Eddy's lawyer and worked out an amicable separation agreement. For now, the William Morris Agency would handle all bookings, and Eddy told the press he planned to be his own personal manager.

"I have nothing but praise for Tom," Eddy told *Billboard*, "he's been a great manager. It is my desire that we remain close friends." Tom also struck a conciliatory tone in the pages of *Billboard*. "I'm very sorry to lose Eddy. He's a fine boy. I'm glad though that we were able to part pleasantly. In any case, he'll continue to be a big star for years to come. But I don't intend to let anyone forget the old Colonel."

No one forgot the Colonel. He soon struck up a management deal with Hank Snow and a young country singer (later pop star) named Tommy Sands. Of course there would be Elvis, and Parker even began booking some of Eddy's shows again through his Jamboree Attractions. As Eddy hoped, he and Tom ultimately resumed their friendship, and over the years Eddy has remained loyal to Tom, chaffing whenever writers come to him looking for stories about his former manager. "They all think they can get me on the phone, and they'll get all the dirt about Tom Parker. They'll never get it from me. I will never betray that man. I know him. I know him like a book, and we're friends. We'll be friends until we both have said good-bye."

—‧—

When Charles Grean heard about the split, he pointed Eddy toward his partner, Joe Csida. Csida-Grean Associates operated two publishing companies, Towne Music and Trinity Music, and in 1954 had launched an artist-management venture. Propped up by silent partner and millionaire Lee Eastman—who would later be the father-in-law of Beatle Paul McCartney—Csida-Grean Associates teemed with potential. They built a vertically integrated machine that controlled the songs, the artists, and ultimately the recordings. Csida-Grean's publishing companies manufactured the songs and matched the songs with their artists. Furthermore, the company often recorded the songs and artists themselves. For example, Csida-Grean independently recorded Betty Johnson, a pop singer in the company's stable, and sold the masters to various record companies. In Eddy Arnold's case, Csida-Grean would obviously defer to RCA and Steve Sholes in the studio, but Charles Grean amply represented the company's interests, freelancing for Sholes on Arnold sessions.

Grean ran the creative end of the partnership, and Csida, an urbane and stealthily aggressive individual, played the deal maker and oversaw the management side. With such combined expertise and financial backing, Csida-Grean could surely transform Eddy Arnold's image from that of a country singer to a generally accepted pop performer. Csida, in turn, hoped some of Eddy's luster would rub off on the company. Eddy brought a name that was easy to sell, an affiliation with the nation's most influential booking agency, and his own money to invest in projects. "I think they thought they had a fish with Eddy," remarked Betty Johnson, Eddy's colleague at Csida-Grean. "Eddy would come in the office, and he was the fish. He was the money guy. Everybody scrambled when he was around."

Csida-Grean had signed just one artist, singer Kathy Godfrey (Arthur Godfrey's sister), but on June 5, 1954, the management firm announced another, much larger, catch. Eddy Arnold officially joined Csida-Grean, where he proved to be a most compliant client. "He indicated if you were going to be his manager," said Joe Csida, "you were the one who had the responsibility to call the shots, and he would do whatever you thought he ought to do."

Eddy's music, of course, made him such a great catch. When he signed with Csida-Grean, he was in the midst of yet another year's string of hits,

riding particularly high on the success of "I Really Don't Want to Know."
Eddy has often pointed to this song as a turning point, representative of the
type of songs he loved. "I like a good sentimental love song, a love song
where two people love each other," Eddy told an interviewer in the 1970s,
"'I Really Don't Want to Know' is a song about the guy. . . . He's in love
with her, and he knows that maybe . . . she wasn't an angel in her lifetime.
But evidently she's an angel to the person singing this song. He's in love
with her. It's just that simple."

Eddy first attempted the song in a Nashville studio, just after he and the
Colonel announced their split in September 1953. With sparse accompaniment—only Eddy on guitar and Grean on bass—Eddy worked through the
number a few times, but couldn't get a satisfactory take. They tried again in
New York on October 23, and Eddy liked what he heard. "I Really Don't
Want to Know" debuted on the country charts in January 1954. The hit
reached number one in May, and ultimately spent thirty-seven weeks on the
charts (his longest stay since "Bouquet of Roses" in 1948 and '49). Other
1954 hits included "My Everything," "Hep Cat Baby," and "This Is the
Thanks I Get (For Loving You)," which Eddy had re-recorded.

"I Really Don't Want to Know" strayed farther from the current crop of
country hits than anything he had done thus far. Hank Garland and Roy
Wiggins stayed home for this session yet the song found a place on the country charts among the honky-tonk sounds of Hank Williams's "I'll Never Get
Out of This World Alive" and "I'll Go on Alone" by freshman Marty Robbins. Curiously, though, "I Really Don't Want to Know" failed to reach the
pop charts, while Les Paul and Mary Ford's hasty cover version reached number eleven. More troubling, though, was the fact that Eddy had not hit the
pop charts since 1949, when "I'm Throwing Rice (At the Girl that I Love)"
spent two weeks there. Eddy and Joe Csida had considerable work ahead.

—— • ——

"Eddy said that he'd like to go down in history not only as a pop singer, but
as a top singer period," Csida recalled. "So that was sort of the goal. We proceeded to work in that direction." Television, Eddy and Joe reckoned, would
pull them in that direction, but Eddy's aim in that medium, according to Joe,
couldn't overshoot the rural audience. "We didn't dare move totally out of the
country sphere. It would be a silly thing to do. You can't force-feed a thing
like that on the public. You have to sort of break it in gradually. . . . It was a
career transition that needed to be handled very, very carefully."

Following in the vein of "The Eddy Arnold Show," Eddy's independently
produced and syndicated radio program, Eddy and Joe set about recreating
Eddy's radio success on television. At its peak, Eddy's independent radio
broadcast had reeled in more than 300 stations. It seemed to follow that an
independent TV show would repeat the success of Eddy's radio ventures with
the added bonus of expanding Csida-Grean's influence to a new medium.

Eddy incorporated Eddy Arnold Enterprises in his hometown of Brentwood to bankroll the syndicated TV project, and Joe Csida took the show's helm as executive producer. Csida hired Ben Park, a Chicago-based NBC man, to produce, direct, and script the music-variety show that promised to be available by January 1955. Park had directed Eddy on the Dinah Shore replacement series and on NBC-TV's "Out on the Farm" that aired during the summer of '54. "Arnold is usually identified as a country artist," wrote *Billboard* in a story most certainly fed by Csida, "but his film series is expected to be aimed at universal appeal."

Eddy featured his boys Hank Garland and Roy Wiggins as well as Csida-Grean's Betty Johnson (who would later be a regular on "Don McNeil's Breakfast Club"). Eddy also recruited the Jordanaires, at the time known primarily for their occasional background vocals in Nashville and appearances on the "Grand Ole Opry." "He actually paid us good money. He paid us the biggest money we ever made in those days. . . . It was a very good experience for us," said Gordon Stoker of the Jordanaires. "Eddy Arnold gave us our first big break. We owe that to him." Dubbed the "Gordanaires" on "Eddy Arnold Time" to protect the show in the event the Jordanaires, who owned their name, left the show, the Jordanaires later entered American vernacular as Elvis Presley's backup singers.

The cast opened production at Chicago's Kling Studios in October and continued working on and off through December. Ben Park delivered on his end with scripts and sets ready to go. Eddy, as planned, had five half hours ready for TV stations by January 1955.

Opening to the strains of "Bouquet of Roses," not "The Cattle Call" (the theme song on his radio shows), "Eddy Arnold Time" promised viewers a heavy peppering of Eddy's songs wrapped around stories starring Eddy as a traveling salesman, pet shop owner, cowboy, or any number of other characters. Standing in front of a rural Tennessee farm scene, Eddy welcomed his viewers with a few familiar songs and introduced the week's story. "Well . . . let's see what the magic stump has for us this time. Wanna know where we'll be in the next part of the show? Well . . . watch." Eddy snapped his fingers over a tree stump and stepped away. A clue to the show's plot magically appeared on the wooden stump.

The plots followed a simple formula: Eddy as the hero, Betty forever in pursuit of Eddy, and the Gordanaires playing any characters that happened to be needed. Occasionally, Ben Park worked Roy and Hank into the script. "Eddy Arnold Time" idealized the old West, farming life, and the pleasures of home, aiming straight for middle-class American families. To please Eddy's country audience and that prospective general audience, Park and Csida threw in a variety of appeals: pop songs, Eddy's country hits, Eddy in a cowboy hat, Eddy in a suit. The gang always closed with a hymn, and the viewers said good-bye watching a heart-warming film montage of Eddy walking up a country road and riding (and standing on!) his tractor.

Betty Johnson, the Jordanaires, and Hank Garland sing a ring around Eddy on the "Eddy Arnold Time" television show. (Eddy Arnold collection)

Eddy and crew filmed editions of the show at a hurried rate, working around the clock at times to accommodate conflicting schedules. For nineteen straight weeks, Eddy and the cast rushed back and forth between Nashville and Chicago to film the shows. The Jordanaires, for example, arrived in Chicago on Monday, filmed through Friday, returned to Nashville for the Saturday night "Opry" broadcast, spent Sunday with their families, and boarded a plane to Chicago on Monday morning.

When Eddy, the Jordanaires, Betty Johnson, and the rest of the cast poured into town, they checked into the ritzy Blackstone Hotel and rushed to Kling Studios in the Windy City's meatpacking district. "When things would get really tense and really tiring," remembered Betty Johnson, "I'm talking about early in the morning, when we had to get the makeup reapplied and the hair done again and everybody's too tired—of course, you're sweating like mad under these lights. Just before a take, Eddy would tell me a corny joke. He loved to tell jokes a little risqué."

The lightheartedness Eddy exhibited backstage also came out in front of the cameras. Unlike his movies of five years before, "Eddy Arnold Time" revealed a more animated Eddy who appeared to know what the audience wanted. Although Eddy's stiffness froze him from time to time, his performance dynamics had improved. "Eddy was very graceful in the way he would sing a song with his guitar," said Betty Johnson. "He would take the guitar off, and he's a big guy, and it was not easy for him to take this cord off and set the guitar down. That was one of the most graceful things he ever did." Eddy laughed, moved, and joked more. His demeanor, like his voice, radiated warmth and ease. Although still not a natural by any means, the TV show revealed marked improvement in Eddy's on-stage entertaining ability.

"All in all," one reviewer commented, "the show rates as one of those few which are ideally suited to a million and one sponsors, and this probably is going to be the least of the worries confronting the property."

—⚫—

As "Eddy Arnold Time" prepared for its 1955 debut, RCA anticipated the tenth anniversary of Eddy's first release on the label. RCA appreciated Eddy's performance over the past decade and planned to let the world know it. The company reserved a multi-page spread in *Billboard* to give Frank Folsom, Joe Csida, and others a forum to praise their man. To celebrate on record, Steve Sholes helped Eddy assemble the album *An American Institution* on which Eddy sang competitors' hits from every one of his RCA years (Spade Cooley's "Shame on You" of 1945 to Hank Snow's "I Don't Hurt Anymore" of 1954). At a February 1955 ceremony in Washington, D.C., with members of Tennessee's congressional delegation on hand, Eddy presented *An American Institution* to the Library of Congress.

Eddy recorded *An American Institution* in early September 1954 and a couple of weeks later re-entered the studio to record three songs for children with his daughter Jo Ann. The session, designed to exploit Eddy's name in the kiddie market, produced a thoroughly cute version of Fred Ebb and Paul Klein's "The Horse in Striped Pajamas." Jo Ann recalled that her dad sort of eased her into the task. "One day he came home and had some sheet music . . . and we went into his little music room at home, and we went over 'Goodnight Sweetheart' (he really didn't tell me why we were doing this at first). Eventually, he told me he wanted me to do these songs with him and record them. Then we worked into practicing what we were going to do. . . . He was really good with me in that he wasn't critical. We just did it, and it was a really fun thing to do."

Eddy and Steve decided to break completely new ground by incorporating the grand, pop sound of Hugo Winterhalter into some recordings. "He was a fine arranger and conductor," said Eddy of Winterhalter. "He arranged all the hits Eddie Fisher had. He was it. He made a trip down here with Steve Sholes. He came out to my house, and we got to talking. We decided we'd do a couple of things with Hugo. . . . I enjoyed old Hugo. Dad gummed, he was a nice guy. He was a Pennsylvania man. Boy, his arrangements were fantastic!"

Hugo Winterhalter, a heavy-set, serious-faced saxophone player, came to RCA under the pop A&R reign of Joe Csida. Winterhalter and the orchestra he conducted had a smash with "Blue Christmas" on Columbia in 1949 and caught Csida's attention. By 1950, Csida had lured Winterhalter to Victor and put him in the studio behind Perry Como and Eddie Fisher. "He would study an artist," said Csida of Winterhalter. "He would know how to do an arrangement that would cover the artist's flaws and highlight his skills. He was a tremendous asset to the A&R staff at RCA."

Hugo endeared himself to his fellow musicians with his relaxed style and quiet yet effective approach to work. A Winterhalter session, whether recording his own records or others', included glorious, massive waves of music. With three saxophones, three French horns, nine violins, three cellos, three violas, a six-person chorus, and four-piece rhythm combo, Winterhalter created a wall of sound. "If Hugo keeps this up," an RCA executive once cracked, "we're going to have to have him recording Beethoven."

On April 28, 1955, Eddy joined Hugo and his gaggle of musicians to record four songs: "The Kentuckian Song," "The Richest Man (In The World)," "I Walked Alone Last Night," and a reinterpretation of "The Cattle Call." To record large instrumental congregations such as Hugo's, RCA rented Webster Hall, an old neoclassic building on New York's East Side that doubled as a club by night. One by one on the morning of the twenty-eighth, RCA staffers and Hugo's musicians weaved their way through the maze of round club tables to the recording area, moving aside napkin holders and salt shakers so they could plop their coats on the tables. Steve Sholes set the control equipment up in front of the bar, and Hugo spread his players throughout the cave of a room. A tiny, five-channel mixer was all Steve had to capture the day's work, so he used his five mikes on the strings, brass, rhythm section, chorus, and, of course, Eddy. Eddy struggled at first to adapt to the large number of instruments ("I wasn't accustomed to hearing that many instruments at one time"), but the final product suggested no such difficulty.

Not since Speedy McNatt's performances of the 1940s had background musicians inspired Eddy to rise above his norm. Hugo's arrangement of "The Kentuckian Song" called for a dreamy harpsichord, lush violin fills, and a soaring backup soprano. Such elements were completely foreign to anything Eddy had done previously, but he matched his beautiful backing note for note. Hugo and his musicians coaxed a tenderness from Eddy: *I see her walking in the rainy April sadness and hear her name in every bluebird call.*"

But how would "The Cattle Call" sound? The song dawned with a French horn that suggested the independent spirit of the West and then rolled into Eddy's opening yodel. The force of Hugo's instrumentation, though, ultimately competed with Eddy's vocals and overwhelmed the song's message. "The Cattle Call" means to communicate the loneliness of

Left to right: Eddy's manager Joe Csida, Eddy, Hugo Winterhalter, and Charlie Grean. (Betty Johnson collection)

the range and a sparse backing does that best. As much as Hugo's tender orchestration lifted "The Kentuckian Song," his powerful wall of sound only diluted "The Cattle Call."

Those in attendance that day at Webster Hall witnessed Eddy and RCA's bravest attempt yet to attract a new, pop audience. Chick Crumpacker, who had replaced Bob McCluskey as RCA Victor's head of country-and-western promotion, saw everything. "To redo 'Cattle Call' with the French horns and everything suggested a way to move Eddy into another, more viable direction, which was pure pop, symphonic pop if you will."

The public agreed. They gave Eddy his first pop chart position in six years and propelled "The Cattle Call" to number one on the country charts for two weeks. However, country purists—who detested any hint of pop—condemned the new version of "The Cattle Call." Distributors told RCA's Brad McCuen that Steve Sholes should forget the trumpets next time, and Joe Csida weathered protests from disc jockeys he met. "We released the record just about the time the disc jockey convention [Nashville's annual junket for record spinners] was being held that year," said Csida. "I remember talking to one of the top jockeys down there about how he liked Eddy's new record. He said, 'Man, I can't play Eddy with all those bugles.' So we met a little resistance on the country side. They didn't like the pop embellishments."

Other disc jockeys joined the chorus Csida heard in Nashville. Al Roberts of WPAW in Pawtucket, Rhode Island, protested to *Billboard*: "I play the older country style version of Eddy Arnold's 'Cattle Call.' . . . I refuse to play the Hugo Winterhalter version on any of my country shows. It's a beautiful number, but it's definitely pop." Harsher criticism came in from Newport News, Virginia and Ted Tatar of WACH: "About Eddy Arnold's new release with Hugo Winterhalter, phooey! I'm not going to air it; I consider this release a pop number and nothing else."

Eddy shrugged his shoulders while the royalties rolled in. He cherished the country audience, but wanted what "The Cattle Call" brought him: a sophisticated sound and pop success. "The Richest Man (In the World)," also from the Winterhalter session, skipped on to the pop charts, too. Eddy charted ten songs in 1955, his most productive year since 1949. Success with a more uptown sound seemed to indicate that Eddy was turning the corner in his search for broader acceptance.

Buoyed by Eddy's chart performance and reemerging pop success in 1955, RCA continued its observance of Eddy's tenth anniversary. The RCA-owned NBC network aired a radio tribute hosted by Tennessee governor Frank Clement, a friend of Eddy's, and RCA itself scheduled a couple of testimonial affairs.

At a posh New York luncheon, RCA officials recounted Eddy's successes until Eddy himself took the spotlight. He rose from his seat and walked to the podium. Eddy uttered a few words, but tears welled in his eyes. It's likely that the Chester County farm and the Victrola his sister Patty sent home years before flashed in his mind. Eddy pictured the family's old Jimmie Rodgers and Carter Family records, all bearing the Victor insignia. Even Patty's Victrola had ole Nipper's picture painted on it. Eddy tried to collect himself and focused again on the audience. "The truth is," Eddy mustered, "this is where I've always wanted to be."

A similar bash was held in Nashville on June 5, which was proclaimed "Eddy Arnold Day." More than 200 industry members and friends gathered at M. T. Gossett's Barn on Estes Road for Eddy's sake. *country-and-western Jamboree* magazine honored Eddy as the "number one male singer of the world"(what ever that meant). "I am flabbergasted by all this to-do," a newspaper quoted Eddy. "I am grateful to everyone for what little success I have had."

Praises rained down on Eddy all night, and the master of ceremonies called name after name of persons connected to Eddy's stardom. "It was quite a to-do—a lot of dignitaries came from all over the country, particularly RCA," Roy Wiggins told researcher Douglas Green. "And they stood up there. Eddy stood up there, any number of people, and bouquets were showered on these people. One of them was Hugo Winterhalter, of course, Tom Parker who deserves it, and a lot of other people. But when I left there, my name had not been mentioned. It hurt. It really hurt because I try real hard."

The omission of "Little" Roy Wiggins from the evening's program symbolized his boss's new path. On Eddy's two most recent smashes, "I Really

Don't Want to Know" and "The Cattle Call," Roy's steel guitar was absent. More and more, Roy stayed home when Eddy recorded, and, when Roy was asked along, Steve Sholes muted his steel guitar. "It was almost like he was ashamed of what we did," concluded Roy. "I have a very distinctive honor. I ruined 80 million Eddy Arnold records."

Obviously, Roy disdained Eddy's refined course, primarily because the new sound squeezed him out of the picture. But Eddy was just doing what he had done dozens of times before: assessing his prospects and doing what was practical from a career standpoint. In 1955, Eddy wanted—and believed he needed—to take a pop avenue, which meant a sharp reduction of steel guitar sound. "The way I was making records earlier was just singing and having a guitar and a steel guitar," Eddy said. "There's no freshness about it. Every record sounds the same."

Eddy and Steve generally excluded Roy from the studio, but Eddy had a heart. Roy remained a fixture on the road and got a piece of a publishing company Eddy financed. On top of it all, Eddy's 1940s' promise of a lifelong financial commitment to Roy remained intact. Despite Roy's bitterness he admitted, "I'd rather have [Eddy's] word than somebody else's contract."

10

*T*wo hundred miles from Nashville, as Eddy looked forward to establishing himself as a pop star, a young Memphian in Sam Phillips's Memphis Recording Service studio was on his way to being the major purveyor of the raucous rock and roll sound. To Eddy Arnold and other brand-name artists, both pop and country, Elvis Presley posed only a minor threat. In 1955, his country- and rhythm and blues–influenced rockabilly had mingled on the country charts with Eddy, Ernest Tubb, and Webb Pierce, and his "I Forgot to Remember to Forget" filled the number one spot for a few weeks.

But Elvis was an exception, the piper of a fad destined to pass—or so many in the country establishment thought. Eddy had encountered this skinny, sideburned boy back in 1954 at a Halloween show in Memphis's Ellis Auditorium. Elvis had made some noise regionally, and after the show went backstage to circulate among its stars. The Jordanaires, Minnie Pearl, and Robert Powers (the "World's Smallest Hillbilly Singer") were there supporting Eddy that night. "Elvis came backstage to meet [us]," said Gordon Stoker of the Jordanaires. "You would have thought [he wanted to meet] Eddy, but he didn't. He came backstage to meet the Jordanaires. He had been hearing us sing on the 'Grand Ole Opry' on Saturday nights, and most of the time . . . we would sing a spiritual, a finger-snapping fast type of number. This was his first love. He wanted to sing in a quartet."

Elvis admired Eddy, too (so much that he would record "How's the World Treating You," "It's A Sin," "I Really Don't Want to Know," and many other Arnold standards during the course of his career); after talking to the Jordanaires, a nervous Elvis asked Oscar Davis, a promoter, to introduce him to Eddy. What Elvis may have muttered to Eddy or any advice that Eddy may have imparted to the young singer that night are long forgotten. It was one of those flashes in time when the veteran meets the rookie: an insignificant moment at the time, but through the lens of history, a symbol of changing times. The boy struck Eddy as nice enough, but Eddy probably never gave Elvis another thought until the next year when some of Elvis's hits competed with Eddy's. Elvis's hits did so well that Steve Sholes signed the boy to an RCA Victor contract in 1955.

Shortly after the signing, Elvis rocketed to number one on the country and pop charts with "Heartbreak Hotel," and released a deluge of hits that chased steel guitarists and fiddlers back to the woods. Country artists, if they wanted to remain afloat, abandoned traditional instruments and incorporated rock's rhythm. Eddy probably thought himself immune to rock and roll as he was moving to a more polished, pop sound anyway. Unfortunately, though, for Eddy, rock and roll was fast becoming America's new pop music. Teenage record buyers devoured this new music and became a market segment to be taken seriously. As rock and roll songs flooded the charts, major record labels scrambled to sign new artists or adapt their existing ones to the curious, novel sound. RCA, at least initially, tried no such tactic with Eddy.

On December 1, 1955, RCA brought Eddy into Webster Hall again to record one of his most memorable songs, "You Don't Know Me." "I had that title in my head for a couple of years and that story," Eddy told interviewer Archie Campbell in 1982. "I didn't physically sit down and put the words down, but it was my story. So I sat down one day with Cindy Walker, who is a very good writer. I told her, 'Cindy . . . I've practically lived it. It's about a boy who's in love with a girl, but he can't tell her. He doesn't have the nerve to tell her that he's really in love with her. He stands and watches her get married and go away. . . . I'm that guy standing out there.'"

Cindy Walker, who had supplied Eddy with "Take Me in Your Arms and Hold Me" (a number one country record in 1949 and Eddy's first Cindy Walker release), recalled discussing the idea for "You Don't Know Me" with Eddy as she was leaving one of Nashville's annual disc jockey conventions. "I went up to the Victor suite to tell Steve Sholes good-bye," she explained, "and just as I was leaving, Eddy came in the door."

Walker remembered him saying, "I got a song title for you . . . 'You Don't Know Me.'"

"But I know you," teased Walker.

"This is serious," replied Eddy, who proceeded to outline his idea.

The songwriter promised to let the idea stew in her head a while. And soon, she remembered, the lyrics tumbled on to the page. "The song just started singing. It just sort of wrote itself": *No, you don't know the one who dreams of you at night and longs to kiss your lips and longs to hold you tight.*

If "I Really Don't Want to Know" had a cousin, "You Don't Know Me" was it. Another tender ballad that shrouds a woman in mystery, "You Don't Know Me" lacked the drama of Hugo Winterhalter's touch, but captured the confusion a man sometimes feels about a woman. Charlie Grean wrote a tight arrangement and assembled an intimate combo lead by the tinkling piano of Marty Gold.

But "You Don't Know Me" lacked the steam to reach the pop charts and only reached number ten on the country charts in 1956. Furthermore, Eddy only charted three songs on the country charts that year. Two other songs, "Mutual Admiration Society" and "I Wouldn't Know Where to Begin," appeared briefly on the pop charts but never touched the country charts.

In 1956, Eddy was mired in Elvis's shadow—as were dozens of other country and pop performers. His 1955 power drive sputtered in 1956, the result of changing tastes and Eddy's continued move into a weakened genre—soft, middle-of-the-road pop music. In the years after Elvis's explosion, established pop entities Teresa Brewer, Eddie Fisher, Dinah Shore, the Four Lads, the McGuire Sisters, and others joined the fiddlers and steel guitarists in the woods. Young Americans were looking for an edge to their music; Eddy's songs offered a pillow.

Moving with the times in 1956, RCA injected an ounce of rock and roll into Eddy's March session in New York. "The Rockin' Mockin' Bird" (*"Other birds nest up in tree tops, but he builds his nest in the record shops"*) stands as a testament to Eddy's pale attempt to rock. His "Easy Rockin' Chair" of ten years earlier rocked with more soul, but it rocked before there was a need to rock. RCA recorded other rock-tinged songs on Eddy with mixed success. He covered Marvin Rainwater's "Gonna Find Me A Bluebird" in 1957 and reached fifty-one on the pop charts, but most of his efforts languished. Upbeat songs like "Little Bit" and "Unbreakable Heart" showed off an above-average ability to adjust to the new sound, but few buyers bit. "He's a laid-back singer," said pianist Bob Davie, who accompanied Eddy during rock's rising tide. "To do rhythm stuff, there's a certain psychology to it. The people who do rhythm are very aggressive on the beat, and they spit out their words. Eddy Arnold would not be Eddy Arnold spitting his words out."

Caught resting backstage at the Ryman Auditorium during rehearsals for a 1957 benefit show (that, incidentally, had nothing to do with the "Grand Ole Opry"), Eddy talked rock with a reporter: "I see it this way, better music, smoother music, is going to stage a resounding comeback. Rock and roll is becoming more modified already—it isn't nearly as rough and rash as it was originally." Eddy's crystal ball needed a wipe of the dust cloth.

— • —

While rock and roll crept up on Eddy, bad news approached on another front. Television stations were turning their back on "Eddy Arnold Time." The reviewer who predicted a rosy picture for the show in late 1954 had erred. Although "Eddy Arnold Time" accumulated big ratings in cities like Jackson, Tennessee, and Grand Junction, Colorado, big-market television stations initially declined to buy the half hour. It wasn't until well into 1956 that New York City viewers could see the show, and even then it was purchased by WRCA television—a station with obvious connections to the singer. Washington, D.C., Pittsburgh, and Los Angeles followed, but came aboard too late. Eddy was losing considerable sums on his investment.

Why did the show fail? Insiders blamed the poor quality of the film's soundtrack, and still others pointed to a lack of commitment on the part of those producing and selling the show. "Eddy Arnold Time" certainly wasn't a waste of air, but stacked against the big shows of the day, it couldn't rate. Eddy, Betty, and the Jordanaires sang like birds, but lacked the charisma to carry a show. The script wanted originality, and no one on the show added spark. Throughout the half hour, the show seemed to just drift along, offering no sense of drama or really good comedy to shake the audience. Although Eddy's stage mannerisms had improved vastly since the movies, he still had handicaps that kept him from coming across as a television natural. "The only talent he didn't have," recalled Joe Csida, "was the talent to lip synch. He was undisciplined. He couldn't sing the song exactly the same way twice. On the TV show it would take ten, twelve takes before lip-synched songs would be acceptable."

Betty Johnson, though enamored of Eddy's way of putting down his guitar, always hoped he could be even more fluid. "He was so beautiful when he would do that motion. Then very quickly he would stiffen up again. . . . We had no choreographer on our show. We didn't have a movement person. I think that would have helped."

Beyond Eddy's awkward movements, the TV show faced other problems. Csida, the show's executive producer, was new to television, and according to Betty Johnson, the show needed more coordination. "This show was like a secret," she claimed. "It wasn't mushrooming. I didn't know what they were doing with it. There didn't seem to be a plan for the show, and if there was, it was kept from the cast."

Still, Eddy had spent freely on the show, putting up the cast at the Blackstone, hiring Ben Park, and employing a well-known agency to sell it. Eddy could have expected better, but these were the early days of television. Standards of TV performance had yet to gel. In retrospect, though, Eddy's first deep dive into television was riddled with kinks that were never smoothed out. "It would have been better if I had just come out, talked, done a song, and talked to the people with me," Eddy concluded. "It could have come off—the natural personality that I have. But we tried to do little sketches—everything was sketches."

A *Billboard* poll of the television industry in 1955 placed "Eddy Arnold Time" sixth in the "Best Music Series, Non-Network" category behind programs starring Liberace, Guy Lombardo, and Frankie Laine, but ahead of "Stars of the Grand Ole Opry." The show finished sixth and fifth in '56 and '57, respectively, but by the end of 1957 "Eddy Arnold Time" vanished from America's television sets. "He was very unhappy with [the shows]," remembered Gordon Stoker, "and he just scratched them all and actually took them all . . . and put them in his office under the steps."

"Eddy Arnold Time" may have disappeared from television, but Eddy remained. Throughout the tenure of his film series, Eddy did numerous guest shots and even competed against himself to a degree on a Thursday night ABC-TV show during the summer of 1956. Every week during that summer, Eddy brought Chet Atkins to Springfield, Missouri, for the live show produced by his old radio friend Charlie Brown. According to Atkins, an ABC executive saw Eddy and Chet perform at the Belle Meade country club in Nashville and decided they'd be just right for the summer series. "We would fly up [to Springfield] every week for about four months . . .," recalled Atkins. "I used to get irritated at Eddy because I thought we'd be safer if we flew when it was daylight. But he'd be late getting out to the airport, and we'd fly into the sunset. And, you know, we never had any bad weather. We didn't have one damn weekend of bad weather. It was amazing."

Eddy breezed through programs that worked around his singing, but the guest shots Eddy did on network comedy and variety shows did little to help his image. He and Joe Csida allowed producers to cast him as a rube. Chances were, if a show scheduled Eddy, he'd be forced back into his Tennessee Plowboy persona. Asked occasionally to play an oaf, he often seemed uncomfortable and distanced from the rest of the cast. A typical appearance was in a 1955 edition of "Caesar's Hour," TV comedian Sid Caesar's program. The story line had Eddy singing in a department store and feeling partially responsible for the injury of Nan Victor, Sid Caesar's wife on the program (Caesar played Bob Victor). A crowd around Eddy pushed Nan to the ground, and Eddy offered to drive her home. Cast as himself, but also as a rube who apparently never visited the city, Eddy was scripted not to know the difference between a cosmopolitan home and a hen house. "Isn't there something I can do for you like dig a post hole or pump some water or chop some wood?" he asked Nan. Bob Victor arrived home from work to find this strong, simple country boy waiting on his wife, touching off a routine that further denigrated Eddy's character and, arguably, Eddy himself. Offering to cook dinner for the Victors, Eddy asked another question, "Do you got any buffalo brains or moose lips?"

Eddy showed comedic ability in the Caesar skit, but clearly the writers crossed a threshold with their patronizing treatment of him. Unfortunately, in the context of network comedies, Eddy seemed only allowed to play a shy, dumb hillbilly. One feels terrible for Eddy as he parroted stupid lines and appeared unsophisticated among a cast of sophisticates. Eddy journeyed to New York and Joe Csida to gain respectability, but on TV shows like Caesar's, he only found ridicule.

But as far as Eddy and Csida seemed to be concerned, inane TV was better than no TV. "Sometimes the directors on the shows were broad-minded enough to see that Eddy could be as much of an asset to the show leaning toward the pop side as he could as the Tennessee Plowboy," said Csida. "There were other directors who have notions about certain performers and that's it. They can't see beyond that. I don't remember whether we struggled against doing that on [the Caesar show]. Apparently, we didn't. Apparently, we thought it would work out all right."

When Eddy appeared most at home on TV it was generally on programs such as CBS-TV's "Ed Sullivan Show" or ABC-TV's "Jubilee U.S.A."— shows that featured few skits and relied on Eddy to sing or emcee. Just as during his days learning the ropes with Pee Wee King, Eddy labored to improve his TV image. He wanted to succeed because regular TV appearances would connect him with an audience without continuing the numbing personal appearance tours that Eddy had begun to scale back in the early 1950s. Unfortunately, though, as the failure of "Eddy Arnold Time" and stereotyped TV roles indicate, national television deemed Eddy Arnold a bit player.

Meanwhile, RCA Victor labored to make sure the recording industry didn't draw the same conclusion about Eddy that television had. Pop standards and similar songs became standard fare on Eddy's recordings as he strove to broaden his audience. "One of America's truly great singing personalities," as RCA promoted Eddy in a 1956 *Billboard* advertisement, "with his first POPULAR smash hit record 'Do You Know Where God Lives.'" Because Eddy was struggling to hit the pop charts on the merits of his music, RCA tried to get the message out through advertising. Their efforts were premature: "Do You Know Where God Lives" never reached the charts.

On the back of Eddy's pop-oriented albums, Joe Csida wrote liner notes emphasizing the versatility of his star while trying not to offend the country audience. "For to say that Eddy is exclusively a country singer (as proud as he is of being thus referred to) is to say that a kiss can only be thrilling in Tennessee and not in New York." Eddy warbled well-worn standards like "It Had to Be You," "September Song," and "I Only Have Eyes for You" to establish a new reputation. He also began to appear on album covers dressed in suits; Eddy had retired the Stetson country gentleman hat years before.

Charles Grean and Steve Sholes supported the move to more popular selections, sending songs and acetates to Eddy for his consideration. From Nashville, Eddy called Steve with his choices, and set a date to record them in New York. Eddy had outgrown his trepidation about New York and moved comfortably in and out of the city. Associates in Gotham remember him relaxing at parties and socializing easily with city folk. "Eddy's great strengths were that he was a completely natural man," observed Joe Csida, "and he had the kind of self-confidence where another person's background or educational training or position just never bothered him."

On the eve of a New York session, Eddy, Steve, and Charlie carefully planned the material for recording in Steve's office and then went out for a casual dinner. There was little need for jitters. Charlie had written out parts for all the musicians, and Eddy had learned the songs back home in Brentwood. Eddy breezed through sessions, Steve Sholes once wrote, because he prepared like a prizefighter. "Once Eddy and I have decided on the songs that are worth recording, Eddy starts to work in earnest. He experiments with different interpretations, tempos, keys and styling to see how the song sounds best when recorded on his tape recorder. . . . When the

Eddy and Steve Sholes with Betty Johnson at her wedding to Charles Grean in 1957. (Betty Johnson collection)

recording dates have been definitely set, Eddy accepts no bookings for a two-week period prior to the sessions. He actually goes into training with plenty of sleep and all the other contributing factors to insure his health and strength for the forthcoming session."

In his preparation for a session, Eddy hid in his special music room at home and digested the songs' lyrics, closing his eyes and listening to each word. He examined meaning and message so he could properly convey the songs. "It amounts to the way I'm telling my story," Eddy said. "If I know what the story is telling, I know how to punctuate. A lot of times they say I'm a 'lyric man.' I am."

Charles Grean never saw anything like Eddy's concentration on lyrics. "He knew how to deliver a song. I remember once when we were doing the film series . . . I was teaching him a song. I'm sitting at the piano, and [after four or five unsuccessful stabs] I remember he said to me, 'Wait! Wait a minute. Let me look at this. . . . I just want to see what this song says.' A lot of singers sing, and they don't know what the hell they're singing. He wanted to get the message. He wasn't interested in the music or anything. He wanted to know what the song was saying, and that is really the secret."

When session day finally arrived, Eddy knew the songs cold and demanded only that the musicians follow his tempo. "I'm a stickler for tempos,"

Eddy told an interviewer. "Sometimes it may be just a little bit too slow, a little too fast or just right. You got to get a song just right and get it . . . in the groove before it will be acceptable to the average person's ear."

There was little rehearsal because Charlie wrote out lead sheets for all the musicians, who, on Eddy's late '50s New York sessions, were exclusively New Yorkers. They were a crack group who often worked three sessions a day, five and even seven days a week. The guys, guitarists Al Chernet and George Barnes, drummer Phil Kraus, and bass player (and Glenn Miller alumnus) Trigger Alpert did so many sessions around Manhattan they often chipped in on a hotel room, where they parked their instruments and slept instead of going home. "You needed people who could go in and get the job done," said pianist Bob Davie, who appeared on many of these sessions and helped Charlie with arrangements. "You couldn't keep the musicians longer if they had another session somewhere. A half-hour overtime was about the most you could do. Your session fell apart if you went to an hour overtime." Eddy's preparation rarely made overtime necessary, and the musicians picked up the songs right away. "They could read fly shit—anything you put in front of them," said Davie.

In the wake of Hugo Winterhalter's success with a fuller Eddy Arnold background sound, Steve frequently worked strings on to Eddy's albums, but he shunned the boldness of the Winterhalter sound. The arrangements of Charlie Grean and Bob Davie called for a soft, lounge atmosphere that brought Eddy's voice to the fore. "He had a great voice and treatment of the song. He didn't just let go of a word," said Davie. "You wanted to follow that line right out to the very last vibration. As an arranger, it is very easy, when you're sitting at home, to overwrite. When you get an Eddy Arnold, you say, 'Just let the piano do a little tinkle here. Stay out of his way.'"

From a New York musician's standpoint Eddy had only one problem—he cut beat, which means he often added two beats to a 4/4 arrangement, changing it, in effect, to 6/4. This habit tangled New York musicians, who rarely made such alterations. "He was the humblest guy I ever knew," recalled Davie. "You would never know that he was a star. He'd walk in and tell the guys, 'I got a meter problem. Excuse me if we have to do another take.'"

As easily as Eddy's sessions went, RCA had difficulty selling the result. Eddy had a loyal core of fans who bought anything he recorded, but others abandoned Eddy on his journey to a new sound. RCA tried various angles to work Eddy into the pop market, none of which proved effective. Eddy recorded four selections from Frank Loesser's musical *The Most Happy Fella*, including "Standing on the Corner." Additionally, he waxed two numbers from the show *Happy Hunting* ("If'n" and "Mutual Admiration Society") with "girl singer" Jaye P. Morgan. ("I liked her. I was her fan. She had a sound that I really liked," said Eddy of his partner.) Chick Crumpacker, whose job it was to promote the Arnold-Morgan collaboration, recalled that Eddy struggled through the session. "They had to jump back and forth a lot, and it broke down. Eddy said, 'Oh hell!' That showed you that he was having trouble even grasping an up-tempo show tune that was definitely safely in the category of pop."

From June 1957 to March 1959, the charts, both pop and country, shunned Eddy Arnold. Eddy and RCA tried everything to prove the singer's versatility and get him over: albums of hymns, a session with Mexican orchestra leader Juan Esquival that was never released, and a return to Hugo Winterhalter that produced an exciting version of "Wagon Wheels" but no big sellers.

In a phrase, Eddy, Joe Csida, and RCA failed in their pursuit of grander things for the best-selling country artist in history. Molding Eddy to the general audience was like trying to jam a square peg into a round hole. No matter how many ads and liner notes RCA used to frame Eddy as a pop artist or how many well-known standards Eddy crooned, the mass audience just didn't buy him. For one thing, as Crumpacker's observation of the Jaye P. Morgan session confirmed, he was ill-suited for the pop material he tried so hard to master. Eddy had not cut his teeth on standards and show tunes, nor were they his staples since he first hit the big time in the late '40s. "It's just like an opera singer can't sing pop songs either, but Eddy wanted to go that way," said Charlie Grean, an architect of Eddy's ill-fitting new approach. "He did a lot of really sharp, hip songs that didn't come off at all." Eddy's interpretation of the songs, while heart felt, couldn't equal the magic Frank Sinatra or Bing Crosby brought to a pop song.

In the stormy weather of rock and roll's heyday, a glut of pop singers knocked around the entertainment industry. If record buyers wanted good ole American pop, they could do better than Eddy, and if Eddy hoped to equal the sales of "Bouquet of Roses," he had chosen the wrong time to explore a new formula. Rock and roll was unforgiving. Although traditional voices rose up against rock, according to RCA's Chick Crumpacker, they didn't help Eddy. "There were millions of people out there who didn't want to make the change, so you dealt with that. But they were less and less your average record buyer. All of these old listeners would call in and protest to a radio station if the deejay played something they considered too modern. But it doesn't mean the converse, that they would go out and buy the old-line performers."

Had Eddy not diverted from the country trail a few years earlier, it's doubtful that his circumstances would have differed significantly. The popular country songs of the late '50s, which already paid tribute to the honky-tonk beat, embraced the rock and roll sound, which Eddy, on the whole, refused to do. Some country disc jockeys around the nation shared Eddy's distaste for rock and roll music, and showed in the pages of *Billboard* that they could lash out against the new sound as violently as they protested Hugo Winterhalter. "It seems that all the good c&w artists are doing r&r," cried Tubby Smith of WHLD in Niagara Falls, New York, "and I won't play the junk they are sending me. . . . When they get done making records for the kids, we'll have forgotten about them. There was a time that I never auditioned a record; just glanced at the artist's name. Today I refuse to play most of them."

Smith's fulminations were lost in the fermenting '50s as country stars like Johnny Cash and Johnny Horton worked rock into their music; and, as Eddy bowed to Elvis in the pop charts, he certainly had to do the same to Cash and Horton on the country side. Eddy was caught in limbo, unacceptable as a pop singer and unwilling or unable to adapt to the changing country scene. "He had that dignity which he was forever fine-tuning and cultivating," said Crumpacker of Eddy. "But there was no way for him to rise above the [pop] mainstream that was slowly sinking in the west with [the advent of] rock and roll. Eddy wouldn't or couldn't have compromised."

As Eddy sorted out his options in light of declining record sales, demand for his live performances plummeted. When he did perform, he played events like the Quad City Autorama in Rock Island, Illinois, a peanut festival in Dothan, Alabama, or any number of benefit appearances around Nashville. Rock and roll stars and popular country singers took Eddy's place on the circuit.

Eddy's mentors seemed to abandon him also. Steve Sholes, though still Eddy's point man at RCA, had watched his stock rise after signing Elvis and moved up to director of pop A&R for the label in 1958. Naturally, the promotion physically distanced Steve from Eddy, and on August 5, 1958, Steve supervised his old friend in the studio for the last time before putting Eddy in the producing hands of Chet Atkins in Nashville. The session produced a lighthearted pop song that in another era might have toppled the charts: "I'm A Good Boy."

While Eddy contemplated the shake-up of producers, RCA also strangled the flow of promotional dollars earmarked for him. The hype generated for Eddy's 1955 anniversary seemed like a dream in 1958. The company diverted an increasingly larger share of its ad dollars to new artists. "The old-line artists, non-rock artists, got caught in the squeeze," Chick Crumpacker recalled. "There wasn't that much money to go around. In the country field, there was never that much. I had to go to my boss . . . and sweat every penny for ads because there was something like a four, five or six to one proportion of total ad money for pop artists [to country artists]." RCA fed Eddy less and less of the promotional pie.

On the management end, Joe Csida's attention to Eddy strayed. Csida had signed Bobby Darin and watched him explode, and even Betty Johnson had raised a few songs up the pop charts. Although he wasn't ignored, Eddy couldn't count on individual attention from Joe Csida. Csida worried about his other artists, publishing interests, and occasional employment offers he received from record companies. Then Charles Grean, who ceased recording with Eddy when Sholes climbed the corporate ladder, left Joe Csida, trading his share of the company for Betty Johnson's contract. That left Csida and Edgar Burton, formerly of Hill and Range Songs, to run the firm; Burton handled the company's purse strings.

In January 1960, Capitol Records lured Csida away to manage its eastern operations. Burton bought Csida's interest in the management-publishing operation and took responsibility for Eddy's career. Burton, though a capable business manager, accomplished little for Eddy. "I don't guess Ed was really the person to manage me," Eddy concluded. His music career seemed to be on autopilot; he was recording every few months and taking gigs whenever they came up with little regard to their impact on his image or popularity. Eddy needed a plan, a strategy to take him into the 1960s. Certainly, some steam still remained bottled inside him: It was 1960, and he was only forty-two.

With his career in the doldrums, Eddy spent more time on his farm in Brentwood, Tennessee, during the late '50s and early '60s than he had since buying the spread in 1950. "I still had the capacity of earning a livelihood, but my popularity went down. I kept working some . . . [but] the records were not selling like they once sold." He was often downcast, perplexed at the turn his career took.

Eddy focused on his business ventures, a thriving real-estate operation that he set up with Roy Wiggins and accountant Charlie Mosely and based out of a small building in downtown Brentwood. Sometimes, though, he'd just lay back on a couch in his office and ponder his lot. His energy seemed sapped at times, and Eddy's daughter Jo Ann saw a change. "It just seemed like he had a different attitude. When you get depressed things happen to you. I remember him going through an inner ear problem, and he'd get irritable. It just wasn't like it had been previously."

From the Arnold kids' perspectives, Dad's slackened work schedule disrupted the routine in Brentwood. "He was at home more. We weren't accustomed to him being there," Jo Ann recalled. "You get used to doing your own thing. We were used to him being gone for six weeks at a time." From where Eddy stood, though, more time with the family was one positive aspect of his diminishing musical fortunes. Although he had brought the family along to New York for his summer replacement work for Perry Como and Dinah Shore and other extended dates when the kids were out of school, Eddy, in his heyday, had little day-to-day contact with them. So, he relished the time he could fish with Dickey or talk with Jo Ann, who was in the midst of her teens.

Eddy's extra time off permitted a rare family vacation, a driving adventure to Canada in 1961. On the way up, Eddy obviously cruised the dial for good music that—as far as Eddy was concerned—did not include rock and roll. Jo Ann, though, liked rock, especially "Transistor Sister," a current hit by Freddie "Boom Boom" Cannon. "He would only let me listen to the rock and roll stations for a short period of time. It drove him insane listening to 'Transistor Sister.' He said, 'I don't know how you listen to this!'"

Eddy and his children, Jo Ann and Dickey, down on the farm. (Eddy Arnold collection)

Eddy and Sally visit their Murfreesboro, Tennessee, record store. (Eddy Arnold collection)

The family enjoyed their time together, taking in sights and cruising north to Canada, sometimes at breakneck speed. Eddy was hell-bent to make time (a residual from his early days of constant road travel), which meant no dallying at rest stops and, according to Jo Ann, early departures from the motels along the way. "It would get him mad when you'd unpack your suitcase and load up the drawers if you were only staying one night."

— • —

"I was trying to find my way," Eddy said of his down days. "I didn't know quite what to do. . . . I was beginning to think it was about all over for me." In fact, Eddy contemplated retirement. He had invested his money wisely and could live comfortably with his family without ever singing a note again.

From the time big royalty statements poured in during the late 1940s, Eddy sought to build a nest egg. The tough days after Will Arnold died when Georgia made shirts from feed bags still smarted. He admired Gene Autry, who invested his profits with astounding results, and watched in amazement as fellow performers frittered their money away. Initially, Eddy made some bad investments with sneaky brokers; a record shop he owned in Murfreesboro, Tennessee, failed in 1950 (he donated the remaining $5,000 worth of discs to orphanages around Nashville). But Eddy soon realized what land could do for him and purchased tracts all around Nashville, especially in the Brentwood area. In 1959, Eddy paid for Roy Wiggins to get his real-estate license from the University of Tennessee's extension school, and, with his accountant Charlie Mosely, established a real-estate and insurance company. The company erected the first subdivision of homes in Brentwood, the Iroquois Estates, and established a waterworks to supply the houses and the rest of Brentwood.

As Nashville expanded, the value of Eddy's heretofore suburban land soared. Eddy often traded land, giving up small parcels of acreage close to Nashville for larger tracts farther out of town. Inevitably, Nashville continued to sprawl, and the value of the land Eddy traded for eventually equaled or exceeded the value of what he had dealt away. Although far removed from his Chester County experience, Eddy also presided over two vast farms (including the one on which he lived), where he raised cattle and horses.

As Eddy wrote in a 1969 autobiography, he stumbled into real estate by accident. "The first piece of real estate I bought from an investment standpoint, other than a home, I bought on a real hunch. I was just driving along the road and I saw a little sign that said a piece of land was for sale. I knew it was on a four-lane highway between Nashville and a small town. Something just told me, 'They're gonna develop this area. It'll all become one city.' I saw that the land was just bushes and briars, but I went out and talked to a banker I knew, out in the little town. . . . I bought that piece of land, almost four acres for $12,500, and sold it later for $150,000 because of its location. I had to hold it for several years, but it was worth it. Later I bought more property behind it that connected with a railroad. I went to an auction sale and bid that in. Now there's a Sears Roebuck store there."

From his perch in Brentwood, Eddy built a small empire that would later include a fried-chicken shop, a record-pressing plant, a line of canned foods, and an investment in Nashville's minor-league baseball team. Around town, he gained as much respect for his business acumen as for his singing. Several businesses invited Eddy to join their boards. Baltimore businessman Louis Grasmick sat on the board of the American Investment Life Insurance Company with Eddy and observed him to be an able member who took his appointment seriously. "He was thorough, insightful, and dedicated," said Grasmick, "and I really have to say that he asked the right questions."

As Eddy vigorously pursued profits in business, he always tried to balance his self-interest with the needs of the community. He performed benefits for Nashville's Parent Teacher Association, a Boy Scout camp on Tennessee's Old Hickory Lake, and tornado victims back in West Tennessee. A Nashville newspaper once reported that Eddy "appeared at fund-raising shows for police benefits, crippled children, farmers clubs and united community campaign kick-offs."

Eddy also found time to support political causes and favorite (mostly Republican) candidates. He wrote newspaper editorials, and frequently performed at campaign rallies for his friend Tennessee governor Frank Clement, who enjoyed Eddy's support despite being a Democrat. Clement, noted in Tennessee for shepherding the state through turbulent racial conflicts and improving roads, schools, and mental-health treatment during the '50s and '60s, was forever urging Eddy to run for office. To scare his rival, Ross Bass, who was then the House of Representatives member for Tennessee's 6th Congressional District, Clement leaked Eddy's name to the press as a possible candidate for the seat in 1964. (Eddy denied the rumors the day after Clement's leak appeared in the newspapers.) A few years later, the three-time governor of Tennessee, who was legally barred from succeeding himself, urged Eddy to take his place as chief executive. Alas, as Eddy told a *Schenectady Gazette* reporter in 1973, such a run would be impractical: "I thought about running and thought about it and the more I thought, the less I wanted to do it. I wouldn't really have enjoyed it, and I felt it was too demanding. Besides, I knew that I couldn't come out of it with the same popularity that I went in with."

The entrepreneurial, charitable, and political sides of Eddy revealed a multidimensional man, an individual capable of thriving outside the music business if he wished. But none of these pursuits, from Eddy's view, surpassed the thrill of performing. Retirement from music would never do. "He didn't want to retire," recalled Sally Arnold of her husband's lull. "If you're on top, you don't want to drop down to second vice president if you're already president. It was very difficult, and all you [could do was] just encourage him to hang in there."

11

*E*ddy's musical endeavors had not ground down completely. Since Steve transferred Eddy's sessions to Nashville, Chet Atkins had helped Eddy launch a few country hits. Eddy's pop hopes dashed, there was little to do but return to his core audience; Atkins helped Eddy through the transition.

Whenever he was asked, Steve Sholes would say one of his proudest accomplishments for RCA was hiring producer/guitarist Chet Atkins. Chet, in the midst of a radio stint in Springfield, Missouri (where he performed on the program "Korn's-A-Krackin'"), sent Steve an audition acetate in 1947. Springfield was just the latest stop for Chet in a radio station ramble through Cincinnati, Knoxville, Richmond, Raleigh, and Nashville, where he appeared for a brief time on the "Grand Ole Opry." Sholes listened to the disc—an exhilarating version of "Canned Heat"—and gave it to Charlie Grean, who, in turn, urged Steve to sign the kid. Chet's hot licks on the record impressed both of them. "I used to play it over and over again. This guy was unbelievable," exclaimed Grean. "Nobody played like this. We signed him up as an artist."

Chet had moved on to Denver, where Steve tracked him down with a contract offer. "I was working with Shorty Thompson's band," Atkins recalled, "and he said, 'Who's going to sing on your records?' I said, 'I am.' And he said, 'Hell, you can't sing.' I said, 'Well, I'm going to sing.' So he came back in an hour and fired me." The skinny, subdued young man with an average voice proved to be a moderately successful recording artist, but tremendously valuable as a session man. His distinguished guitar backed various RCA recording artists starting in the late 1940s, and when other responsibilities kept Steve in New York, Chet coordinated Nashville sessions on a freelance basis. By 1958, when Steve assumed the top pop A&R slot, Chet was a full-timer, overseeing Nashville sessions in the company's newly opened studios.

Chet had met Eddy a year before he approached RCA in 1947, when the guitarist was working with Red Foley on the "Opry." He stumbled upon the rising star while Eddy and the boys were rehearsing backstage at the "Grand Ole Opry." "The first thing that struck me about him was the volume he

151

had," said Chet. "I never heard a singer sing with so much volume. He was rehearsing and, boy, he was knocking out the walls in that little dressing room with his volume. I never heard anything like that before." Chet ran into Eddy a few other times around WSM, and when he moved on to his next radio gig, Chet made sure to get an autographed photo of the Tennessee Plowboy. After signing with RCA in 1947, Chet landed back in Nashville on a more or less full-time basis, and, in addition to backing the Carter Family and lining up musicians for sessions organized by music publisher Fred Rose, he found work supporting Eddy on the Mutual radio programs. Eddy warmed to Chet and in the early '50s asked the guitarist to join Roy Wiggins behind him on the road. "I thought about taking it," recalled Chet, "and I talked to my next door neighbor. . . . He was in the insurance business. He said, 'You should not do this. Your earning power is going to be from now until you're about fourty or so, and you shouldn't tie yourself down to one salary.' I didn't take the job. So he hired Hank Garland, but he never held it against me."

In the years of Eddy's star treatment in Chicago and New York, Nashville's reputation as a recording center blossomed. Chet, Owen Bradley (who had opened his own studio), and various other producers harnessed Nashville's most talented session musicians in the 1950s to produce a quality of sound that rivaled New York, Chicago, and Los Angeles. The construction of free-standing, state-of-the-art recording studios around what became known as Music Row, and the availability of trained recording engineers also fueled Nashville's escalating reputation. It was into this current of instrumental and technical expertise that Chet plugged Eddy.

In this setting, Chet and Eddy chose steps likely to get Eddy selling again in the country field. Initially, Eddy caught a wave of folk and historical themes flooding country music. The Kingston Trio had captured the 1958 Grammy Award for Best country-and-western Performance with their version of the old folk song "Tom Dooley," and Johnny Horton jammed the charts with odes to earlier American times. In 1959, Horton's "Battle of New Orleans" and "Johnny Reb" joined Johnny Cash's "Frankie's Man Johnny" (his reworking of the traditional ballad "Frankie and Johnny") and Marty Robbins's "El Paso" on the charts. Eddy weighed in with the LP *Thereby Hangs A Tale,* a collection of traditional songs and ballads including "Tennessee Stud," adapted by an Arkansas schoolteacher, Jimmie Driftwood (who was also responsible for "Battle of New Orleans"). In 1959, "Tennessee Stud" galloped to the country chart's top five and to forty-eight on the pop side, handing Eddy his biggest hit since 1955. Initially though— as RCA engineer Bill Porter told Country Music Foundation researcher John Rumble in 1995—it seemed that "Tennessee Stud" might not ever leave the starting gate. "Eddy had a hard time doing that song," said Porter. "For some reason, he couldn't figure out where to come in, and we did seventy-two takes on that song—not all the way through, but seventy-two starts. I never will forget it. . . . It was about eight bars in. He had a little trouble trying to adjust to one of the parts to come back in again. And even Chet was starting to get upset with him. It was really funny."

He followed up on the ballad theme in 1961, recording "(Jim) I Wore A Tie Today," written by Cindy Walker about two old cowboy partners and lifelong friends:

> *Jim, I did ev'rything that I could*
> *But your fever just wouldn't die down.*
> *So I tied your horse to the wagon bed*
> *And last night I brought you to town.*
> *But when I got there you were gone, Jim*
> *And there was nothin' nobody could do.*
> *I bought you a suit and a tie, Jim.*
> *And today I wore one too.*
>
> *Jim, I wore a tie today.*
> *The first one that I ever wore.*
> *And you'd have said I looked like a dummy*
> *Out of a dry goods store.*
>
> *Jim, they said a lot of things*
> *But I don't know a thing they said.*
> *My mind kept wand'rin' off down the trail*
> *Back to the times that we've had.*
>
> *Ridin' herd through the sun and the rain*
> *Pannin' for gold on the cuff.*
> *We've done ev'rything in the book, I guess*
> *And a lot they never thought up!*
>
> *Well, Jim, you're riding on ahead.*
> *I guess that's how it has to be.*
> *But when you reach those streets paved with gold,*
> *Jim, stake a claim out for me.* *

"(Jim) I Wore A Tie Today" remains one of Eddy's finest performances, the combination of a wrenching story and a sympathetic voice to interpret it. Eddy's classic effort, though, shot over the heads of country-music fans. They allowed the song only one week on the charts.

Ironically, while Eddy struggled to sell records in the valley of the late '50s and early '60s, the quality of his singing voice peaked. Years of singing on an almost daily basis had perfected Eddy's baritone. He seemed to warm

---

each lyric he sang. Up to this point, Eddy's voice had hinted at the perfection yet to come: sweetness on "Bouquet of Roses," whimsy on "Cuddle Buggin' Baby," tenderness on "I Really Don't Want To Know" and "The Kentuckian Song." The varied vocal effects and qualities matured with satisfying results by the time he returned to the Nashville scene. Eddy's audible struggles with the New York pop sound had evolved into effortlessness. Each line poured onto the record with confidence and lingered long enough for the listener to distill it, and—in a way that never seemed so natural— Eddy accented the various messages of songs with deep feeling. His claim to be a singing storyteller—a "lyric man"—achieved its greatest validity during this time.

Eddy's voice, in the glory of maturity, also melded with his instrumentation. Speedy McNatt and Hugo Winterhalter challenged him before, but now he waltzed gracefully with his Nashville accompaniment. Chet Atkins's brisk, dancing guitar shadowed Eddy, and the tight rhythm section stayed out of the way, laying down a solid floor for Eddy and his instrumental partners. In his role of producer, Chet also recruited Anita Kerr to write arrangements for instruments and background vocals, which were most often provided by Kerr's quartet and, at times, the Jordanaires. Kerr, a professional piano player since her early teens, came to Nashville from Memphis in the late '40s, where she formed a vocal group that soon wove its way into the fabric of the city's radio broadcasts and recording sessions. When Chet began organizing sessions for Steve Sholes around 1950, he often employed Kerr for her background singing and prowess on the keyboard.

By the time of Eddy's return to Nashville in the late '50s, Anita Kerr was writing arrangements—primitive arrangements by New York standards, but nonetheless a stab at formalizing the off-the-cuff approach to recording that was so popular in studios around town. New York musicians considered Kerr's arrangements primitive because she simply wrote chord sheets for the rhythm section and expected them to inject their own fills throughout the course of a song. "They couldn't read music, but they could read chord changes," said Kerr. "If I had written out every note for them, they wouldn't have been able to read it."

On her arrangements for Eddy's sessions, Kerr eschewed the dramatics of Hugo Winterhalter and asked her players and vocalists to just tinge Eddy's records with their flourishes. Kerr's almost laissez-faire way of arranging also allowed Eddy to be Eddy Arnold, not confining him to a strict note-by-note arrangement. "We would talk it through," said Kerr of her arrangements for Eddy. "I wouldn't tell him what I [was] going to write because I wouldn't know until I got in front of the score paper. We would set the right key, and we would say, 'Eddy will sing it through once, then the Anita Kerr Singers will sing a few lines or the piano will play a few lines, and then Eddy will come in at this point and sing it on out.' We always tried to keep them under three minutes because the radio stations [ignored them if they were longer]."

The new instrumental environment was Eddy's first extended encounter with what was becoming known as the "Nashville Sound," a term as hard to define as "jazz" or "rock." The sound sprang from the fraternity of freelance musicians who made their living recording sessions at different studios around Nashville. Among the players who scurried around town to various dates were drummers Buddy Harman and Louis Dunn; bass players Junior Huskey, Bob Moore, and Henry Strzelecki; pianists Floyd Cramer, Bill Pursell, and Hargus "Pig" Robbins; and guitarists Harold Bradley, Velma Williams Smith, Ray Edenton, Grady Martin, and Hank Garland. The list stretches on, but in the late '50s and early '60s, Chet used these musicians on Eddy's sessions most often.

These musicians probably spent more time with one another than they did with their families. In the morning, rhythm guitarist Ray Edenton might play with one contingent of Nashville session folk at Owen Bradley's famed Quonset hut studio, and meet up with another that afternoon for a session at Starday Sound Studios. "Back in those days we were working three and four sessions a day, seven days a week," explained vocalist Louis Nunley, who performed with the Anita Kerr Singers. "There weren't very many studios, so they had to use them all the time. So you'd go from one session to the next to the next to the next. Grab a sandwich and eat it while you were learning the song."

This constant contact and delirious pace bonded the musicians and background vocalists. Indeed, they often knew each other's thoughts and anticipated their licks and turns in the studio. The musicians grew accustomed to the quirks of producers, engineers, and singers, and the acoustic limitations of each studio around Nashville. In addition, with so little arranging (in the New York sense of written-out parts), producers relied on musicians and background vocalists to learn a tune quickly by ear and then kick in ornamentation to help distinguish a record from its competition.

The Nashville approach during the period of Eddy's return to Music City studios, Chet Atkins told *Billboard* in 1960, departed drastically from the New York style of recording. "A New York record always sounds mechanical. The musicians are inhibited by the sheet music in front of them. Sidemen blow the notes and do what they're told. The A&R man has to dream up all the ideas and sometimes he can't help but run dry.

"Down here," Chet went on, "we have arrangements, but we never write them down. We create them in the studio. Every musician offers suggestions, so we have seven or eight creative minds at work for every record. The A&R man acts as an editor, pulling these ideas together and unifying them."

The tight, in-step rhythm section left its mark on all Nashville recording but, ultimately, only partly defined the "Nashville Sound." The label became associated with a relaxed feel, a feel that was the antithesis of rock and roll and hardly sympathetic to the honky-tonk style. When someone called a record "Nashville," they often referred to a middle-of-the road sound, a sound that increasingly embraced soothing strings and the angelic voices of the Anita Kerr Singers or the Jordanaires.

Eddy was one of the pioneers of this "Nashville Sound"—one of the first truly big country singers with a gentle touch and attraction to strings. Before Eddy's re-recording of "The Cattle Call" with Hugo Winterhalter in 1955, strings or any other symphonic instruments rarely embellished (or "destroyed," some critics might have said) country hits. "The Cattle Call," however, hardly ignited a stampede of strings, and it was not until around 1960 that violins and other orchestral instruments eased on to other artists' country recordings. Chet Atkins, wearing his recording-artist hat, waxed an album with strings during the late '50s as did Ray Price, and in the early '60s Owen Bradley incorporated them on Decca hits like Patsy Cline's "So Wrong" and Bill Anderson's "Still." At RCA, strings lifted Skeeter Davis's "The End of the World" in 1963, and in early 1964, Jim Reeves enjoyed remarkable sales on the string-laden "Welcome to My World" (which Eddy would cover in 1971) and "Love Is No Excuse," Reeves's duet with Dottie West.

Eddy, of course, had not stopped using strings with his mid-'50s recording of "The Cattle Call." Charlie Grean included violin, viola, and cello on *Wanderin',* a 1955 album of traveling songs, and *A Little on the Lonely Side,* one of Eddy's 1950s collections of pop songs. Grean stepped a little further, putting brass on the 1956 Jaye P. Morgan sessions and woodwinds on Eddy's 1957 kiddie album, *When They Were Young.* In Nashville, Chet had included strings on "(Jim) I Wore A Tie Today" and assembled an ensemble for another album of pop hits, *Let's Make Memories Tonight.* On and off from 1960 to 1964, Chet worked in strings until they became part of Eddy's version of the "Nashville Sound."

The strings adapted many of the same characteristics of the Nashville rhythm section, pursuing a feeling rather than a strict adherence to sheet music. Anita Kerr introduced a core of string musicians to RCA in the late 1950s that would, like the rhythm musicians, become a mainstay in all Nashville studios throughout the 1960s. Kerr saw Brenton Banks—a music instructor at Tennessee State College—playing piano in a Nashville jazz combo and, after the show, asked him if he read music. Banks smiled and invited her to a violin concerto he was performing. Banks, as Kerr witnessed, definitely could read, and Kerr paid him on a freelance basis to head a string ensemble for RCA's sessions. "We had tried strings from [Nashville's] symphony orchestra," explained Kerr. "They either were ahead of the beat [or behind the beat]. I knew that Brenton, besides being a violinist, was a good pianist. I knew he really played the piano with a beat. . . . In those days, those [symphony] violinists weren't raised on hearing rhythm. . . . All they played really was symphony music. They just weren't raised with a lot of other kinds of music. They needed that help."

Before Brenton Banks could go to work for Anita Kerr, one problem had to be solved. Banks, a black man, was unable to get a union card from the

American Federation of Musicians in Nashville until Chet Atkins pulled some strings among the members there. When Banks—with union card in hand—arrived for his first RCA session in 1959, he recalled finding three violinists with their pencils brandished and ready to write out their parts. "I said, 'Put the pencil away,'" recalled Banks, "I never used a pencil. When you do that you get a different type of music, much more mechanical. . . . When I came up, classical music was considered dance music, which was a different approach than most people think about classical music. I approached [country] as the same thing. It was dance music, and you don't get in the way of the flow of the music." Banks urged his violinists to listen to the rhythm section—to absorb the bass, drums, and guitars—and let the bass do the counting. "We matched that rhythm. We didn't make our own rhythm. . . . Our thing was to mesh right on the spot." Slowly, the strings blended with the rhythm section and the singer. "Everybody's in there together," continued Banks. "We're listening to one another, and we can feel one another. We feel the same tempos. The blend is marvelous because it makes it all one thing. People can dance to it if they want to dance, or they can just listen if they want to listen. But all the components are there. That is the root of the Nashville Sound."

One of Banks's first sessions, if not the first, was with Eddy Arnold. Demonstrating why Nashville players suited Eddy so well, Banks studied the singer for clues about how to adapt to him. "He sang in tune. He had a nice feel. He had a nice voice. All the components were there. It was just a matter of playing his kind of music, playing the way he sang—feeling the way he felt when he sang a song. Sort of intangibles, but they're so important when it comes to the overall feel of his music. . . . He made such an impression on me because he knew what the song was about. He knew how it felt. He knew how it went. All those things make an artist. It was a pleasure to work with him. I knew I didn't have to try to help him. I just had to fit in with him." Banks and his players—including at different times Sollie Fott, Lillian Hunt, Howard Carpenter, Sheldon Kurland, and others—complemented Eddy throughout the 1960s as his reliance on strings grew. Over the years, few recording string sections rivaled the Nashville ensemble's ability to produce quality work so cheerfully and quickly.

"We did what they wanted, and it went fast," said violinist Sheldon Kurland. "Three-hour sessions would take two hours. We would do four songs in record time. They could keep us if they wanted to, but there was no reason. I felt that we were about as efficient . . . and good sounding as you could get. It came from playing day after day after day with each other."

Eddy's mature voice, Chet's production, the Nashville rhythm sections, and—more and more often—the strings produced some of the finest music of Eddy's career. He sang country songs, pop songs, and folk songs with striking clarity and pleasing background instrumentation. Standing out among Eddy's recorded performances during that period are the pop songs "Mister and Mississippi," "Sometimes I'm Happy," and "Smile"; traditional compositions like "The Streets of Laredo" and "Old Folks"; and new country songs such as "Yesterday's Memories," "Molly," and "Cowpoke." Eddy's voice had reached the peak of its abilities and—unlike his days in the more formal New York pop surroundings—had found comfort in the breezy Nashville session atmosphere.

However, despite a healthy recording schedule—Eddy came into Nashville from Brentwood to record about five or six times a year—the results failed to produce any major hits, indicating that America's interest in Eddy was still on the wane. Although the quality of his music reached new heights, Eddy failed to capitalize on it, and—except for a skimpy live appearance schedule, a daily radio spot on CBS, and occasional network TV guest spots—Eddy's music career was practically a recording career only. Eddy also claimed a steady gig on NBC-TV's "Today on the Farm," which brought him to Chicago once a week in 1960 and 1961; but "Today on the Farm" aired at the suicidal time of 7:00 Saturday mornings, and though farmers may have been watching, few other potential record buyers were. An article in *Billboard* noted that the show spotlighted "farm news, weather reports and other info of interest to farm families." Jim Reeves, Skeeter Davis, and Chet Atkins all guest starred from time to time, and one Saturday Eddy's daughter Jo Ann came along to do the weather.

Even as a self-absorbed teenager, Jo Ann knew something was eating away at Dad. "He seemed more down," she said. "There wasn't a whole lot going on for him. He didn't know what to do. All the spotlight was on rock and roll at the time. . . . There's nothing worse for a performer to feel like people don't want to come [to shows], or that they don't appreciate your work."

— • —

Chet and Eddy searched for ways to make America appreciate Eddy's music again. In the early '60s, Eddy tried hymns, Christmas songs, and a contemporary folk album with the Needmore Creek Singers (really the Anita Kerr Singers, but renamed for Eddy's old swimming hole to add a homespun flavor). Eddy also decided to re-record a couple of albums' worth of his old hits.

Eddy never shied from rewriting his recording history. As far back as 1949, he updated "The Cattle Call" of 1944 and, of course, did it again with Hugo Winterhalter. Eddy waxed his old theme song for a fourth time in 1961, and ended up with the definitive version—sparser than Hugo Winterhalter's interpretation and not as rushed as the first two versions. Eddy finally radiated "The Cattle Call's" feeling seventeen years after trying the first time.

Not so successful, though, was Eddy's 1960 album *Eddy Arnold Sings Them Again,* which attempted to update twelve of Eddy's smash hits. Eddy brought Roy Wiggins back to the studio, but "Bouquet of Roses," "I'll Hold You in My Heart," and "It's A Sin" tasted different with lush strings and background vocals. "We did it for money," Eddy told a radio interviewer years later. "Let's be honest, but you can make honest money. Many of those old songs were not available in stereo. We thought we should update them." Many of the new renditions showed up on greatest hits packages for years to come, replacing the original, best-selling versions.

Eddy preferred the modern version to the older, cruder renditions, so much so that he tried a similar album in 1961. (Writer Cy Coben remembered Eddy dancing around his Brentwood living room to the re-recordings while he and Sally watched.) *One More Time* reconsidered hits like "The Richest Man (In the World)" and "The Kentuckian Song," which didn't stray too far from the originals, but when Roy Wiggins appeared to do the older songs—"Don't Rob Another Man's Castle," "I'm Throwing Rice (At the Girl That I Love)," and a couple of others—the 1949 smashes mutated into the early '60s, middle-of-the-road "Nashville Sound." Eddy and Roy recut these old songs in the RCA studio on the evening of September 19, 1961; they have not worked on a record since.

Eddy's 1958 reconfiguration of "That's How Much I Love You" was perhaps the most radical reworking of older material Eddy and Chet undertook to resuscitate his record sales. The song, of course, was the first smash hit of Eddy's career, but it was now refashioned in a rock-influenced style. Other veteran artists were trying to conjure up old magic with rock-flavored versions of their old hits. Billy Eckstine's "Prisoner of Love" (originally waxed in 1946) and Guy Mitchell's "My Heart Cries for You" (first done in 1950), for example, found second—albeit short—lives in rock form during the late '50s. The new "That's How Much I Love You" ripped open with a piercing guitar solo by Hank Garland, and a heavy rock beat carries Eddy's more macho interpretation through to the end (*"That's how much I love you, woman!"* Eddy sang this time). A housewife who wistfully recalled the song from her teenage years would have lost her hair curlers when the needle dropped down on this new translation. The song, with its rocket-fueled instrumentation, might have fared well against the hits of the day, but RCA chose not to release it as a single and instead banished the song to a 1959 Arnold album on the company's Camden budget label. But, the new "That's How Much I Love You," like selections from *Eddy Arnold Sings Them Again,* replaced the original hit on subsequent greatest hits albums.

As hard as Eddy and Chet grasped for an invigorating spark, earth-shattering sales and strong hits still eluded Eddy Arnold. Off in the distance, unhappy rumblings could be heard from RCA's headquarters. Eddy's contract with RCA was to expire on May 31, 1963, and from what Eddy heard, the label had second thoughts about re-signing him. Bob Yorke, a veteran of RCA's West Coast operations, had moved into the position of vice president of commercial records creation in 1960, which meant he now controlled the company's A&R operations. Chet reported to Yorke through the manager of pop A&R, Ben Rosner; Steve Sholes, who in 1961 had taken over RCA Record's West Coast post, also answered to Yorke.

In Eddy's opinion, Yorke wanted him off the label. Yorke's philosophy was to focus on the youth market, and Eddy, an elder statesman and slipping source of sales, did not fit into this mold. By 1962, Yorke had slashed RCA's artist roster in half, and, although Eddy had thus far survived, Yorke had more confidence in veterans such as Elvis, Chet, Harry Belafonte, Henry Mancini, Van Cliburn, and Lena Horne. New talent, though, received most of Yorke's attention, and he gobbled up current acts like trumpeter Al Hirt, pianist Peter Nero, teen idol Paul Anka, and vocalist Ann Margaret. "Our future," Yorke told a *Billboard* reporter, "basically lies with our ability to develop new artists."

Fortunately for Eddy, the recording division's vice president and general manager, George Marek, still believed in him. Angered by Yorke's ingratitude toward one of the label's top-sellers ever, Marek dispatched Yorke to Nashville to personally re-sign Eddy. "The guy running the record company [Marek] said: 'You go down there and sign him again.' So he came down here, and I played golf with him," Eddy said, "but I never would talk to him about a record contract. I was PO'd at him. The thought that I had sold so many records, and I had been good for the label! I wouldn't sign with him at all. So Ben Rosner [manager of pop A&R] fixed up a contract, and I signed with him. . . . I treated Yorke nice. I just didn't talk business with him." Eddy signed a five-year contract—two years fewer than the last long-term deal he signed in 1955. Still, Eddy remained hitless. He would turn to an old friend and manager, Joe Csida, hoping he could revive his career.

In September 1962, Joe Csida left Capitol Records and returned to managing the talent he had handed over to Edgar Burton in 1960. Shortly after Csida returned, Bobby Darin, the firm's biggest client, bought the Csida-Burton publishing companies and, with them, the services of Burton. Csida turned his attention back to the other artists of whom Eddy was the biggest. Without the publishing companies and other artists distracting him, Csida might be able to focus better on Eddy. However, no sooner was Csida back with Eddy than other interests came courting. In March of '63, rumors swirled that a group of music industry executives wanted Joe to head a new recording company for them in Nashville. Joe remained mum on the speculation until May, when a new record-production plant—partially owned by Eddy—named him its eastern representative. In an issue of *Billboard* announcing the appointment, Csida informed the magazine about his Record Representation, Inc., a new service to represent writers, producers, and managers in contract negotiations. As far as the record company, Csida simply told *Billboard,* "If the time comes when it seems advisable for me to become president of the new company, I will make whatever adjustments are necessary in my present operation."

The writing was on the wall. Csida was going to preside over this as-yet-to-be-named label, apparently, it seemed, at Eddy's behest. "He had a bunch of friends in Nashville who decided they were going to put together a record company," said Csida. "And Eddy recommended to them that they should get me to be the guy to run it. They did, and we made a deal. The company was called Recording Industries Corporation. The label was RIC. I signed a three-year deal with them as president of RIC." Csida said he signed the pact on the condition that the owners would ante up $1 million in capital for RIC within a year. In February of 1964, *Billboard* announced the news that RIC had raised the $1 million through a stock offering. Csida—the trade magazine wrote—had started to deal out his artists to other managers so he could focus on his new job.

Csida offered Eddy to Gerard W. Purcell, "Jerry" to everyone in the business. A native of New York City, Gerard Purcell was born in 1915 and experimented with various professions before settling on artist management. A former official in the New York City firemen's union, Purcell tasted what an association with the music industry could do for him in the late '40s when he bought a piece of the publishing rights to Perry Como's hit "Far Away Places" and two other songs for $5,000. He then sold his share of the songs for $25,000, and used the proceeds as a springboard to artist management. Alan Dale, a former vocalist with Carmen Cavallaro's band, signed with Purcell first, and Toni Arden, another big-band alumna, followed. Each had modest success in the 1950s before drowning in the tide of rock and roll.

By the 1960s, Purcell managed poet Maya Angelou and the popular Irish folk group Tommy Makem and the Clancy Brothers, and came upon his biggest finds yet, Al Hirt and Gale Garnett, who both obtained RCA recording contracts through Purcell's work. Hirt, who played trumpet with Tommy and Jimmy Dorsey and Horace Heidt, blared on the scene in 1964 with a huge hit, "Java," and Garnett followed his success during the same year with "We'll Sing in the Sunshine." Purcell's name was well able to open doors in the entertainment industry, particularly at RCA, where he enjoyed a friendship with A&R man Ben Rosner; his often forceful demeanor made some staffers quaver. "He was a strong personality who knew how to stand up and fight for the artists and got a lot done for them, too," said Gordon Bossin, an RCA promotion man.

Bossin also recalled that Purcell wisely labored to woo the RCA promotion team. "He knew that without the support of all us guys, his artists had a tough way to go. . . . If we called him and said, 'It's really crucial that Eddy come in and spend a weekend and visit the jocks. . . . It'll help bust the record, but without it, I'm having trouble,' he would be one of the most cooperative managers, always."

— • —

Joe Csida, according to Jerry Purcell, offered to "throw in" Eddy Arnold (who seemed to be close to retiring) at no charge if Purcell agreed to buy at least one of his other artist management contracts. Jerry said he declined Csida's offer and asked only for permission to work with Eddy. Csida agreed. "Do what he says and don't worry," Eddy recalled Csida telling him when Purcell took over his affairs. Jerry, who knew Eddy superficially through his contact with RCA, figured his new client needed more attention and immediately discussed an image change for Eddy. Jerry and Eddy decided to take the act uptown, which meant Eddy had to get away from appearing at rural festivals and appeal to a more sophisticated crowd. "I had nice shoes made in England," Purcell recalled of Eddy's image change. "I had clothes made for him—tuxedoes that were all custom made. [Eddy said], 'For that tuxedo, I could buy six suits!' Then I had his shirts made out in California. Everything was custom made." Like WSM's Irving Waugh almost twenty years before, Jerry thought Eddy needed to find something to do with his hands when he sang live, so he hired teachers to improve Eddy's hand and microphone technique.

Purcell then put Eddy in finer venues around America. He asked Eddy to cut the concert booking ties he had with Tom Parker (who placed the singer in rodeos and fairs), and arranged for Eddy to tour major cities with an orchestra and Roger Miller, the young singer who had set the charts on fire with "Lock, Stock and Teardrops," "Dang Me," and other hits. The idea was to reintroduce Eddy to the audiences through a younger, country singer so people would get a taste of Eddy's new tuxedo-clad image. The plan worked. Crowds amassed to see Roger Miller while others came for Eddy, but in the end they all got a clear sight of what the new Eddy Arnold was all about. Jerry had also lowered ticket prices to attract people to the shows, which, along with a costly promotion effort, led to a $20,000 loss on the tour that Eddy split with his new manager. Despite this financial problem, Eddy was pleased with the tour. "You have hit upon what I wanted to do all my life," Eddy told him.

Purcell enjoyed an inside track to many of the nation's top television variety shows and planned to roll Eddy into that arena, too. However, in February of 1965, less than a year after adding Eddy to his roster, Purcell picked up the trade papers and saw that Joe Csida had resigned from RIC. Csida, Purcell read, wanted to reactivate his talent management firm, and presumably resume his management relationship with Eddy. Contrary to the *Billboard* report of the previous year, according to Csida, RIC had actually fallen short of the $1 million in capital, raising only about $300,000 and promising the balance by the end of 1964. It was for this reason, Csida said, that he departed the recording industry yet again.

"Joe wanted me to come back then with him, and I was in a tizzy," recalled Eddy. "I liked Joe very much. I liked Jerry very much, and I liked what Jerry was doing for me. As a country boy would say, 'I didn't know whether to go blind or wind my watch.'"

Eddy did neither. He called a meeting in Joe's Manhattan apartment and addressed his two suitors. "Gentlemen, this is one of the hardest decisions of my lifetime. I like both of you people very, very much and respect you. But I have to make a decision for my long term." Eddy turned to the man he signed with more than ten years before. "Joe, something tells me in the back

Eddy Arnold's new look. (Gerard W. Purcell collection)

of my mind that another record deal will come to you. Another company will want to hire you because you have record company experience. And I would take it that you'd probably want to take it again. If I went back with you, you'd have to farm me out again. I like what Jerry's been doing with me. It hurts for me to have to make a decision, but I wanted to do it this way. I'm going to stay with Jerry." Eddy spoke again to both. "Now, if you gentlemen want to get together to make some kind of settlement, that's up to you, but I wanted both of you to hear it from me at the same time."

And so the marriage of Jerry Purcell and Eddy Arnold commenced. Jerry was Eddy's third manager in seven years and, to Eddy, represented the only way to reinvigorate his career. Jerry, with his entertainment contacts and tenacity, perhaps held the key to popular acceptance. He also embodied the strategic thinking that Eddy's management had lacked in the past few years. When Jerry arranged television and concert appearances, they supported the new Eddy Arnold image, and, just to make sure they did, Jerry always accompanied his client to his jobs. Despite their divergent backgrounds—Nashville and New York—the two struck a good friendship. "You got to have somebody who knows a country boy, and I can't say Purcell knew a country boy when I got with him, but, by gosh, he spent some time learning." With not as much as a signed contract, the two lit off to explore the 1960s.

12

*J*erry Purcell, in addition to booking the Roger Miller tour, took a hard look at Eddy's recording prospects. "Eddy was very cold," remembered Purcell. "Eddy was somebody you never could ignore or be impolite to, but he wasn't in a position of power [at RCA]. . . . He was being treated as a has-been, and that upset me very much. I didn't feel that we were getting full cooperation."

Specifically, Purcell claimed that Chet Atkins and RCA Nashville failed to find the best songs for Eddy and, in general, refused to pay the singer the proper degree of attention. Not a matter of conjecture was RCA's promotion of Eddy's records, which had lagged and needed bolstering. For example, in contrast to RCA's blizzard of promotion tied to Eddy's tenth anniversary, the company barely celebrated his twentieth. Observances centered on a record shop window display and a few salad bowls. "Put Eddy Arnold on display in your window," an RCA trade advertisement urged record store owners, "and you'll enter the big RCA Victor window display contest for February. You'll be eligible to win beautiful Dansk salad bowl or candelabra sets." In light of RCA's lackluster campaign, Jerry hired his own promotion people.

Jerry Purcell could be intimidating. When the RCA people dealt with him in 1964, they met a large man who tolerated little foolishness. With sharp, dark eyes, he looked out for his client's interests, and in 1964 he demanded that RCA record Eddy in New York. Chet conceded to Jerry's wishes, and RCA New York assigned Eddy to Jim Foglesong, a young producer who, in addition to being an alumnus of Fred Waring's Pennsylvanians, had produced Julie Andrews, the Ames Brothers, and Robert Goulet at Columbia before joining RCA. According to Foglesong: "Chet called me one day and he said, 'Eddy Arnold has wanted to record an album with Marty Gold, the arranger, for a long time. He's always wanted to do this. I don't really enjoy recording in New York. I spoke to Steve [Sholes], and Steve recommended that I call you. I said, 'I'd be thrilled to work on an album with Eddy Arnold; that would be a fantasy come true.'" Foglesong also remembered that Chet warned him to forgo anything up-tempo and to focus on the ballads that Eddy could handle with journeyman ability.

Foglesong met with Eddy and the New York rehearsal pianist Walter Fleischer to finalize the album set from a list of songs Eddy brought with him. "Marty [Gold] came in a couple of days later and sat with us," continued Foglesong. "Then we went over all the songs again. . . . Everything was written out. So we would routine every song. How are we going to open it? How are we going to end it? What key it should be in. Are we going to change keys in the middle of the thing? So Marty made all these notations and took the music and probably took about two weeks minimum to write all the arrangements."

Marty Gold knew Eddy from his work in New York during the 1950s, and, by 1964, Gold had established a reputation as a great arranger just as Hugo Winterhalter had been. Gold, however, relied only on an army of strings to produce a full sound, unlike Winterhalter, who applied brass as well as strings. "Marty played a large string section even for those days," said Foglesong. "Twelve violins, three violas, and three cellos. That's what Marty needed for his sound." Eddy chose the songs—country hits that had crossed over to the pop charts like Don Gibson's "Oh, Lonesome Me," Patsy Cline's "I Fall to Pieces," and Jim Reeves's "Four Walls"—and Gold wove a lush, sugary sound around Eddy's vocal interpretations.

Though the sales were average, the album's message was clear. Eddy would go for the country fan with country music, but polish the sound and his image to reach the mature, pop audience. For the album cover shoot, Eddy donned a tuxedo and posed against a sparse, rustic background to drive home the juxtaposition of country and class. Everything about the album emphasized the change: the cover photo, the country songs with lush instrumentation, and the title itself, *Pop Hits from the Country Side.* Much of this new emphasis was due to Purcell, who oversaw the presentation of his artist. The album charted a new course for Eddy. His subsequent albums during the 1960s—all recorded back in Nashville—relied on strings and sophisticated, precise arrangements.

Arnold and Foglesong's New York session lasted from Monday, July 27, through Wednesday, the 29th. In the midst of their work, a young Australian musician, fresh from a job with RCA in South Africa, popped into the studio. Bill Walker had just flown into New York on his way to work with Jim Reeves (like Eddy, an RCA artist), whom Walker had met in South Africa during the filming of Reeves's movie, *Kimberly Jim.* Walker—an arranger, pianist, and conductor schooled at the Sydney Conservatory of Music—helped Reeves cut the film soundtrack in Johannesburg; Reeves so admired Walker's work that he invited him to America to write scores for a television show he was planning. Walker was to continue on to Nashville after a few days in Manhattan, where Steve Sholes was showing him around. At the 24th Street studios, Walker met Eddy Arnold for the first time.

On July 31, two days after Eddy's session packed up, Sholes gave Walker tickets to a Broadway production of *Oliver!,* a show that Walker had arranged and conducted in Johannesburg. Walker relished the idea of sitting in a Broadway theater and comparing his version of *Oliver!* against what unfolded on the stage before him. However, Steve Sholes awaited him in the theater lobby with bad news about Jim Reeves. "Jim's plane is missing," Steve informed Bill. "You better get down to Nashville."

— • —

If any country singer was achieving what Eddy wanted to achieve throughout the late 1950s and early '60s, it was Jim Reeves. An international star, Reeves shined brightest for RCA's Nashville division, fine-tuning an easygoing approach reminiscent of what Eddy pioneered, but with infinitely more success than Eddy was having. In 1959, while Eddy managed two moderate hits, Jim Reeves spent fourteen weeks at number one on the country charts and reached number two on the pop charts with "He'll Have to Go." Eddy had never reached the top ten of the pop charts, and now Reeves was doing it in a style that Eddy first made acceptable to modern country music. A long string of country and pop hits followed "He'll Have To Go" as Reeves continued to refine his tender vocal approach and tone down the country elements of his background instrumentation.

Reeves frequently appeared on network radio and television and—with *Kimberly Jim* in the can—perhaps had an acting career ahead of him, too. But just as Reeves began consolidating his different successes into mainstream American popularity, he perished in a plane crash. At the controls of a single-engine plane, Reeves was returning to Nashville from Batesville, Arkansas, with his pianist, Dean Manuel, when they encountered a rainstorm. Flying by sight, Reeves tried desperately to negotiate his way to the airport, but his engine stalled and the plane nosedived into a dense wooded area near Brentwood. Throughout the Saturday evening and Sunday, search parties—Eddy, John D. Loudermilk, Ernest Tubb, Stonewall Jackson, Chet Atkins, and Eddy's son Dickey among them—combed the woods and fields around Brentwood, finding nothing. Reeves's plane dropped through the wooded patch without splintering many tree branches, thus preserving a leafy umbrella that hid the wreckage. Finally, on Sunday, August 2, rescuers discovered the wreckage just a few hundred yards from a busy Brentwood thoroughfare. "I don't know how many times I flew with a helicopter over that very spot and couldn't see it," Eddy said to an interviewer years later. The crash immolated Dean Manuel and threw Reeves thirty feet, badly dismembering him.

Bill Walker arrived in Nashville while the search was still in progress. It was a grim welcome. The death of Jim Reeves, while tragic in itself, left Walker out of work in a foreign land. But Chet Atkins worked through the Tennessee congressional delegation to get the Australian a green card and, for months, Walker worked odd music jobs. Meanwhile, Walker persuaded Chet Atkins to record an Eddy Arnold album of songs in Afrikaans, the official, Dutch-derived language of South Africa. With Jim Reeves's death, perhaps Eddy could fill a void in South Africa. "Bill Walker and his former wife taught me that lyric," said Eddy. "His former wife was from South Africa. They worked with me phonetically. We *worked* on it, I want you to know."

In January of 1965, Chet included Walker on Eddy's first recordings for domestic release since New York's *Pop Hits from the Country Side.* Taking a cue from Marty Gold, Walker doubled the typical number of string instrumentalists on the session and added oboe, clarinet, and saxophone to construct the largest Nashville ensemble to back Eddy up to that point. Eddy and Jerry liked what Walker could do. He was constructing a sort of Marty Gold beachhead in Nashville, but with more concessions to country music. "It was like finding a gold mine," said Purcell. "Bill Walker was part of the new middle-of-the-road sound. . . . We wanted more class."

The resulting album, *The Easy Way,* covered current country songs like Johnny Cash's "Understand Your Man" and "Bad News" by John D. Loudermilk (the young fan from the 1940s had become a songwriter, recording artist, and RCA staffer) and permitted Nashville elements such as Floyd Cramer's tinkling piano and Harold Bradley's guitar. The strings came through clearly, though, and Eddy included a few pop hits like "We'll Sing in the Sunshine" and "Taking A Chance on Love." On *The Easy Way,* Eddy had zeroed in on a comfort zone, and he and Jerry threw their support behind Walker. It was clear that Walker was having a great influence on the direction of Arnold's sound. "I was just thankful to get the gig and be paid," said Walker. "I didn't care at that point about credit or anything. All I wanted to do was make enough money to eat on." Subsequently, Purcell and Eddy hired Walker as his conductor and musical director.

Walker added a new twist to Eddy's adaptation of the Nashville Sound. He brought a formality to Eddy's sessions that heretofore never existed. Anita Kerr might write out parts for the strings and background vocals and jot down chords for the rhythm section, but basically she asked the musicians to improvise. The Nashville Sound relied heavily on "head" arrangements, literally the off-the-top-of-your-head method where musicians, singers, and producers threw their ideas in a pile and out popped a song. When Eddy walked in the door for a session, he knew the songs. However, the musicians, often just in from another session across town or across the street, were seeing the songs for the first time and deciding how to record them by talking with Anita, Chet, or each other. On Eddy's new sessions, though, Bill Walker changed everything.

"There was more written stuff after Bill came in," remembered Louis Nunley, who sang backup for Eddy. "He did do more writing for the group and for the instruments. That was what school he came from, the European school. He wasn't really used to all this faking stuff." When the musicians sat down to record, Bill had written music on their stands, although many of them couldn't read a note. A musician unable to read, however, could be certain to have keen ears and quickly picked up his parts when Walker hummed them or played them on the piano.

In terms of the songs themselves, Chet kept a file in which he squirreled away appropriate material for each of RCA's Nashville singers. Songwriters deluged Chet with material, and if their songs didn't work, Chet and his Nashville staff foraged through publishing company catalogs for material. In the normal course of events, Chet gave Eddy a stack of demonstration discs, and, with Walker's help, Eddy pared down his song choices to a few that appealed to him. "Chet would give me maybe twenty songs," said Walker, "and let me go through them with Eddy. Sometimes we'd sit in Chet's office. Sometimes we'd sit in Brentwood out in Eddy's office. Sometimes I'd just take the songs myself and play [them] over and think about them and then get with Eddy the next day and see how they laid for him—if he felt good, if he liked the lyric."

"Chet was very good at picking songs," continued Walker. "Eddy was pretty good, too, but Chet had a real flair. He could imagine things pretty good, and I could hear arrangements pretty good. I would think [songs] could sound better than the way the composer put it down [and make changes]. I think all together it worked pretty good." Each arrangement passed through Chet for approval; once recording day arrived, Walker was in the studio making sure each instrumentalist followed his part.

"Bill Walker had pretty much figured out what he wanted everybody to do . . .," recalled guitarist Wayne Moss, a frequent contributor to Eddy's sides in the 1960s. "He would have large string sections and large background vocal group sections. He played celeste . . . or he would play vibes. But he generally had a piano player other than himself. That freed him up to direct except on the second verse where he'd be playing celeste. He kept it all together, and all Eddy had to concentrate on was his own performance."

—– • —–

On January 13, 1965, Eddy, Chet, and Bill hit pay dirt. In the studio to record some additional tracks for *The Easy Way* LP, Eddy had some extra time and turned to "What's He Doin' in My World." "We weren't even going to do that song," said Walker, "and Chet sent me out to write the strings, and Anita went out and sketched out the voice parts. The rhythm section learned the song, and we came back in and did it."

The song never made it on to *The Easy Way,* but "What's He Doin' in My World" represented Eddy's easy way much better than anything on the album. With dignity, Eddy admonished his girl about a third party in their relationship, while Bill Walker's beefed-up string arrangements cried the tears that Eddy was too proud to shed. When the last measure faded, Sheldon Kurland, who played violin on the track, knew Eddy had a hit. "I just loved it. I remember coming home and telling my wife. I just loved the song, and I loved the way he sang it. It was one of the first sessions I ever worked." Usually Kurland's predictions of success inexplicably brought failure, but not that day.

RCA released the song as a single, and in March of 1965, "What's He Doin' in My World" entered the country charts at number forty-one, while Roger Miller's "King of the Road" pushed the broom at number one. Over the next nine weeks, Eddy floated up through a school of hits, including Dick Curless's "A Tombstone Every Mile" and Dave Dudley's "Two Six Packs Away." Eddy rose above them to number one by June, but Buck Owens's "Before You Go" bounced Eddy out after only two weeks. Eddy, however, had found his first number one in almost ten years, since 1955. "It did very well," Eddy modestly remembered, "which told us there was still some life left in me record-wise."

In June of '65, while the long-awaited number one still lingered near the top, Eddy recorded the bulk of *My World*. A mixture of the middle-of-the-road and country sound, *My World* revolved around what would be Eddy's biggest hit since "Bouquet of Roses." Originally slated for album filler, "Make the World Go Away" far outpaced the welcome success of "What's He Doin' in My World." "I remembered hearing [Timi Yuro] singing 'Make the World Go Away,'" said Eddy. "I had already heard Jim Reeves and Ray Price and somebody else. They didn't register on me very much. But I heard [Yuro] sing almost a rock version of it. . . . So I said to Chet, 'That might fit this album.' So I found the song, and I checked to see how many records the girl had sold. If she had sold a half million records or a million records, I wouldn't attempt it. But she had sold—about two years before—50,000 records. That's all she had sold. I said, 'That don't bother me if that's what she sold.' I did 'Make the World Go Away.' And we were in the studio, and I was just doing it for the album, and we started listening to the playbacks, and we all looked at one another and said, 'That sounds like a single record.'"

Bill Walker recalled that Chet wasn't so sure if the Hank Cochran composition would make such a good single. "Chet wasn't really decided on doing that song at that one point because there had been four or five records of it. And then when we did it, it turned out so good. He still buried it." What Walker meant was that Chet placed "Make the World Go Away" fourth on side one of the album, instead of highlighting it. The liner notes even labeled the song "older, but well worth an encore." Well worth it, indeed. Highlighted by Floyd Cramer's piano, drummer Jerry Carrigan's steady brush beat, and a piercing string performance, the song was eventually released as a single. Eddy's even vocals soared to number one during the first week of December of 1965, making it his second number one song of the year. "He sang it so good," said Anita Kerr who arranged the background vocals on "Make the World Go Away." "I remember thinking that if this is not a hit something's wrong."

Then—in among hip representatives of Motown, the British Invasion, and the surfing sound, as well as "adult" poppers like Dean Martin and Al Martino—the song appeared on the pop charts and steadily passed the Temptations, the Beatles, the Vogues, and others to peak at number six. The accompanying album, *My World*, flew to number one on the country

Eddy with singer Jeannie Seely and her husband, Hank Cochran, the source of "Make the World Go Away." (Don Mackin collection)

album charts and seven on the pop album charts, remaining on the pop chart for more than a year. Eddy Arnold was back on top of country music and in full view of his dream of popular, widespread recognition. "It was almost the beginning of what I call a second career," he proclaimed.

Jerry Purcell fanned the flames of Eddy's revival, booking him on countless TV shows—"The Steve Lawrence Show," "The Danny Kaye Show," "The John Gary Show," "The Telephone Hour," "Nightlife," Johnny Carson's "Tonight Show," and on and on. On the personal appearance side, Jerry started Eddy's 1966 off with a bang, negotiating an appearance with the Dallas Symphony. Although Eddy had worked with the Nashville Symphony back in the '50s, he was amazed by the Dallas Symphony's willingness to back him. "It was the biggest shock of my life," Eddy told a reporter in 1983. "My gosh! I had had hit records, but I said, 'They're out of their minds. What in the hell am I going to do with a symphony?' But we talked back and forth, and finally I just sort of decided I'd do what I always do, but expand it to a symphony. I was already appearing around the country with strings, so I just added more string parts, threw a couple of guitar players in and added a drummer to make the symphony swing. The symphony players loved it. They had a ball. They even played a hoedown!"

After the Dallas appearance, pops concerts with large city symphonies became standard fare for Eddy. If not always symphonies, strings always appeared on stage behind Eddy after he hooked up with Purcell. As in the studio, Bill Walker stood behind Eddy on the road, going over arrangements with string players he hired in different cities, conducting the orchestra, and recruiting Nashville rhythm men to come along. "At first, we never took anybody," Walker recalled. "I used to pick up the whole band everywhere, and it got so bad. I'd pick up these terrible bass players and terrible drummers. I just really harassed [Eddy] to death and finally we took a bassist, a drummer, and guitar players with us." Among the Nashville musicians to join Eddy from time to time were drummers Terry Waddell, Jerry Carrigan, and Eddy's nephew Jerry Arnold (W. D.'s son, who also backed Eddy on a few sessions).

From Dallas, Eddy headed to Hollywood to do the "Danny Kaye Show," and a week later boarded a plane for Great Britain. "Make the World Go Away" was finally slipping on the American charts, but Jerry believed new life awaited the song abroad and scheduled a grueling sixteen-day media and personal appearance tour in the United Kingdom to prove it. As Eddy traversed the Atlantic with Bill Walker and Jerry, he was already booked to appear on almost every imaginable British Broadcasting Corporation (BBC) television and radio show: "Saturday Club," "Top of the Pops," "Juke Box Jury," the "The Eamon Andrews Show," the "The Murray Cash Show," "Music to Midnight," and "Pop Inn." Eddy also looked forward to concert appearances all around the U.K.—including Belfast in Northern Ireland—that would surely brighten the international luster of "Make the World Go Away." But when Eddy hit the ground in London, a damp English fog rolled in.

The RCA promotion people in England, actually employees of British Decca that distributed and promoted RCA product, stretched a sign across the terminal to greet the American star: "Welcome Eddie Arnold, Grand Ole Opry Star." Nothing could have made Eddy feel less at home. If there were two things the mild-mannered Eddy Arnold hated most, it was the frequent misspelling of his first name and the label "Grand Ole Opry Star," a billing that Eddy shed in 1948 when he bid adieu to WSM's Saturday night hoedown.

But troubles only began with the offending sign. The promotion people wanted Eddy to plug another song during his U.K. visit. "They had a guy who did promotion for RCA in London that had a political deal with the music publisher," Eddy recalled. "They were trying to get me to release another song published by them." Jerry squashed their attempts, threatening to take Eddy home until they backed down. Eddy remembered, "I said right now 'Make the World Go Away' is in the top ten of the pop charts in the United States; why would you think it wouldn't become a hit here? Either release it or I'm going home. . . . I went on the BBC on a Friday night," Eddy continued. "They had one of these programs where you lip synch your records,

'Top of the Pops,' and I went on and did a lip synch job of 'Make the World Go Away' on Friday night. Monday morning it was a hit."

BBC radio, indeed, picked up on Eddy's American smash, and coupled with Eddy's maddening schedule of U.K. appearances, propelled "Make the World Go Away" as high as number ten on the British record charts. But the problems with the promotion man didn't end with Eddy and Jerry's insistence that "Make the World Go Away" be promoted. The nameless promotion man, it seems, had a friend who owned a club.

"Let's go see a friend of mine who has this big dance hall," Jerry remembered the staffer proposing to him and Eddy. The two Americans went along, but Jerry's eyebrows arched when the promotion man drove to the back car park and escorted them in through a service entrance. As Eddy and Jerry stood in the back of the club, they saw a dance floor packed with people and a disc jockey spinning records. The promotion man stepped away to whisper something in the disc jockey's ear, and, at that, Jerry walked back out the service entrance and around to the front of the club where he saw "Eddy Arnold: Live Appearance Tonight" on a sign beckoning passersby. The club may have spelled Eddy's name correctly, but a live appearance was out of the question. Jerry rushed inside and promptly excused himself and Eddy.

Eddy's *scheduled* appearances went somewhat more smoothly. Eddy and Bill performed at a number of regal concert halls, but also at less-appealing venues of the like that Eddy hadn't seen since his honky-tonk days. "It was unreal what happened," said Jerry. Eddy's manager remembered dank dance halls and one dive that had no piano. In cold and snowy Liverpool, he played a club that catered to Irish expatriates, who became so boisterous that Bill Walker feared the premises would erupt in rioting.

Eddy could deal with the gamy venues, but the February chill of Great Britain enervated him. On a swing through Scotland, Eddy retired in an icy bed that, he thought, would leave him a pneumonic wreck by morning. In no time, Eddy sprang from the bed to call the desk clerk, who seemed to be turning the hotel heat on and off again. "If you don't turn the heat up in my room, I'm coming down there to the lobby because I know you have a heater there, and I'm going to sleep on the couch in the lobby . . . with a nightcap on!"

Eddy ventured across the vast Atlantic to Great Britain one more time during the '60s for more television spots, but, except for appearances in Canada, he has yet to go abroad again. "I'm not a good traveler. I don't like to go to foreign countries. . . . I'm a very sentimental person. I get very homesick. That's the reason I don't go. I don't want to go. I have all the work here I'll ever want to do."

— • —

When the country-pop star arrived home from Britain's cold, he found a world that had warmed considerably. In late February, welcoming applause

On the road again, promoting "WGNU: The Sound of Granite City, Ill." (Gerard W. Purcell collection)

engulfed Eddy on a West Coast swing through Bakersfield, Los Angeles, and San Francisco and on through the Midwest, where he performed in St. Louis, Chicago, Akron, and Cleveland. After only eleven dates on the tour, he had grossed more than $74,000, and Eddy's latest hit, "I Want to Go with You," had begun an ascent to number one. The song, another Hank Cochran composition recorded in the flowing, easygoing Eddy Arnold fashion, commenced a six-week stay at number one on the country charts in April 1966.

With "I Want to Go with You" high on the charts and its follow-up—the Roger Miller–penned "The Last Word in Lonesome Is Me"—rising fast, late-night favorite Johnny Carson presented Eddy a gold record for *My World* on "The Tonight Show." Eddy appeared with Johnny on May 18, and the next day he made a triumphant concert appearance at New York's Carnegie Hall—the most celebrated of all concert venues in the city and indeed around the world. Jerry enlisted country stars Jim Ed Brown, Skeeter Davis, and George Hamilton IV to open for Eddy, and Bill Walker gathered a nineteen-piece orchestra to replicate the sounds of Eddy's new hit records for the live audience.

As the opening performers ran through their hits on that Thursday evening, Eddy waited backstage with little hint of nervousness. Like a boxer's training camp, Eddy's vigorous schedule of late had conditioned him for success. The wild sales of Eddy's records and enthusiastic crowd responses he had seen throughout February and March were not lost on

Eddy. He knew he was a hot commodity again and was poised to give the Carnegie Hall audience a real treat. When Bill Walker struck up the band, the tuxedo-garbed Eddy Arnold strode out on the stage, and, although Eddy had never worked a concert in Manhattan, the audience welcomed him as if he were local hero Frank Sinatra. Just twenty years before, Eddy might have looked out from a typical stage to see a ranch audience packed in among a grove of trees, but this night Eddy saw a sea of ties, pearls, and furs floating in the grandeur of Carnegie Hall.

Bill Walker feared that the orchestra's sound would bounce off the hard stage floor and overpower the star, but Eddy's powerful vocals soared above the accompaniment. He wove the recent smashes, "Make the World Go Away" and "The Last Word in Lonesome Is Me," with covers of traditional songs like "John Henry" and "Cottonfields," and—paying tribute to his old New York sound—Eddy dished out a lively version of "The Richest Man (In the World)," a Hugo Winterhalter collaboration that sold well for Eddy in 1955.

About halfway through the little more than one-hour show, Eddy dismissed the orchestra, took his guitar, grabbed a stool, and tenderly ran through his standards. To the biggest ovations of the night, Eddy and his guitar performed "Bouquet of Roses," "I Really Don't Want to Know," and snatches from the other hits of his career. A review in *Variety* hailed this segment of the show: "In this quiet solo setting, Arnold delivered another varied book of old folk songs and more contemporary ballads in a way that totally entranced the audience. It was the kind of palpable impact achieved by only a handful of great showmen."

The rest of the trade press chimed in behind *Variety*. "Arnold Delivers Haymaker At His Carnegie Hall Bow," blared *Billboard*. "Arnold Great At Carnegie Hall," *Record World* raved. "Arnold: Country Boy Who Conquered Carnegie," cackled *Cashbox*.

Eddy gave himself top reviews, too. "It was very successful, very successful. I tore up the place. That audience was on fire. It sure was, and I was, too. That was really a time in my life that I never dreamed would come about. A country boy from Tennessee in Carnegie Hall—never in my life, never! As a boy growing up, I didn't even know what Carnegie Hall was."

When Eddy tried to leave, the crowd forced him back again and again. "It was a wonderful experience for me," remembered Bill Walker, "but it was a great concert for Eddy. It was SRO. I've never forgotten this. The place was jammed, and [there] was a wonderful standing ovation."

"Arnold could not get off," wrote Herm Schoenfeld in *Variety*. "He received one of those insistent ovations usually reserved by claquers for their favorite operatic divas. And being no prima donna, Arnold obliged with a full quota of encores which even then did not leave his devoted fans sated." With hands clasped in gratitude and satisfaction, Eddy finally headed off the stage, but when he looked across the orchestra seats and on up through the four curving, crowded balconies nobody seemed ready to go home. Women cried, men hollered their appreciation, and camera flashes sporadically blinked among the people. Out of sight and in the wings, Eddy grinned. He had just capped the journey he had always hoped to finish.

With a sophisticated sound, a love song–laden repertoire, pop hits, and acceptance in venues of the stature of Carnegie Hall, Eddy realized he had arrived where he wanted to be. He shattered the Tennessee Plowboy mold and approached a Sinatra-like presence in American entertainment.

13

The day after his monumental Carnegie Hall performance, Eddy performed at the Brooklyn Academy of Music, another prestigious New York venue. In July, he returned to the road for an extensive summer tour of midsize American towns: Minot, North Dakota; Casper, Wyoming; Oshkosh, Wisconsin; Wellington, Ohio; Reading, Pennsylvania; Asbury, New Jersey, among others. As Eddy wound his way through America in the summer of 1966, he could turn on the radio to hear another of his pop-country hits, "The Tip of My Fingers" (written by Bill Anderson), and switch on the television to see guest spots he had filmed earlier.

As Eddy basked in what amounted to a second career, long-overdue awards showered on him. *Billboard* proclaimed Eddy to be the Country Male Vocalist of 1966 and his *I Want To Go With You* the Favorite Country Album. The Music Operators of America named him Most Popular Juke Box Artist of the Year in 1966, and for performances in 1965 the National Academy of Recording Arts and Sciences (NARAS) nominated Eddy for Grammy awards in the categories of best country-and-western single, best country-and-western album, and best country-and-western vocal performance by a male—although he failed to win in any of the areas. In 1967, the Country Music Association bestowed their first "Entertainer of the Year" award on him.

Even the White House acknowledged Eddy's new station in the corridors of American entertainment. President Johnson invited Sally and Eddy to a state dinner held for His Imperial Majesty, Haile Selassie, the emperor of Ethiopia. Eddy knew LBJ from the President's tenures as a U.S. senator and vice president, and had performed at his Texas ranch a couple of times for visiting foreign dignitaries. This time, though, LBJ spared Eddy from singing for his supper and instead had opera singers Richard Tucker and Nedda Casei serenade the Ethiopian leader and the other White House guests.

Actually, Eddy and Sally almost missed their chance to dine as guests of the White House. The Arnolds arrived in the city a day early for the dinner that was to be held on Valentine's Day, 1967. On the big day, Sally and Eddy dressed early to reach 1600 Pennsylvania Ave. at 8:00 P.M., but when they

177

"Somebody Like Me." Eddy says hello to Phoenix. (Eddy Arnold collection)

left their room on the ninth floor of Washington's International Inn and pressed the elevator's "down" button, no elevator came. They waited and waited, hesitating to walk down nine flights of steps and rumple Sally's long, pink dress. The Arnolds rushed back to their room and called the desk. Even the service elevator, the clerk informed them, was out of commission, but a repair man would see to the problem. So, Eddy and Sally stood by while a mechanic tried to revive the stalled lift. Soon, though, it became apparent that the Arnolds would be late if they hung around any longer.

"I pulled up my full-length dress [that] I just had hand pressed," Sally told a reporter a few days later, "and down the nine flights we ran." As Secretary of Defense Robert McNamara and Vice President Hubert Humphrey arrived alongside private citizens like Benny Goodman, Eddy and Sally's cab dashed to the White House. They were the last to arrive at the building's east entrance, but made it in time to be properly introduced and enjoy the Florida pompano, roast filet of beef White House, duchess potatoes, fresh asparagus, garden salad, roquefort mousse, and savarin jubilee. "Moose lips and buffalo brains" were worlds away—frozen in the 1950s on the "Caesar's Hour" television show.

More than any dinner or industry award, Eddy probably found the most gratification with his induction into Nashville's Country Music Hall of Fame. Even though he was helping to remold country music into a "country-politan" style and moving in entertainment circles more familiar to George Burns than George Jones, he loved Nashville and its people. He counted those who kept their feet in traditional country music among his friends and welcomed their acceptance. The Country Music Association slated the Hall of Fame induction for October 2, 1966, when they would enshrine the late banjo player Uncle Dave Macon, Judge George D. Hay, Cedarwood Publishing's Jim Denny (who had died three years before), and Eddy. Organizers kept the news from Eddy, but told Jerry Purcell, who had a heck of a time getting Eddy to the ceremonies.

"I was sick," said Eddy. "I had the flu. I had not planned to go. As a matter of fact, I was home in bed." He had even scotched plans to attend Dickey's football game that night, but Jerry succeeded in luring him off the Brentwood farm for a trade magazine dinner where Eddy was to be honored. The magazine people would be hurt, Jerry implored, if Eddy skipped the event. So, ever the gentleman, Eddy met Jerry at the dinner and accepted his kudos. Award in hand, Eddy headed for the exit, home on his mind, but Jerry suggested they stop by the Municipal Auditorium to see the inductees to the Hall of Fame. "I said, 'I need to go home, I'm sick.' I wasn't planning on going because I just didn't feel like going."

Jerry drove the reluctant Eddy over to the auditorium, where he walked in only to see his family seated at a table. Something was up. He sat down, and Jo Ann broke into tears, sparking her father to do the same. She hadn't seen him cry so hard since her wedding the year before. "I was the first one he hugged when they called his name," recalled Jo Ann. "It was a real emotional night, one of my fond memories. . . . We all had a good cry." Eddy and Sally walked to the front as tears streamed from Eddy's eyes. *Billboard* publisher Hal B. Cook read the plaque that would hang in the Hall of Fame while Eddy stood by wiping tears from his eyes:

> Born near Henderson, Tennessee, Eddy Arnold first gained widespread recognition in 1946. After a humble beginning, he rose to great heights as a performer and as a recording artist, selling millions of records. He has been a powerful influence in setting music tastes. His singing, warm personality, and infectious laugh have endeared Eddy to friends and fans everywhere.

"It's a long road," Eddy sputtered to those gathered around. "I'm a very emotional person, and I thank you." For a few minutes, Eddy and Sally stood holding hands as the Nashville establishment roared. "Could we go now?" Eddy cried. They stepped down from the stage only to be besieged by well-wishers.

No one deserved a place in a country hall of fame more than Eddy Arnold. More successfully than any of his peers, with his soft baritone, he began in the 1940s to touch Americans who had never considered listening to country music. He turned heads and ears in major cities and areas around the nation as quickly as in the South. He helped create new markets for so-called rural music, and the country-music industry prospered as a result. Frankly, much of urban America—especially in the North—found country music indigestible. Eddy dished out a compromise in the late '40s and '50s and introduced those unbelievers to Nashville. By the early 1960s, Eddy was growing up with his fans who liked his romantic approach, offering a middle-of-the-road sound in a genre dominated by Hank Williams's disciples. He gave older fans a reason to remain interested in country music during the 1960s while attracting explorers from the world of Perry Como and Frank Sinatra as one of the prime figures of the more acceptable Nashville Sound.

To describe the Nashville Sound as an "acceptable" strain of country music means that it was more acceptable to an audience who heretofore had ignored country music or had found nothing to relate to in the popular drinking-and-cheating songs that gushed out of Nashville. The classic, unadorned, rural sound was just as "acceptable"—but to a different audience. The Eddy Arnold of the mid-1960s kept a foot in country music by recording with Nashville musicians and incorporating the occasional country theme or instrumental embellishment. In many ways, though, Eddy was really an easy-listening or middle-of-the-road singer—a country singer in name only—and his forays out of country were bound to anger those fans who protested new directions.

Rumblings similar to those Eddy faced in 1955 resurfaced just after the Country Hall of Fame induction. Some—those who abhorred anything that seemed nontraditional—worried that Eddy was the devil himself, lurking in

An overwhelmed Eddy joins the Country Music Hall of Fame. (Eddy Arnold collection)

Nashville and waiting to steal the soul of country music. Blood first spilled in the November 1966 pages of *Music City News,* a Nashville organ that capitalized the word "country" (as in "Country Music") just as the Bible capitalizes God's name. Honky tonk–influenced singer Faron Young (of "Live Fast, Love Hard, Die Young" fame) presided over the magazine. In an editorial entitled "Which Road, Country Music?" the publication left names unmentioned but could have only meant Eddy Arnold when it criticized country music's new middle-of-the-road direction: "We believe the way of the past is still the way of the future. If the past is dead, then we cannot understand why the harmonica and dobro—and even folk music—have seen a new birth. While the popular music people learn from Country Music, we continue to move away from our great heritage. . . . These are the ingredients of greatness," the editorial concluded, "and it would do well for those who have strayed so far from the 'Songs of the soil' to return to those days for this 'second birth.'"

The *Music City News* editorial coincided with an angry letter to the magazine from one James Kennison of Valley Station, Kentucky. "All of those people who voted to place 'pop' singer Eddy Arnold in the Country Music Hall of Fame . . . should be forced to resign from the Country Music Association immediately," the angry man seethed. "They couldn't have done anything more detrimental to Country Music. . . . The new Hall of Fame building isn't even finished yet and they have already ruined it," Kennison raged. "There is no reason now why Connie Francis, Andy

Williams, Patti Page, and Steve Lawrence shouldn't be added to the Hall of Fame. They sing Country songs now and then and sound more Country than Tuxedo Eddy does."

The commotion in the pages of *Music City News* wouldn't die with the passions of James Kennison. In December, another reader fell in behind the magazine's clarion call: "This is a stand AGAINST those deviationists among us who would sell us out to the so-called 'pop' field, and there are several big names that fit in this category," wrote Edward Wilson of Murfreesboro, Tennessee. "It would appear that those individuals who would have wind instruments classed as 'Country' are more interested in immediate dollar returns than the preservation of true Country Music." Interestingly, and quite tellingly, the only defense of Eddy in the pages of *Music City News* came from a man in Bridgeton, New Jersey. "Those people who voted to put Mr. Arnold in the Country Music Hall of Fame," wrote Dom Macera in response to all the criticism, "are people who have been in Country Music for a long time and know what Mr. Arnold has done for country music."

Buck Owens also followed the anti-innovation theme in the magazine. With his Bakersfield Sound—a California brand of honky-tonk music— Owens was emerging as the preeminent country artist of the 1960s. In an insert in *Music City News,* he issued his manifesto—a sort of five command- ments of country music—to atone for his experiments with rock music, while implicitly condemning others who didn't sound "country":

> *I shall sing no song that is not a country song.*
> *I shall make no record that is not a country record.*
> *I refuse to be known as anything, but a country singer.*
> *I'm proud to be associated with country music.*
> *Country music and country music fans have made me what I am*
> *today. And I shall not forget it.*

The purists in country music marched in step against the heretics, but, as Eddy would say many times, the hearty welcomes he received elsewhere dulled his ears to the uproar. His phenomenal record sales and constant demand on the concert and TV variety-show circuit provided ample affirma- tion of his career decisions. That said, though, he rarely resisted a chance to fire a volley over the bow of traditionalism. "It's the respect," Eddy told the *National Observer* during the same month Buck Owens's pledge to country music ran. "Our music had to have respect. As soon as we [country musi- cians] started respecting ourselves then the people started respecting us too. When they took all those goldarned hayseeders off the air, that's when we started going to town. Now much of our music is modernized, radio stations all over the country are playing country songs, and many more of our artists are on nationwide television." Eddy even went as far as to tell the *Pensacola (Fla.) Journal* that "pop singer" might be a more appropriate classification for him. "Country music has been good to me and it still is. But, like I say, I don't really consider myself a country singer anymore."

An irate Pensacolan read the article, clipped it, and sent it with a vitriolic letter to the Country Music Hall of Fame. "I was in Nashville last November and visited the Country Music Hall of Fame. It was a disgrace to Country Music to see Eddy Arnold in the Country Hall of Fame," fumed M. R. Burkes. "In this article he says himself that he is not a country music singer. This statement alone should be enough to take him out of the Hall of Fame."

—— • ——

RCA's Nashville operation spearheaded the move away from absolute traditionalism in country music and, in doing so, grew to be one of the leading studios in town. Since the late 1950s, when Chet Atkins took over supervision of country recordings for Steve Sholes, RCA Nashville's influence had ballooned. Chet took on the added responsibility of supervising the administrative end of the Nashville operation in 1960, and, over the next seven years, his staff grew from three people to eighteen. Felton Jarvis and Bob Ferguson—onetime manager of Ferlin Husky—produced many sessions for RCA in Nashville. On top of them, a crack group of A&R staffers—including, at one time or another, Anita Kerr, Jack Clement, and John D. Loudermilk—helped guarantee RCA the songs and the singers to maintain its preeminence on the 1960s Nashville scene. The public faces—those of the singers—who represented RCA's success included (along with Eddy) Connie Smith, Don Gibson, Jim Ed Brown, Dottie West, Skeeter Davis, George Hamilton IV, and Willie Nelson. On the technical side, RCA boasted some of the finest of Nashville's recording engineers. Incredibly, all four of its engineers—Al Pachucki, Jim Malloy, Chuck Seitz, and William Vandevort—were nominated for Grammy awards in 1966. They kept RCA's Nashville studios humming, controlling the sound board and setting recording levels and mike positions for singers and instrumentalists on an unbelievable 1,211 sessions in 1967. Not all of these sessions were for RCA artists; other national and local labels used RCA's Nashville facilities, particularly after the company christened a larger studio—Studio A as it was known—in 1965.

In RCA's old, cramped Studio B on 1610 Hawkins Street, Chet looked out on a crowded room of music people. Eddy, or whoever happened to be recording, stood in the back of the small room surrounded by tall baffles that prevented leakage into the singer's mike. The background vocal group stood just feet away from the star. The drummer was jammed against the left wall near the rest of the rhythm section, and the electric instrumentalists sat on the right side of the studio with any orchestral instruments on the date. The sight resembled a New York subway car at rush hour. Studio B legend tells of a date when lilting rocker Roy Orbison just couldn't be heard over a large ensemble of musicians huddled around him, prompting the producer to stick Orbison's head and a mike in a closet among an insulating row of hanging coats.

Studio A, though, could easily accommodate a soft voice like Orbison's among 100 musicians, and by 1966 most of RCA's sessions had moved to the new facility. But, according to engineer Al Pachucki, the new studio was sterile compared to the gritty Studio B. The sound of the bass disappeared in the room, and the drums flooded other microphones, forcing the engineers to build a hut over the drums and hang black burlap on the white walls to improve the sound. Still, the studio could accommodate more musicians, which was critical as Chet and his staff employed strings more often to broaden their singers' appeal.

"I tried to make crossover records all the time," declared Chet. "I didn't try to make pop records, but for a long time I didn't use country fiddle or steel [guitar] because that would keep a record from crossing over. I had a lot of success with Jim Reeves doing that before I had records with Eddy. It worked."

Engineer Chuck Seitz saw wheels turning in Chet's head as Chet tried to make those crossover records. "Chet worked on a song, and he concentrated on that song. He tried to mold it to that artist, and he tried to make it commercial. I heard him say many a time that he felt that he was in tune with the country public, and that if he liked it, the public would like it, too. And if he didn't like it, that they wouldn't like it. That's the way he worked with everyone."

By the mid-1960s, Chet's Nashville team accounted for almost 20 percent of RCA's sales even without Elvis, who had transferred most recording to Hollywood, where Tom Parker had him making B-grade movies. Chet and company's collective touch so resembled alchemy that out-of-town Victor artists lined up to benefit from the Nashville Sound. Perry Como waxed his popular *The Scene Changes* album in Nashville with the Anita Kerr Singers and Floyd Cramer's piano in the background, and New Orleans–based trumpeter Al Hirt, Hollywood's Ann Margret, and New Yorker Paul Anka trekked to Nashville behind Como.

Nobody in Chet's stable, nobody, squeezed more from RCA's Nashville setup than Eddy Arnold. On April 24, 1967, Eddy was back in the studio to cut more pop-oriented records. The session birthed a pop hit and number one country song, "Turn the World Around." Chet Atkins and Bill Walker developed with Eddy a winning recording procedure, characterized mostly by Eddy's preparedness, Walker's lush arrangements, and Atkins's let-it-happen supervision.

The raw material for Eddy's session—the songs—was more easily mined in light of Eddy's resurgent success. "After I had 'What's He Doin' in My World,' I really started getting the good songs," said Eddy. "The publishers started bringing me their good songs. It's funny how that works." Writers and publishers flooded Eddy and Chet with numbers, some offering to cut both men in on the potential publishing profits should they record their

Eddy with Elvis, former RCA chief Frank Folsom, and Col. Tom Parker on the set of Elvis's 1968 movie, *Speedway*. (Eddy Arnold collection)

songs. Eddy had welcomed the gratitude of Wally Fowler and others in the '40s but refused any writing or publishing credit in the 1960s. "I never wanted to be political about songs," Eddy continued. "I didn't want a writer to think he had to give me half of his copyright to get me to record it. . . . I wanted the writer to bring me his good songs and for the most part they would because they knew they didn't have to share the copyright with me. If I liked the song, I'd record it." Songs by some of country's best writers—Hank Cochran, Merle Kilgore, Cindy Walker, Jean Chapel, and Cy Coben—gave Eddy a well of quality work to draw upon, which translated to an added advantage in the studio.

To sit in on an Eddy Arnold session, which rarely happened because Eddy liked closed sessions (and disliked visits from meddlesome writers who wanted their songs recorded *their* way), meant seeing a process that dropped into place like a needle in a groove. With songs in hand and arrangements decided, Eddy arrived at the studio ready to work. "[Eddy] always knew his material," recalled background vocalist Louis Nunley. "Not everybody did. You could depend on Eddy. He always knew his songs and was ready to record when he walked in."

Eddy politely greeted the musicians and background singers (some of whom playfully called him "Edert") as he saw each of them, but before the audiotape rolled, he concentrated on Chet and Bill—the men in charge of the music. Pleasure and socializing followed business. "He liked funny stories," said Nunley, "and we'd always have something new for him when we came in the studio. He would meet us as we came in and say, 'Stop! Stop! Don't tell it now. Wait 'til after the session. You'll ruin my throat.' When he starts laughing, he laughs all over. It just tore his throat all to pieces."

Perhaps a reflection of his farming childhood that allowed little procrastination, Eddy seemed a zealot to drummer Jerry Carrigan when it came to the work ethic. "We got into a habit that was not really good. All the session players did. We would sign the doggone time card about halfway through the session so we could get out of there, go get lunch, and go to another session. I remember one day, he looked over there, and he saw that going on and he said, 'What are you fellows doing?' I said, 'We're signing the time card.' He said, 'Uh-uh. You don't even know that you'll live until the session's over. I don't want you to do that on my session. When you finish your work, then you sign that. Let me have that.' I gave it to him, and he tore it up and threw it in the wastebasket.

"Eddy was quite sure of himself and prepared in every way. . . . He expected you to do it right," said Carrigan. "He was hard-nosed. The attitude was 'Do it right or you're gone.' He didn't have time for people who would not work or apply themselves."

Certainly, if there is common sentiment about Eddy's recording approach, it was that he tolerated little shenanigans during the session and always knew his material. "I cannot be uptight when I go into the studio," Eddy explained. "I got to be loose. I've got to be able to stop and tell a little joke with the conductor or with the producer . . . but then when I do it, I want to be serious because I have a one-track mind. I got to put my mind right on it. I got to think seriously about it." Elvis Presley's Nashville sessions for RCA might go into hours of overtime because Elvis spent little time with his repertoire before the session; but not Eddy. When the band and vocalists internalized the material, Eddy pounced on the song and often speared it in fewer than five takes.

"Gentlemen have to be prepared," former RCA staffer John D. Loudermilk said in reference to Eddy. "They can't make it up as they go along. They have to have it already planned. He was like that. Jim Reeves would make it up as he [went] along. Sometimes he would say things that he was sorry for later. Like anybody who is not prepared, once you go out on the stage and forget your routine, next time you'll memorize it."

Eddy Arnold sessions always progressed with uneventful splendor, about as exciting and exacting as a chess game in the park. He might edge closer to the guitar player if he wanted the feel of the guitar or quietly have a word with Chet (who Eddy ironically called "Loudmouth"), if the tempo strayed or the band blared too loudly. "Eddy never got flustered," recalled bassist Henry Strzelecki. "I never saw Eddy get angry. . . . If Eddy thought something needed fixing, he would do it again. He would never blame anybody else. . . . He would say, 'I think I can do better than that.' He never belittled the band members. He would say, 'Let's do it again.' He commanded the respect of the musicians who worked with him."

"How did that sound, Chet?" Eddy asked when he wrapped up a take.

"Let's hear it," Chet dryly answered.

The two huddled, and if the take lacked what Eddy and Chet wanted, Eddy walked back to the musicians, "Well, boys, we're going to take another one."

Other sessions around town might explode with the dynamite of an emotional producer or the egotism of the star, but Eddy and Chet navigated sessions with firm coolness. Chet, especially, revealed little emotion, giving the musicians and singers time to work things out before stepping in to correct a problem. "Chet had already done his homework with Eddy before they ever came to the studio," said guitarist Wayne Moss. "About all Chet had to do was say, 'That sounds great, Eddy . . . take two . . . try one more . . . let's go to the next song.'"

Atkins learned well from mentor Steve Sholes, who never made a scene in the studio and approached his singers and musicians with respect. "Chet would always give the musicians and the artists the direction to go in . . . [and] make it clear what he was looking for," observed engineer Al Pachucki. "I can see Chet right now. He would sit in that chair, fold his hands, put them inside his belt, and darn near go to sleep. He knew the people he had to work with, and he left it up to them. When things weren't going right, he would get out in the studio and rectify the situation. He always did it in a very calm . . . very professional way."

Chet attacked sessions so gently that a few wondered if he really did anything. Recording engineer Jim Malloy wondered just that one evening during a Dottie West session when, after two hours, Dottie and the band had failed to put even one song to bed. They endeavored to cut four songs in three hours (as was the standard in the industry), but nothing was working right. Behind the glass, suffering in quiet disgust, Chet mashed his forehead down on the recording console, lifting his head occasionally to survey the wreckage, only to rest it again. Seemingly at his saturation point, Chet asked Malloy to turn down the studio monitor.

"Well," Malloy thought, "we're going to fix this damn thing now and get on with this thing!"

"You know what?" Chet looked at Malloy.

"What?"

"There are greenflies getting in here. We got to put a screen door on this building." Chet sauntered out of the control room, into his office, found a fly swatter, rejoined Malloy, and squashed the trespassing insect on the control room's glass window. "I guess I need to go out and talk with these people for a minute," Chet said to Malloy.

According to Malloy, they tied up Dottie's four songs over the next hour. "Chet was so secure within himself and in his own knowledge," explained

Malloy, "he didn't have to be running around the studio like a chicken with his head cut off like some of these people do—hollering and screaming and complaining about this and complaining about that. Chet knew the worst thing that could happen is that he could pick up the guitar himself and play the whole thing."

If a producer has one job, it is to coax a great song from a singer. Chet got the best out of Eddy by letting Eddy Arnold be Eddy Arnold. To Chet, Eddy was, in many ways, still the larger-than-life "Opry" star who shook the walls backstage at the Ryman Auditorium when Chet first met him in 1946. Chet remained somewhat intimidated by Arnold, deferring to him in the studio and only subtly steering him if the star went flat or needed help with phrasing. "I do remember that he would sing much better if I got some pretty girls in the control room," said Chet. "I'd invite some of the office girls in, pretty girls, and he'd perform a lot better. He would sing and dance around, kind of do a little show." If Chet could get Eddy to concentrate on his long-hewn ability to put across a song, he figured he had succeeded. "He reads music, you know, and I always felt that was a little to his detriment. I'd always tell him, 'Put a little more Eddy Arnold in it. Forget those damn notes!' Because he has a heck of a style."

That Eddy Arnold style created hit after hit in the 1960s and helped make Chet Atkins a well-regarded producer. For the remainder of the '60s, following "Turn the World Around" in 1967, Eddy raised nine more hits up the country charts, seven of which crossed over to the pop charts. His LPs regularly topped the country album charts and performed solidly on the pop ones. *The Best of Eddy Arnold* LP, released in 1967, went gold, spending more than a year on the pop album charts and almost 100 weeks on the country charts; to capitalize on Eddy's Hall of Fame induction, RCA repackaged twenty-six of his albums using new cover photos and a logo that resembled the Hall of Fame plaque. As Eddy approached the age of fifty in 1968, his appeal was never more potent.

Actually, as the mid-'60s became the late '60s, all of Eddy's songs seemed more at home on the pop or easy-listening charts than the country charts. The concessions to country found in the sessions immediately around "Make the World Go Away" in the mid-'60s, tinkling pianos or an occasional banjo lick, vanished on hits like "Here Comes the Rain, Baby" and "Please Don't Go." And Eddy's covers of country hits like Wynn Stewart's "It's Such A Pretty World Today" or Roger Miller's "Little Green Apples" left few remnants of the songs' original country-ness. Furthermore, when Eddy covered a song, he more frequently opted to sample pop songs such as "The Summer Wind," popularized by Frank Sinatra, Louis Armstrong's "What A Wonderful World," or the Bee Gees' "I Started A Joke."

When Eddy tried The Casinos' 1967 pop hit "Then You Can Tell Me Goodbye" in 1968, he found a song tailored to his deep baritone and Bill Walker's sophisticated arrangements. Eddy says he was inspired to cut the song after hearing John D. Loudermilk perform it. The low, lonely sound of

Eddy with Bill Walker. (University of Maryland collection)

Harold Bradley's electric guitar in concert with a whispering flute introduced the song and cleared a blue path for Eddy's yearning baritone.
Bradley's guitar was soon overpowered by twelve stringed instruments that,
as the song's drama soared, eventually gave way to the forceful pulsing of a
massive brass section. The brass, including four trombones and two trumpets, intensified as Eddy's hope that his girl will stay brightened. But, in the
end, she appears to be leaving and the soft strings return to ease Eddy's fall.

Eddy had struck the definitive version of the John D. Loudermilk–
penned classic, and somehow, in the absence of any hint of a country sound,
"Then You Can Tell Me Goodbye" spent two weeks at number one on the
country charts. The song peaked during October of '68 as unmistakably
country songs like Jeannie C. Riley's "Harper Valley P.T.A.," Conway
Twitty's "Next in Line," and Waylon Jennings's "Only Daddy That'll Walk
the Line" surrounded Eddy's refined style. His pendulum had swung decidedly to the pop side.

"We were having such huge success in the pop market . . . ," recalled Bill
Walker, who was largely responsible for the advent of Eddy's new sound. "I
might have gone too far to the right. I think I was pretty excited about how
accepted he was on the West Coast and in New York. He opened up a
whole new market for himself. I mean suddenly, instead of just selling to the

country market, he was selling all over the United States, in England, Australia, everywhere. I think I aimed my arranging at that, and I should have stayed a little more back. I think I went a bit too far with him."

"Chet gave me an absolutely free hand with arrangements," Walker continued. "He could have come in and said, 'Bill, that's not country enough.' He could have come in and said it, but he never did. The very first time I used a bunch of what I call secondary sevenths [a harmony style rarely—if ever—heard in traditional country music] Chet had a little bit of a worry about it. But then when he saw which direction we were going, he left it alone." As Walker indicated, Chet's eyes were wide open as Eddy's pop sound carried to new markets. Eddy's eyes were peeled too. In the warmth of his realized goals, Eddy couldn't have cared less to hear anything that resembled a twang. "When we'd go on tour," said Bill Walker, "I can't tell you how many people used to walk up and say, 'Why don't you have a steel guitar with the band?' Eddy wouldn't have one. I would have had one, but he wouldn't have it."

The strings hummed the melody of Eddy's success, and he loved them. "When I hear violins it gives me something!" Eddy rejoiced. "Sometimes I hear those violins, and they just thrill me. I love to be in the studio when you're singing and all those beautiful strings are wrapped around you. There's something sensational about that."

14

*C*ountry music had finally achieved the respectability and economic via- bility first suggested when the art form exploded commercially in the 1940s. Country songs frequently found favor among the pop audience, and stars like Hank Snow and Johnny Cash seemed equally at home abroad as in front of American audiences. Increasing favor across all audiences—inter- national and domestic, country and pop—bolstered country music's stature in the 1960s, as did Nashville's status in the industry as a recording center on par with New York and Los Angeles. A remarkable growth of full-time country music radio stations also signaled the regard and popularity the music had earned; the Country Music Association counted 127 new country radio stations that took to the air from 1961 to 1965.

As the clamor for more and more recorded music to fuel this boom reached uproarious levels, a proliferation of publishing companies, agents, writers, and aspiring performers invaded Nashville. The Nashville studios hummed night and day, seven days a week, producing a variety of country music sounds—from the status quo of the Nashville Sound to styles influ- enced by Hank Williams or rock and roll. The record companies unceasingly rained product on the market. "You'd make a bunch of records," explained Chet Atkins, "and just throw them out and see what stuck to the wall. If you got one started at just one little place, you could spread it all over the coun- try usually. That was the M.O. in those days."

Eddy Arnold's international success helped draw attention to the Nashville scene, and his name was a fixture in the country-music works. In that his records performed so well in the country market, he shared a great deal with other Nashville stars like George Jones and Webb Pierce; and he also shared with country singers Johnny Cash and Roger Miller the ability to appeal to pop audiences. The similarities with most country performers, though, ended there. Eddy Arnold's serious, sweetly arranged sound fac- tored him out of the pack.

With the success generated by "Make the World Go Away," "I Want to Go with You," and other triumphs, Eddy Arnold broke away from main- stream country music. Yes, strings were more plentiful than ever before on

191

country records, but rarely did producers or arrangers use them as extensively as Chet Atkins and Bill Walker did on Eddy's records. Although many have characterized the 1960s as the decade of the airy, urbane Nashville Sound, Buck Owens and many others performed and recorded in a more traditional vein through the '60s.

The subject matter of Eddy's songs also distinguished him from his hit-making country colleagues. His innocent expressions of hurt in the 1967 number one hits "Lonely Again" and "Turn the World Around" blushed next to other number one songs from that year: Loretta Lynn's "Don't Come Home A'Drinkin' (With Lovin' on Your Mind)" or Marty Robbins's "Tonight Carmen," for example. Merle Haggard's themes of desperation in "Branded Man" and "The Fugitive" also seemed more at home with the traditional, Jimmie Rodgers/Hank Williams–inspired ideals of country music than Eddy's 1967 outings.

Eddy was unique in the country genre, placing country hits with a decidedly un-country style. He seemed without compatriots in sound on the Nashville scene—an anomaly. But if Eddy looked hard enough, he could see traces of himself in the work of a few youngsters around him. Seeds he had sown almost twenty years before as the Tennessee Plowboy had grown up in the attitudes of many hit makers of the 1960s. Among them were George Hamilton IV, John D. Loudermilk, and Jim Ed Brown—not necessarily the absolute giants of country music in the 1960s, but palpable forces nonetheless.

In many respects, Hamilton, Loudermilk, and Brown are the "thinking man's" country musicians, men who on their respective journeys have thought to put their music in historical perspective. They have demanded that country music be regarded for its reflection, not parody, of American common people. In their youth, they admired Eddy Arnold's music for pure entertainment value, and, as they matured, came to respect Eddy's no-nonsense approach to his craft. George Hamilton IV, who sang rock and roll in the 1950s and as a country singer hit big in 1963 with "Abilene," first glimpsed Eddy's style at the Carolina Theater in Winston-Salem. "When I saw him in person I was very impressed with what a gentleman he was," said Hamilton, a son of a suburban businessman. "He had a lot of class and dignity, which I hadn't previously associated with country music. I loved the music, but a lot of the people wore flashy costumes and rhinestones and all that. The first time I saw Eddy, he had a Stetson hat on, but it was kind of on the back of his head and he was wearing sports clothes. . . . He seemed to avoid the rhinestones and glitter. It was a much more reserved stage presence—sort of a gentlemanly, dignified presence on stage. And that caught my attention."

That style drew a teenage Hamilton to Nashville, where he often traveled by bus to see his favorite "Grand Ole Opry" stars. In the early '50s, when young Hamilton made his journeys over the mountains to Nashville, Eddy was no longer an "Opry" star. But, at a coffee shop near the WSM studios,

Hamilton stumbled on Roy Wiggins and the Willis Brothers, who told him where to locate the onetime king of the Ryman Auditorium. It was Saturday morning, Wiggins told the boy, and he could probably find Eddy Arnold in his downtown Brentwood office. "Now looking back on it," said Hamilton, "I realize they were playing a practical joke on Eddy as well, sending a spook out there. But I got in a taxicab, and I went all the way to Brentwood."

The cab dropped Hamilton in front of the boxy, brick building where Eddy Arnold took care of business (and still sees to business today). Hamilton knocked on the glass door and, through the dimness of an office on a day off, saw a head pop into the hallway and peer at him. The head became a body that began walking toward the door. It was Eddy Arnold with a furrowed brow. Hamilton's hero opened the door.

"Yes?" Eddy asked. Hamilton heard music drifting from the back of the office.

"Mr. Arnold, I'm George Hamilton from North Carolina," the boy panted, "and you're one of my very favorites. I just think you're wonderful, and it's so good to meet you."

"Well . . . thank you," Eddy responded. "Come in, young man. Have a seat."

For a quarter of an hour, Eddy chatted with this young fan. He listened to Hamilton talk about his musical aspirations while the playing from the back room—which George had determined to be a man singing and strumming the guitar—continued. "Son," Eddy advised, "you just work hard at it and be yourself, and you got as good a chance as anybody. One of these days maybe I'll be sitting in the audience watching you sing."

George rose to leave with a signed photo of his hero. Eddy even called a cab for the boy. But there was one more thing: who was playing in the back? "That's Marty Robbins," Eddy told young George. "He's a neighbor of mine, and he's singing me a few new songs of his." The whole experience astonished Hamilton. Looking back on it, he wondered if he'd open his doors to a youngster so willingly and leave a Marty Robbins cooling his heels for fifteen or twenty minutes. But Eddy's lesson stuck with Hamilton. Fame is no excuse for ungraciousness.

The other lesson Hamilton, Brown, and Loudermilk took from Eddy was musical in nature. Country music could be performed seriously and with a progressiveness that could appeal across populations and geographical areas. "He managed to bring a lot of class and dignity to our music," said Hamilton, "and be a really good ambassador for country music in areas where it had often been . . . the object of derision and laughter. There's no way anybody could go to an Eddy Arnold concert and go 'yee-haw' or talk about straw in your ears and hicks and hillbillies because he just absolutely was the personification of all that was good about American folk music."

The music of George Hamilton IV and others who had looked to Eddy for inspiration ultimately proved distinct from Eddy Arnold's sound. But they copied his sobriety and straightforward approach to the music. They had seen that Eddy didn't need to be a rhinestone cowboy or take on any other guise to deliver his music, so they never wore cowboy hats or fashioned rebel mystiques to convey an image of something or somebody they were not. Such were Eddy Arnold's professional brothers in the 1960s.

— · —

As Eddy's style became more pop, his live appearances underscored the phenomenal resurgence he enjoyed in the 1960s. More than 15,000 fans jammed the Convention Hall in Asbury Park, New Jersey, for two Eddy Arnold shows in July 1967. With their Kodaks and Polaroids, giddy fans deluged the foot of the stage, snapping photos much to the distraction of Eddy, who was trying to perform his catalog of hits as well as a couple of Broadway show tunes: "As Long As She Needs Me" from *Oliver!* and the title song from *Hello, Dolly!* The flashing cameras blinded Eddy and his musicians one too many times, forcing Eddy to stop the show and allow the shutterbugs to shoot at will for a few minutes. He ordered the zealous fans back to their seats and resumed his routine for the charged fans who, one reviewer observed, "were thunderously cheering."

Increasingly, Eddy's live work brought him to the coasts, and he was as likely to be found in Asbury Park or Sacramento, California, as Atlanta or Memphis. He flew west for his Los Angeles nightclub debut in October 1967, performing in the Ambassador Hotel's storied Cocoanut Grove where stars like Andy Griffith, Carol Channing, and Omar Sharif waited in the audience. Bill Walker wanted to include so many orchestral instruments that an extension to the club's small stage had to be built, delaying rehearsals. "Eddy Arnold Wins Over 'Sophisticates'," the *Los Angeles Herald-Examiner* hailed in the wake of a performance that the paper said "emphasized a sweet blend of pop and country music." The applauding fans and reviews turned up in town after town, following him back across the nation to another appearance at Carnegie Hall in New York during March 1968, where RCA Records' vice president and general manager, Norman Racusin, honored him for sales in excess of 50 million platters. At this Carnegie Hall gig, Bill Walker's earlier fears of the orchestra overpowering Eddy surfaced. "Throughout the evening," *Billboard* pointed out, "his banter with the audience exuded a charm not evident in his comments to the orchestra, usually to play softer." But despite Eddy's dissatisfaction with his backing, the reviewer decided that "in one number after another, Arnold showed why he has sold more than 50 million records for RCA."

Eddy's performances, like his studio work, generally went off so well because he prepared. Eddy and Bill decided the repertoire for the tour, and Eddy, retreating to his private music room on the Brentwood farm, committed the song lineup and arrangements to memory. He seldom responded to hollered requests from the audience and less often strayed from the original

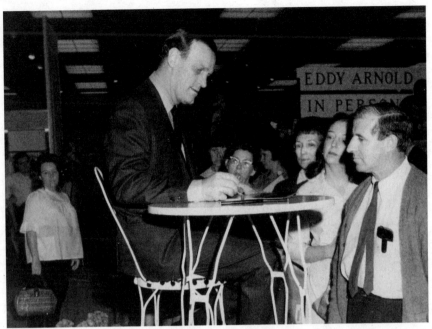

Lining up for autographs. (Gerard W. Purcell collection)

arrangements. Improvisation had no place in Eddy's tightly scripted, formulaic shows. With the songs and their order of performance in his head, he could concentrate on reaching the audience in front of him.

"There's a lot you have to learn as a performer. I mean a *performer*," said Eddy of his overtures to the audience. "I'm not just talking about a guy who sings and makes records. You have to learn how to perform. There's so many things you need to do and you *do not* need to do to get the attention of an audience and hold them. It's not easy to learn, and nobody can teach that to you. You got to learn it. You got to look at [the audience]. I've gone to see acts perform, both lady singers and male singers, and I watch them and they come out there and they can sing like a million dollars, but they can never look at the audience. You got to learn to look at the audience whether you can see them or not. Many times you can't see them. . . . I have people who come [backstage] all the time and say to me, 'You looked like you were just singing that song to me.' I say, 'I was.' That's what I want them to think.

"I used to come off the stage in my early days and I'd say to myself: 'What can I do to get to those people?' After a while it came to me, and I don't know how to explain it, only you got to look at them and you got to have your timing down, your rhythm of going from one song to another or from one subject to another—just like a man making a speech. . . . I had it all going pretty good when I did Carnegie Hall."

Eddy struck a bond with his audience. Many of the older fans felt like they had completed an odyssey with Eddy, from simplicity in the '40s to prosperity in the '60s. In step with Eddy as he journeyed to popular circles, they had realized their own versions of the American Dream. And for those who shared no historical connection with Eddy, he wooed them with his unwavering voice, aura of simplicity, and good-natured humor. Eddy often peppered his shows with jokes, some risqué, that lit an auditorium with laughter as he bit his lip to restrain his own guffaws. "He'd have those people right in the palm of his hand," said drummer Jerry Carrigan. "It was unbelievable. He had that charm."

Eddy's shows also benefited from his involvement in every development leading to showtime. In addition to warming up his voice by running the scale, he stood alongside Bill Walker as he rehearsed the orchestra and as the theater's "techies" assembled and adjusted the lighting and sound. Such technical aspects of staging a show were familiar to Eddy, and he knew their value in pulling off a good performance. In the late '60s, Speedy McNatt took his son to an Eddy Arnold rehearsal in Memphis (where Speedy worked for a trucking company) and told the boy, an aspiring musician, to watch closely as Eddy interacted with the sound and lighting crew. Eddy walked to the edge of the stage, turned, and assessed the setup, complimenting the work he saw and endearing himself to the workers with his praise. Commending the guys in front of their peers opened the door for Eddy to change certain microphone placements or lighting configurations he disliked. While other performers might criticize, Eddy used a heap of diplomacy to get his way.

Such were the ingredients of a stellar Eddy Arnold show. He perfected his act and, to preserve his good standing in America's eyes, worked harder in the late '60s than at any point since the early '50s. Jerry escorted him out on the road for a series of thirty-city tours, and he logged thousands of miles in the air, flying to Hollywood for TV dates.

On one of these hops to Hollywood, Eddy had a hero experience similar to the excitement of coming upon Gene Autry on the train to New York twenty years previously. This time, Bing Crosby caught Eddy's eye. Eddy and Bill Walker had spent the night in San Francisco on their way to Los Angeles, Eddy recalled, but in the morning couldn't fly out of the fog-enveloped city. "So they were using a small airport back inland a little bit," continued Eddy. "They bussed us there and a United Airlines [jet] came in. . . . I saw a limo sitting out waiting, and I saw people getting off the plane. They were lined up walking, and I saw Bing get off the plane. He'd been to Los Angeles, and he was getting off because he lived in San Francisco at the time. He got right by me, and I just whispered, 'Bing.' He said, 'Yeah.' I said, 'I'm Eddy Arnold.' He said, 'Why hello, boy, how are you?' He shook hands with me. He was in line," Eddy sighed. "He had to keep moving."

Television was voracious in its appetite for Eddy. "I was on television enough that I became known nationally. I wasn't just a little boy down

Not exactly a Rat Pack kind of guy, Eddy does TV with Dean Martin and Frank Sinatra. (Eddy Arnold collection)

South. I did [Red] Skelton's show, a special with Danny Kaye, a special with Danny Thomas, [the] 'Ed Sullivan Show.' I did a lot of guest appearances." One evening for NBC, Eddy stepped in for Johnny Carson and hosted "The Tonight Show," interviewing guests Ginger Rogers and Henny Youngman.

On February 9, 1968, just days after America watched Viet Cong forces launch the punishing Tet Offensive against U.S. and South Vietnamese troops, an old reliable face—Eddy Arnold's—hosted his first prime-time network show since the early '60s. Actually an NBC documentary, "American Profile: Music from the Land" examined country music from its commercial Nashville manifestation on down to its still-thriving roots in the hills of Virginia. Among a corps of others, Buck Owens, Earl Scruggs, Marty Robbins, and John D. Loudermilk appeared with Eddy. Eddy's recording of "Then You Can Tell Me Goodbye" had its genesis on the program after Eddy heard Loudermilk perform it, but equally significant was the NBC brass's enthralled reaction to Eddy's television appearance.

The network invited him to return to their airwaves as host of the "Kraft Music Hall," a summer series of variety shows that for many years had spotlighted various entertainers. As Jerry Purcell recalled, the show's producers originally asked Eddy to make a guest appearance during a segment on country music that they had asked Dinah Shore to host; Eddy agreed to be a guest in exchange for the opportunity to host the program himself. Under an arrangement with NBC, Eddy starred in six shows starting on April 24, 1968, and Johnny Carson's sidekick, Ed McMahon, picked up the reins from June 12 through the summer. "Eddy Arnold was the program's tower of dignity," wrote a *San Francisco Examiner* critic of his work at the helm of the show. "He has in his voice the resonance common to 'Kraft Music Hall' back in the radio days when we called it 'KMH' and the continuing star was Bing [Crosby]." Periodically, the "Kraft Music Hall" featured Eddy into 1969 and on through the early 1970s.

With his semi-regular television appearances on NBC, Eddy fulfilled the hope for television glory that began in the 1950s with the syndicated "Eddy Arnold Time" show. With the passing of the years, a bundle of pop hits, and a dedicated manager, Eddy finally achieved a high profile on television. The medium had eluded him since the late '40s while he succeeded fabulously in radio and records. But by the late '60s, Eddy had joined television's establishment, fraternizing on screen with Dean Martin, Frank Sinatra, Carol Channing, Jackie Gleason, and others who appeared on the ever-popular variety show circuit. This wide television exposure completed Eddy's full-court press on the American home. He had their ears *and* eyes.

—— • ——

As Eddy anticipated his first "Kraft Music Hall" special, a jolt of tragic news jarred him. A heart attack took the life of his friend and mentor Steve Sholes on Monday, April 22 as he drove from Nashville's Metropolitan airport to a meeting of the Country Music Foundation. The attack struck Sholes on the Silliman Evans Memorial Bridge, and he lost control of his rental car. The car slammed into guard-rails on both sides of the bridge and traveled the entire length of the bridge before stopping. Miraculously, no other drivers on the bridge were hurt, but Steve Sholes was dead at the age of fifty-seven. "It was so sudden," recalled one of Sholes's staffers. "Steve was such a legend and a very different kind of man in that position. In that position . . . you thought of very aggressive types, very often cigar-chomping. . . . Steve was very gentle."

Sholes's sudden demise stunned Eddy. Only a few months before he had hosted an industry tribute to Steve in New York, and now Steve was dead. To Eddy, Sholes represented RCA. Sholes was the only constant for him there since just after World War II, and, although Chet now produced Eddy, Steve was Eddy's man at RCA. After the unfriendly Bob Yorke's departure in October 1963, Steve had returned from the West Coast to become vice president of pop A&R. Once again Chet reported to Steve, and with Steve entrenched in New York, Eddy felt as if there was someone in the corporate offices he could trust. In many ways, Eddy thought of himself as aligned with Steve, not RCA: "He was the greatest thing that happened to me, Steve was. Because he liked me."

Chet Atkins, too, shared a special bond with Sholes and claimed he only ran RCA's Nashville operation out of deference to him. "I started quitting when he died," Atkins said. "I worked for him. I didn't work for RCA. They paid me, but I really worked for Steve and tried to please him."

Toward the end of Steve's life, corporate intrigue nibbled away at his influence. Although beloved by many at RCA and across the industry, RCA's higher brass contained his influence in the company. Sholes radiated a jovial demeanor, but he suffered some behind closed doors. After bringing Elvis to RCA, Steve expected to rise above the pop A&R department, but RCA dampened these hopes by shipping him out to the West Coast in 1962 and hiring Eddy's detractor Bob Yorke to supervise him. When he returned to the East Coast after Yorke's departure, RCA's pop division was hemorrhaging at an alarming rate. Chet's country operations and Elvis Presley's sales plugged the dike, but the rest of the division seemed vulnerable. "The '60s really were hard times," said Chick Crumpacker, who worked then in RCA's special products area. "We had Elvis, and whoever was in second place was so far down that it was almost unrecognizable. Capitol came in with the Beatles. That was another body blow." Sholes labored as he always had for his beloved RCA, but by 1966, RCA restructured and placed him under a vice president unfriendly to him in the record division. At the time of his death, Sholes's influence had waned, but he maintained enough clout to shepherd Eddy's interests in RCA. With his death, though, Eddy lost an advocate, and promotion and sales of his records probably suffered as a result.

Coolness also prevailed on the RCA Nashville front as Jerry Purcell voiced dissatisfaction with Chet Atkins's treatment of Eddy. In late 1968, Eddy's record sales, though still healthy, faltered a bit. Jerry cast partial blame for the lag on Chet Atkins, charging that Eddy's longtime producer failed to find the best songs for Eddy and give Eddy adequate overall attention. Jerry demanded that he and Eddy, not Chet, assume a greater responsibility for picking Eddy's songs. Indeed, Eddy already had a significant role in picking songs, but he chose from material provided by Chet and his A&R staff. Jerry Purcell wanted Eddy and himself to completely control the song-selection process. "I wanted to voice my opinion," said Jerry Purcell, "and Eddy, being very kind, very affable, and having a lot of respect for people, [sometimes didn't speak up]. I was more pragmatic. . . . If I liked a song, I liked it. Eddy . . . he put his trust in people that he worked with [at RCA]. Now, that's a good quality. It's a very good quality, one I admire. But picking hit songs is a very tough job, and you got to be very pragmatic. If you don't like it, you got to say you don't like it, and if you like it, you got to fight."

In response to Jerry's demand, Chet stated, in effect, that as long as RCA Nashville recorded the artists, RCA Nashville picked the songs. But Jerry was not to be ignored as long as Eddy sold records. As Eddy's career rebounded in the mid-1960s, Jerry's name, already a force in New York and Los Angeles circles, caught fire in the country industry. In 1965, his Gerard W. Purcell Associates opened operations in Nashville, and soon promoted

Jerry Purcell. (Gerard W. Purcell collection)

as many as 150 concerts a year featuring the city's top talent, including Johnny Cash, Dottie West, Skeeter Davis, Roger Miller, Connie Smith, and Sonny James. By 1968, in the heat of his tussle with Chet Atkins, Jerry formed GWP Productions, which contracted with RCA to take over production responsibilities for his client Al Hirt, as well as his own label, GWP Records. Jerry also teamed with former RCA Records executive Andy Wiswell to independently produce Broadway original cast albums and sell the results to large record companies. Evolving from a promoter-manager-publisher, Jerry fast became a music-industry mogul.

Jerry and Chet's mutual distrust stemmed from Jerry's demand that Eddy record 1964's *Pop Hits from the Country Side* album in New York and flare-ups over the control of Al Hirt's recording sessions in the mid-'60s. For Eddy's part, he seemed more frustrated with what he sensed was the refusal of RCA's marketing department to promote his records, not the kind of songs Chet gave him. However, Chet admitted that his decision to pass on "Rain Drops Keep Falling on My Head" angered Eddy (it eventually became a major pop hit for B. J. Thomas in 1969). "I think Eddy held that against me for a while," said Chet, "but, you know, I didn't think Eddy could sing the song. . . . I just didn't think it fit Eddy. But everybody in town turned it down."

Eddy, though, still pointed to promotion as RCA's weakness. "I wanted the company to help me a little bit. Chet can't get out on the street and merchandise the record. He can just make the record. . . . As I look back on it, I think it was just sort of a time that I had to be reborn," said Eddy. "Chet . . . he produced good records with me."

Ultimately, Chet never conceded the control of song selection, but at the end of the '60s, he began assigning Eddy to other producers. "Now . . . *that* I didn't like," declared Eddy. "Chet started farming me out 'cause the poor guy got so dad-gummed busy. . . . I'd been lucky with him, and I didn't care about going with other producers." Chet first enlisted another producer to assist him when Eddy cut *The Warmth of Eddy* album in July 1969. Danny Davis, who at MGM Records had produced hits with Connie Francis, Johnny Tillotson, and Herman's Hermits (and in earlier days led a New York band frequently booked by Jerry Purcell), came to Nashville as executive producer to lighten Chet's load.

By this time, Eddy also parted with another studio partner, arranger Bill Walker, who had moved on to the next step in his American experience as musical producer on Johnny Cash's popular network variety show. He was replaced in Eddy's camp by arranger and conductor Cam Mullins. Years later, Walker reteamed with Eddy for occasional concert and studio work.

The needle that finally burst Eddy's 1960s chart bubble was the Chet Atkins and Danny Davis–produced *The Warmth of Eddy*. The album lacked originality (at least half the songs were covers of others' hits) and missed the crackle of Bill Walker's dramatic arrangements that seemed to inspire Eddy. Eddy himself sounded sluggish and only managed to place one song from the album on the country charts, "You Fool," which staggered to number sixty-nine. It was Eddy's worst showing on the country charts in twenty-five years of recording, but of greater concern was the flimsy hit's failure to make the pop charts. Only one Eddy Arnold country charter—1966's "The First Word"—had failed to cross over since "What's He Doin' In My World" broke loose in 1965.

Country music's indulgence of Eddy's "symphonic pop" appeared to have waned, and the pop arena finally decided that little room existed for Eddy's brand of singing (Eddy's recordings have yet to reappear among the top 100 songs on the pop singles charts). *The Warmth of Eddy* drew the line that demarcated Eddy's fall from 1960s preeminence. His last country hit of the 1960s, "Since December," managed only a seventy-three showing before disappearing after two weeks.

The reason for Eddy's chart slide in 1969 is elusive; in fact, no single culprit hampered Eddy. Certainly, changes at RCA affected Eddy's status on the charts, but shifting tastes and times can probably take most of the responsibility. Ferment in musical tastes victimized many veteran pop singers, including Frank Sinatra. In 1967, Sinatra—with daughter Nancy—spent four weeks at number one with "Somethin' Stupid," but, by 1969, an "Ole Blue Eyes" number one hit was unthinkable. The assassinations of

prominent political leaders, campus unrest, questions about U.S. involvement in the Vietnam War, increasing drug use, and other factors rendered
Eddy Arnold and other older singers irrelevant among teenagers, who every
year made up a larger share of America's record buyers. In a pop music
world of social messages and psychedelia, songs like "You Fool" seemed
anachronistic.

Few artists in Nashville had stepped forward as boldly as Eddy with a
sound that so liberally incorporated symphonic instruments and so willingly
rejected traditional country stylings. But by 1969 Eddy could no longer
record in such a middle-of-the-road vein and expect to have country chart
success. The big songs of the day rose from a new generation of singers
(including Tammy Wynette, Conway Twitty, and Charley Pride) and made
only sparse use of symphonic instruments.

At the initial signs of erosion in the country market and rejection in the
pop market, Eddy acted. In the days after Christmas, 1969 and into the new
year, the elite of Nashville's guitar corps joined Eddy in the studio to assemble the album *Love and Guitars*. Chet, who rarely played on Eddy's sessions
anymore, led a pack of guitars that also included Jerry Reed Hubbard, Ray
Edenton, and Harold Bradley. The guitars gently lifted Eddy's baritone
through a heavy dose of contemporary Nashville songs like the Merle
Haggard and Bonnie Owens–penned "Today I Started Loving You Again,"
Jeannie Seely's "Just Enough to Start Me Dreamin'," and Johnny Darrell's
"With Pen in Hand."

"Soul Deep," a swinging acoustic tribute to a woman, debuted on the
country charts in February of 1968 and bubbled up to twenty-two—a vast
improvement over his last two efforts. A follow-up single not included on
the album—"A Man's Kind of Woman" and its flip side "Living Under
Pressure"—wandered to twenty-eight. Both songs spent almost three
months on the charts with a sound that abandoned the lush arrangements
for a skeletal instrumental structure. The listener still could look forward to
Eddy's easy-going style, but with an acoustic accompaniment more in step
with the times. The *Love and Guitars* album could not be considered completely country, but it was certainly closer than Eddy's collaborations with
Bill Walker's arrangements. Eddy had compromised for the country market
and received a mildly enthusiastic response, and although there was little
chance now of making much of a splash in the pop market, *Love and Guitars*
did stick its toe into *Billboard*'s top 200 pop albums chart for three weeks.

This new, contemporary path led Eddy to one of his finest album performances ever: a collaboration with independent producer Lee Hazlewood.
Hazlewood helped Nancy Sinatra's boots walk up the charts many times,
and he had a reputation as a young, hip producer. In a Hollywood studio,
Hazlewood paired Eddy with a batch of equally hip, folk-rock songs, particularly a few penned by southern California folk singer John Stewart. On the
resulting LP, *Standing Alone*, Eddy's versions of Stewart's "July, You're A
Woman Now," "She Believes in Me," and "Some Lonely Picker" departed

from Eddy's standard themes of simple love and yearning and grappled with self-doubt and haunting old lovers. In the Eddy Arnold tradition, the songs told a story, but these stories were not so obvious. Eons away from "Bouquet of Roses" or even "Make the World Go Away," the compositions grew from the secret experiences of their writer and were open to any number of interpretations. Who was the *"Gypsy girl named Shannon, a daughter of the devil,"* and why does Eddy sing, *"Julie get the gun. Julie throw it in the river. Let it roll far on out to sea"*? Mystery shrouded the songs. They engaged the mind and presented puzzles to be solved, the solutions to be applied to the listener's life. Eddy Arnold was recording message songs in every sense of the term's late '60s and early '70s meaning.

Optimism also sprang from *Standing Alone.* Eddy's interpretation of Roger Whitaker's "New World in the Morning" energized the album, and John Stewart's "She Believes in Me" opened Eddy's 1970s with the glory of dawn: *"She believes that ships come home singing from the sea."*

RCA marketed Eddy's first session outside Nashville in six years to the album market only, and as with much great art, the public allowed *Standing Alone* to do just that—stand alone (the album made a brief appearance on the country LP charts). But the album proved Eddy's ability to adapt to the 1970s and mirrored the maturity of a new breed of country music found in the work of artists like Glen Campbell and Kris Kristofferson—despite the collective yawn from America.

*   *   *

Campbell and Kristofferson had little reason to fear competition from Eddy Arnold, but in the singles market Eddy continued to score moderate hits. Much was changing in Eddy's recording world. In the studio, he rarely recorded with his beloved string ensembles. Instead, producers added any strings and other sweetening in separate sessions. Eddy preferred the live setting, but the industry—as Eddy learned—stood still for no one. Chet Atkins supervised Eddy in the studio one final time in June of 1970 (producing the moderately successful single, "From Heaven to Heartache"), but by October of that year longtime RCA engineer Jim Malloy took over producing chores for Eddy.

Malloy had left RCA in the late '60s to begin producing and found the new role suited him, capturing the Country Music Association's 1970 "Producer of the Year" award for his work on Sammi Smith's "Help Me Make It through the Night." Eddy assumed Malloy's relatively younger view would keep him musically plugged into the times. "He's got a good ear," Eddy told a radio interviewer in early 1971. "He listens well. He's sort of tuned in to what is happening today. That's important."

Under Malloy's guidance, the folk-rock feel fell by the wayside for a return to a more string-based sound arranged by Cam Mullins. The themes remained mature (but not elderly—Eddy was sensitive about the age he

Two RCA guys in camel hair. Chet Atkins hands Eddy RCA's Golden Boot Award. (Don Mackin collection)

On the "Kraft Music Hall" with Loretta Lynn. (Don Mackin collection)

projected on record). The songs, however, were not as hip as the Hazlewood partnership. On his first LP with Jim Malloy, *Portrait of My Woman*, Eddy echoed the thoughts and concerns of a middle-aged man: the faithfulness of a longtime wife, death, and divorce. On the following single release, Eddy took a turn toward topical material, addressing middle America's growing concern with crime, an issue brought to the fore by President Richard M. Nixon's rhetoric. "A Part of America Died" and "Call Me" were penned by Harry Koch—a policeman—and lashed out at the overemphasis on criminals' rights and a citizenry unappreciative of police and increasingly tolerant of drug use. On "A Part of America Died," Eddy condemns a policeman's murder while a disembodied chorus singing "The Old Rugged Cross" hovers behind him. "I think it's timely," Eddy said then. "I think it's something that should be said now."

> *Somebody killed a policeman today*
> *And a part of America died.*
> *A piece of our country he swore to protect*
> *Will be buried with him at his side.*
>
> *The suspect who shot him will stand up in court,*
> *With counsel demanding his rights*
> *While a young widowed mother must work for her kids*
> *And spend many long, lonely nights.*
>
> *The beat that he walked was a battlefield, too*
> *Just as if he'd gone off to war.*
> *Though the flag of our nation won't fly at half mast*
> *To his name, they will add a gold star.*
>
> *Somebody killed a policeman today.*
> *Maybe in your town or mine.*
> *While we slept in comfort behind our locked doors,*
> *A cop put his life on the line.*
>
> *Now his ghost walks the beat*
> *On a dark, city street*
> *And he stands at each new rookie's side.*
> *He answered the call. Of himself, gave his all*
> *And a part of America died.* *

Like the *Standing Alone* material, "A Part of America Died" deviated from Eddy's normal fare—rarely had Eddy (a Nixon stalwart and friend of George C. Wallace) aired his political inclinations on record. Optimistic that his appeal to the "silent majority" would sell, he called RCA representatives around the country to check its progress. Don DeLacy, a left-leaning promoter based in Boston, got one such call about "A Part of America Died." "[The song was] not anti–civil rights," recalled DeLacy, "but certainly on the side of government, on the side of police, law and order . . . that side of it. I was quite liberal and had been arrested several times for civil disobedience. [Eddy] called me as a promotion person to ask me what I thought of the record. He didn't know my political position, and I had an awful lot of difficulty dancing around so that I didn't get fired for saying the wrong thing. I guess the one thing that was important for me not to say was that I liked the record." Liberal New Englanders, DeLacy told Eddy, couldn't be counted on to impel the song. Ultimately, "A Part of America Died" reached the *Billboard* country chart's top-fifty, evidently without the help of the Northeast.

—. —

Eddy's work with Jim Malloy, both political and nonpolitical, sold well considering that Eddy was a fifty-three-year-old surrounded by youngsters. When Eddy tracked his sales and chart performance, he could be proud of his resilience after almost thirty years of recording. None of his competitors from the 1940s—Ernest Tubb, Jimmy Wakely, or George Morgan, for example—and few from the 1950s sold and charted as well as Eddy. Eddy's willingness to explore new directions and his foresight in light of changing trends preserved his viability.

15

$\mathcal{A}$s Eddy's career cooled, he and his family enjoyed a comfortable material life derived from his mountain-high success in the recording industry and vast dividends from profitable business investments (there were unprofitable investments, too—like a failed fried-chicken shop). A self-made man if ever one existed, Eddy had pursued musical and business opportunities throughout his years, parlaying those winnings into financial reward and an enviable reputation in the music business.

Eddy maintained a rigorous work schedule, but more frequently found time to enjoy what the world had given him, especially his fourty-two-foot cabin cruiser, the "Sally K," which he stored on Old Hickory Lake outside Nashville. Eddy, as he told an interviewer in 1971, also found time to ponder the spiritual aspect of his life: "I'm not a religious fanatic. I believe in God. I believe there's a supreme being. I read the Bible. I've gotten to where I read it much more than I did several years ago. Many times I read it from an informational standpoint. I want to know. . . . I'm much more inquisitive now than I used to be about life, about the Almighty. I'm sorry for the man who doesn't feel the presence of the Almighty."

Eddy's two children, Jo Ann and Dickey, had left the roost, and he spent more time on his marriage, which could use some attention after years of Eddy's absences. He still hit the road, though, headlining at Las Vegas's International Hotel in 1970—his first appearance in the Nevada city since 1953—and debuting at the Waldorf Astoria's Empire Room in New York City. Every three months on the average throughout 1970 and 1971 he placed a song on the charts, although few were big hits. Physically, Eddy had the energy to tackle the 1970s, his fourth decade in the business.

Eddy looked ahead down a straight, level, unobstructed road, but when he glanced away the road buckled. In the late summer of 1971, Eddy's world, and every assumption in it, shattered.

— • —

Dickey Arnold graduated from the University of Alabama in the spring of 1971. On Sunday afternoon, August 1, 1971, he headed off from Nashville to

Tuscaloosa, Alabama, with his friend and college roommate, Larry Mathis, to pick up some clothing Mathis had left at school. As the two cruised down U.S. Route 11 into Bessemer, Alabama, a car driven by thirty-six-year-old Willie Terrell darted out from a side road and slammed Dickey's sports car on the side where Dickey was seated. The impact sent Dickey through the windshield, jamming some food he had been eating down his throat.

Paramedics arrived at a terrible scene. A passenger in Terrell's car, Laura Lewis, was dead, and Dickey was not far from sharing her fate (Mathis sustained relatively minor injuries). The rescuers loaded Dickey on board and dashed for the nearest hospital. The paramedics dug the food from Dickey's throat, but as they hurriedly surveyed the damage to his body, they realized the nearest hospital would be useless. Dickey had suffered serious head injuries, so they drove on a little farther to the better-equipped Lloyd Nolan Hospital in the suburbs of Birmingham. Dickey was dead on arrival at the hospital, but the staff revived him. His hold on life was the width of a hair, and he was likely to expire at any second.

Meanwhile, back in Nashville, Eddy and Sally relaxed away the Sunday afternoon on their boat out on Old Hickory Lake. The hospital got through to Jo Ann and told her that the family should get to Birmingham: Dickey was slipping away. Jo Ann called her parents on the cabin cruiser, and Eddy and Sally sprinted to their car and sped back to Brentwood. Eddy, Sally, and Jo Ann converged on the farm and caught a plane waiting to rush them to Birmingham. Steve Sholes had expired in a car, and, in 1969, former governor Frank Clement—Eddy's good friend—had died in a wreck. Now an automobile accident seemed likely to take his son, too.

The trip to Birmingham seemed interminable, but, thankfully, Dickey's heart was still pumping when the Arnolds reached the hospital. A couple of times that evening, he had drifted into death only to emerge seconds later with the frantic help of the hospital's medical team. On Monday, one day after the accident, a hospital spokesman told the press that "patient Arnold is unconscious in the intensive care unit. The next forty-eight hours will be critical. . . . It is now up to the Lord." The car crash had inflicted serious brain damage on Dickey, and eventually he fell into a coma, which would last in varying degrees of severity for more than nine weeks. "It almost destroyed us," said Eddy.

Chet Atkins and Jim Malloy drove down to Birmingham a few days later, and as Malloy recalled, Dickey's situation seemed hopeless: "We walked in that hospital room, and I never saw so many tubes coming out of one person in my life. I had never seen a sight like this before. There were bags and tubes . . . hanging everywhere." Although doctors initially gave Dickey a less than one in ten chance of coming out of the coma, the hospital allowed Sally to move into a room across from the intensive care unit so she could spend time with Dickey whenever the doctors and nurses vacated the room.

While Eddy commuted back and forth between Nashville and Birmingham, Sally tried to get through to her comatose son, carrying on a monologue about Dickey's school, friends, family, and his father's records. "The doctors think perhaps he got to where, when he was coming to, he would follow my voice around," recollected Sally. "You could see his eyes moving. The eyes weren't open, but you could see him following my voice around." Dickey improved to a semi-comatose state, and when his vital signs stabilized seven and a half weeks after the wreck, doctors okayed his transfer from Birmingham to St. Thomas Hospital in Nashville. In the ambulance to Nashville, as Sally fed him, Dickey showed further signs of recovery when Sally asked him to pick up a napkin and wipe his mouth. "He reached down and got his napkin and wiped his mouth. His eyes were still closed," said Sally. "That was the first time I directed him to do a certain thing." After two weeks in Nashville, Dickey awoke.

—▪—

Eddy sharply cut his schedule to remain close to Dickey, but there were a few obligations that Eddy felt he had to fulfill. One job, about a month after Dickey's accident, took Eddy to the Mill Run Theater, near Chicago, where he donned his entertaining boots and revealed few signs of his son's tenuous condition. "Like a self-effacing country minister who came to dinner and got a wee bit tipsy on . . . brandy," wrote the *Chicago Daily News,* "Arnold turned up the resonators of human love to stereo fidelity and sang romantic, comic and neo-sacred songs of great variety." But Eddy's thoughts, hidden to the reviewer, remained with his son. "When he went on that stage he was Eddy Arnold, and he done a good show," said Gabe Tucker, who had returned to Eddy yet again, this time as a promotion director. "It was hard for him to do."

When Dickey finally regained consciousness, he came home to Brentwood and an immense rehabilitation effort ensued. At first, Dickey couldn't remember ever having attended the University of Alabama, but slowly his memory returned until he could wearily piece together the events leading up to the crash. As he realized the extent of his injuries, his temper flared, but Sally and Eddy soothed him as best as they could. Dickey's speech was restricted, and he had also lost feeling and movement in various parts of his body, making physical therapy another challenge. Some experts had urged Eddy and Sally to send Dickey far afield for rehabilitation, to which Sally remembered replying, "No way. That little thing will lie there and have one hour of rehab, and he'll have twenty-three hours with no one around. We'll rehab him right here." The Arnolds rented rehabilitation equipment and put Dickey downstairs in their recreation room, where he could exit the house through a sliding glass door without dealing with steps.

A team of therapists descended on the Arnold's Brentwood home and helped Dickey regain his speech and his ability to walk and write. The process was arduous, requiring a great deal of Sally and Eddy's time and strength, so Eddy refused most bookings and stayed close to Brentwood.

Eddy helped Dickey walk and carried him when he needed to be carried, responsibilities that most fathers have when their child is small. But when Dickey was small Eddy missed many of Dickey's early developments. "I guess I was just trying to be a father," Eddy said of that time in his life. "My wife worked very hard, and I tried to be as much help to her as I could." Eddy walked Dickey around the house, and, on the advice of therapists, bought his son a dog, a bull mastiff that, to Eddy's amusement, often tripped Dickey with its leash and chewed the fallen young man's shoes.

Eddy also found a trough to bathe his son, and every morning Eddy lugged the long tub in through the sliding glass door. "I dragged that thing in there right by his bed," said Eddy, "and I got me a water hose. I had it rigged up where I could put [the hose] on the faucet, and I filled [the trough] with hot water. I put pillows in the bottom of it, and then I'd pick him up, and I'd put him in it. And I'd keep running the hot water. We were told, and it sounded logical to us, that maybe the heat and the water would bring the feeling back in his arm. I did that every day, and then I'd give him a good rubdown with cream. We became pretty good nurses."

Eddy resolved not to miss any aspect of Dickey's recovery, and, in many ways, life changed for Eddy Arnold. Family responsibilities beckoned, and for a time, Eddy became a father first and a performer second. Eddy tied his happiness less and less to hit records and more often to Dickey's gradual improvements. "I had a booking [in] Lake Tahoe," Eddy recalled. "I was booked in a hotel out there, and I got a call from home, from my wife and [Dickey]. He had just said a word. She woke me up. I was already sleeping out there, and she put me on the phone with him. He was able to say 'Daddy,' and that was the most beautiful sound—the prettiest sound—I had heard in a long time."

Dickey progressed amazingly well in light of the crushing accident. His perseverance, reinforced by Sally and Eddy's sweat, carried him back to relative normalcy. In time, after hurdling psychological barriers, Dickey slid behind the steering wheel of a car again, went to work, and moved out on his own. Initially, Dickey hesitated to leave the Brentwood farm, but after a year he summoned the will to accompany his dad to a week long concert engagement in Detroit. "That was wonderful," Eddy told a reporter at the time. "He's gaining confidence in himself. Oh, he still falls occasionally, but the trouble keeping his equilibrium reduces itself with each passing day."

As for Eddy, his career changed forever. Although he remained in the public eye, his TV appearances and visits to the recording studio slackened. Eddy seemed to be decreasing his activity, anyway, before 1971; Dickey's bad luck forced an even slower pace. He scaled back his touring and played smaller venues. Instead of 7,500-seat arenas, he filled 3,000-seat showrooms, and in place of Carnegie Hall, he seemed more at home in theaters and per-

The mature performer. (Gerard W. Purcell collection)

forming arts centers. But whatever the size of the audience, he still garnered mostly upbeat reviews. "Deceptively simple, melodic and soothing, his program is low-keyed polish," reported the *New York Times* in 1974 after yet another Manhattan performance.

Eddy's slower pace reflected a workload commensurate with the stride of a man approaching his late fifties, but he wasn't ready to lay down the plow for good. Eddy enjoyed a viable career in the 1970s. Record sales and concert revenues remained respectably constant, although Jerry and Eddy remained dissatisfied with RCA. In June 1972, Eddy left his longtime home and moved to MGM. "We didn't have another Steve Sholes around," explained Jerry Purcell, who still found RCA's attention to Eddy lacking.

More than thirty years before, Frank Walker (Eddy's first contact at RCA) had asked Eddy to join him after he hopped to MGM, but Eddy was reluctant to spoil his good relationship with Steve Sholes and company. But 1973 was not 1946, and MGM (owned by Phonogram International of Holland) offered a bright new talent, president and producer Mike Curb, as an exciting lure to Eddy. Curb had previously led the popular group the Mike Curb Congregation, that had enjoyed soft-pop hits on its own, as well as backing other artists, including Sammy Davis, Jr. on his best-seller, "The Candy Man." His bubblegum work with the Osmonds had also paid nice dividends for the label. With industry veteran Don Costa and other producers, Curb helped Eddy fire off eight country hits from 1973 to 1975. On his first album for MGM, Eddy mostly covered old 1950s rock and roll ballads, and found a hit with a version of Brook "Rainy Night in Georgia" Benton's "So Many Ways." In deference, it seems, to Dickey, Eddy also tried "My Son, I Wish You Everything."

Despite this success, Eddy's MGM recordings—created alternately in Los Angeles and Nashville—rang remarkably shallow. MGM's instrumentation efforts sounded tinny, lacking the fullness and soul of the Nashville Sound, and furthermore, Eddy's voice occasionally strayed off key on the recordings. Eddy's three MGM albums of new material, in their recording and packaging, seemed pasted together and allowed to go to market without proper care. By 1975, Eddy's cover of Vic Dana's pop hit "Red Roses for A Blue Lady" briefly reached the sixtieth spot on the country charts, and his last MGM outing, "Middle of A Memory," perished at number eighty-six.

When Mike Curb left MGM in 1974, Eddy soon followed him. "It wasn't the same without him there. . . . I asked out of my contract. I told Purcell, 'Get me out. . . . Mike's gone. It's not the same. I'd rather not be under contract to anyone.'" Curb formed his own label, and Eddy returned to open arms at RCA, where Jerry Bradley—Owen Bradley's son—had replaced Chet as head of the company's Nashville operations.

Eddy found a new world at RCA. The studio system of record making was fading, and labels more often turned their artists over to freelance, independent producers. Rarely now did record company producers, like Chet Atkins or Decca's Owen Bradley, preside over a community of artists, choose their songs, and give them a sound. Independent producers, many of whom owned studios, flooded the recording industry, and happily took a lump sum from a record company in return for an album. The record company benefited by avoiding the expenses associated with full-time employees. Another problem that concerned recording executives was the increasing use of alcohol and drugs among country's stars that could possibly lead to scandals. "Big companies couldn't afford to have a whole lot of wild things going on in their studio," recalled master producer Owen Bradley, who had retired from Decca in the mid-1970s and pursued independent production. "The [stars] . . . if they got stoned that was their problem. . . . The company didn't get in trouble."

On his first outing with RCA since 1972, Eddy was teamed with Owen Bradley. Almost thirty years had elapsed since Bradley and Arnold worked in the studio together, but they obviously still knew how to work well with each other. "He knew how to get a sound," said Eddy of Owen. Eddy and Owen made sure their first collaboration since "Bouquet of Roses" would be memorable; they slammed a home run at their first at bat with the single "Cowboy." The song lassoed the thirteenth position on the country charts in the summer of 1976 and remained on the charts for more than three months. Eddy had his biggest hit since the tail end of his salad days in 1969. "We almost had a [pop hit]," said Eddy. "It almost got going." Appropriate for America's bicentennial, "Cowboy" captured a young boy's dream of the West. Eddy also reminded fans that his voice could still deliver a knockout punch even as he approached the age of sixty. He glided through the song's refrain with an unveiled falsetto previously reserved for "The Cattle Call."

On television with Lynn "I Never Promised You a Rose Garden" Anderson. (Gerard W. Purcell collection)

Owen returned for Eddy's next album, *I Need You All the Time,* and throughout the 1970s and 1980s a series of respected independent producers—in addition to Bradley—helped Eddy achieve a string of moderate country hits. Charles Grean returned in 1978 to help Eddy on the hit "I'm the South," and Bob Montgomery, who worked with Buddy Holly in the 1950s and penned Eddy's 1967 hit "Misty Blue," supervised two strong-selling LPs: *A Legend and His Lady* and *A Man for All Seasons.* Recording-artist-turned-producer Norro Wilson also coordinated two albums for Eddy.

Incredibly, the 1980s opened for the impervious-to-time Eddy Arnold with more spark than the 1970s, when the Bob Montgomery–produced *A Legend and His Lady* birthed two top ten country hits in 1980: "Let's Get It While the Gettin's Good" and "That's What I Get for Loving You." Montgomery's influence obviously helped fuel the rise of the two hits, but Eddy never cottoned to the producer's method of melding his vocal performance to the instrumentation. "Bob would mix me, as a vocalist, down in the music so much that it really didn't sound like Eddy Arnold, and I wasn't too happy about that," complained Eddy. "I like Bob Montgomery personally, but he would make that mix so tight and EQ [equalize the treble and bass sounds] me so much until it might sound good on radio, but it didn't sound good on the record player."

With or without Bob Montgomery, the string of hits had to peter out sometime, and in 1984 Eddy slipped off the charts and has yet to return. Country music's periodic youth movements had eroded Eddy's position from time to time over the years, but never knocked him off his feet. In the mid-'80s, though, youth won out, and RCA lost interest in Eddy. He made some albums with Bill Walker that were marketed through television, but generally concentrated on occasional concert appearances and stints on the then-new cable TV channel, The Nashville Network.

—　·　—

One Sunday afternoon in the late 1980s, Eddy lounged around his Brentwood home, watching television, and thinking of earlier years. He commented to Sally that the name Eddy Arnold probably meant nothing to a generation of Americans.

"Who's fault is that?" Sally retorted.

Picking up on the challenge implied in Sally's question, Eddy called on his occasional guitarist Harold Bradley to work with him on a new project at Bradley's Barn Studio in Mount Juliet, Tennessee. Their work during the early '90s produced three albums of Eddy Arnold love songs for RCA, but none of the cuts made the charts. Eddy badly wants to chart in the 1990s, which would mean six decades of hit making for him. "I'd like to have one more, and then I'll go out to pasture."

If Eddy is to succeed in his final quest, he will have to overcome formidable obstacles. His voice suffers from the frailties of age, although his ability to phrase his lyrics and drive home their message can still make an Eddy Arnold song an entirely enjoyable experience. Eddy also battles his environment. Current country-music radio stations and record buyers ignore Eddy Arnold and the music of his contemporaries. Just as the pop market finally rejected him in the late 1960s, the country market has brand-ed the almost-eighty Eddy Arnold irrelevant. But Eddy has faced down adversities before.

That Eddy believes enough in himself to strive for a hit in an era of "hot, new country music" and radio stations with mere six-month memories explains much about the way Eddy has attacked his career. Impervious to any criticism but his own, Eddy has often sailed directly into the winds of prevailing wisdom. At times, he has been defeated. But, as we approach the millennium, Eddy has once again summoned the gumption to try for more hits, making video versions of his songs, and playing periodic shows around the country where crazed fans still "handle" him backstage. "They even get after me," jokes Sally Arnold of her husband's fans. "I can't mistreat him [they tell me]. I can't do anything wrong. They even think he writes all those songs. Some lady—I was backstage—she came up to me, and she said, 'You better be good to him because I sat there and listened to all those songs he has written for you.' You think they're kidding, but they're not!"

Some of those fans Sally Arnold meets backstage would love nothing more than for Eddy to bring back "Little" Roy Wiggins and sing as if his career ended in 1949, when he released "Don't Rob Another Man's Castle." But Eddy refuses to live too far back in his recorded past, conjuring the old hits with his guitar for a few minutes only during his performances. He rel-ishes the new career that came to him in the 1960s after "What's He Doin' in My World" and "Make the World Go Away" shot up the charts, and chooses to identify his name and image with that second career.

The prevailing wisdom probably would have advised against bathing his 1960s recordings with pop choruses and strings, but that wisdom may have also discouraged the young Arnold from leaving the family farm during the Great Depression. The struggles of Jackson, Memphis, and St. Louis would have dispatched less-determined pioneers back to the fields of Chester County. Safer souls may have buckled to critics' opinions and remained at the "Grand Ole Opry" or stuck to a winning formula instead of pursuing the risky route of a polished, pop-oriented New York sound. But Eddy turned a deaf ear to detractors and doubters, keeping his eye on the goal of popular acceptance through a smooth, pop-influenced sound.

Eddy climbed the edifice of mass acceptance for ten years during the 1950s and early '60s, weathering rejection in television, lukewarm sales in the record market, and vitriolic protests from country-music hard-liners. Then he tasted five glorious years of mass appeal in the 1960s. Had Eddy decided to remain the Tennessee Plowboy he could have counted on unqualified loyalty from the country world for the rest of his career, but he wasn't always comfortable with what the label "country" implied, and believed that great numbers of Americans would love his voice and songs if he could only reach them.

Eddy feels pride in his accomplishments as the Tennessee Plowboy. He knows that in those days he dominated the country charts as no one else had before or has since. But, in talking to Eddy in his cluttered Brentwood office, it's difficult to determine if he holds his early days in the high esteem that historians do. Many view Eddy's late 1940s success and wonder why he abandoned (or "sold out," some charge) his golden formula that, for a time, helped define country music and bring rural music to the masses. But Eddy looks at the 1940s within the context of a long career and sees the phenomenal era as a launching pad for what was to come. "He doesn't know who he is historically," theorized John D. Loudermilk in 1995. "He's not old enough yet to really understand who he is. . . . Eddy is still in the developmental years."

If, as Loudermilk suggests, Eddy remains in the developmental years, he remains there only at the expense of those who would pin him to a time and place in history. Eddy's ongoing desire to find new hits and speak to people through his songs and stories has refreshed him by providing new challenges. He would rather RCA refrain from releasing the older music, so it won't compete with today's. "When they start talking to me," says Eddy, "I say, 'Play some of the later stuff.' The sound is better, and that's what I do today. I don't want to create a second career on something I did fifty years ago that I don't do anymore."

Due, in large measure, to Eddy's avoidance of the rocking chair, accolades from the popular American music establishment have bypassed him. Lifetime achievement awards from the National Academy of Recording Arts and Sciences and even the federal government would seem appropriate as Eddy nears his eightieth birthday as one of the top-selling artists in recording history. But these awards often go to those who have died or hung up their hats from the performing life. Like a man with fresh dreams, Eddy Arnold presses on.

In addition, Eddy's influence on country music often languishes in the shadow of the contributions of Ernest Tubb, Jimmie Rodgers, Hank Williams, and others who adhered to a rawer, more traditional sound throughout their careers. Michael Corcoran of the *Dallas Morning News* represents the frequently aired opinion that Eddy was un-hip and therefore not as influential as Hank Williams. "Unlike the stodgy performers of the day like Eddy Arnold, George Morgan and Roy Acuff," Corcoran posited in 1993, "Hank Williams exuded a raw energy and a sexual spark. He snapped his songs right into hearts and made country-music blues for white folks at a time when most Nashville hits were about gunfights and trains. Country music has never been the same." When Hank Williams first captured hearts—and he did capture hearts—most big hits were Eddy Arnold hits, and Eddy Arnold hits had little to say about gunfights and trains. Certainly, country music has never been the same since Hank, but the "stodgy" Eddy Arnold made a deep and distinctive imprint on the music as well.

Eddy in the 1990s, his seventh decade in the music business. (Gerard W. Purcell collection)

"Eddy was kind of a pioneer in many ways," says Danny Dill, Eddy's employee from the road. "He was singing good when singing good was not popular. He always had that niche in there that he was a little better than anybody else. He was a little more smooth."

Eddy Arnold, the gentleman and the legend, looms large on the Nashville scene, but mostly as an elder statesmen, not for his art. Artistic praise tends to fall on figures like bluegrass father Bill Monroe and, again, Hank Williams—those who indeed exhibited more creativity as songwriters and innovators. Songs pay tribute to Williams (Alan Jackson's "Midnight In Montgomery" and Johnny Cash's "The Night Hank Williams Came to Town," for example), but the name "Eddy Arnold" is absent from the soundtrack of today's country music.

Eddy's migration from country music's roots apparently has had a price, but not one that Eddy dwells upon. He basks in the glow of the zenith he reached in the 1960s and can smile to himself when he sees the acceptance today of a country troubadour like Vince Gill. Although the fact is often obscured, Eddy blazed a path through country music that's recognizable today. When Vince Gill or Reba McIntyre croons songs that are in every way pop ballads and Nashville doesn't gasp in shock, they have Eddy Arnold to thank.

Over the years, with Hugo Winterhalter, Bill Walker, Chet Atkins, and others, Eddy relentlessly incorporated symphonic instruments until the country-music market bowed to him. The formula shook to life in the mid-1960s, when Eddy Arnold's desire to bring his talent to the pop market converged with Jerry Purcell's superior management and marketing abilities and Chet Atkins's prowess in the studio. Eddy's warm baritone and elaborate, optimistic, Bill Walker–influenced instrumental backing came to represent the Nashville Sound and country music's ability to reach a mass audience. In the process, Eddy's sound avoided definitive classification. Certainly, his work emanated from Nashville and incorporated various elements of the best the town had to offer, yet it communicated a compromise to a middle-of-the-road sound that appealed to many Americans who may have otherwise snubbed country music.

The acquisition of Sinatra-like popularity must have dazzled Eddy Arnold in the 1960s when he reflected on the nineteenth-century-like farm life he forsook in order to take on an aspiring entertainer's grubby, tiring existence. Yet, there he stood, in the midst of contrast, often clad in a tuxedo and surrounded by a mass of musicians as he entertained an ermine crowd. Almost twenty years before, however, he wore a Stetson hat and, with a mere handful of musicians behind him, nervously thrilled simple country folks. Between 1946 and 1966, and with the help of a diverse group of people like Sally Arnold, WSM's Harry Stone, RCA's Steve Sholes, Tom Parker, and Jerry Purcell, Eddy went through an extreme and often rocky transformation. Shedding a relatively primitive, rustic presentation, Eddy had reinvented himself by the 1960s, presenting a polished, sophisticated image to reach the American mass audience and beyond.

And with all the discussion of musical compromises, longevity, Bill Walker's arrangements, and a country versus pop sound, it should be remembered that Eddy Arnold's voice was the common denominator that allowed him to sing his way through various musical styles and to garner new audiences. "He was just one of the greatest damn singers that's ever been," declared Chet Atkins. That rigid, yet sweet, voice of "Mommy Please Stay Home with Me" warmed and became wise over the years until it was rich in timbre and agile in phrasing. The voice brought Eddy twenty-eight number one country hits, acceptance in the pop markets, and record sales that are approaching 90 million in 1997.

— · —

Some long-forgotten reporter quoted Eddy Arnold's aspirations decades ago in a newspaper that's now tattered and yellowed with time: "When I finally put my guitar in the case the last time, I want to be remembered just as a singer, not as a country singer or pops singer—just a singer." His journey over many years and musical styles tells the story. Eddy Arnold accomplished his goal.

SESSIONOGRAPHY
Discography of Eddy Arnold Recordings, 1944–1996

The sheer breadth of Eddy Arnold's recording career makes it one of history's most remarkable. For more than fifty years, Americans and people around the world have found fresh Eddy Arnold material in their record stores, and in 1997 he plans to release new material on Curb Records. His songs have sold steadily over years of changing musical tastes, styles, and formats, from 78-rpm records to compact discs. Eddy adapted to the times and his own desires in order to preserve a beachhead in the industry, and certain efforts proved more successful than others.

To follow Eddy's career on record is to hear a sweet, immature voice with rustic instrumentation evolve into a confident baritone lifted by lush symphonic arrangements. The contrast is remarkable and denotes the two paths his distinguished musical career has followed. As one observes the blooming transformation of Eddy's voice, it is difficult to ignore his instrumental backing. From the start, Eddy boasted the best in his background, from the brilliance of steel guitarist Roy Wiggins and fiddler Speedy McNatt in the Tennessee Plowboy days through the Charles Grean–arranged New York experiments and on into the Chet Atkins–led 1960s. Mistakes, both vocally and instrumentally, certainly mar his records from time to time, and, since the mid-1980s, Eddy's voice has occasionally suffered from the wear of age. The flourishes and failings are all part of Eddy Arnold's musical journey and are quite available for public consumption.

The Eddy Arnold fan will find little of his early music on compact discs or in any other repackaged form. Eddy has discouraged the Bertelsmann Music Group (BMG), owner of the RCA label, from releasing the early material, preferring that they concentrate on recordings he has made since the "Make the World Go Away" days of the mid-1960s. The result has been that few Eddy Arnold songs, early or otherwise, have been re-released on the RCA label in recent years. Furthermore, the buyer should be careful of the Eddy Arnold "greatest hits" albums currently available on RCA—many of the cuts are re-recordings of the original hit versions. On the bright side, Bear Family Records of Germany repackaged the thoroughly enjoyable RCA albums *Thereby Hangs A Tale* (1959) and *Cattle Call* (1963) on one compact disc in 1990, and BMG-Germany re-released Eddy's singing jaunt across America— *Have Guitar, Will Travel* (1959)—in 1995. But, alas, those in search of the overwhelming bulk of Eddy's recorded output are destined to dusty searches through used record stores—not such a bad way to spend a Saturday afternoon!

In the future, those yearning for Eddy Arnold recordings can hope either for a European label to come forward with a venerable collection of Eddy's music or for RCA/BMG and Eddy himself to see fit to release a comprehensive retrospective (along with the more than 100 unreleased songs tantalizing us in the RCA/BMG archives).

The following is the most complete sessionography that could be compiled from RCA and MGM original log sheets and other information. When songs were issued as 78s or 45s, the release number follows the matrix or master number. Following the sessionography is a discography of extended-play and long-play (LP) records issued through Eddy's career by RCA and its subsidiary labels, MGM and Curb. I have tried to avoid listing collections of previously released material, promotional, bootleg, or television-marketed releases (of which, albeit, there have been many). An asterisk (*) is placed next to titles that I recommend for their historical value or promise of just plain good listening. A dagger (†) denotes an unreleased performance.

Sessionography for RCA and MGM Recordings

EA = Eddy Arnold. Full names of session players, producers, etc., are given on first usage, otherwise last name only

RCA VICTOR

Session: December 4, 1944, WSM Studios, Nashville
Producer: unknown
Musicians: EA (gtr), Speedy McNatt (vln), Butterball Paige (b and gtr), Gabe Tucker (b and trpt), Roy Wiggins (steel gtr)

Mother's Prayer* (Wallace Fowler)	D4-AB-517-1	Bluebird 33-0520A
Mommy Please Stay Home with Me* (Arnold-Fowler-Hall)	D4-AB-518-1	Bluebird 33-0520B
The Cattle Call (Tex Owens)	D4-AB-519-1	Bluebird 33-0527A
Each Minute Seems a Million Years (Alton "Cook" Watson)	D4-AB-520-1	Bluebird 33-0527B

Session: July 9, 1945, Brown Brothers Studios, Nashville
Producer: Steve Sholes
Musicians: EA (gtr), McNatt (vln), Paige (gtr), Golden Stewart (b), Dempsey Watts (gtr), Wiggins (steel gtr)

Did You See My Daddy Over There? (Bill Showmet)	D5-AB-493	Bluebird 33-0535A
Many Tears Ago (Jenny Lou Carson)	D5-AB-494	Bluebird 33-5040A
I Walk Alone (Herbert Wilson)	D5-AB-495	Bluebird 33-0535B
You Must Walk the Line (Arnold-Fowler-Hall)	D5-AB-496	Bluebird 33-5040B

Session: November 21, 1945, RCA Victor Studios, Chicago
Producer: Sholes
Musicians: EA (gtr), McNatt (vln), Paige (gtr), Rollin Sullivan (elec mandolin), Watts (b), Wiggins (steel gtr)

(I'll Have To) Live and Learn (Zeke Clements)	D5-AB-1218	RCA 20-1801B
Be Sure There's No Mistake (Arnold-Watson)	D5-AB-1219	RCA 20-2058B
I Couldn't Believe It Was True (Arnold-Fowler)	D5-AB-1220	RCA 20-2241A
I Talk to Myself About You (Fred Rose)	D5-AB-1221	RCA 20-1801A

Session: March 20, 1946, RCA Victor Studios, Chicago
Producer: Sholes
Musicians: EA (gtr), Owen Bradley (pno), Lloyd George (b), McNatt (vln), John Sullivan (gtr), R. Sullivan (elec mandolin), Wiggins (steel gtr)

All Alone in This World Without You (McAlpin-Bradley-Wade)	D6-VB-1870	RCA 20-1855B
Can't Win, Can't Place, Can't Show (Paul Westmoreland)	D6-VB-1871	RCA 20-1855A
What Is Life Without Love (Arnold-McAlpin-Bradley)	D6-VB-1872	RCA 20-2058A
That's How Much I Love You* (Arnold-Fowler-Hall)	D6-VB-1873	RCA 20-1948A (78 rpm)
Why Didn't You Take That Too? (Sessons-Butler)	D6-VB-1874†	
Chained to A Memory (Jenny Lou Carson)	D6-VB-1875	RCA 20-1948B

Session: September 24, 1946, RCA Victor Studios, New York
Producer: Sholes
Musicians: EA (gtr), Lloyd George (b), Eddie McMullen (steel gtr), McNatt (vln), Harold Spierer (pno), J. Sullivan (gtr), R. Sullivan (elec mandolin)

What A Fool I Was (Stu Davis)	D6-VB-2890†	
Easy Rockin' Chair* (Fred Rose)	D6-VB-2891	RCA 20-2481B
To My Sorrow (V. J. McAlpin)	D6-VB-2892	RCA 20-2481A
It's A Sin (Rose-Turner)	D6-VB-2893	RCA 20-2241B

Session: May 18, 1947, RCA Victor Studios, Chicago
Producer: Sholes
Musicians: EA (gtr), Bradley (pno), Adrian McDowell (vln), Jack Shook (gtr), R. Sullivan (elec mandolin), James Swinney (b), Wiggins (steel gtr)

I'm Somebody Nobody Loves (Jenny Lou Carson)	D7-VB-728†	
That Little Boy of Mine (Meroff-King-Hirsch)	D7-VB-729†	
Don't Bother to Cry (Bob Merrill)	D7-VB-730	RCA 20-2332A
Me Too (Fred Rose)	D7-VB-731†	
I'll Hold You In My Heart (Till I Can Hold You in My Arms)* (Arnold-Horton-Dilbeck)	D7-VB-732	RCA 20-2332B
Bouquet of Roses* (Nelson-Hilliard)	D7-VB-733	RCA 20-2806B
What A Fool I Was (Stu Davis)	D7-VB-734	RCA 20-2700B
Little Angel With the Dirty Face (Dale Parker)	D7-VB-735†	
Wondering What to Do (Arnold-Homesley)	D7-VB-736†	

Session: August 19–20, 1947, RCA Victor Studios, New York[1]
Producers: Sholes and Charles Green
Musicians: EA (gtr), Grean (b), Jack Kelly (pno), Ben Lambert (vln), Shook (gtr), R. Sullivan (elec mandolin), Wiggins (steel gtr)

August 19

The Prisoner's Song (Guy Massey)	D7-VB-1525
Rockin' Alone (In An Old Rocking Chair) (Bob Miller)	D7-VB-1526

---

[1]On August 19, Eddy and members of the band also backed Texas Jim Robertson on one number, "Answer to Rainbow at Midnight" (RCA 20-2455A).

It Makes No Difference Now (Davis-Tillman)	D7-VB-1527	RCA 20-2489A
Will the Circle Be Unbroken (My Family Circle) (Arr. Eddy Arnold)	D7-VB-1528	
Seven Years With the Wrong Woman (Bob Miller)	D7-VB-1529	
Molly Darling* (Will Hays)	D7-VB-1530	RCA 20-2489B
I'm Thinking Tonight of My Blue Eyes (Carter-Marcotte)	D7-VB-1531	
Who at My Door Is Standing (Slade-Everett)	D7-VB-1532	

August 20

Then I Turned and Walked Slowly Away (Red Fortner)	D7-VB-1534	RCA 20-3174A
Texarkana Baby (Clark-Rose)	D7-VB-1535	RCA 20-2806A
(In the) Hills of Tomorrow (Arnold-Bradley-Beasley)	D7-VB-1536	
My Daddy Is Only A Picture (Tommy Dilbeck)	D7-VB-1537	RCA 20-3013B
Say You'll Be Mine (Arnold-Selph)	D7-VB-1538†	
There's Not A Thing (I Wouldn't Do for You) (Billy Hughes)	D7-VB-1539	RCA 21-0002A
I've Got A Lifetime to Forget (Jenny Lou Carson)	D7-VB-1540†	
Anytime* (Herbert Lawson)	D7-VB-1541	RCA 20-2700A

Session: December 17, 1947, RCA Victor Studios, New York
Producers: Sholes and Grean
Musicians: EA (gtr), Grean (b), Lambert (vln), Sam Liner (pno), Shook (gtr), R. Sullivan (elec mandolin), Wiggins (steel gtr)

A Heart Full of Love (For A Handful of Kisses) (Arnold-Nelson-Soehnel)	D7-VB-2821	RCA 20-3174B
My Heart Cries for You (Like A Baby) (Cindy Walker)	D7-VB-2822†	
I've Got Other Fish to Fry (Arnold-Rule)	D7-VB-2823†	
This Is the Thanks I Get (For Loving You) (Tommy Dilbeck)	D7-VB-2824†	
You Know How Talk Gets Around (Fred Rose)	D7-VB-2825	
Just A Little Lovin' (Will Go A Long, Long Way) (Arnold-Clements)	D7-VB-2826	RCA 20-3013A
Till the End of the World (Vaughn Horton)	D7-VB-2827†	
Save A Little Corner in Your Heart (Allen-Bohme)	D7-VB-2828†	

Session: December 20–22, 1948, RCA Victor Studios, New York
Producer: Sholes
Musicians: EA (gtr), Harold Bradley (gtr), Grean (b), Lambert (vln), Jack Pleis (pno), Shook (gtr), Wiggins (steel gtr)

December 20

M-O-T-H-E-R (A Word That Means the World) (Johnson-Morse)	D8-VB-4082	
I Wouldn't Trade the Silver in My Mother's Hair (For All the Gold in the World) (Little-Coots)	D8-VB-4083	
That Wonderful Mother of Mine (Hager-Goodwin)	D8-VB-4084	
Bring Your Roses to Her Now (Ennis-Giles-Large)	D8-VB-4085	
I Wish I Had A Girl Like You, Mother (Nelson-Nelson-Arnold)	D8-VB-4086	
My Mother's Sweet Voice (Dale Parker)	D8-VB-4087	
There's No Wings on My Angel (Arnold-Coben-Melsher)	D8-VB-4088	
The Echo of Your Footsteps (Jenny Lou Carson)	D8-VB-4089	RCA 21-0051A

December 21

Why Didn't You Take That Too (Sessons-Butler)	D6-VB-1874†	
That Little Boy of Mine (Meroff-King-Hirsch)	D6-VB-729†	
This Is the Thanks I Get (For Loving You) (Arnold-Dilbeck)	D7-VB-2824	
My Heart Cries for You (Like A Baby) (Cindy Walker)	D7-VB-2822†	
Don't Rob Another Man's Castle* (Jenny Lou Carson)	D8-VB-4096	RCA 21-0002B
I've Got Other Fish to Fry (Arnold-Rule)	D7-VB-2823†	
Me Too (Fred Rose)	D7-VB-731†	
Little Angel with the Dirty Face (Dale Parker)	D7-VB-735	RCA 21-0300A

December 22

Many Tears Ago (Jenny Lou Carson)	D5-AB-494	RCA 20-1871A
I Walk Alone (Herbert Wilson)	D5-AB-495	RCA 20-2128B
Show Me the Way Back to Your Heart (Nelson-Soehnl-Arnold)	D8-VB-4104	RCA 21-0083B
Homesick, Lonesome and Sorry (Vaughn Horton)	D8-VB-4105†	
One Kiss Too Many (Nelson-Nelson-Arnold)	D8-VB-4106	RCA 21-0051B
I Was Foolish When I Fell in Love with You (Herbert Lawson)	D8-VB-4107†	
Something Old, Something New, Something Borrowed, Something Blue (Arnold-Coben-Grean)	D8-VB-4108†	
I Tied A Little String Around My Finger (Nelson-Douglas-Arnold)	D8-VB-4109†	

Session: April 5, 1949, RCA Victor Studios, New York
Producer: Sholes
Musicians: EA (gtr), Grean (b), Lambert (vln), Danny Perri (gtr), Jack Pleis (pno), Wiggins (steel gtr)

I'm Throwing Rice (At the Girl That I Love)* (Nelson-Nelson-Arnold)	D9-VB-1237	RCA 21-0083A
Shepherd of My Heart (Jenny Lou Carson)	D9-VB-1238	
Why Should I Cry? (Zeke Clements)	D9-VB-1239	RCA 21-0300B
C-H-R-I-S-T-M-A-S (Carson-Arnold)	D9-VB-1240	RCA 21-0124A

Session: September 13–14, 1949, RCA Victor Studios, New York
Producer: Sholes
Musicians: same as April 5

September 13

To the Last Beat of My Heart (Parker-Arnold)	D9-VB-2232†	
Take Me in Your Arms and Hold Me (Cindy Walker)	D9-VB-2233	RCA 21-0146B
Evil Tempt Me Not (Parker-Arnold)	D9-VB-2235	
When Jesus Beckons Me Home (Gene Arnold)	D9-VB-2236	
Will Santy Come to Shanty Town* (Arnold-Nelson-Nelson)	D9-VB-2237	RCA 21-0124B
Beautiful Isle of Somewhere (Pounds-Fearis)	D9-VB-2238	
The Lily of the Valley (Arr. by Eddy Arnold)	D9-VB-2239	
Softly and Tenderly (Will Thompson)	D9-VB-2240	

September 14

Mama and Daddy Broke My Heart (Spade Cooley)	D9-VB-2241	RCA 21-0146A
You Touched Me (Butcher-Arnold)	D9-VB-2243†	
Chained to A Memory (Jenny Lou Carson)	D6-VB-1875	RCA 20-1948B (78) 47-3310B (45)

The Cattle Call (Tex Owens)	D4-AB-519	RCA 20-2128A
The Nearest Thing to Heaven (Russell-Jolson)	D9-VB-2242	
Something Old, Something New, Something Borrowed,		
Something Blue (Arnold-Coben-Grean)	D8-VB-4108†	

Session: April 26–27, 1950, RCA Victor Studios, New York
Producer: Sholes
Musicians: EA (gtr), L. Braun (b), Lambert (vln), Perri (gtr), Wiggins (steel gtr), Skeeter Willis (vln), Vic Willis (pno)

April 26

A Prison Without Walls (Nelson-Rollins)	EO-VB-4267	RCA 21-0382B
Cuddle Buggin' Baby (Red Rowe)	EO-VB-4268	RCA 21-0342A
Enclosed, One Broken Heart (Sallis-Arnold)	EO-VB-4269	RCA 21-0342B

April 27

Tie Me to Your Apron Strings Again (Goodwin-Shay)	EO-VB-4270	RCA 21-0412B
Behind the Clouds (Jenny Lou Carson)	EO-VB-4284†	
A Million Miles from Your Heart (Jenny Lou Carson)	EO-VB-4285	RCA 21-0444B
At the Close of A Long, Long Day (Moll-Marvin)	EO-VB-4292†	
C-H-R-I-S-T-M-A-S (Carson-Arnold)	EO-VB-1240	RCA 21-0124A

Session: August 20–21, 1950, Brown Brothers Studios, Nashville
Producer: Sholes
Musicians: Chet Atkins (gtr), Anita Kerr (org), Shook (gtr), Wiggins (steel gtr), Guy Willis (gtr), S. Willis (gtr), V. Willis (pno), Chuck Wright (b)

August 20

If I Never Get to Heaven (Carson-Botkin)	EO-VB-5500†	
The Lovebug Itch* (Carson-Botkin)	EO-VB-5501	RCA 21-0382A

August 21

White Christmas (Irving Berlin)	EO-VB-5502	RCA 21-0390A
Santa Claus Is Comin' to Town (Gillespie-Coots)	EO-VB-5503	RCA 21-0390B

Session: November 9–10, 1950, Brown Brothers Studio, Nashville
Producer: Sholes
Musicians: same as April 20–21, 1950, without Atkins

November 9

There's Been A Change in Me* (Cy Coben)	EO-VB-5839	RCA 21-0412A
Precious Little Baby (Lee Roberts)	EO-VB-5840†	
Through A Stranger's Eyes (Jessie Mae Robinson)	EO-VB-5841†	

November 10

Open Thy Merciful Arms (Don Whiston)	EO-VB-5844
Jesus and the Atheist (Austine-Richards)	EO-VB-5845

Session: December 13, 1950, RCA Victor Studios, New York
Producer: Sholes
Musicians: same as November 9–10, 1950, with R. Rio (org) replacing Anita Kerr

Something Old, Something New (Arnold-Coben-Grean)	EO-VB-6280	RCA 21-0476B
Behind the Clouds (Jenny Lou Carson)	EO-VB-4284†	
Precious Little Baby (Lee Roberts)	EO-VB-5840†	

Kentucky Waltz (Bill Monroe)	EO-VB-6279	RCA 21-0444A
Jesus and the Atheist (Austine-Richards)	EO-VB-5845	RCA 21-0495A
I'm Writing A Letter to the Lord (Kennedy-Stone)	EO-VB-6282	RCA 21-0425B
May the Good Lord Bless and Keep You (Meredith Willson)	EO-VB-6281	RCA 21-0425A

Session: January 27, 1951, Brown Brothers Studios, Nashville
Musicians: EA (gtr), H. Bradley (gtr), Farris Coursey (drm), Marvin Hughes (org), Wiggins (steel gtr), G. Willis (gtr), S. Willis (vln), V. Willis (pno), Wright (b)

Tennessee Hillbilly Ghost (Smith-Peterson)	EO-VB-908

Session: April 16–18, 1951, RCA Victor Studios, New York
Producer: Sholes
Musicians: EA (gtr), Wiggins (steel gtr), G. Willis (gtr), S. Willis (vln), V. Willis (pno), Wright (b)

April 16

Rollin' and Tossin' (Ed Nelson, Jr.)	E1-VB-1783†	
I Wanna Play House with You (Cy Coben)	E1-VB-1784†	
Call Her Your Sweetheart (Leon Payne)	E1-VB-1785	RCA 20-4413A (78) 47-4413A (45)[2]
He Knows (Nash-Arnold)	E1-VB-1790	RCA 21-0495B
Puppy Love (Jenny Lou Carson)	E1-VB-1791†	
I Wish I Knew (Sandy Oakton)	E1-VB-1792†	

April 17

Heart Strings (Merle Moore)	E1-VB-1788	RCA 20/47-4273B
Bundle of Southern Sunshine (Sunny Clapp)	E1-VB-1789	RCA 20/47-4413B
When You and I Were Young, Maggie (J. Butterfield)	E1-VB-1793	
A Sinner's Prayer (McEnery-Davis)	E1-VB-1794	

April 18

I Wanna Play House with You (Cy Coben)	E1-VB-1784	RCA 21-0476A
Roll Along Kentucky Moon (Bill Halley)	E1-VB-2007	
Trouble in Mind (Richard Jones)	E1-VB-2008	RCA 20/47-6365B
When My Blue Moon Turns to Gold Again (Walker-Sullivan)	E1-VB-2009	
No One Will Ever Know (Foree-Rose)	E1-VB-2010†	
Wild Flower (Spencer-Rowe-Spencer)	E1-VB-2011†	
White Azaleas (Bob Miller)	E1-VB-2012	
I'll Still Belong to You (Cargill-Clark)	E1-VB-2017†	
Somebody's Been Beating My Time (Zeke Clements)	E1-VB-2018	RCA 20/47-4273A

Session: September 13, 1951, RCA Victor Studios, Hollywood, California
Producer: unknown
Musicians: same as April 16–18, 1951

That Little Boy of Mine (Meroff-King-Hirsch)	D7-VB-729

---

[2]From this point on, 78s and 45s in the RCA catalog shared the same four-digit number—the prefix "20" indicates 78 rpm, and "47" indicates 45 rpm.

Session: December 10, 1951, RCA Victor Studios, New York
Musicians: Frank Carroll (b), Marty Gold (org), Cy Levitan (pno), Perri (gtr),
Jack Saunders (drm)

The Old Rugged Cross (George Bennard)	E1-VB-4615	RCA 20/47-5196A
Have Thine Own Way, Lord (Pollard-Stebbins)	E1-VB-4616	RCA 20/47-5196B
Take My Hand, Precious Lord (Thomas A. Dorsey)	E1-VB-4617	RCA 20/47-4490B
Open Thy Merciful Arms (Don Whiston)	E0-VB-5844	RCA 20/47-4490A

Session: January 8, 1952, Brown Brothers Studio, Nashville
Producer: Sholes
Musicians: Atkins (gtr), J. Gordy (pno), W. Lenk (drm), Wiggins (steel gtr), G. Willis (gtr),
Wright (b)

Anything That's Part of You (Dixon-Wrubel)	E2-VB-5017	RCA 20/47-4569B
Easy on the Eyes (Arnold-Coben)	E2-VB-5018	RCA 20/47-4569A

Session: January 17, 1952, RCA Victor Studios, New York
Producer: Sholes
Musicians: EA (gtr), Gold (celeste), Wiggins (steel gtr), G. Willis (gtr), S. Willis (vln),
V. Willis (pno), Wright (b)

That's What Love Is All About (Dave Bohme)	E2-VB-5557†	
Someone Calls Me Daddy (Stuart Hamblen)	E2-VB-5558	RCA 20/47-4646A
(Don't Ever Take the) Ribbons from Your Hair (Helen Hudgins)	E2-VB-5559	RCA 20/47-4646B
This Is the Thanks I Get (For Loving You) (Tommy Dilbeck)	D7-VB-2824†	

Session: May 15, 1952, Brown Brothers Studio, Nashville
Producer: Sholes
Musicians: same as January 17, 1952, with Hank Garland (gtr) and without Gold

A Full Time Job (Gerry Teifer)	E2-VB-6249	RCA 20/47-4787A
Shepherd of My Heart (Jenny Lou Carson)	E2-VB-6250	RCA 20/47-4787B
Ya Gotta Be Mine (Boudleaux Bryant)	E2-VB-6251†	
Puppy Love (Jenny Lou Carson)	E2-VB-6252†	
I'll Do as Much for You Someday (Nelson-Nelson, Jr.)	E2-VB-6253†	

Session: June 16, 1952, RCA Victor Studios, New York
Producer: Sholes
Musicians: EA (gtr), Gold (org), Grean (b), Allen Hanlon (gtr), Phil Kraus (drm),
Levitan (pno)

My Desire (Thomas A. Dorsey)	E2-VB-6594	RCA 20/47-5020B
When I've Done My Best (Thomas A. Dorsey)	E2-VB-6595	RCA 20/47-5197B
I Want To Thank You, Lord (Alberta Hunter)	E2-VB-6596	RCA 20/47-5020A
Have Thine Own Way, Lord (Pollard-Stobbins)	E2-VB-4616†	

Session: July 24, 1952, RCA Victor Studios, New York
Producer: Sholes
Musicians: unknown, but probably includes musicians from June 16 and August 7, 1952,
sessions

Smokey the Bear (Nelson-Rollins)	E2-VB-6822	BY-38B (78)/WBY-38B (45)

Horace the Horse (Coben-Grean)	E2-VB-6823	BY-38A (78)/WBY-38A (45)

Session: August 7, 1952, RCA Victor Studios, New York
Producer: Sholes
Musicians: EA (gtr), Al Chernet (gtr), Garland (gtr), Gold (pno), Grean (b), Wiggins (steel gtr)

I'd Trade All of My Tomorrows (For Just One Yesterday) (Jenny Lou Carson)	E2-VB-6877	RCA 20/47-4954B
Older and Bolder (Cy Coben)	E2-VB-6878	RCA 20/47-4954A
Lovin' Up A Storm (Thelma Blackmon)	E2-VB-6879	

Session: December 1–2 & 4, 1952, RCA Victor Studios, New York
Producer: Sholes
Musicians: EA (gtr), George Barnes (gtr), Chernet (gtr), Garland (gtr), Gold (pno), Grean (b), Kraus (drm), Litvan (org), Wiggins (steel gtr)

December 1

The Missouri Waltz (Hush-A-Bye, Ma Baby) (Shannon-Eppel)	E2-VB-7788	RCA 20/47-5192B
Condemned Without A Trial (Blair-Robertson)	E2-VB-7789	RCA 20/47-5108A

December 2

You Always Hurt the One You Love (Fisher-Roberts)	E2-VB-7792	RCA 20/47-5193B
I'm Waiting for Ships That Never Come In (Yellen-Olman)	E2-VB-7794	RCA 20/47-5188A
Moonlight and Roses (Bring Mem'ries Of You) (Lemare-Black-Moret)	E2-VB-7793	RCA 20/47-5192A
The Old Rugged Cross (George Bernard)	E2-VB-4615†	
Have Thine Own Way, Lord (Pollard-Stebbins)	E2-VB-4616†	
Someday, Somewhere (Thomas A. Dorsey)	E2-VB-7795	RCA 20/47-5197A
Today (Evening Song) (Thomas A. Dorsey)	E2-VB-7796	

December 4

Angry (Mecum-Cassard-Brunies-Brunies)	E2-VB-7797	RCA 20/47-5189B
I Got Bad News for You (Rose-Willis)	E2-VB-7798†	
When Your Hair Has Turned to Silver (I Will Love You Just the Same) (Tobias-De Rose)	E2-VB-7797	RCA 20/47-5189A
I'm Gonna Lock My Heart (And Throw Away the Key) (Eaton-Shand)	E2-VB-7800	RCA 20/47-5193A
Ready, Willing, and Able (Grean-Gold)	E2-VB-8001	
I'm Gonna Sit Right Down and Write Myself A Letter (Young-Ahlert)	E2-VB-8002	RCA 20/47-5188B
Eddy's Song (Grean-Coben)	E2-VB-8003	RCA 20/47-5108B

Session: March 31, 1953, RCA Victor Studios, New York
Producer: Sholes
Musicians: same as December 1–2 & 4, 1952, without Barnes

Your Left Over Kisses (Ab Green)	E3-VB-1025†	
How's the World Treating You (Atkins-Bryant)	E3-VB-1026	RCA 20/47-5305B
Free Home Demonstration (Coben-Grean)	E3-VB-1027	RCA 20/47-5305A
A Second Fling (Nelson-Javits)	E3-VB-1028	RCA 20/47-5634B
Mama, Come Get Your Baby Boy (Merritt-Alton)	E3-VB-1029	RCA 20/47-5415A
If I Never Get to Heaven (Jenny Lou Carson)	E0-VB-5500	RCA 20/47-5415B

This Is the Thanks I Get (For Loving You)
    (Tommy Dilbeck)   D7-VB-2824†

Session: September 21, 1953, Thomas Production Studios, Nashville
Producer: Sholes
Musicians: EA (gtr), Grean (b)

I Really Don't Want to Know (Barnes-Robertson)   E3-VB-2215†

Session: September 26, 1953, Thomas Production Studios, Nashville
Producer: Sholes
Musicians: EA (gtr), Garland (gtr), Ernie Newton (b), Shook (gtr), Wiggins (steel gtr)

I'll Never Get Over You (Floyd Tillman)	E3-VB-2246	RCA 20/47-5525B
My Everything (Lacy-Wilson)	E3-VB-2247†	
Unfaithful Love (Floyd Wilson)	E3-VB-2248†	

Session: October 22, 1953, RCA Victor Studios, New York
Producer: Sholes
Musicians: EA (gtr), Chernet (gtr), Gold (pno), Grean (b), Kraus (drm, vibes), Litvan (org)

It Is No Secret (What God Can Do) (Stuart Hamblen)	E3-VB-2456
Crying in the Chapel (Artie Glenn)	E3-VB-2457
Beyond the Sunset (Brock-Brock)	E3-VB-2458†

Session: October 23, 1953, RCA Victor Studios, New York
Producer: Sholes
Musicians: same as October 22, 1953, without EA on guitar

Whispering Hope (Alice Hawthorne)	E3-VB-2468†	
The Chapel on the Hill (Arnold-King-Frank)	E3-VB-2469	RCA 20/47-5753
I Really Don't Want to Know* (Barnes-Robertson)	E3-VB-2215	RCA 20/47-5525A

Session: November 9, 1953, RCA Victor Studios, New York
Producer: Sholes
Musicians: EA (gtr), Chernet (gtr), Garland (gtr), Grean (b), Kraus (drm),
Wiggins (steel gtr)

This Is the Thanks I Get (For Loving You)		
(Tommy Dilbeck)	D7-VB-2824†	
I Was Foolish When I Fell in Love with You		
(Herbert Lawson)	D8-VB-4107†	
Through A Stranger's Eyes (Jesse Mae Robinson)	E0-VB-5841†	
My Everything (Lacy-Wilson)	E3-VB-2247	RCA 20/47-5634A

Session: December 29, 1953, RCA Victor Studios, New York
Producer: Sholes
Musicians: EA (gtr), Atkins (gtr), Garland (gtr), Gold (org, pno), Grean (b), Litvan (org),
Saunders (vibes)

Robe of Calvary (Twomey-White-St. Clair-Rivers)	E3-VB-2902	RCA 20/47-5601A
Prayer (Lisbona-Bryan)	E3-VB-2903	RCA 20/47-5601B
The Chapel on the Hill (Arnold-King-Frank)	E3-VB-2469	RCA 20/47-5753A
I Called on the Master (Brady-Wingert)	E3-VB-2962	
'Twas the Dawn of a Beautiful Day (Glenn Wagoner)	E3-VB-2963	
When It's Round-Up Time in Heaven (Jimmie Davis)	E3-VB-2964	

The Touch of God's Hand (Bob Nolan)   E3-VB-2965   RCA 20/47-5753B

Session: December 30, 1953, RCA Victor Studios, New York
Producer: Sholes
Musicians: same as December 29, 1953, without Litvan and Saunders

Just Call Me Lonesome (Rex Griffin)	E3-VB-2974	RCA 20/47-6198B
Hep Cat Baby (Cy Coben)	E3-VB-2975	RCA 20/47-5805B
The Mills of the Gods (Kane-Team)	E3-VB-2976	
A Dozen Hearts (Odom-Grean)	E3-VB-2977	RCA 20/47-6773B

Session: February 14, 1954, Thomas Production Studio, Nashville
Producer: Sholes
Musicians: EA (gtr), Garland (gtr), Louis Innis (gtr), Bob Moore (b), Polk Moore (drm), Wiggins (steel gtr)

When You Said Goodbye (Danny Dill)	E4-VB-3609	RCA 20/47-6365A
Hep Cat Baby (Cy Coben)	E4-VB-3610†	
If She Will (Nagel-Carver-Adams)	E4-VB-3611†	
Live Fast, Love Hard, Die Young (Joe Allison)	E4-VB-3612†	

Session: April 22, 1954, RCA Victor Studios, New York
Producer: Sholes
Musicians: EA (gtr), Tony Gottuso (gtr), Grean (b), Kraus (drm)

No One to Cry To (Willing-Robin)	E4-VB-3987	
When You Said Goodbye (Danny Dill)	E4-VB-3609†	
This Is the Thanks I Get (For Loving You) (Tommy Dilbeck)	D7-VB-2824	RCA 20/47-5805A

Session: September 13, 1954, RCA Victor Studios, New York
Producer: Sholes
Musicians: same as December 1–2 & 4, 1952

Shame on You (Spade Cooley)	E4-VB-5442	
Cold, Cold Heart (Hank Williams)	E4-VB-5443	
So Round, So Firm, So Fully Packed (Travis-Stone-Kirk)	E4-VB-5444	
I Love You So Much It Hurts (Floyd Tillman)	E4-VB-5445	
Christmas Can't Be Far Away (Boudleaux Bryant)	E4-VB-5446	RCA 20/47-5905A
Someday (You'll Want Me to Want You) (Jimmie Hodges)	E4-VB-5447	
Sittin' on Santa Claus' Lap (Cy Coben)	E4-VB-5448	RCA WY-490B (45)
Slow Poke (King-Stewart-Price)	E4-VB-5449	

Session: September 14, 1954, RCA Victor Studios, New York
Producer: Sholes
Musicians: same as September 13, 1954, without Barnes and Kraus

You Can't Be True, Dear (Ebeler-Cotton-Otten-Griffin)	E4-VB-5450
(Now and Then There's) A Fool Such As I (Bill Trader)	E4-VB-5451
Tennessee Waltz (King-Stewart)	E4-VB-5452
Do You Miss Me (Coben-Grean)	E4-VB-5453

Session: September 15, 1954, RCA Victor Studios, New York
Producer: Sholes
Musicians: same as September 13, 1954

I've Been Thinking* (Boudleaux Bryant)	E4-VB-5441	RCA 20/47-6000A
Don't Forget (Ebb-Leyden)	E4-VB-5413	RCA 20/47-6000B
I Always Have Someone to Turn To (Sornoff-Kenner)	E4-VB-5454	RCA 20/47-6001B
I Wouldn't Know Where to Begin (Johnny Marks)	E4-VB-5455	RCA 20/47-6699B

Session: September 16, 1954, RCA Victor Studios, New York
Producer: Sholes
Musicians: same as September 13, 1954

I'm Your Private Santa Claus (Cy Coben)	E4-VB-5463	RCA 20/47-5905B
I Don't Hurt Anymore (Rollins-Robertson)	E4-VB-5464	
Oh, My Achin' Heart (Tim Spencer)	E4-VB-5465†	
(Gonna Get Myself A) Brand New Sandman (Tommy Dilbeck)	E4-VB-5466	
Two Kinds of Love (Nelson-Nelson-Thorp)	E4-VB-5467	RCA 20/47-6069B
In Time (Bellah-Cross)	E4-VB-5468	RCA 20/47-6069A
Each Time You Leave (Scotty Wiseman)	E4-VB-5469	
It Took A Miracle (John Peterson)	E4-VB-5470	RCA 20/47-6001A

Session: September 22, 1954, Thomas Production Studios, Nashville
Producer: Sholes
(EA duets with Jo Ann Arnold)
Musicians: EA (gtr), James Burks, Jr. (vibes), Garland (gtr), Grean (b), Hughes (pno), Shook (gtr)

A Present for Santa Claus (Avis Allen)	E4-VB-5511	RCA WY-490A (45)
The Horse in Striped Pajamas (Ebb-Klein)	E4-VB-5512	RCA WY-492A (45)
Why, Daddy? (Tepper-Bennett)	E4-VB-5513	RCA WY-492B (45)

Session: April 3, 1955, RCA Victor Studios, Nashville
Producer: Sholes
Musicians: EA (gtr), Coursey (drm), Garland (gtr), Sam Hollingsworth (b), Hughes (celeste, pno), Shook (gtr), Wiggins (steel gtr)

Unchained Melody (Zaret-North)	F2-WB-0291
His Hands (Stuart Hamblen)	F2-WB-0292
Silver Moon (Donnolly-Rosburg)	F2-WB-0293
Making Believe (Jimmy Work)	F2-WB-0294

Session: April 28, 1955, Webster Hall, New York
Producer: Sholes
Musicians: George Duvivier (b), Garland (gtr), John Guarmiori (pno), Clifford Loeman (drm), orch acc cond Hugo Winterhalter, voc acc

The Cattle Call (Tex Owens)	F2-PB-3528	RCA 20/47-6139B
The Richest Man (In the World)* (Boudleaux Bryant)	F2-PB-3529	RCA 20/47-6290A
The Kentuckian Song* (Irving Gordon)	F2-PB-3530	RCA 20/47-6139A
I Walked Alone Last Night (Arthur-Wolf)	F2-PB-3531	RCA 20/47-6290B

Session: May 30, 1955, RCA Victor Studios, Nashville
Producer: Sholes
Musicians: Coursey (drm), Garland (gtr), Hughes (pno), Newton (b), Shook (gtr), Wiggins (steel gtr), string acc, voc acc

Home on the Range (traditional)	F2-WB-2299
Wanderin' (traditional)	F2-WB-3900
On Top of Old Smoky (traditional)	F2-WB-3901
Sweet Betsy from Pike (traditional)	F2-WB-3902

Session: May 31, 1955, RCA Victor Studios, Nashville
Producer: Sholes
Musicians: same as May 30, 1955, without Coursey, Shook, and Wiggins

The Lonesome Road (Austin-Shilkrot)	F2-WB-3911
The Wayfaring Stranger (traditional)	F2-WB-3912
Sometimes I Feel Like A Motherless Child (traditional)	F2-WB-3913
Barbara Allen (traditional)	F2-WB-3914

Session: June 1, 1955, RCA Victor Studios, Nashville
Producer: Sholes
Musicians: Garland (gtr), Hughes (pno, celeste), Newton (b), Wiggins (steel gtr), string acc, voc acc

Across the Wide Missouri (Drake-Shirl)	F2-WB-3915
Down in the Valley (traditional)	F2-WB-3916
Red River Valley (traditional)	F2-WB-3917
I Gave My Love A Cherry (traditional)	F2-WB-3918

Session: June 2, 1955, RCA Victor Studios, Nashville
Producer: Sholes
Musicians: same as June 1, 1955, with Shook (gtr)

Careless Love (traditional)	F2-WB-3919	
The Rovin' Gambler (traditional)	F2-WB-3920	
If She Will (Carver-Adams-Coben)	F2-WB-3921†	
That Do Make It Nice* (Arnold-Ebb-Klein)	F2-WB-3922	RCA 20/47-6198A
I'll Be Satisfied (Don Robertson)	F2-WB-3923	

Session: December 1, 1955, Webster Hall, New York
Producer: Sholes
Musicians: Barnes (gtr), Carroll (b), Chernet (gtr, banjo), Gold (pno), Kraus (drm), voc acc

I'll Be Satisfied (Don Robertson)	F2-WB-3923	
Do You Know Where God Lives (Cy Coben)	F2-WB-8123	RCA 20/47-6407A
Bayou Baby (A Cajun Lullaby) (Merle Travis)	F2-WB-8124	RCA 20/47-6407B
You Don't Know Me* (Walker-Arnold)	F2-WB-8125	RCA 20/47-6502B

Session: March 15, 1956, RCA Victor Studios, New York
Producer: Sholes
Musicians: Trigger Alpert (b), Barnes (gtr), Bob Davie (pno), Hanlon (gtr), Kraus (drm)

Sixteen Tons (Merle Travis)	G2-WB-2914	
Don't Fence Me In (Cole Porter)	G2-WB-2915	
The Rockin' Mockin' Bird* (Singleton-McCoy)	G2-WB-2916	RCA 20/47-6502A

Session: May 14, 1956, Webster Hall, New York
Producer: Sholes
Musicians: same as March 15, 1956, with string acc

| Sometime (Kahn-Fiorito) | G2WB-4330 |
| I Don't Know Why (I Just Do) (Turk-Ahlert) | G2WB-4331 |

Don't Take Your Love from Me (Henry Nemo)   G2WB-4332
I Only Have Eyes for You (Dubin-Warren)   G2WB-4333

Session: May 15, 1956, Webster Hall, New York
Producer: Sholes
Musicians: Barnes (gtr), Sam Bruno (b), Chernet (gtr), Davie (pno), Kraus (b),
Eddy Manson (hca), string acc

Casey Jones (The Brave Engineer) (Seibert-Newton) G2WB-4334   RCA 20/47-6601A
The Ballad of Wes Tancred (Myrow-Wells)   G2WB-4335   RCA 20/47-6699A
September Song (Weill-Anderson)   G2WB-4336
It Had to Be You (Kahn-Jones)   G2WB-4337

Session: May 22, 1956, RCA Victor Studios, Nashville
Producer: Atkins
Musicians: Atkins (gtr), Buddy Harman (drm), Moore (b), Shook (gtr)

Warm All Over (Frank Loesser)   G2WB-0283
Big D (Frank Loesser)   G2WB-0284
Don't Cry (Frank Loesser)   G2WB-0285
Standing on the Corner (Frank Loesser)   G2WB-0286

Session: May 29, 1956, RCA Victor Studios, Nashville
Producer: Sholes
Musicians: Garland (gtr), Sam Hollingsworth (b), Hughes (pno), Doug Kirkham (drm),
Shook (gtr), Wiggins (steel gtr)

You Were Mine for A While (Hicks-Freeman)   G2WB-0301   RCA 20/47-6601B
How Did You Know (Joan Hager)   G2WB-0302
I'd Like to Be (Hugh Ashley)   G2WB-0303†

Session: June 28, 1956, Webster Hall, New York
Producer: Sholes
Musicians: Barnes (gtr), Davie (pno), Lessberg (b), Bunnie Shawker (drm),
Eddy Thomas (gtr), string acc cond Charles Grean

The Way You Look Tonight (Kern-Fields)   G2WB-5868
A Little on the Lonely Side (Robertson-Cavanaugh) G2WB-5869
That Old Feeling (Brown-Fain)   G2WB-5870
You'll Never Know (Gordon-Warren)   G2WB-5871

Session: June 29, 1956, Webster Hall, New York
Producer: Sholes
Musicians: same as March 15, 1956

The Very Thought of You (Ray Noble)   G2WB-5884†
I Cried for You (Freed-Arnheim-Lyman)   G2WB-5885
Take A Tiger by the Tail (Schuster-Lowe)   G2WB-5886
A Good Lookin' Blonde (Zep Turner)   G2WB-5887   RCA 20/47-6773A

Session: August 23, 1956, Webster Hall, New York
Producer: Sholes
Musicians: Barnes (gtr), Chernet (gtr), Davie (pno), Kraus (drm), Jack Lessberg (b),
string acc cond Grean

The Way You Look Tonight (Kern-Fields)   G2WB-6857
A Little on the Lonely Side (Robertson-Cavanaugh) G2WB-6858

That Old Feeling (Brown-Fain)	G2WB-6859	
You'll Never Know (Gordon-Warren)	G2WB-6860	
The Very Thought of You (Ray Noble)	G2WB-6861	
I Cried for You (Freed-Arnheim-Lyman)	G2WB-6862	

Session: October 4, 1956, Webster Hall, New York
Producer: Sholes
(EA duets with Jaye P. Morgan)
Musicians: Barnes (gtr), Davie (pno), Lessberg (b), Billy Mure (gtr), Shawker (drm), brass acc

If'n (Dubey-Karr)	G2WB-7737	RCA 20/47-6708A
Mutual Admiration Society (Dubey-Karr)	G2WB-7738	RCA 20/47-6708B
One (Warren Spencer)	G2WB-7739	RCA 20/47-6842B
Do You Love Me (Floyd Wilson)	G2WB-7740	RCA 20/47-6842A

Session: March 7, 1957, Webster Hall, New York
Producer: Sholes
Musicians: Domenic Cortese (accordian), Lessberg (b), Joe Marshall (drm), Mure (gtr), William Rowland (pno), Thomas (gtr)

Daddy's Little Boy (Billy Collins)	H2WB-2152	
Don't Ever Take the Ribbons from Your Hair (Helen Hudgins)	H2WB-2153	
Little Man You've Had A Busy Day (Sigler-Hoffman-Wayne)	H2WB-2153	
Little Lady Make Believe (Tobias-Simon)	H2WB-2155	

Session: April 9, 1957, Webster Hall, New York
Producer: Sholes
Musicians: same as October 4, 1956, with Eddy Thomas (gtr) replacing Mure

Gonna Find Me A Bluebird (Marvin Rainwater)	H2WB-3364	RCA 20/47-6905A
Little Bit (Joan Hager)	H2WB-3365	RCA 20/47-6905B
What A Way to Die (Wolfe-Moore)	H2WB-3366†	

Session: April 11, 1957, Webster Hall, New York
Producer: Sholes
Musicians: same as October 4, 1956, with Perri (gtr) replacing Mure, orch acc cond Grean

Scarlet Ribbons (For Her Hair) (Segal-Denzig)	H2WB-3419	
When He Was Young (Manson-Ebb)	H2WB-3420	RCA 20/47-7040A
Specially for Little Girls (Peter Cadby)	H2WB-3421	
Say Goodnight (Moore-Grean)	H2WB-3422	

Session: April 12, 1957, Webster Hall, New York
Producer: Sholes
Musicians: Barnes (gtr), Danny Herd (pno), Lessberg (b), Perri (gtr), Terry Snyder (drm), voc acc

Daddy's Little Girl (Burke-Gerlach)	H2WB-3423	
Little Miss Sunbeam (Willems-Fort)	H2WB-3424	RCA 20/47-7040B
Little Johnny Everything (Csida-Grean)	H2WB-3425	
My Little Buckaroo (Scool-Jerome)	H2WB-3426	

Session: June 25, 1957, RCA Victor Studios, New York
Producer: Sholes
Musicians: Barnes (gtr), Ernie Calabria (gtr), Davie (pno), Shawker (drm), Gene Traxler (b), voc acc

Crazy Dream (Bryant-Bryant)	H2WB-4855	RCA 20/47-6975A
The Biggest Fool in Tennessee (Raleigh-Coleman)	H2WB-4856	
What A Way to Die (Moore-Wolfe)	H2WB-4857	
Open Your Heart (Cindy Walker)	H2WB-4858	RCA 20/47-6975B
The Day You Left Me (Cindy Walker)	H2WB-4886†	

Session: June 28, 1957, RCA Victor Studios, New York
Producer: Sholes
Musicians: same as June 25, 1957, without voc acc

Gimme A Little Kiss (Will Ya, Huh?)	
(Turk-Smith-Pinkard)	H2WB-4915
Two Sleepy People (Loesser-Carmichael)	H2WB-4916
Why Don't We Do This More Often (Newman-Wrubel)	H2WB-4917
Paradise (Brown-Clifford)	H2WB-4918

Session: July 22, 1957, RCA Victor Studios, New York
Producer: Sholes
Musicians: Andy Ackers (pno), Chernet (gtr), Lessberg (b), Mure (gtr), Shawker (drm), voc acc

My Darling, My Darling (Frank Loesser)	H2WB-5368
Hands Across the Table (Parish-Delettre)	H2WB-5369
You're My Everything (Dixon-Young-Warren)	H2WB-4370
Everything I Have Is Yours (Adamson-Lane)	H2WB-4371

Session: July 23, 1957, RCA Victor Studios, New York
Producer: Sholes
Musicians: same as July 22, 1957, with John Pizzarelli (gtr) replacing Mure, without voc acc

Let's Fall in Love (Koehler-Arlen)	H2WB-5701
I'm Yours (Harburg-Green)	H2WB-5702
Ev'ry Time We Say Goodbye (Cole Porter)	H2WB-5703
A Lovely Way to Spend An Evening	
(Adamson-McHugh)	H2WB-5704

Session: July 25, 1957, Webster Hall, New York
Producer: Sholes
(EA and Hugo Winterhalter billed equally)
Musicians: Kraus (drm), Don Lamond (drm), Lessberg (b), Mundell Lowe (gtr), Henry
Rowland (pno), orch and voc acc cond Hugo Winterhalter

Wagon Wheels* (Hill-De Rose)	H2PB-5753	RCA 20/47-7089A
Molly Darling (Will Hays)	H2PB-5754†	
Wandering Star (Wayne-Frisch)	H2PB-5755†	
You've Made Up for Everything (Cindy Walker)	H2PB-5756	RCA 20/47-7089B

Session: December 5, 1957, RCA Victor Studios, Nashville
Producer: Atkins
Musicians: Floyd Cramer (pno), Garland (gtr), Harman (drm), Roy Huskey, Jr. (b), voc acc

Too Soon to Know (Don Gibson)	H2PB-7346	RCA 20/47-7143A
I Need Somebody (Sharp-Teifer)	H2PB-7347	RCA 20/47-7143B
All It Takes (Spielman-Pleskow-Discant)	H2PB-7348†	

Session: February 5–6 & 19, 1958, RCA Victor Studios, Nashville
Producer: Atkins
Musicians: Boyce Hawkins (org), Hughes (pno), voc acc

February 5
I Am Thine, O Lord (Crosby-Doane)   J2WB-0375
Jesus Is Calling (Crosby-Stebbins)   J2WB-0376
Pass Me Not (Crosby-Doane)   J2WB-0377
Near the Cross (Crosby-Doane)   J2WB-0378

February 6
Close To Thee (Crosby-Vail)   J2WB-0383
Rescue the Perishing (Crosby-Doane)   J2WB-0384
Safe in the Arms of Jesus (Crosby-Doane)   J2WB-0385
Tell Me the Story of Jesus (Crosby-Sweney)   J2WB-0386

February 19
Praise Him, Praise Him (Crosby-Allen)   J2WB-0402
Blessed Assurance (Crosby-Knapp)   J2WB-0403
Though Your Sins Be as Scarlet (Crosby-Doane) J2WB-0404
He Hideth My Soul (Crosby-Kilpatrick)   J2WB-0405

Session: February 26, 1958, RCA Victor Studios, Nashville
Producer: Atkins
Musicians: Jerry Byrd (b), Cramer (pno), Harman (drm), Grady Martin (gtr), Shook (gtr), voc acc

Take Her for A Boat Ride (Cy Coben)   J2WB-0429
Peck-A-Cheek (Darin-Coben)   J2WB-0430   RCA 20/47-7221A
Before You Know It (Stuart-Reiter-Schnapf)   J2WB-0431   RCA 20/47-7221B

Session: March 20, 1958, RCA Victor Studios, Nashville
Producer: Atkins
Musicians: same as February 26, 1958, with Huskey (b) replacing Jerry Byrd

The Day You Left Me (Cindy Walker)   J2WB-0468   RCA 20/47-7292A
Sweet Night of Love (Boudleaux Bryant)   J2WB-0469†
Little Swallow (Farnsworth-Furtado)   J2WB-0470
When A Fellow Falls in Love (Floyd Wilson)   J2WB-0471†

Session: June 2, 1958, RCA Victor Studios, Nashville
Producer: Atkins
Musicians: Atkins (gtr), Cramer (pno), Garland (gtr), Harman (drm), Moore (b), Velma Williams Smith (gtr)

Real Love (Phil Everly)   J2WB-3235†
I'll Do as Much for You Some Day (Nelson-Nelson, Jr.) J2WB-3236†
That's How Much I Love You (Arnold-Fowler-Hall) J2WB-3237

Session: June 13, 1958, RCA Victor Studios, Nashville
Producer: Sholes
Musicians: Atkins (gtr), Moore (b)

Real Love (Phil Everly)   J2WB-3260   RCA 20/47-7292B

Session: July 29, 1958, RCA Victor Studios, Nashville
Producer: Atkins
Musicians: Atkins (gtr), Byrd (b), Cramer (pno), Harman (drm), Martin (gtr)

Singing the Blues (Melvin Endsley)   J2WB-3306
Kisses Sweeter Than Wine (Campbell-Newman)   J2WB-3307

Wabash Cannon Ball (Hughie Cannon)	J2WB-3308	
Unbreakable Heart (Allison-Allison-Wyatt)	J2WB-3309	

Session: August 5, 1958, RCA Victor Studios, New York
Producer: Sholes
Musicians: Barnes (gtr), Al Casamenti (gtr), Davie (pno), Lessberg (b), Herbert Lovelle (drm), voc acc

My Woman (Zeno Goss)	J2WB-6117†	
I'm A Good Boy* (Moore-Grean)	J2WB-6118	RCA 47-7340A[3]
The Dark at the Top of the Stairs (Tom Glazer)	J2WB-6119†	
Till You Come Back Again (Buddy Killen)	J2WB-6120	RCA 47-7340B

Session: September 14, 1958, RCA Victor Studios, Nashville
Producer: Atkins
Musicians: Atkins (gtr), Garland (gtr), Harman (drm), Hughes (pno), Moore (b), voc acc

Oklahoma Hills (Guthrie-Guthrie)	J2WB-3380
Missouri (Duncan-Penny)	J2WB-3381
Mister and Mississippi (Irving Gordon)	J2WB-3382
Idaho (Jessie Stone)	J2WB-3383

Session: September 18, 1958, RCA Victor Studios, Nashville
Producer: Atkins
Musicians: same as September 14, 1958, with Floyd Cramer (pno) replacing Hughes

Indiana (Back Home Again in Indiana) (MacDonald-Hanley)	J2WB-3384
Carry Me Back to Old Virginny (James Bland)	J2WB-3385
Georgia on My Mind (Gorrell-Carmichael)	J2WB-3386
Kentucky Babe (Buck-Geibel)	J2WB-3387

Session: September 19, 1958, RCA Victor Studios, Nashville
Producer: Atkins
Musicians: same as September 14, 1958

Carolina in the Morning (Kahn-Donaldson)	J2WB-3388
Beautiful, Ohio (MacDonald-Earl)	J2WB-3389
Stars Fell on Indiana (Parish-Perkins)	J2WB-3390
On Miami Shores (Jacobi-LeBaron)	J2WB-3391

Session: December 4, 1958, RCA Victor Studios, Nashville
Producer: Atkins
Musicians: same as September 14, 1958, with Jimmy Selph (gtr), string acc

Just A Little Lovin' (Clements-Arnold)	J2WB-6950	
I'll Hold You in My Heart (Till I Can Hold You in My Arms) (Dilbeck-Arnold-Horton)	J2WB-6951	RCA 7435B
Chip Off the Old Block (James Lee)	J2WB-6952	RCA 7435A

---

[3]From this point forward, RCA ceased issuing EA's records on 78. All recordings had the prefix "47" (indicating 45 rpm) followed by four digits. The following entries include only the last four digits, followed by A or B (indicating A- or B-side, as before).

Session: December 10, 1958, RCA Victor Studios, Nashville
Producer: Atkins
Musicians: same as September 14, 1958, with Wiggins (steel gtr)

Love Will Find Out the Way (Goldman-Paxton-Weiss) J2WB-6964
I'll Have Nothing to Lose (Bonnie Guitar) J2WB-6965

Session: April 15, 1959, RCA Victor Studios, New York
Producer: Herman Diaz
Musicians: Ernie Ardi (gtr), Lee Erwin (pno), Juan Esquivel (pno), Arthur Marotti (drm),
Bob Rosengarden (drm), orch and voc acc cond Juan Esquivel

When Day Is Done (DeSylva-Katscher) K2PB-2410†
Someone to Watch Over Me (Gershwin-Gershwin) K2PB-2411†

Session: April 24, 1959, RCA Victor Studios, Nashville
Producer: Atkins
Musicians: Atkins (gtr), Cramer (pno), Ray Edenton (gtr), Harman (drm), John D.
Loudermilk (gtr), Moore (b), voc acc

Little Sparrow (Crutchfield-Crutchfield) K2WB-0524
What's the Good (Of All This Love) (Moore-Davie) K2WB-0525 RCA 7542B

Session: April 27, 1959, RCA Victor Studios, Nashville
Producer: Atkins
Musicians: Atkins (gtr), Byrd (b), Edenton (gtr), Harman (drm), Kirkham (drm),
Loudermilk (gtr)

Tennessee Stud* (Jimmie Driftwood) K2WB-0526 RCA 7542A

Session: July 13 & 21, 1959, RCA Victor Studios, Nashville
Producer: Atkins
Musicians: Atkins (gtr), Harman (drm), Loudermilk (gtr, hca), Moore (b), Williams Smith
(gtr), voc acc

July 13
Jesse James (traditional) K2WB-1419
Johnny Reb, That's Me (Bill Graham) K2WB-1420 RCA 7661A
Tom Dooley (Arr. Warner-Lomax-Lomax) K2WB-1421
Nellie Sits A-Waitin' (Crutchfield-Nelson) K2WB-1422

July 21
The Wreck of the Old '97 (Whitter-Noell-Lewey) K2WB-1426
Boot Hill (Crumbacker-Wilson) K2WB-1427 RCA 7661B
Riders in the Sky (Stan Jones) K2WB-1428

Session: July 24, 1959, RCA Victor Studios, Nashville
Producer: Atkins
Musicians: same as July 13, 1959, without Loudermilk

The Battle of Little Big Horn (Nancy Chase) K2WB-1434
The Red Headed Stranger (Linderman-Stutz) K2WB-1435
The Ballad of Davy Crockett (Blackburn-Bruns) K2WB-1436
Partners (Danny Dill) K2WB-1437

Session: September 15, 1959, RCA Victor Studios, Nashville
Producer: Atkins
Musicians: Atkins (gtr), Cramer (pno), Garland (gtr), Harman (drm), Loudermilk (gtr), Moore (b), voc acc

Sittin' by Sittin' Bull (Jimmie Driftwood)	K2WB-1468	RCA 7619B
Did It Rain (Crutchfield-Dinning-Robertson)	K2WB-1469	RCA 7619A

Session: November 24, 1959, RCA Victor Studios, Nashville
Producer: Atkins
Musicians: Atkins (gtr), Cramer (pno), Garland (gtr), Harman (drm), Moore (b), Williams Smith (gtr), Wiggins (steel gtr), voc acc

A Heart Full of Love (For A Handful of Kisses) (Arnold-Nelson-Soehnel)	K2WB-1548
Anytime (Herbert Lawson)	K2WB-1549
I Wanna Play House with You (Cy Coben)	K2WB-1550
The Lovebug Itch (Carson-Botkin)	K2WB-1551

Session: November 25, 1959, RCA Victor Studios, Nashville
Producer: Atkins
Musicians: same as November 24, 1959, with string acc

Just A Little Lovin' (Will Go A Long Way) (Clements-Arnold)	K2WB-1554
I Walk Alone (Herbert Wilson)	K2WB-1555
It's A Sin (Rose-Turner)	K2WB-1556
I'll Hold You in My Heart (Till I Can Hold You in My Arms) (Dilbeck-Horton-Arnold)	K2WB-1557

Session: December 9, 1959 & January 18, 1960, RCA Victor Studios, Nashville
Producer: Atkins
Musicians: same as November 25, 1959, without Atkins

You Don't Know Me (Walker-Arnold)	K2WB-1578
I Really Don't Want to Know (Robertson-Barnes)	K2WB-1579
Molly Darling (Adapt. Hays-Arnold)	K2WB-1580
Bouquet of Roses (Nelson-Hilliard)	K2WB-1581

January 18

Texarkana Baby (Clark-Rose)	L2WB-0045

Session: February 16, 1960, RCA Victor Studios, Nashville
Producer: Atkins
Musicians: Atkins (gtr), Cramer (pno), Garland (gtr), Harman (drm), Huskey (b), string acc, voc acc

My Arms Are A House (Kennedy-Alstone)	L2WB-0062	RCA 7727A
The Lovebug Itch (Carson-Botkin)	L2WB-0063	
Little Sparrow (Crutchfield-Crutchfield)	L2WB-0064	RCA 7727B

Session: May 31, 1960, RCA Victor Studios, Nashville
Producer: Atkins
Musicians: Atkins (gtr), Cramer (pno), Garland (gtr), Karl Garvin (trumpet), Harman (drm), Moore (b), Williams Smith (gtr), voc acc

There's A Star Spangled Banner Waving
    Somewhere (Roberts-Darnell-McEnery)   L2WB-0172†
Catch Me A Kiss (Tepper-Bennett)   L2WB-0173†
Now I Think as A Man (Roberts-Katz)   L2WB-0174

Session: June 1 & 8–9, 1960, RCA Victor Studios, Nashville
Producer: Atkins
Musicians: Atkins (gtr), Loudermilk (gtr), Moore (b), Williams Smith (gtr), voc acc

June 1

If I Had My Life to Live Over (Vincent-Tobias-Jaffe)	L2WW-0178
How's the World Treating You (Bryant-Atkins)	L2WW-0179
I Don't Want to Walk Without You (Loesser-Styne)	L2WW-0180

June 8

Have I Told You Lately That I Love (Scott Wiseman)	L2WW-0181
I Wish I Didn't Love You So (Frank Loesser)	L2WW-0182
You're Nobody 'Till Somebody Loves You	
(Morgan-Stock-Cavanaugh)	L2WW-0183
Love Me (Stoller-Leiber)	L2WW-0184†

June 9

You Gotta Have Love (Nash-Atkins)	L2WW-0185
I'm Alone Because I Love You (Schuster-Young)	L2WW-0186
Love and Marriage (Cahn-Van Heusen)	L2WW-0187
Answer Me, My Love (Winkler-Rauch-Sigman)	L2WW-0188
Love Me (Stoller-Leiber)	L2WW-0189

Session: September 2, 1960, RCA Victor Studios, Nashville
Producer: Atkins
Musicians: same as November 24, 1959, without Wiggins

Just Out of Reach (V. F. Stewart)	L2-WW-0268	RCA 7794B
Before This Day Ends (McAlpin-Wilson-Drusky)	L2-WW-0269	RCA 7794A
Golden Girl (John D. Loudermilk)	L2-WW-0270†	

Session: February 1, 1961, RCA Victor Studios, Nashville
Producer: Atkins
Musicians: EA (gtr), Atkins (gtr), Louis Dunn (drm), Bill Pursell (pno), Williams Smith (gtr), Strzelecki (b), string acc, voc acc

If I Never Get to Heaven (Carson-Botkin)	M2WW-0526
I Love You Because (Leon Payne)	M2WW-0527
I Don't Want to Set the World on Fire	
(Seiler-Marcus-Benjamin-Durham)	M2WW-0528
Hey Good Lookin' (Hank Williams)	M2WW-0529

Session: February 8, 1961, RCA Victor Studios, Nashville
Producer: Atkins
Musicians: same as February 1, 1961, without EA on guitar

Will You Always (Robertson-Blair)	M2WW-0534	
Hold Me (Little-Oppenheim-Schuster)	M2WW-0537	
(Jim) I Wore A Tie Today* (Cindy Walker)	M2WW-0538	RCA 7861A
Just Call Me Lonesome (Rex Griffin)	M2WW-0539	RCA 7861B

Session: February 15, 1961, RCA Victor Studios, Nashville
Producer: Atkins
Musicians: Kirkham (drm), Pursell (pno), Williams Smith (gtr), Strzelecki (b), string acc, voc acc

Let's Make Memories Tonight (Gene Nash)	M2WW-0546
It's Been So Long, Darlin' (Ernest Tubb)	M2WW-0547
Take Me in Your Arms and Hold Me (Cindy Walker)	M2WW-0548
You're the Only Star (In My Blue Heaven) (Gene Autry)	M2WW-0549
Are You Sincere (Wayne Walker)	M2WW-0550

Session: May 26, 1961, RCA Victor Studios, Nashville
Producer: Atkins
Musicians: Cramer (pno), Harman (drm), Kirkham (drm), Martin (gtr), Williams Smith (gtr), Strzelecki (b), voc acc

Lonely People (Powell-Kearney)	M2WW-0680
One Grain of Sand (LaRue-Maxwell-Maxwell)	M2WW-0681†
The Worst Night of My Life (Crutchfield-Crutchfield)	M2WW-0682†

Session: July 14, 1961, RCA Victor Studios, Nashville
Producer: Atkins
Musicians: EA (gtr), Cramer (pno), Martin (gtr), Williams Smith (gtr), voc acc

One Grain of Sand (LaRue-Maxwell-Maxwell)	M2WW-0883	RCA 7926A
The Worst Night of My Life (Crutchfield-Crutchfield)	M2WW-0884	RCA 7926B

Session: September 6, 1961, RCA Victor Studios, Nashville
Producer: Atkins
Musicians: Cramer (pno), Garland (gtr), Harman (drm), Williams Smith (gtr), Strzelecki (b), voc acc

I'd Trade All My Tomorrows (For Just One Yesterday) (Jenny Lou Carson)	M2WW-0944
That Do Make It Nice (Arnold-Ebb-Klein)	M2WW-0945
This Is the Thanks I Get (For Loving You) (Dilbeck-Arnold)	M2WW-0946
The Kentuckian Song (Irving Gordon)	M2WW-0947
The Richest Man (In the World) (Boudleaux Bryant)	M2WW-0948

Session: September 19, 1961, RCA Victor Studios, Nashville
Producer: Atkins
Musicians: same as September. 6, 1961, with Roy Wiggins (steel gtr) replacing Garland

Then I Turned and Walked Slowly Away (Fortner-Arnold)	M2WW-0957
Don't Rob Another Man's Castle (Jenny Lou Carson)	M2WW-0958
What A Fool I Was (Stu Davis)	M2WW-0959
I'm Throwing Rice (At the Girl I Love) (Nelson-Nelson-Arnold)	M2WW-0960
The Cattle Call (Tex Owens)	M2WW-0961

Session: December 5, 1961, RCA Victor Studios, Nashville
Producer: Atkins
Musicians: Atkins (gtr), Cramer (pno), Garland (gtr), Harman (drm), Moore (b), Williams Smith (gtr), voc acc

I'll Do as Much for You Someday (Nelson-Nelson, Jr.)   M2WW-1072   RCA 7984B
Tears Broke Out on Me (Hank Cochran)   M2WW-1073   RCA 7984A
The Wall Came Tumbling Down (Berry-Resnick)   M2WW-1074†

Session: February 5, 1962, RCA Victor Studios, Nashville
Producer: Atkins
Musicians: Dunn (drm), Edenton (gtr), Martin (gtr), Williams Smith (gtr), Strzelecki (b),
voc acc

Ole Faithful (Kennedy-Carr)   N2WW-0555
A Cowboy's Dream (traditional)   N2WW-0556
Sierra Sue (Joseph Carey)   N2WW-0557
Tumbling Tumbleweeds (Bob Nolan)   N2WW-0558
Leanin' on the Old Top Rail (Kenny-Kenny)   N2WW-0559†

Session: February 23, 1962, RCA Victor Studios, Nashville
Producer: Atkins
Musicians: EA (gtr), Edenton (gtr), Harman (drm), Martin (gtr), Williams Smith (gtr),
Strzelecki (drm), voc acc

The Wayward Wind (Newman-Lebowsky)   N2WW-0620
Carry Me Back to the Lone Prairie (Arr. Eddy Arnold)   N2WW-0621
Cowpoke (Stan Jones)   N2WW-0622
Where the Mountains Meet the Sky (Williams-Kaye)   N2WW-0623

Session: March 5, 1962, RCA Victor Studios, Nashville
Producer: Atkins
Musicians: Edenton (gtr), Kirkham (drm), Martin (gtr), Williams Smith (gtr),
Strzelecki (drm), voc acc

The Streets of Laredo (traditional)   N2WW-0637
Cool Water (Bob Nolan)   N2WW-0638
Leanin' on the Old Top Rail (Kenny-Kenny)   N2WW-0639
White Christmas (Irving Berlin)   N2WW-0640
C-H-R-I-S-T-M-A-S (Carson-Arnold)   N2WW-0641

Session: March 6, 1962, RCA Victor Studios, Nashville
Producer: Atkins
Musicians: William Ackerman (drm), Ken Carllile (gtr), Pursell (pno), Williams Smith (gtr),
Strzelecki (b), voc acc

Christmas Can't Be Far Away (Boudleaux Bryant)   N2WW-0642
Santa Claus Is Comin' to Town (Gillespie-Coots)   N2WW-0643
I Heard the Bells on Christmas Day (Henry
     Wadsworth Longfellow, adapted by John Marks) N2WW-0643
Will Santy Come to Shanty Town
     (Arnold-Nelson-Nelson-Nelson, Jr.)   N2WW-0644
Winter Wonderland (Smith-Bernard)   N2WW-0645

Session: March 7, 1962, RCA Victor Studios, Nashville
Producer: Atkins
Musicians: Ken Carllile (gtr), Dunn (drm), Pursell (pno), Williams Smith (gtr),
Strzelecki (b), voc acc

Jingle Bell Rock (Beal-Boothe)   N2WW-0647
Up on the Housetop (traditional)   N2WW-0648

Jolly Old Saint Nicholas (traditional)   N2WW-0649
It Came Upon A Midnight Clear (Willis-Sears)   N2WW-0650
O Little Town of Bethlehem (Redner-Brooks)   N2WW-0651
Silent Night (traditional)   N2WW-0652

Session: May 4, 1962, RCA Victor Studios, Nashville
Producer: Atkins
Musicians: Cramer (pno), Paul Ferrara (drm), Jerry Reed Hubbard (gtr), Martin (gtr),
Strzelecki (b), voc acc

After Loving You (Miller-Lantz)   N2WW-0726   RCA 8048B
She Called Me Baby (Harlan Howard)   N2WW-0727
Tender Touch (Kirby-Dickens)   N2WW-0728   RCA 8102B
A Little Heartache (Wayne Walker)   N2WW-0729   RCA 8048A

Session: July 6, 1962, RCA Victor Studios, Nashville
Producer: Atkins
Musicians: Atkins (gtr), Hughes (vibes), McCoy (hca), Pursell (pno), Williams Smith (gtr),
Strzelecki (b), Joseph Tanner (gtr), voc acc

Comin' Green (Hackady-Naylor)   N2WW-0787
My Own True Love (David-Steiner)   N2WW-0788
My Darling Nellie Gray (B. R. Handy)   N2WW-0789
Old Folks (Hill-Robison)   N2WW-0790

Session: July 31, 1962, RCA Victor Studios, Nashville
Producer: Atkins
Musicians: Ackerman (drm), H Bradley (gtr), Cramer (pno), McCoy (hca), Williams Smith
(gtr), Strzelecki (b), voc acc

The Green Leaves of Summer (Webster-Timokin)   N2WW-0819
The Battle of New Orleans (Jimmie Driftwood)   N2WW-0820
Does He Mean That Much to You (Robertson-Rollins) N2WW-0821   RCA 8102A

Session: August 1, 1962, RCA Victor Studios, Nashville
Producer: Atkins
Musicians: same as July 31, 1962, with string acc

My Shoes Keep Walking Back to You (Ross-Wills) N2WW-0825
She Thinks I Still Care (Liscomb-Duffy)   N2WW-0826
Black Cloud (Bill Brock)   N2WW-0827
May You Always (Markes-Charles)   N2WW-0828
Moody River (Gary Bruce)   N2WW-0829
Charlie's Shoes (Roy Baham)   N2WW-0830

Session: September 5, 1962, RCA Victor Studios, Nashville
Producer: Anita Kerr
Musicians: Billy Byrd (gtr), Dunn (drm), Hughes (pno), Williams Smith (gtr),
Strzelecki (b), voc acc

The Unclouded Day (J. K. Alwood)   N2WW-0879
I Love to Tell the Story (Hankey-Fischer)   N2WW-0880
Love Lifted Me (Rowe-Smith)   N2WW-0881
Take My Hand, Precious Lord (Thomas A. Dorsey) N2WW-0882
Open Thy Merciful Arms (Don Whiston)   N2WW-0883
Wonderful Words of Life (P. P. Bliss)   N2WW-0884

Session: September 6, 1962, RCA Victor Studios, Nashville
Producer: Anita Kerr
Musicians: same as September 5, 1962, with string acc

God Walks These Hills with Me (McAlpin-Hughes)	N2WW-0885	
He Lives Next Door (Gene Nash)	N2WW-0886	
The Voice in the Old Village Choir (Kahn-Woods)	N2WW-0887	
May the Good Lord Bless and Keep You		
(Meredith Wilson)	N2WW-0888	
Go Little Prayer (Wetherell-Fredrickson-Wilson)	N2WW-0889	
Where We'll Never Grow Old (James Moore)	N2WW-0890	

Session: February 13, 1963, RCA Victor Studios, Nashville
Producer: Atkins
Musicians: H. Bradley (gtr), Harman (drm), Joe Layne (pno), Pursell (pno),
Williams Smith (gtr), Strzelecki (b), voc acc

I Don't Cry No More (Harlan Howard)	PPA4-0122	RCA 8445B
A Million Years or So (Charlie Williams)	PPA4-0123	RCA 8207A
Lonely Balladeer (Kirby-Dickens)	PPA4-0124	RCA 8160B
Yesterday's Memories (Hank Cochran)	PPA4-0125	RCA 8160A

Session: May 31, 1963, RCA Victor Studios, Nashville
Producer: Atkins
Musicians: Arnold (drm), H. Bradley (gtr), Cramer (pno), Edenton (gtr), Jerry Kennedy (gtr),
Strzelecki (b), voc acc

Just A Ribbon* (Scott-Resnick)	PPA4-0316	RCA 8207B
I Met Her Today (Robertson-Blair)	PPA4-0317	RCA 8253B
Rhinestones (Merle Kilgore)	PPA4-0318†	

Session: September 3, 1963, RCA Victor Studios, Nashville
Producer: Atkins
Musicians: Arnold (drm), Cramer (pno), Reed Hubbard (gtr), Layne (org), Moss (gtr),
Williams Smith (gtr), Strzelecki (b), voc acc

Sweet Adorable You* (Baker Knight)	PPA4-0393	RCA 8363A
Jealous Hearted Me (A. P. Carter)	PPA4-0394†	
I Thank My Lucky Stars (Wayne Walker)	PPA4-0395	RCA 8445A

Session: September 10, 1963, RCA Victor Studios, Nashville
Producer: Atkins
Musicians: Atkins (gtr), Ken Buttrey (drm), Cramer (pianist), Kennedy (gtr),
Williams Smith (gtr), Strzelecki (b), voc acc

Jealous Hearted Me (A. P. Carter)	PPA4-0416	RCA 8253A

Session: October 8–10, 1963, RCA Victor Studios, Nashville
Producer: Atkins
Musicians: Arnold (drm), Atkins (gtr), H. Bradley (drm), Edenton (gtr), Kennedy (gtr),
Layne (vibes), Strzelecki (b), voc acc

October 8

Jeff Canady (Danny Dill)	PWA4-0468	
The Song of the Coo Coo (Bill Faier)	PWA4-0469	RCA 8296B
Gotta Travel On (Clayton-Lazar-Ehrlich-Six)	PWA4-0470	
Time's A Gettin' Hard (Lee Hays)	PWA4-0471	

October 9
Green, Green (McGuire-Sparks)   PWA4-0478
Where Have All the Flowers Gone (Pete Seeger)   PWA4-0479
The Young Land (Jerry Fuller)   PWA4-0480
The Folk Singer (Merle Kilgore)   PWA4-0481
Molly* (Steve Karliski)   PWA4-0482   RCA 8296A

October 10
Cotton Fields (Huddie Ledbetter)   PWA4-0487
Blowin' in the Wind (Bob Dylan)   PWA4-0488
Poor Howard (Harlan Howard)   PWA4-0489
It Comes and Goes (Bill Anderson)   PWA4-0490

Session: February 13–14, 1964, RCA Victor Studios, Nashville
Producer: Atkins
Musicians: Floyd Robinson (gtr), Cramer (pno), Edenton (gtr), Harman (drm), Kennedy (gtr),
Strzelecki (b), string acc, voc acc

February 13
A Little Bitty Tear (Let Me Down) (Hank Cochran)   RWA4-1113
Lonely People (Stough-Powell-Kearney)   RWA4-1114
No Other Arms-No Other Lips
    (Whitney-Kramer-Zaret)   RWA4-1115
(I Wanna Go Where You Go, Do What You Do)
    Then I'll Be Happy (Friend-Clare-Brown)   RWA4-1116
The Minute You're Gone (Jimmy Gately)   RWA4-1117
Sometimes I'm Happy (Youmans-Caesar)   RWA4-1118

February 14
Roamin' Through the Countryside (Kendall Hayes)   RWA4-1119
Laughing on the Outside (Crying on the Inside)
    (Wayne-Raleigh)   RWA4-1120
(I Got A Woman Crazy for Me) She's Funny
    That Way (Whiting-Moret)   RWA4-1121
It Only Hurts for A Little While (David-Spielman)   RWA4-1122
Smile (Chaplan-Parsons-Turner)   RWA4-1123
After Loving You (Miller-Lantz)   RWA4-1124

Session: March 26, 1964, RCA Victor Studios, Nashville
Producer: Atkins
Musicians: Arnold (drm), Harman (drm), Reed Hubbard (gtr), Kennedy (gtr), Layne (vibes),
Pursell (pno), Williams Smith (gtr), Strzelecki (b), voc acc

This Is the Place (Alex Zanetis)   RWA4-1175†
Why (Cindy Walker)   RWA4-1176   RCA 8363B
So Used to Loving You (Sonny Curtis)   RWA4-1177†

Session: July 27–29, 1964, RCA Victor Studios, New York
Producer: Jim Foglesong
Musicians: Sandy Block (b), Dick Hyman (pno), Osie Johnson (drm), Art Marotti (perc),
Art Ryerson (gtr), string acc cond Gold, voc acc

July 27
Four Walls (Moore-Campbell)   RPA1-6301
The End of the World (Dee-Kent)   RPA1-6302
I Fall to Pieces (Cochran-Howard)   RPA1-6303
Faded Love (Wills-Wills)   RPA1-6304

July 28

Half as Much (Curley Williams)	RPA1-6305
Oh, Lonesome Me (Don Gibson)	RPA1-6306
Lonely Street (Sowder-Belew-Stevenson)	RPA1-6307
Till I Waltz Again with You (Sidney Prosen)	RPA1-6308

July 29

I Can't Help It (If I'm Still in Love with You) (Hank Williams)	RPA1-6309
Tennessee Waltz (Stewart-King)	RPA1-6310
Gone (Smokey Rogers)	RPA1-6311
Your Cheatin' Heart (Hank Williams)	RPA1-6312

Session: November 19, 1964, RCA Victor Studios, Nashville
Producer: Atkins
Musicians: Buttrey (drm), Moss (gtr), Pursell (pno), Williams Smith (gtr), Strzelecki (b), Bill Walker (vibes), voc acc

Huisie In Die Berge (Hendrick Susan)	RPA4-1609
Ruiter In Die Nag [Oh Bury Me Not On The Lone Prairie] (Anton De Waal)	RPA4-1610
Die Swaeltjie [The Swallow] (De Wall-Roodt)	RPA4-1611
Jou Dwalende Hart [I Can't Cry Anymore] (Friedman-De Waal)	RPA4-1612
O, Boereplaas (C. F. Visser)	RPA4-1613
Totsiens My Blondenooi (Saul-Comrinck)	RPA4-1614

Session: November 20, 1964, RCA Victor Studios, Nashville
Producer: Atkins
Musicians: Buttrey (drm), Kennedy (gtr), Smith (piano and vibes), Williams Smith (gtr), Strzelecki (b), Walker (vibes), voc acc

Alleen In Droomland (Dutoit-De Waal)	RPA4-1615
Maanskyn En Rose [Moonlight and Roses] (Black-Moret)	RPA4-1616
My Boerenooi [Londonderry Air] (Combrinck-De Waal)	RPA4-1617
Boereseun (Deur Danie Bosman)	RPA4-1618
Silwer Hare Tussen Goud (Anton De Waal)	RPA4-1619
Jy Ken My Nie [You Don't Know Me] (Walker-Walker-Arnold)	RPA4-1620

Session: January 11, 1965, RCA Victor Studios, Nashville
Producer: Atkins
Musicians: Cramer (pno), Carrigan (drm), Reed Hubbard (gtr), Kennedy (gtr), Williams Smith (gtr), Strzelecki (b), Walker (vibes), orch acc cond Walker, voc acc

I've Been to Town (Rod McKuen)	SWA4-1033
He'll Have to Go (Wilson-Wilson)	SWA4-1034
Bad News (John D. Loudermilk)	SWA4-1035
It's My Pleasure (Ollie Jones)	SWA4-1036
We'll Sing in the Sunshine (Gale Garnett)	SWA4-1037

Session: January 12–13, 1965, RCA Victor Studios, Nashville
Producer: Atkins
Musicians: H. Bradley (gtr), Carrigan (drm), Cramer (pno), Moss (gtr), Williams Smith (gtr), Strzelecki (b), Boots Randolph (saxophone), string acc, voc acc

January 12

My Heart's Not Made That Way (Merle Kilgore)	SWA4-1042	
Baby I've Got It (Merle Kilgore)	SWA4-1043	
Understand Your Man (Johnny Cash)	SWA4-1044	
Tell 'Em Where You Got Your Blues (Sutton-Kilgore)	SWA4-1045	
The Easy Way (Kilgore-Sutton)	SWA4-1046	RCA 8679B
Taking A Chance on Love (Latouche-Fetter-Duke)	SWA4-1047	

January 13

What-Cha Gonna Do? (Floyd Huddleston)	SWA4-1056	
What's He Doin' in My World* (Belew-Moore-Bush)	SWA4-1057	RCA 8516A
Laura Lee (Sullivan-Wood)	SWA4-1058	RCA 8516B

Session: June 18, 1965, RCA Victor Studios, Nashville
Producer: Atkins
Musicians: Edenton (gtr), Harman (drm), Reed Hubbard (gtr), Kennedy (gtr), Smith (pno), Strzelecki (b), Walker (vibes), string acc, voc acc

I'm Letting You Go (Bill Grammar)	SWA4-2549	RCA 8632A
You've Still Got A Hold on Me (Merle Kilgore)	SWA4-2550†	
The Days Gone By (Stillman-Stone)	SWA4-2551	RCA 8632B
Please Buy My Flowers (Turner-Dunham)	SWA4-2552†	

Session: June 24, 1965, RCA Victor Studios, Nashville
Producer: Atkins
Musicians: Carrigan (drm), Cramer (pno), Martin (gtr), Williams Smith (gtr), Strzelecki (b), string acc, voc acc

Taking Chances (Lester Vanadore)	SWA4-2560	RCA 8965B
As Usual (Alex Zanetis)	SWA4-2561	
Too Many Rivers (Harlan Howard)	SWA4-2562	
I'm Walking Behind You (Billy Reid)	SWA4-2563	
If You Were Mine, Mary (Chip Taylor)	SWA4-2564	

Session: June 25, 1965, RCA Victor Studios, Nashville
Producer: Atkins
Musicians: same as June 24, 1965, with Walker on vibes

Mary Claire Melvina Rebecca Jane (White-Nix)	SWA4-2565	RCA 8818B
Make the World Go Away (Hank Cochran)	SWA4-2566	RCA 8679A
Here Comes My Baby (West-West)	SWA4-2567†	
You Still Got A Hold on Me (Merle Kilgore)	SWA4-2568	

Session: October 25, 1965, RCA Victor Studios, Nashville
Producer: Atkins
Musicians: Cramer (pno), Edenton (gtr), Harman (drm), Kennedy (gtr), Moss (gtr), Strzelecki (b), strings cond Walker, voc acc

I'll Always Be in Love with You (Green-Ruby-Stept)	SWA4-2819	
Pardon Me (Galbraith-Mareno)	SWA4-2820	
A Good Woman's Love (Cy Coben)	SWA4-2821	
I Want to Go with You* (Hank Cochran)	SWA4-2822	RCA 8749A

Session: October 26–27, 1965, RCA Victor Studios, Nashville
Producer: Atkins
Musicians: H. Bradley (gtr), Cramer (pno), Edenton (gtr), Harman (drm), Kennedy (gtr), Strzelecki (b), string acc cond Walker, voc acc

October 26
You'd Better Stop Tellin' Lies (About Me)

(Vaughn Horton)	SWA4-2823	RCA 8749B
Love Me Like That (Don Deal)	SWA4-2824	
Come Live with Me and Be My Love (Cindy Walker)	SWA4-2825	
Good-Bye Sunshine (Cindy Walker)	SWA4-2826	

October 27

Somebody Loves You (Tobias-De Rose)	SWA4-2827	
One Kiss for Old Times' Sake (Resnick-Young)	SWA4-2828	
The Last Word in Lonesome Is Me (Roger Miller)	SWA4-2829	RCA 8818A
Don't Forget I Still Love You (Guy Louis)	SWA4-2830	
After Losing You (Lee McAlpin)	SWA4-2831	

Session: April 18, 1966, RCA Victor Studios, Nashville
Producer: Atkins
Musicians: Cramer (pno), Edenton (gtr), Harman (drm), Kennedy (gtr), McCoy (b), Strzelecki (b), string acc cond Walker, voc acc

Don't Touch Me (Hank Cochran)	TWA4-0773
A Thing Called Sadness (Chuck Howard)	TWA4-0774
My Home Town Sweetheart (Dee-Kent)	TWA4-0775
Millions of Roses (Dee-Kent)	TWA4-0776

Session: April 19, 1966, RCA Victor Studios, Nashville
Producer: Atkins
Musicians: Carrigan (drm), Cramer (pno), Edenton (gtr), Kennedy (gtr), McCoy (b, hca), Strzelecki (b), string acc cond Walker, voc acc

The Other Side of Lonely (Walker-Sykes)	TWA4-0777	
The Tip of My Fingers (Bill Anderson)	TWA4-0778	RCA 8869A
That's A Lie (Turner-Williams)	TWA4-0779	
Don't Laugh at My Love (Kenneth Rogers)	TWA4-0780	

Session: April 20, 1966, RCA Victor Studios, Nashville
Producer: Atkins
Musicians: H. Bradley (gtr), Cramer (pno), Edenton (gtr), Harman (drm), Kennedy (gtr), McCoy (b, hca), Strzelecki (b), string acc cond Walker, voc acc

Long, Long Friendship (Cindy Walker)	TWA4-0781	RCA 8869B
After the Laughter (Comes The Tears) (Ray Griff)	TWA4-0782	
Somebody Like Me (Wayne Carson Thompson)	TWA4-0783†	
Misty Blue (Bob Montgomery)	TWA4-0784	RCA 9182A
Here Comes My Baby (West-West)	TWA4-0785†	

Session: May 14, 1966, RCA Victor Studios, Nashville
Producer: Atkins
Musicians: H. Bradley (gtr), Cramer (pno), Edenton (gtr), Harman (drm), Martin (gtr), Strzelecki (b), Walker (celeste), orch acc cond Walker, voc acc

Oh So Far from Home (Jerry Crutchfield)	TWA4-0879	
The First Word (Tubert-Sherrill)	TWA4-0880†	
Somebody Like Me (Wayne Carson Thompson)	TWA4-0783	RCA 8965A
Here Comes My Baby (West-West)	TWA4-0785	
Why (Cindy Walker)	TWA4-1176	

Session: August 31, 1966, RCA Victor Studios, Nashville
Producer: Atkins
Musicians: Cramer (pno), Harman (drm), Martin (gtr), McCoy (vibes and bass), Moss (gtr),
Strzelecki (b), string acc cond Walker, voc acc

When Your World Stops Turning
   (Tubert-Strasser-Winters)   TWA4-1272
Come By Me Nice and Slow (Beasley Smith)   TWA4-1273
Mary Who (Crutchfield-Richey)   TWA4-1274
Lonely Again (Jean Chapel)   TWA4-1275   RCA 9080A

Session: September 1, 1966, RCA Victor Studios, Nashville
Producer: Atkins
Musicians: same as August 31, 1966, with Edenton (gtr) replacing Martin

Ev'ry Step of the Way (Allen-Stillman)   TWA4-1276
You Made Up for Everything (Cindy Walker)   TWA4-1277
Lay Some Happiness on Me (Chapel-Jennings)   TWA4-1278
Did It Rain (Crutchfield-Dinning-Robertson)   TWA4-1279
I Love You Drops (Bill Anderson)   TWA4-1256
The First Word (Tubert-Sherrill)   TWA4-0880   RCA 9027A

Session: September 22, 1966, RCA Victor Studios, Nashville
Producer: Atkins
Musicians: same as September 1, 1966

It's Only Love (Hank Cochran)   TWA4-1354
Love on My Mind (Cindy Walker)   TWA4-1355   RCA 9080B
There's Always Me (Don Robertson)   TWA4-1356
At Sunset (Ray Griff)   TWA4-1357
The Angel and the Stranger (Freda Anne)   TWA4-1358   RCA 9027B

Session: December 15–16, 1966, RCA Victor Studios, Nashville
Producer: Atkins
Musicians: Carrigan (drm), Cramer (pno), McCoy (vibes, b), Moss (gtr), Strzelecki (b),
Pete Wade (gtr), strings cond Walker, voc acc

December 15
The Wheel of Hurt (Singleton-Snyder)   TWA4-1586
That's All I Want from You (Rotter-Rotha)   TWA4-1587
Meet Me at the Altar (Deal-Deal)   TWA4-1588
Baby (Ray Griff)   TWA4-1589
I Guess I'll Never Understand (Blair-Robertson) TWA4-1590

December 16
That's All That's Left of My Baby (Allen-Haynes) TWA4-1591
Bear with Me A Little Longer (Darrell Glenn)   TWA4-1592
Calling Mary Names (Wayne Thompson)   TWA4-1593   RCA 9182B
He's Got You (Hank Cochran)   TWA4-1594
Nobody's Darling But Mine (Jimmie Davis)   TWA4-1595

Session: April 24, 1967, RCA Victor Studios, Nashville
Producer: Atkins
Musicians: H. Bradley (gtr), Carrigan (drm), Cramer (pno), Edenton (gtr), Moss (gtr),
Strzelecki (b), orch acc cond Walker, voc acc

Love Finds A Way (Robertson-Blair)	UWA4-2370	
How Is She? (Marijohn Wilkin)	UWA4-2371	
Turn the World Around* (Ben Peters)	UWA4-2372	RCA 9265A
When There's A Fire in Your Heart (Kilgore-Williams)	UWA4-2373	
The Long Ride Home (Washington-Alexander)	UWA4-2374	RCA 9265B

Session: July 3 & 5, 1967, RCA Victor Studios, Nashville
Producer: Atkins
Musicians: same as April 24, 1967, with Charles McCoy (vibes, b, chimes)

July 3

Walk with Me (Don Robertson)	UWA4-2549	
It's Such A Pretty World Today (Dale Noe)	UWA4-2550	
I'll Love You More (Hank Cochran)	UWA4-2551	
The World of Ours (Cette Nutt La) (DeBout-Le Senechel-Harrison)	UWA4-2552	RCA 9387A
Release Me (And Let Me Love Again) (Miller-Stevenson)	UWA4-2553	

July 5

There's This About You (Chapel-Calongne)	UWA4-2554	
Here Comes Heaven (Byers-Tubert)	UWA4-2555	RCA 9368A
Baby That's Living (Jean Chapel)	UWA4-2556	RCA 9368B
Castle Made of Walls (Cy Coben)	UWA4-2557	
Don't Keep Me Lonely Too Long (Melba Montgomery)	UWA4-2558	

Session: October 30–31 & November 1, 1967, RCA Victor Studios, Nashville
Producer: Atkins
Musicians: same as April 24, 1967, with Ray Stevens (vibes)

October 30

Dear Heart (Mancini-Livingston-Evans)	UWA4-2900	
Nothing But Time (Williams-Jones)	UWA4-2901	
No Matter Whose Baby You Are (Chapel)	UWA4-2902	RCA 9525B
Here Comes The Rain, Baby (Newbury)	UWA4-2903	RCA 9437A

October 31

There You Go (Allison)	UWA-2904
When the Wind Blows (In Chicago) (Murphy-Turner)	UWA-2905†
Sunny (Bobby Hebb)	UWA-2906
From This Minute On (Peters)	UWA-2907

November 1

All the Time (Walker-Tillis)	UWA-2908	
The World I Used to Know (Rod McKuen)	UWA-2909	RCA 9437B
A Song for Shara (Tubert-Tapp)	UWA-2910	
In the Misty Moonlight (Cindy Walker)	UWA-2911	
Secret Love (Webster-Fain)	UWA-2846	

Session: April 1–3, 1968, RCA Victor Studios, Nashville
Producer: Atkins
Musicians: same as April 24, 1967, with William Sanders (b)

April 1

What Now My Love (Becaud-Sigman-Delance)	WWA4-1996
Can't Take My Eyes Off You (Crewe-Gaudio)	WWA4-1997

Honey (Bobby Russell)	WWA4-1998	
Am I That Easy to Forget (Belew-Stevenson)	WWA4-1999	

April 2

What A Wonderful World (Weiss-Douglas)	WWA4-2000	RCA 9667B
Gentle on My Mind (John Hartford)	WWA4-2001	
By the Time I Get to Phoenix (Jimmy Webb)	WWA4-2002	
Then You Can Tell Me Goodbye*		
(John D. Loudermilk)	WWA4-2003	RCA 9606A

April 3

It's Over (Rodgers)	WWA4-2004	RCA 9525A
The Sunshine Belongs to Me (Thompson)	WWA4-2005	
I Really Go for You (Chapel)	WWA4-2006	
Evergreen (Belew-Givens)	WWA4-2007	

Session: July 9–10, 1968, RCA Victor Studios, Nashville
Producer: Atkins
Musicians: same as April 1–3, 1968, with Richard Morris (vibes, celeste, bells)

July 9

I'll Never Smile Again (Ruth Lowe)	WWA4-3233†	
Apples, Raisins and Roses (Carr-Shuman)	WWA4-3234	RCA 9606B
Little Girls and Little Boys (Tubert)	WWA4-3235	
Turn Around, Look at Me (Jerry Capehart)	WWA4-3236	

July 10

All I Have to Do Is Dream (Bryant-Bryant)	WWA4-3237	
Until It's Time for You to Go (Buffe Sainte-Marie)	WWA4-3238	
The Summer Wind (Mayer-Mercer-Bradtke)	WWA4-3239	
The Olive Tree (Springfield-Lampert)	WWA4-3240	

Session: August 13, 1968, RCA Victor Studios, Nashville
Producer: Atkins
Musicians: H. Bradley (gtr), David Briggs (pno), Carrigan (drm), Edenton (gtr), Kenneth Krause (perc), Sanders (b), Strzelecki (b), James Wilkerson (gtr), orch acc cond Walker, voc acc

Just Across the Mountain (Mercer-Kent)	WWA4-4766	
They Don't Make Love Like They Used To		
(Red Lane)	WWA4-4767	RCA 9667A
My Dream (Vernon-Hughes)	WWA4-4768	
Walkin' in Love Land (Vernon-Hughes)	WWA4-4769	
I'll Never Smile Again (Ruth Lowe)	WWA4-4770	

Session: October 24, 1968, RCA Victor Studios, Nashville
Producer: Atkins
Musicians: H. Bradley (gtr), Briggs (pno), Carrigan (drm), Edenton (gtr), Morris (vibes and bells), Moss (gtr), Sanders (b), Strzelecki (b), orch acc cond Walker, voc acc

Sweet Marilyn (Lana Chapel)	WWA4-4964
Suddenly My Thoughts Are All of You	
(Clint Ballard, Jr.)	WWA4-4965
Little Green Apples (Bobby Russell)	WWA4-4966
Take A Little Time (John D. Loudermilk)	WWA4-4967

Session: November 14, 1968, RCA Victor Studios, Nashville
Producer: Atkins
Musicians: Briggs (pno), Carrigan (drm), Morris (timp and vibes), Moss (gtr), Sanders (b),
Strzelecki (b), Wade (gtr), Wilkerson (gtr), orch acc cond Walker, voc acc

I'm in Love with You (Tubert-James)	WWA4-4968
Since You've Been Loving Me (Dallas Frazier)	WWA4-4969
Town and Country (Bobby Russell)	WWA4-4970
I Get Baby on My Mind (Ben Peters)	WWA4-4971

Session: December 4 & 21, 1968, RCA Victor Studios, Nashville
Producer: Atkins
Musicians: H. Bradley (gtr), Briggs (pno), Carrigan (drm), Edenton (gtr), Morris (timp, marimba, bells, vibes), Wayne Moss (gtr), Sanders (b), Strzelecki (b), orch acc cond Bill Walker,
voc acc

December 4

I Love How You Love Me (Mann-Kolber)	WWA4-4972	
Tender Is Her Name (George Tidwell)	WWA4-4973	
My Lady of Love (Eddie Miller)	WWA4-4974	RCA 74-0175B[4]
Wichita Lineman (Jimmy Webb)	WWA4-4975	

December 21

The Song of Long Ago (Mercer-Carmichael)	WWA4-7509
As Long as I Love (Carter-Montgomery)	WWA4-7510
Old Love, New Love (Brown-Bloodworth)	WWA4-7511†
Sweet Bird of Youth (Ray Griff)	WWA4-7512

Session: January 29, 1969, RCA Victor Studios, Nashville
Producer: Atkins
Musicians: Larry Butler (pno), Buttrey (drm), Reed Hubbard (gtr), Huskey (b), Morris (perc),
Moss (gtr), Strzelecki (b), Wade (gtr), orch acc cond Walker, voc acc

Just A Bend in the Road (Judy West)	XWA4-1184	
Heaven Below (Jerry Fuller)	XWA4-1185	RCA 0120B
Please Don't Go (Reed-Rae)	XWA4-1186	RCA 0120A
Walking Through the Memories of My Mind (Eddie Miller)	XWA4-1187†	

Session: April 15, 1969, RCA Victor Studios, Nashville
Producer: Atkins
Musicians: H. Bradley (gtr), Briggs (pno), Carrigan (drm), Moss (gtr), Shook (gtr), Strzelecki
(b), orch acc cond Cam Mullins, voc acc

The Glory of Love (William Hill)	XWA4-1250	
Faithfully (Styne-Grossman)	XWA4-1264	
But for Love* (Cashman-Pistilli-West)	XWA4-1326	RCA 0175A
Then She's A Lover (Bobby Russell)	XWA4-1345	
You Gave Me A Mountain (Marty Robbins)	XWA4-1437	

---

[4]RCA began using the prefix "74" for record numbers above "9000" for their 45
releases; they also continued to use the old "47" prefix on the remaining 9000 numbers.

Session: July 15, 1969, RCA Victor Studios, Nashville
Producers: Atkins and Danny Davis
Musicians: H. Bradley (gtr), Briggs (pno), Carrigan (drm), Hughes (vibes), Strzelecki (b),
Wade (gtr), orch acc cond Mullins, voc acc

You Don't Need Me Anymore (Robertson-Blair)	XWA4-2232	RCA 0226B
What Have I Done for Her Lately? (Blair-Kay)	XWA4-2233	
San Francisco Is A Lonely Town (Ben Peters)	XWA4-2234	
You Fool (Martha Sharp)	XWA4-2235	RCA 0226A

Session: July 22, 1969, RCA Victor Studios, Nashville
Producer: Atkins
Musicians: H. Bradley (gtr), Briggs (pno), Carrigan (drm), Huskey (b), Wade (gtr),
Chip Young (gtr), orch acc cond Mullins, voc acc

Band of Gold (Musel-Taylor)	XWA4-2236
Shadows of Her Mind (Kris Kristofferson)	XWA4-2237†
To Sleep with You (Bob Tubert)	XWA4-2238
Then I'll Be Over You (Ben Peters)	XWA4-2239

Session: July 23, 1969, RCA Victor Studios, Nashville
Producer: Atkins
Musicians: Buttrey (drm), Beegie Cruser (pno), Hughes (perc), McCoy (gtr), Jerry Stembridge
(gtr), Strzelecki (b), orch acc cond Mullins, voc acc

I Started A Joke (Gibb-Gibb-Gibb)	XWA4-2240
Cycles (Gayle Caldwell)	XWA4-2241
My Way (Anka-Revaux-Francois)	XWA4-2242
Yesterday, When I Was Young (Kretzmer-Aznavour)	XWA4-2243

Session: October 9, 1969, RCA Victor Studios, Nashville
Producer: Atkins
Musicians: James Capps (gtr), James Colvard (gtr), Cruser (pno), Donald Kane (b), Morris
(perc, timp, vibes), Stembridge (gtr), Terry Waddell (drm), orch acc cond Hank Levine, voc acc

Morning of My Mind (Dick Wilson)	XWA4-2480	RCA 0282B
For My Woman's Love (Ben Peters)	XWA4-2481	
Since December (Cochran-Martin)	XWA4-2482	RCA 0282A
I Always Dress My Very Best (Belew-Pitts)	XWA4-2483†	

Session: December 23, 1969, RCA Victor Studios, Nashville
Producer: Atkins
Musicians: Atkins (gtr), H. Bradley (gtr), Carrigan (drm), Colvard (gtr), Hughes (perc),
Robbins (pno), Stembridge (gtr), Strzelecki (b)

Mary in the Morning (Cymbal-Lendell)	XWA4-2722
With Pen in Hand (Bobby Goldsboro)	XWA4-2723

Session: December 29, 1969, RCA Victor Studios, Nashville
Producer: Atkins
Musicians: Atkins (gtr), Colvard (gtr), Edenton (gtr), Harman (drm), Reed Hubbard (gtr),
Hughes (perc), Ferrell Morris (drm, vibes), Robbins (pno), Dale Sellers (b), Stembridge (gtr),
Strzelecki (b)

Shadows of Her Mind (Kris Kristofferson)	XWA4-2724
When the Wind Blows (In Chicago) (Murphy-Turner)	XWA4-2725
Just Enough to Start Me Dreamin' (Hank Cochran)	XWA4-2726

Session: December 30, 1969, RCA Victor Studios, Nashville
Producer: Atkins
Musicians: Atkins (gtr), Colvard (gtr), Edenton (gtr), Harman (drm), Hubbard (gtr), Hughes (perc), Morris (drm, vibes), Billy Sanford (gtr), Sellers (gtr), Jerry Smith (pno), Strzelecki (b)

I Just Can't Help Believin' (Mann-Weil)	XWA4-2727	
(Today) I Started Loving You Again (Haggard-Owens)	XWA4-2728	RCA 9801B
I'll Give You Three Guesses (Mercer-Mancini)	XWA4-2729	

Session: December 31, 1969, RCA Victor Studios, Nashville
Producer: Atkins
Musicians: same as December 29, 1969

A Man's Kind of Woman (George Rizzo)	XWA4-2730	RCA 9848A
Leaving on A Jet Plane (John Denver)	XWA4-2731	
Soul Deep (Wayne Carson Thompson)	XWA4-2732	RCA 9801A

Session: March 26, 1970, RCA Victor Studios, Nashville
Producer: Atkins
Musicians: Carrigan (drm), Edenton (gtr), Boyce Hawkins (pno), Hubbard (gtr), Huskey (b), Martin (gtr), Sellers (gtr), Wade (gtr), string acc cond Bill McElhiney, voc acc

Living Under Pressure (Baker Knight)	ZWA4-1358	RCA 9848B
A Man's Kind of Woman (George Rizzo)	ZWA4-1359†	
Fools (Ed Carrell)	ZWA4-1360	

Session: May 11, 1970, probably RCA Victor Studios, Hollywood, California
Producer: Lee Hazlewood
Musicians: Max Bennett (b), Chuck Berghofer (b), Al Casey (gtr), David Cohen (gtr), Gary Coleman (perc), Guerin (drm), Michel Rubin (keyboard), string acc, voc acc

Some Lonely Picker (John Stewart)	ZPA3-8255
Seven Bridges Road (Steve Young)	ZPA3-8256
July, You're A Woman (John Stewart)	ZPA3-8257†

Session: May 13, 1970, probably RCA Victor Studios, Hollywood, California
Producer: Hazlewood
Musicians: Bennett (b), Berghofer (b), Casey (gtr), Cohen (gtr), Coleman (perc), Milton Holland (drm), Larry Knechtel (keyboard), orch acc, voc acc

July, You're A Woman (John Stewart)	ZPA3-8257
Gentle Is My Love (Ben Peters)	ZPA3-8258†
Where Love Has Died (Jim Owen)	ZPA3-8259
All That Keeps Ya' Going (Hoover)	ZPA3-8260

Session: May 15, 1970, probably RCA Victor Studios, Hollywood, California
Producer: Hazlewood
Musicians: Bennett (b), Berghofer (b), Casey (gtr), Cohen (gtr), Gene Estes (perc), Guerin (drm), Knechtel (keyboard), George Tipton (perc), orch acc

New World in the Morning (Roger Whittaker)	ZPA3-8261
She Believes in Me (John Stewart)	ZPA3-8262
My Way of Life (Sonny Curtis)	ZPA3-8263
How Do I Love Thee (Freeman-Sparks)	ZPA3-8264†
Closest I Ever Came (Mac Davis)	ZPA3-8265
Each Road I Take (Leads Back to You)	ZPA3-8266

Session: June 29, 1970, RCA Victor Studios, Nashville
Producer: Atkins
Musicians: H. Bradley (gtr), Ralph Gallant (drm), Martin (gtr), Sellers (gtr), Smith (pno),
Stembridge (gtr), Strzelecki (b), string acc, voc acc

Ten Times Forever More (David-Bacharach)	ZWA4-1659	RCA 9889B
From Heaven to Heartache (Ben Peters)	ZWA4-1660	RCA 9889A

Session: October 9 & 12–13, 1970, RCA Victor Studios, Nashville
Producer: Jim Malloy
Musicians: H. Bradley (gtr), Briggs (pno), Carrigan (drm), Edenton (gtr), Farrell Morris
(perc), Norbert Putnam (b), Shook (gtr), string acc cond Cam Mullins, voc acc

October 9

Wait for Sunday (Glenn McGuirt)	ZWA4-1837	
Here We Go Again (Steagall-Lanier)	ZWA4-1838	
Baby I Will (Ben Peters)	ZWA4-1839	
I Really Don't Want to Know (Robertson-Barnes)	ZWA4-1839	RCA 9935B

October 12

Anything That's Part of You (Don Robertson)	ZWA4-1841	
I Was Born to Love You (Robertson-Blair)	ZWA4-1842	
Portrait of My Woman* (Glen Sherley)	ZWA4-1843	RCA 9935A
Not One Minute More (Robertson-Dinning-Blair)	ZWA4-1844†	

October 13

It Ain't No Big Thing (But It's Growing) (Merritt-Merritt-Hall)	ZWA4-1845	RCA 9993B
She's Everywhere (Dobbins-Whitehead)	ZWA4-1846	
Heaven Everyday (Foster-Rice)	ZWA4-1847	
Forty Shades of Green (Johnny Cash)	ZWA4-1848	

Session: February 24, 1971, RCA Victor Studios, Nashville
Producer: Malloy
Musicians: Carrigan (drm), Morris (drm), Ron Oates (org), Eberhard Ramm (French horn),
Stembridge (gtr), Strzelecki (b), voc acc

A Part of America Died* (Harry Koch)	AWA4-1190	RCA 9968A
Call Me (Harry Koch)	AWA4-1191	RCA 9968B

Session: March 12, 1971, RCA Victor Studios, Nashville
Producer: Malloy
Musicians: Briggs (pno), Carrigan (drm), Morris (perc), Sanford (gtr), Shook (gtr), Stembridge
(gtr), Strzelecki (b), string acc cond Bergen White (added later), voc acc (added later)

I Love Her (Dobbins-Whitehead)	AWA4-1235	
'Cause I Got You (Scoggins-Parker)	AWA4-1236	
I Love You Dear (Jack Moran)	AWA4-1237	RCA 0559A
Welcome to My World (Winkler-Hathcock)	AWA4-1238	RCA 9993A

Session: June 1–3, 1971, RCA Victor Studios, Nashville
Producer: Malloy
Musicians: Briggs (pno), Carrigan (drm), Edenton (gtr), Morris (perc), Stembridge (gtr),
Strzelecki (b), orch acc, voc acc (added later)

June 1
For the Good Times (Kris Kristofferson)   AWA4-1239
Help Me Make It Through the Night
    (Kris Kristofferson)   AWA4-1240
(They Long to Be) Close to You (Bacharach-David) AWA4-1241
Ramblin' Rose (Sherman-Sherman)   AWA4-1242

June 2
I Can't Stop Loving You (Don Gibson)   AWA4-1243
Long Life, Lots of Happiness (Owen McGovern, Jr.) AWA4-1244   RCA 0559B
Roses to Reno (Sykes-Walker)   AWA4-1553
Ruby, Don't Take Your Love to Town (Mel Tillis) AWA4-1554

June 3
Poor Boy (Ortiz-Ortiz)   AWA4-1555
Take My Hand for A While (Buffy Sainte-Marie)   AWA4-1556
Love Story (Where Do I Begin) (Sigman-Lai)   AWA4-1557
My Sweet Lord (George Harrison)   AWA4-1558

Session: September 16, 1971, RCA Victor Studios, Nashville
Producer: Malloy
Musicians: same as June 1–3, 1971, with Jerry Shook (gtr) replacing Ray Edenton

Loving Her Was Easier (Than Anything I'll Ever
    Do Again) (Kris Kristofferson)   AWA4-1800
Take Me Home, Country Roads
    (Danoff-Nivert-Denver)   AWA4-1801
Easy Loving (Freddie Hart)   AWA4-1802
Put A Little Love in Your Heart
    (Holiday-Myers-DeShannon)   AWA4-1803

Session: December 2, 1971, RCA Victor Studios, Nashville
Producer: Malloy
Musicians: H. Bradley (gtr), Briggs (pno), Billy Grammar (gtr), McCoy (b),
Terry Waddell (drm), string acc, voc acc

Lonely People (Harlan Howard)   AWA4-1994   RCA 0641A
You May Be Too Much for Memphis Baby
    (But You're Not Enough for L.A.) (Paul Hampton) AWA4-1995
If It's Alright with You (O'Dell-Henley)   AWA4-1996   RCA 0641B

Session: March 21, 1972, RCA Victor Studios, Nashville
Producer: Malloy
Musicians: Carrigan (drm), Edenton (gtr), Farrell Morris (perc), Strzelecki (b), Wade (gtr),
Jerry Whitehurst (pno), string acc

Born to Lose (Frankie Brown)   BWA4-1219
Just Out of Reach (V. F. Stewart)   BWA4-1220   RCA 0705A
Here We Go Again (Steagall-Lanier)   BWA4-1221
It's Four in the Morning (Jerry Chesnut)   BWA4-1222

Session: March 23, 1972, RCA Victor Studios, Nashville
Producer: Malloy
Musicians: H. Bradley (gtr), Morris (perc), Waddell (drm), Wade (gtr), Whitehurst (pno),
string acc, unknown (b)

It Keeps Right on A Hurtin' (Johnny Tillotson)	BWA4-1223	
The Last Letter (Rex Griffin)	BWA4-1224	RCA 0747B
Poison Red Berries (Mickey Newberry)	BWA4-1225	RCA 0705B
Rainy Night in Georgia (Tony Joe White)	BWA4-1226	

Session: April 5 & 10, 1972, RCA Victor Studios, Nashville
Producer: Malloy
Musicians: same as March 23, 1972, with Pat Merola (b)

April 5

The Birthmark Henry Thompson Talks About		
(Frazier-Owens)	BWA4-1266	
My Special Angel (Jimmy Duncan)	BWA4-1267	
Suddenly There's a Valley (Meyer-Jones)	BWA4-1270	

April 10

An Angel Sleeps Beside Me Every Night		
(Gary Paxton)	BWA4-1264	RCA 0842B
I'm Givin' Her Love (Tom Hartman)	BWA4-1265	
Sweet Bunch of Daisies (Arr. by Eddy Arnold)	BWA4-1268	RCA 0842A
Let It Be Me (Curtis-Delanoe-Becaud)	BWA4-1269	

Session: May 26, 1972, RCA Victor Studios, Nashville
Producer: Malloy
Musicians: H. Bradley (gtr), Ken Malone (drm), Morris (perc), Wade (gtr), Whitehurst (pno), string acc (added later), voc acc (added later)

Carolyn (Tommy Collins)	BWA4-1472	
Lucy (Alex Harvey)	BWA4-1473	RCA 0747A
More Than A Friend (Harry Middlebrooks)	BWA4-1474	
She Was Alone (Wayne Carson)	BWA4-1475	

Session: August 9, 1972, RCA Victor Studios, Nashville
Producer: Malloy
Musicians: same as May 26, 1972, with Shook (gtr) replacing H. Bradley

Song Sung Blue (Neil Diamond)	BWA4-1476	
She's Gone Again (Ed Penney)	BWA4-1477	
When You Say Love (Foster-Rice)	BWA4-1478	
Daddy Don't You Walk So Fast (Callander-Stephens)	BWA4-1479	

Session: October 31, 1972, MGM Studios, New York
Producers: Mike Curb and Don Costa
Musicians: unknown

Only You (And You Alone) (Ram-Rand)	73L4739	
Among My Souvenirs (Leslie-Nicholls)	72L4246	
So Many Ways (Bobby Stevenson)	72L4394	MGM K14478A
Once in A While (Edwards-Green)	72L4245	MGM K14478B

Session: January 24, 1973, location unknown
Producers: Curb and Costa
Musicians: unknown

If the Whole World Stopped Lovin' (Ben Peters)	73L4739	MGM K14535A
Some Sunday Morning (Jerome-Heindorf-Koehler)	73L4735	
My Son! I Wish You Everything (Otis-Stallman)	73L4736	MGM K14535B

I Almost Lost My Mind (Ivory Joe Hunter)	73L4733	
My Special Angel (Jimmy Duncan)	73L4734	
At the End of A Long Long Day (Marvin-Moll)	73L4738	

Session: August 21–22, 1973, Jack Clement Recording Studios, Nashville
Producer: Malloy
Musicians: H. Bradley (gtr), Jim Lance (gtr), Morris (drm), Shook (gtr), Strzelecki (b), Whitehurst (pno), Joe Zinkman (b), string acc (added later), vocal acc (added later)

August 21

If I Ever Make It (Ben Peters)	73L5581	
Love Is So Elusive (Dave Burgess)	73L5584	
I'm Glad You Happened to Me		
(Rogers-White, Jr.-Johnson)	73L5583	MGM K14672B
Love Me Back Together (Ray Griff)	73L5580	

August 22

I'd Prefer to Do It Again (Jud Strunk)	73L5588	
She's Got Everything I Need		
(Wayne Carson Thompson)	73l5585	MGM K14672A

Session: December 3, 1973, Monument Recording Studios, Nashville
Producer: Malloy
Musicians: Lance (gtr), Shook (gtr), Strzelecki (b), Waddell (drm), Whitehurst (pno), string acc

You Don't Know Me (Walker-Arnold)	?
Welcome to My World (Winkler-Hathcock)	?
The Cattle Call (Tex Owens)	?
I Want to Go with You (Hank Cochran)	?
Don't Rob Another Man's Castle (Jenny Lou Carson)	?
Anytime (Herbert Lawson)	?
Bouquet of Roses (Nelson-Hilliard)	?
Turn the World Around (Ben Peters)	?
What's He Doin' in My World (Belew-Moore-Bush)	?
I Really Don't Want to Know (Robertson-Barnes)	?
I'll Hold You in My Heart (Till I Can Hold You	
in My Arms) (Dilbeck-Horton-Arnold)	?
The Last Word in Lonesome (Roger Miller)	?
May the Good Lord Bless and Keep You	
(Merdith Willson)	?
Make the World Go Away (Hank Cochran)	?
Take Me in Your Arms and Hold Me (Cindy Walker)	?

Session: December 7, 1973, MGM Recording Studios, probably in Los Angeles
Producers: Mike Curb and Don Costa
Musicians: unknown

I Wish That I Had Loved You Better (Chick Rains)	73L5920	MGM M14734A
Just for Old Times Sake (Tepper-Bennett)	73L5914	MGM M14711A
Oh, Oh, I'm Falling in Love Again		
(Hoffman-Manning-Markwell)	73L4739	MGM K14600A
Anyway You Want Me (That's How I Will Be)		
(Schroeder-Owens)	73L4737	MGM K14600B
Butterfly (Gerard-Bernet-Barnes-David-Curb)	73L5913	MGM M14679A
I Got This Thing About You (Ben Peters)	73L5915	MGM M14711B

Session: January 24, 1974, Columbia Recording Studios, Nashville
Producer: Dick Glasser
Musicians: H. Bradley (gtr), Edenton (gtr), Malone (drm), Morris (perc), Robbins (pno),
Strzelecki (b), Wade (gtr)

Love Me (Sanders-Mabry-Westberry)	75N6797	
Middle of A Memory (B. Johnston)	?	MGM M14827A
Still Loving You (T. Shondell)	75N6799	

Session: March 15, 1974, MGM Recording Studios, probably in Los Angeles
Producers: Curb and Costa
Musicians: unknown

A Place in the Sun (Miller-Wells)	74L6288	
Let Me Call You Baby Tonight (Jordan-Duncan)	74L6287	
Eve's Garden (Neal Davenport)	74L6285	
Let It Be Love (Ben Peters)	74L6286	MGM M14734B

Session: April 30, 1974, MGM Recording Studios, Los Angeles
Producers: Curb and Costa
Musicians: unknown

Sunshine Blue (Bill Graham)	74L6338	
Memories Are Made of This (Gilkyson-Dehr-Miller)	74L6339	
If You Could Only Love Me Now (Burgess-Pfrimmer)	74L6341	MGM M14769B
My Lonely Room (Bill Graham)	74L6340	

Session: December 4, 1974, Fred F. Carter Studios, Goodlettsville, Tennessee
Producer: Curb
Musicians: H. Bradley (gtr), Harman (drm), Morris (perc), Sellers (gtr), Shook (gtr),
Smith (pno), Strzelecki (b), string acc (added later)

What in the World's Come Over You (Jack Scott)	?
You Stand at Every Crossroad (Foster-Munn-Clingon)	74N6701
The Great Mail Robbery (Today I'm Bringing	
Daddy's Letter Home) (Joseph Allen)	74N6702

Session: February 13, 1975, Columbia Recording Studios, Nashville
Producer: Glasser
Musicians: H. Bradley (gtr), Capps (gtr), Harman (drm), Morris (perc), Smith (gtr),
Stembridge (gtr), John Williams (b), string acc (added later), voc acc (added later)

Nearer, My Love, to You (Kent-Stanton)	75N6810	
The Same Old Way (Foster-Rice)	75N6811	
I Will (Dick Glasser)	75N6812	MGM M14780B

Session: February 21, 1975, Columbia Recording Studios, Nashville
Producer: Glasser
Musicians: H. Bradley (gtr), Harman (drm), Morris (perc), Robbins (pno), Smith (gtr),
Strzelecki (b), Wade (gtr), string acc (added later)

I Need You Now (Crane-Jacobs)	?†	
I Just Had You on My Mind (S. Richards)	75N6818	MGM M14827B
Red Roses for A Blue Lady (Tepper-Brodsky)	75N6820	MGM M14780A

Session: August 7, 1975, Jack Clement Recording Studios, Nashville
Producer: Glasser
Musicians: H. Bradley (gtr), Malone (drm), Tony Migliore (pno), Morris (perc), Williams (b), string acc (added later), voc acc (added later)

Livin' It Down (Ben Peters)	GWA4-2484†
That's All She Wrote (Jerry Fuller)	GWA4-2485
If I Were Lovin' You (Graham-Castleberry)	GWA4-2486†

Session: August 8, 1975, Jack Clement Recording Studios, Nashville
Producer: Glasser
Musicians: H. Bradley (gtr), Lance (gtr), Malone (drm), Migliore (kybds), Morris (perc), Robbins (pno), Williams (b), string acc (added later)

Burning Bridges (Walter Scott)	GWA4-2487†
Making Love to You Again (Steve Gibb)	GWA4-2488†
You Took Her Off My Hands (Now Please Take Her Off My Mind) (Howard-McDonald-Stewart)	GWA4-2489†

Session: August 21, 1975, Jack Clement Recording Studios, Nashville
Producer: Glasser
Musicians: H. Bradley (gtr), Lance (gtr), Malone (drm), Migliore (kybds), Smith (pno), Strzelecki (b), string acc (added later), voc acc (added later)

Leavin' Is So Hard To Do (Harry Middlebrooks)	GWA4-2490†
Permanently Lonely (Willie Nelson)	GWA4-2492†
Corner of My World (Steagall-Peters)	GWA4-2491†
Gettin' Away From It All (George Tomsco)	GWA4-2493

Session: April 19–20, 1976, Bradley's Barn Studios, Mount Juliet, Tennessee
Producer: Owen Bradley
Musicians: H. Bradley (gtr), Edenton (gtr), Harman (drm), Smith (pno), Strzelecki (b), Wade (gtr), string acc (added later), voc acc (added later)

April 19

She's Just An Old Love Turned Memory (John Schweers)	FWA4-0863	
My Woman's Eyes (Kirk-Peters)	FWA4-0864	
We Found It in Each Other's Arms (Cochran-Lane)	FWA4-0865	
Goodnight, Irene (Ledbetter-Lomax)	FWA4-0866	RCA PB-10794B
Put Me Back Into Your World (Lorene Mann)	FWA4-0867	RCA PB-10794A
Freedom Ain't the Same as Being Free (Jackie Johnson)	FWA4-0868	RCA PB-11031A

April 20

Don't Let the Good Times Roll Away (Burgess-Pfrimmer)	FWA4-0869	RCA PB-10701B
I Wouldn't Be So Sad (If We Hadn't Been So Happy) (Wayne Parker)	FWA4-0870	
Remember the Good (Mickey Newbury)	FWA4-0871	
Cowboy* (Fraser-Shannon)	FWA4-0872	RCA PB-10701A

Session: December 29–30, 1976, Bradley's Barn Studios, Mount Juliet, Tennessee
Producer: O. Bradley
Musicians: H. Bradley (gtr), Edenton (gtr), Harman (drm), Moore (b), Robbins (pno), Sellers (gtr), string acc (added later), voc acc (added later)

December 29
(I Need You) All the Time (Bryant-Bryant)   FWA5-1180   RCA PB-10899A
Till You Can Make It on Your Own (McBee-Owens) FWA5-1181   RCA PB-11031B
The Hand That Rocks the Cradle (Ted Harris)   FWA5-1182†

December 30
Easy (Chick Rains)   FWA5-1183†
Fraulein (Lawton Williams)   FWA5-1184
Hurtin' Song (Redington-McCoy)   FWA5-1185

Session: January 5, 1977, Bradley's Barn Studios, Mount Juliet, Tennessee
Producer: O. Bradley
Musicians: H. Bradley (gtr), Edenton (gtr), Harman (drm), Mike Leech (b), Ron Oates (pno), Sellers (gtr), string acc (added later), voc acc (added later)

You Slip Into My Mind (Putnam-Haynes)   FWA5-1186
(I Can't Help It If) You're Always on My Mind
  (Bill Nash)   FWA5-1187
I've Never Loved Anyone More (Hargrove-Nesmith) FWA5-1188   RCA PB-10899B
Easy (Chick Rains)   FWA5-1189

Session: August 23, 1977, Bradley's Barn Studios, Mount Juliet, Tennessee
Producer: O. Bradley
Musicians: same as January 5, 1977

Where Lonely People Go (Floyd Huddleston)   GWA5-2697   RCA PB-11133A
I Don't Want to Be A Memory (Springfield-Lampert) GWA5-2698†

Session: August 24, 1977, Bradley's Barn Studios, Mount Juliet, Tennessee
Producer: O. Bradley
Musicians: same as August 23, 1977, with Pete Wade (gtr) replacing Dale Sellers

Penny Arcade (Bryant-Bryant)   GWA5-2699   RCA PB-11133B
Give Myself A Party (Don Gibson)   GWA5-2700†
I've So Much to Be Thankful For (Mullan-Douglass) GWA5-2701†

Session: unknown date in 1978, unknown studio, New York
Producer: Joel Diamond
Musicians: unknown

Country Lovin' (Bernstein-Adams)   HWA5-5054   RCA PB-11257A
I've So Much to Be Thankful For (Mullan-Douglas) HWA5-5055   RCA PB-11257B

Session: June 7, 1978, Music City Music Hall Studios, Nashville
Producer: Charles Grean
Musicians: H. Bradley (gtr), Lloyd Green (steel gtr), Jim Lance (gtr), Terry McMillan (hca), Mark Morris (drm, vibes and timp), Oates (pno), Steve Schaffer (b), string acc

You Are My Sunshine (Davis-Mitchell)   HWA5-1518   RCA PB-11319B
I'm the South (Foster-Carruth)   HWA5-1519   RCA PB-11319A
Session: October 11, 1978, The Soundshop Studios, Nashville

Producer: Bob Montgomery
Musicians: Carrigan (drm), Steven Gibson (gtr), Oates (pno), Schaffer (b), Reggie Young (gtr), string acc (added later), voc acc

If Everyone Had Someone Like You
   (Bobby Springfield)   HWA5-5267   RCA PB-11422A
If I Ever Had to Say Goodbye to You (Steve Gibb)   HWA5-5268   RCA PB-11752A
You're A Beautiful Place to Be (Van Stevenson)   HWA5-5269   RCA PB-11422B

Session: February 12–13, 1979, The Soundshop Studios, Nashville
Producer: Montgomery
Musicians: James Capps (gtr), Carrigan (drm), Oates (kybds, pno), Schaffer (b), Young (gtr), string acc (added later)

February 12
You and I (Steve Gibb)   JWA5-7568
The Love of My Life (Kenny O'Dell)   JWA5-7569   RCA PB-11537B
Somebody Loves You (Harry Middlebrooks)   JWA5-7571
You're So Good at Lovin' Me (Bobby Springfield)   JWA5-7572   RCA PB-11668B
I Still Long to Hold You Now and Then (Jerry Fuller)   JWA5-7573

February 13
What in Her World Did I Do (Wayne-Fischer)   JWA5-7570   RCA PB-11537A
                                               PB-11752B
Goodbye (Butler-Killen)   JWA5-7574   RCA PB-11668A
Undivided Love (Van Stephenson)   JWA5-7576   RCA PB-12039B

Session: July 31, 1979, The Soundshop Studios, Nashville
Producer: Montgomery
Musicians: same as February 12–13, 1979, with voc acc (added later)

That's What I Get for Loving You (Bobby Springfield)   JWA5-7751   RCA PB-12039A
A Daisy A Day (Jud Strunk)   JWA5-7752
Happy (Lance-Oates)   JWA5-7753
My World Begins and Ends with You (Pippin-Keith)   JWA5-7754
It Ain't Over Yet (Steve Stone)   JWA5-7755
You Cared Enough (To Give Your Very Best)
   (Slate-Keith)   JWA5-7756   RCA PB-11918B

Session: December 11, 1979, The Soundshop Studios, Nashville
Producer: Montgomery
Musicians: same as February 12-13, 1979

If She Looked at Me (Kenny O'Dell)   JWA5-8009
Let's Get It While the Gettin's Good*
   (Bobby Springfield)   JWA5-8010   RCA PB-11918A
Sally K. (Grant-Burgess)   JWA5-8011

Session: February 29, 1980, The Soundshop Studios, Nashville
Producer: Montgomery
Musicians: same as July 31, 1979

Two Hearts Beat Better Than One
   (Hoffman-Page-Kennedy)   KWA5-8305   RCA PB-12226B
Happy Everything (Stephens-Black)   KWA5-8306
The Rose (Amanda Broom)   KWA5-8307

Don't Look Now (But We Just Fell in Love)
   (Slate-Silbar)   KWA5-8308   RCA PB-12136A
There Are Women (Then There's My Woman)
   (Lorber-Silbar-Jobe)   KWA5-8309   RCA PB-12136B

Session: March 13, 1980, The Soundshop Studios, Nashville
Producer: Montgomery
Musicians: same as July 31, 1979

Love Can Move Mountains (Harry Middlebrooks)   KWA5-8366
I Wish That I Had Loved You Better (Chick Rains) KWA5-8367
Lovin' in the Good Old Days (Lance-Oates-Oates) KWA5-8368
If the World Should Ever Run Out of Love
   (Johnny Slate)   KWA5-8369
Bally-Hoo Days* (Pippin-Henley-Vanhoy-Keith-Slate) KWA5-8370   RCA PB-12226A

Session: October 29–30, 1980, The Soundshop Studios, Nashville
Producer: Montgomery
Musicians: same as July 31, 1979

October 29
One of Those People (Dennis William Wilson)   KWA5-8574†
I Keep Falling in Love with You Over and
   Over Again (Bobby Springfield)   KWA5-8575†
I Know A Good Thing When I Feel It
   (Bobby Springfield)   KWA5-8576†
Hold Me (Till the Last Waltz Is Over) (Bill Nash) KWA5-8577†
Being Loved by You (Johnson-Stone)   KWA5-8578†
I'll Be Over (Slate-Keith-Roberts)   KWA5-8579†

October 30
I'm Still Feeling It (Ben Peters)   KWA5-8580†
Roses and Rainbows (DuBois-Newton)   KWA5-8581†
Easin' on Back (Goodrum-Newton)   KWA5-8582†
Kiss and Tell (Lee Morgan)   KWA5-8583†
You and I (Morrison-Robb-Keith)   KWA5-8584†

Session: July 30, 1981, Columbia Recording Studios, Nashville
Producer: Norro Wilson
Musicians: Gene Chrisman (drm), Morris (perc), Pursell (pno), Billy Sanford (gtr), Strzelecki
(b), Wade (gtr), string acc (added later), voc acc (added later)

Don't It Break Your Heart (Jordan-David)   LWA5-6521   RCA PB-13000B
Honey I Don't Love You (Parker-Potter)   LWA5-6522
This Ain't Tennessee and She Ain't You
   (Bastain-Shaw)   LWA5-6523

Session: August 10, 1981, Music City Music Hall Studios, Nashville
Producer: Wilson
Musicians: Capps (gtr), Chrisman (drm), Sanford (gtr), Wade (gtr), Bobby Wood (pno), Bob
Wray (b), voc acc

Don't Throw Our Love to the Wind (Dave Burgess) LWA5-6524
In Love with Loving You (Stegall-Monk)   LWA5-6525   RCA PB-13094B
Missouri Woman (Leslie-Horton)   LWA5-6526

Session: October 13, 1981, Music City Music Hall Studios, Nashville

Producer: Wilson
Musicians: Briggs (pno), Carrigan (drm), Lance (gtr), Leech (b), Bobby Thompson (gtr), Wade (gtr), strings and voc acc (added later)

Memories of Us (Martin-Kirby)	LWA5-6601	
Don't Give Up on Me (Ben Peters)	LWA5-6602	RCA PB-13094A
All I'm Missing Is You (Wayland Holyfield)	LWA5-6603	RCA PB-13000A
I Keep Running (Cindy Walker)	LWA5-6604	

Session: May 28, 1982, Music City Music Hall Studios, Nashville
Producer: Wilson
Musicians: Briggs (pno), Chrisman (drm), Lance (gtr), Leech (b), Wade (gtr), Young (gtr)

All But One (Holyfield-Wilson)	MWA5-8638†	
Long Lost Lover (Greenebaum-Gemeiner)	MWA5-8639†	
Wooden Heart (Wise-Weisman-Twomey-Kaempfert)	MWA5-8640	RCA PB-13452B

Session: August 19, 1982, Music City Music Hall Studios, Nashville
Producer: Wilson
Musicians: unknown (but personnel probably includes musicians who appear in November 1982 sessions)

The Valley Below (Knutson-Barlow-Burgess)	MWA5-8750	RCA PB-13339A
How's the World Treating You (Bryant-Atkins)	MWA5-8751†	
The Blues Don't Care Who's Got 'Em (Lee-Holyfield)	MWA5-8752	RCA PB-13452A

Session: November 1, 1982, Music City Music Hall Studios, Nashville
Producer: Wilson
Musicians: H. Bradley (gtr), Edenton (gtr), Sonny Garrish (steel gtr), Harman (drm), Lance (gtr), Leech (b), McCoy (hca), Gary Prim (pno), Sanford (gtr), voc acc (added later)

Let Me Put the Love Back in Your Life (Schroeder-Grover)	MWA-8958†
My Broken Heart Made Someone Happy (Holyfield-Arledge)	MWA-8959
Take A Chance on Love (Black-Holmes)	MWA-8960†

Session: November 23, 1982, Music City Music Hall Studios, Nashville
Producer: Wilson
Musicians: same as November 1, 1982, without Sonny Garrish

We're Love Makers (Bobby Springfield)	MWA5-9002
Hold Me (Till The Last Waltz Is Over) (Bill Nash)	MWA5-9003
Son (Reed-Roberts)	MWA5-9004
Sweetheart (Gibb-Gibb)	MWA5-9005

Session: November 30, 1982, Music City Music Hall Studios, Nashville
Producer: Wilson
Musicians: same as November 1, 1982

Close Enough to Love (Ben Peters)	MWA5-9006
All This Could Have Been Mine (Schroeder-Mandel-Sachs)	MWA5-9007
Making Memories (Rhett Davis)	MWA5-9008

Session: (all dates in 1989) February 22, April 7, May 8, May 16, May 31, June 30, Bradley's Barn Studios, Mount Juliet, Tennessee
Producer: H. Bradley
Musicians: Beegie Adair (pno), H. Bradley (gtr), Ferguson (b), Harman (drm), Lance (gtr), synths (added later), saxophone (added later)

February 22
To Each His Own (Livingston-Evans)	WWA5-0012	
It's Been A Long, Long Time (Cahn-Styne)	WWA5-0008	
You Don't Miss A Thing* (Fred Knipe)	?	RCA 2750-7-RA[5]
And I Love You So (Don McLean)	WWA5-0005	

April 7
That's My Desire (Loveday-Kressa)	WWA5-0013
As Time Goes By (Herman Hupfield)	WWA5-0004
You'll Never Know (Gordon-Warren)	WWA5-0009
Say A Long Goodbye (Shannon-Johnson)	?

May 8
The Nearness of You (Washington-Carmichael)	WWA5-0002
Can't Help Falling in Love (Weiss-Peretti-Creatore)	WWA5-0006
Always (Irving Berlin)	?†
I'll Never Stop Loving You (Cahn-Brodsky)	?†

May 16
I Love You Because (Leon Payne)	WWA5-0001
But Beautiful (Burke-Van Heusen)	?†
You Are So Beautiful (Preston-Fisher)	WWA5-0011
The Way You Look Tonight (Fields-Kern)	WWA5-0003

May 31
You Belong to Me (King-Stewart-Price)	WWA5-0007
Yours (Sherr-Rodriguez-Roig)	?†
You Must Have Been A Beautiful Baby (Warren-Mercer)	WWA5-0010
(You May Not Be An Angel But) I'll String Along with You (Dubin-Warren)	WWA5-0015

June 30
I Only Have Eyes for You (Dubin-Warren)	WWA5-0014
It's Been A Long, Long Time (Cahn-Styne)	WWA5-0008
I'm in the Mood for Love (Fields-McHugh)	?†
Snowfall (Fred Knipe)	?

Session: November 8, 1989, Bradley's Barn Studios, Mount Juliet, Tennessee
Producer: H. Bradley
Musicians: H. Bradley (gtr), Briggs (pno), Ferguson (b), Harman (drm), Lance (gtr), string acc (added later), synths (added later), voc acc (added later)

Somebody Loves You (Harry Middlebrooks)	?
If I Had You (Mayo-Chater)	?
(I'd Choose) You Again (Overstreet-Schlitz)	?

---

[5]RCA once again changed their numbering system—the "A" at the end of the catalog number indicates A-side.

Session: September 6, 1990, Bradley's Barn Studios, Mount Juliet, Tennessee
Producer: H. Bradley
Musicians: H. Bradley (pno), Ferguson (b), Harman (drm), Tony Migliore (synths),
Wade (gtr), string acc (added later), voc acc (added later)

A Lady Like You (Stegall-Weatherly)	?	
Over (Jerry Fuller)	?	
Surround Me with Love (Holyfield-Wilson)	?	

Session: September 17, 1990, Bradley's Barn Studios, Mount Juliet, Tennessee
Producer: H. Bradley
Musicians: H. Bradley (gtr), Harman (drm), Johnny Johnson (b), Migliore (synth),
Johnny Minick (pno), string acc (added later), voc acc (added later)

Just One Time (Don Gibson)	?	RCA 2750-7-RB
Can I Put You in A Love Song (Fred Knipe)	?	
To Have and to Hold (Don McLean)	?	

Session: October 21, 1991, Bradley's Barn Studios, Mount Juliet, Tennessee
Producer: H. Bradley
Musicians: H. Bradley (gtr), Capps (gtr), Harman (drm), Stephen Hill (vocals), Robbins (pno),
Wade (gtr), string acc (added later), synths (added later), voc acc (added later)

Afraid (Fred Rose)	?	
Out of the Blue* (Fred Knipe)	?	RCA 62598-7A
When the Wind Blows (In Chicago) (Murphy-Turner)	?	

Session: December 18, 1991, Bradley's Barn Studios, Mount Juliet, Tennessee
Producer: H. Bradley
Musicians: same as October 21, 1991, without Stephen Hill and with Gary Prim (kybds)
and Johnson (b)

How's the Weather Back in Tennessee (Weatherly-Durrill)	?	
I've Just Got A Feelin' 'Bout You (Fred Knipe)	?	
On A Night Like This (Jones-McGuire)	?	RCA 62598-7B

Session: February 4, 1992, Bradley's Barn Studios, Mount Juliet, Tennessee
Producer: H. Bradley
Musicians: H. Bradley (gtr), Capps (gtr), Harman (drm), Johnson (b), Minick (pno), Robbins
(pno), Wade (gtr), string acc (added later), synths (added later), voc acc (added later)

She Makes My Roses Grow (Wayne Carson)	?
Last of the Love Song Singers (Wayne Carson)	?

Session: July 20, 1992, Bradley's Barn Studios, Mount Juliet, Tennessee
Producer: H. Bradley
Musicians: H. Bradley (gtr), Ferguson (b), Harman (drm), Minick (pno), Robbins (pno),
Wade (gtr), string acc (added later), voc acc (added later)

I've So Much to Be Thankful For (Douglas-Mullan)	?
If You Could Only Love Me Now (Burgess-Pfrimmer)	?†

Discography

EXTENDED PLAYS

1952	To Mother	EPA-239
	Eddy Arnold Sings	EPA-260
	Eddy Arnold's Favorite Sacred Songs	EPA-261
	Country Classics	EPB-3027
	All-Time Hits from the Hill (Vol. 1)	EPB-3031
	All-Time Hits from the Hills (Vol. 2)	EPA-328
1953	The Old Rugged Cross	EPA-427
	All Time Favorites, Vol. I	EPA-428
	All Time Favorites, Vol. II	EPA-429
	Christmas Greetings by Eddy Arnold	EPA-473
	Open Thy Merciful Arms	EPA-500
	Songs of Hope and Inspiration	EPA-544
1954	I Really Don't Want to Know	EPA-573
1955	Top Hits Round-Up	EPA-624
	Cattle Call	EPA-712
	An American Institution	EPB-3230
1956	All-Time Favorites	EPA-786
	Anytime	EPA-787
	The Chapel on the Hill	EPA-788
	Hits from "The Most Happy Fella"	EPA-900
	Wanderin'	EPA-912
	Tennessee Waltz	EPA-913
	Cold, Cold Heart	EPA-914
	Slow Poke	EPA-915
1957	A Little on the Lonely Side	EPA-972
	The Very Thought of You	EPA-973
	September Song	EPA-974
	When They Were Young	EPA-1-1484
	Songs from Happy Hunting	EPA 4037
1958	My Darling, My Darling, Vol. I	EPA-1-1575
	My Darling, My Darling, Vol. II	EPA-2-1575
	My Darling, My Darling, Vol. III	EPA-3-1575
	Eddy Arnold Time	EPA-4109
	Specially for the Little Ones	EPA-4220
	Eddy Arnold	EPA-5019
	Bouquet of Roses	EPA-5055
1959	Kentucky Waltz	EPA-5087
1960	Tennessee's Eddy Arnold	EPA-5126
	Take Me in Your Arms	EPA-5150

78 RPM ALBUMS

1948	All Time Hits from the Hills	P-195
1949	To Mother	P-239
	Eddy Arnold Sings	P-260
1950	Eddy Arnold's Favorite Sacred Songs	P-261
1951	All Time Hits from the Hills (Vol. 2)	P-328
1952	Country Classics	P-3027

LONG PLAYING ALBUMS

1952	Country Classics	LPM-3027
	All-Time Hits from the Hills, Vol. I	LPM-3031
1953	All-Time Favorites	LPM-3117
1954	When It's Round-Up Time in Heaven	LPM-3219
	Eddy Arnold—An American Institution	LPMX-3230
1955	Wanderin'*	LPM-1111
1956	All-Time Favorites*	LPM-1223
	Anytime*	LPM-1224
	The Chapel on the Hill	LPM-1225
	A Dozen Hits	LPM-1293
1957	A Little on the Lonely Side	LPM-1377
	When They Were Young	LPM-1484
1958	My Darling, My Darling	LPM-1575
	Praise Him, Praise Him	LPM-1733
1959	Have Guitar, Will Travel*	LPM/LSP-1928
	Thereby Hangs A Tale*	LPM/LSP-2036
1960	Eddy Arnold Sings Them Again	LPM/LSP-2185
	You Gotta Have Love	LPM/LSP-2268
1961	Let's Make Memories Tonight	LPM/LSP-2337
1962	One More Time	LPM/LSP-2471
	Christmas with Eddy Arnold	LPM/LSP-2554
1963	Cattle Call*	LPM/LSP-2578
	Our Man Down South*	LPM/LSP-2596
	Faithfully Yours	LPM/LSP-2629

1964	Folk Song Book*	LPM/LSP-2811
	Sometimes I'm Happy, Sometimes I'm Blue*	LPM/LSP-2909
	Pop Hits from the Country Side*	LPM/LSP-2951
1965	The Easy Way	LPM/LSP-3361
	My World*	LPM/LSP-3466
1966	I Want to Go with You*	LPM/LSP-3507
	The Best of Eddy Arnold	LPM/LSP-3565
	The Last Word in Lonesome	LPM/LSP-3622
	Somebody Like Me	LPM/LSP-3715
1967	Lonely Again	LPM/LSP-3753
	Turn the World Around*	LPM/LSP-3869
1968	The Everlovin' World of Eddy Arnold*	LPM/LSP-3931
	The Romantic World of Eddy Arnold	LPM/LSP-4009
	Walkin' in Love Land*	LSP-4089
1969	Songs of the Young World*	LSP-4110
	The Glory of Love	LSP-4179
	The Warmth of Eddy	LSP-4231
1970	Love and Guitars*	LSP-4304
	The Best of Eddy Arnold, Vol. II	LSP-4320
	Standing Alone*	LSP-4390
1971	Portrait of My Woman*	LSP-4471
	Welcome to My World	LSP-4570
	Loving Her Was Easier	LSP-4625
1972	Lonely People	LSP-4718
	Eddy Arnold Sings for Housewives and Other Lovers	LSP-4738
1973	The Best of Eddy Arnold, Vol. III	LSP-4844
1976	Eddy*	APL1-1817
1977	I Need You All the Time	APL1-2277
1979	Somebody Loves You	AHL1-3358
1980	A Legend and His Lady	AHL1-3606
1981	A Man for All Seasons*	AHL1-3914
1982	Easin' on Back to Love	AHL1-4126
	Don't Give Up on Me	AHL1-4263
1983	Close Enough to Love	AHL1-4661
1990	You Don't Miss A Thing*	3020-2/4 R
	Hand-Holdin' Songs	9963-1-R
1993	Last of the Love Song Singers: Then and Now*	07863-66046-2/4

Camden (an RCA Victor Label)

Albums

1959	Eddy Arnold*	CAL/CAS-471
1960	More Eddy Arnold*	CAL/CAS-563
1963	Country Songs I Love to Sing* [later titled "Songs I Love to Sing"]	CAL/CAS-741
1964	Eddy's Songs*	CAL/CAS-798
1965	I'm Throwing Rice (At the Girl I Love) and Other Favorites by Eddy Arnold*	CAL/CAS-897
1971	Then You Can Tell Me Goodbye Chained to A Memory	CAS-2501 CXS-9007
1973	I Love How You Love Me Echoes	ACL1-0099 ACL-7025
1974	Misty Blue	ACL1-0458

MGM

Long Playing Albums

1973	So Many Ways/If the Whole World Stopped Lovin' She's Got Everything I Need	SE-4878 SE-4912
1974	I Wish That I Had Loved You Better	M3G-4961
1975	World of Eddy Arnold	M-4992
1976	Eddy Arnold: World of Hits	MJB-5017

Curb

Albums

1995	Greatest Songs	D2-77767

BIBLIOGRAPHY

General

Billboard magazine. 1940–1971.

Court trial papers. *Arnold, A. A. et al. v. D. S. Parker et al.* 846. Chancery Court at Henderson, Tenn. 1929.

Court trial papers. *Upson, Dean R. v. Arnold, Richard E.* 67214. Chancery Court at Nashville, Tennessee. 1949.

Journal of the Academy for the Preservation of Old-Time Country Music. 1992–1994.

McNatt, Howard. Unpublished diaries. 1937–1940

MGM Records. Recording sheets 1973–1975. Unpublished. Courtesy of Polygram Records Inc.

RCA Records. Recording sheets 1944–1982. Unpublished. Courtesy of Bertelsmann Music Group.

Reference Material

Allen, Bob, ed. *The Blackwell Guide to Recorded Country Music.* Cambridge, Mass.: Blackwell Publishers, 1994.

Arnold, Eddy. *It's a Long Way from Chester County.* Old Tappan, N.J.: Hewitt House, 1969.

Csida, Joseph. *The Music/Record Career Handbook.* New York: Billboard Publications, 1980.

Davis, Skeeter. *Bus Fare to Kentucky: The Autobiography of Skeeter Davis.* New York: Birch Lane Press, 1993.

Delmore, Alton. *The Delmore Brothers: Truth Is Stranger Than Publicity,* 2nd ed. Nashville: Country Music Foundation Press, 1995.

Dennisoff, R. Serge. *Waylon: A Biography.* Knoxville: University of Tennessee Press, 1987.

Escott, Colin, with George Merritt and William MacEwen. *Hank Williams: The Biography.* Boston: Little, Brown, 1994.

Goldblatt, Burt, and Robert Shelton. *The Country Music Story: A Picture History of Country and Western Music.* Indianapolis: Bobbs-Merrill Company Inc., 1966.

Hall, Wade. *Hell-Bent for Music: The Life of Pee Wee King.* Lexington: University of Kentucky Press, 1996.

Harris, Sheldon. *Blues Who's Who: A Biographical Dictionary of Blues Singers.* New York: Da Capo, 1979.

Hemphill, Paul. *The Nashville Sound: Bright Lights and Country Music.* New York: Simon and Schuster, 1970.

Jasper, Tony. *The Top Twenty Book: The Official British Record Charts, 1955–1993.* London: Blandford, 1994.

Jones, Lewis P. *Cemeteries in Chester County.* Henderson, Tenn.: White Printing, 1992.

Katz, Ephraim. *The Film Encyclopedia.* New York: Harper Perennial, 1994.

King, Lee Nell. *The History of the Friendship Community of Chester County, Tennessee.* Henderson, Tenn.: White Printing, 1996.

Larkin, Colin, ed. *The Guiness Encyclopedia of Popular Music,* Vol. 1. Middlesex, England: Guiness Publishing, 1992.

Lipsitz, George. *The Sidewalks of St. Louis: Places, People, and Politics in an American City.* Columbia: University of Missouri Press, 1991.

Malone, Bill C. *Country Music, U.S.A.,* 2nd ed. Austin: University of Texas Press, 1985.

McCloud, Barry, and contributing writers. *Definitive Country: The Ultimate Encyclopedia of Country Music and Its Performers.* New York: Perigee, 1995.

Paris, Mike, and Chris Comber. *Jimmie the Kid: The Life of Jimmie Rodgers.* London: Eddison Press Ltd., 1977.

Sanjak, Russell. Updated by David Sanjak. *Pennies from Heaven: The American Popular Music Business in the Twentieth Century.* New York: Da Capo, 1996.

Savage, William W. *Singing Cowboys and All That Jazz: A Short History of Popular Music in Oklahoma.* Norman: University of Oklahoma Press, 1983.

Shestack, Melvin. *The Country Music Encyclopedia.* New York: Thomas Crowell Company, 1974.

Snow, Hank, with Jack Ownbey and Bob Burris. *The Hank Snow Story.* Urbana: University of Illinois Press, 1994.

Stambler, Irwin, and Grellun Landon. *The Encyclopedia of Folk, Country & Western Music.* New York: St. Martin's Press, 1984.

Tindall, George Brown. *America: A Narrative History,* Vols. 1 and 2. New York: Norton, 1984.

Variety's Film Reviews, 1949–1953. New York: R. R. Bowker, 1983.

Variety Radio Directory. New York: Variety, 1938–1941.

Whitburn, Joel. *Pop Memories, 1890–1954.* Menomonee Falls, Wis.: Record Research, 1986.

Whitburn, Joel. *Top Country Singles, 1944–1993.* Menomonee Falls, Wis.: Record Research, 1986.

Whitburn, Joel. *Top Pop Singles, 1955–1993.* Menomonee Falls, Wis.: Record Research, 1994.

Wolfe, Charles K. *Tennessee Strings: The Story of Country Music in Tennessee.* Knoxville: University of Tennessee Press, 1977.

Prologue

Author Interviews: Jim Foglesong

Chapter 1

Corlew, Robert C. *Tennessee: A Short History.* Knoxville: University of Tennessee Press, 1981.

Federal Writers' Project of the Works Projects Administration for the State of Tennessee. *Tennessee: A Guide to the State.* New York: The Viking Press, 1939.

Gibson, Arrell M. *The Chickasaws.* Norman: University of Oklahoma Press, 1971.

Reid, S. E. *A Brief History of Chester County.* Jackson, Tenn.: McCowat-Mercer Press, 1967.

Swanton, John R. *The Indians of the Southwestern United States.* Washington, D.C.: Smithsonian Institution Press, 1979.

Tennessee Historical Commission. "Historic Front Street." Historical Marker 4C33.

Williams, Samuel Cole. *Beginning of West Tennessee: In the Land of the Chickasaws, 1541–1841.* Johnson City, Tenn.: The Watauga Press, 1930.

Author Interviews: Eddy Arnold, Moselle Jones

Chapter 2

Arnold, A. A. et al. v. D. S. Parker et al. 846. Chancery Court at Henderson, Tenn. 1929.

Arnold, Eddy. Interview with producers. "The Eddy Arnold Story" (radio documentary). 1973.

"Chester County in Good Shape for New Year." *Chester County Independent.* January 2, 1930.

Deen, Dixie. "Eddy Arnold: His World." *Music City News.* April 1966.

"Farmers Are Urged to Improve Farm Methods." *Chester County Independent.* May 27, 1930.

"Farmers Told How to Meet Drought Emergency." *Chester County Independent.* August 14, 1930.

"First Airplane Mail Carrier." *Nashville Banner.* May 15, 1918.

"French Troops Make Attack Near Hailles." *Nashville Banner.* May 15, 1918.

"Hot Weather and Low Prices Cut Egg Production." *Chester County Independent.* August 14, 1930.

Latham, Willard. Interview with producers. "The Eddy Arnold Story" (radio documentary). 1973.

Moore, David. Interview with producers. "The Eddy Arnold Story" (radio documentary). 1973.

"To Unveil Marker on Shiloh Field." *Nashville Banner.* May 15, 1918.

Victor Talking Machine Company advertisement. *Nashville Banner.* May 15, 1918.

Author Interviews: Eddy Arnold, Odessia Austin, Tauso Branch, Robert Jones, Exie Latham, Jamie Nash, David Weir

Chapter 3

Deen, Dixie. "Eddy Arnold: His World." *Music City News.* April 1966.

Prima, James Neal. *Lion of the Valley: St. Louis, Missouri.* Boulder, Colo.: Pratt Publishing Co., 1981.

Workers of the Writers' Program of the Works Projects Administration in the State of Missouri. *Missouri: A Guide to the "Show Me" State.* New York: Hastings House, 1959.

Author Interviews: Earl Aldrich, Eddy Arnold, Stephen Davis, Don McNatt, Lynn McNatt, Melton McNatt, Gabe Tucker

Chapter 4

Arnold, Eddy. Interview with Archie Campbell. "Yesteryear in Nashville" (television show). 1982.

Arnold, Eddy. Interview with Lorraine Crook and Charlie Chase. "Music City Tonight" (television show). May 24, 1995.

"Camp Talent 37G Weekly." *Billboard.* January 24, 1942.

Eddy Arnold advertisement. *Billboard Music Year Book.* Cincinnati: Billboard Publishing, 1944.

"Eddy Arnold . . . Marco Polo with a Guitar." *Radio Mirror.* August 1943.

"Eight Thousand Enlisted Men Pack Ft. Sam Houston Service Club." *The Military Service.* December 12, 1941.

Federal Writers' Project of the Works Projects Administration for the State of Tennessee. *Tennessee: A Guide to the State.* New York: The Viking Press, 1939.

Green, Douglas, ed. "The Grand Ole Opry, 1944–45: A Radio Log Kept by Dick Hill of Tecumseh, Nebraska." *Journal of Country Music* Vol. V, No. 3.

King, Pee Wee, with John Rumble. "The Camel Caravan: A Scrapbook." *Journal of Country Music* Vol. X, No. 1.

King, Pee Wee. Interview with Douglas Green. Country Music Foundation Oral History Project. March 8, 1974.

Kitsinger, Otto. Liner notes to *Pee Wee King and His Golden West Cowboys.* Vollersode, Germany: Bear Family Records, 1994.

"My True Romance by Eddy Arnold." *True Romance,* unknown date in 1949.

Pearl, Minnie, with Joan Dew. *Minnie Pearl: An Autobiography.* New York: Simon and Schuster, 1980.

"Traveling Show Here Next Week." *The Reveille.* October 29, 1941.

Upson, Dean R. v. Arnold, Richard E. 67214. Chancery Court at Nashville, Tennessee. 1949.

Wolfe, Charles K. *The Grand Ole Opry: The Early Years, 1925–1935.* London: Old Time Music, 1975.

World of Country Music. Cincinnati: Billboard Publishing, 1966.

Author Interviews: Eddy Arnold, Sally Arnold, Harold Bradley, Owen Bradley, Dolly Denny, Danny Dill, Rollin Sullivan, Gabe Tucker, Irving Waugh, Roy Wiggins

Chapter 5

Carlton, Joe. "Oberstein Leaves Victor." *Billboard.* May 29, 1948.

Chase, Sam. "Down Memory Lane with Victor's Folsom." *Billboard.* September 12, 1960.

"Disking Starts, Ban's Over." *Billboard.* November 18, 1944.

McNatt, Howard. Interview with producers. "The Eddy Arnold Story" (radio documentary) 1973.

Miller, Neville. "The Recording Ban." *Billboard.* May 8, 1943.

Orodenker, M. H. "Folk Record Reviews." *Billboard.* June 9, 1945.

"Sholes' Life Reads Like History Lesson in A&R." *Billboard.* March 20, 1961.

Sholes, Steve. Interview with Mike Lipskin. Country Music Foundation Oral History Project. January-March, 1968.

"Thar's Gold in Them Thar Hillbilly and Other American Folk Tunes." *Billboard.* September 26, 1942.

Upson, Dean R. v. Arnold, Richard E. 67214. Chancery Court at Nashville, Tennessee. 1949.

Walker, Frank B., "Dean Dies at 74." *Billboard.* October 26, 1963.

Wiggins, Roy. Interview with Douglas Green. Country Music Foundation Oral History Project. April 25, 1974, and May 9, 1974.

Wolfe, Charles K. *The Grand Ole Opry: The Early Years, 1925–1935.* London: Old Time Music, 1975.

Author Interviews: Eddy Arnold, Owen Bradley, Joe Csida, Jim Foglesong, Bob McCluskey, Rollin Sullivan, Gabe Tucker, Roy Wiggins

Chapter 6

"American Folk Tunes." *Billboard.* November 8, 1947.

"American Folk Tunes." *Billboard.* February 28, 1948.

Bivin, Virginia. "Honest, Eddy, Virginia Doesn't Have Your Signature." *Nashville Banner.* August 19, 1955.

Carlton, Joe. "Oberstein Leaves Victor." *Billboard.* May 29, 1948

Hurst, Jack. *Nashville's Grand Ole Opry.* New York: Harry N. Abrams, Inc., 1975.

"Show's Star." *Nashville Tennessean.* December 31, 1946.

Sippel, Johnny. "Folk Talent and Tunes." *Billboard.* November 25, 1950.

Upson, Dean R. v. Arnold, Richard E. 67214. Chancery Court at Nashville, Tennessee. 1949.

Wiggins, Roy. Interview with Douglas Green. Country Music Foundation Oral History Project. April 25, 1974 and May 9, 1974.

Author Interviews: Eddy Arnold, Owen Bradley, Jack Burgess, Joe Csida, Danny Dill, Charles Grean, John D. Loudermilk, Rollin Sullivan, Roy Wiggins, Chuck Wright

Chapter 7

Arnold, Eddy. Interview with Ralph Emery. "Eddy Arnold: An Inside Look" (television show). 1991.

Arnold, Eddy. Interview with Ralph Emery. "The Ralph Emery Show" (radio show). May 26, 1980.

Broadcasting Yearbook. Washington, D.C.: Broadcasting Publications, Inc., 1950.

"Corn of Plenty." *Newsweek.* June 13, 1949.

"Eddy Arnold to Get 3 Awards on Coast Guard Show Tonight." *Washington Star.* March 27, 1949.

Review of "Hometown Reunion." *Variety.* September 22, 1948.

"RMA Monthly Reports on TV and Radio Set Production." Television Rates and Factbook. October 1, 1949.

Sippel, Johnny. "Folk Talent and Tunes." *Billboard.* April 16, 1949.

Author Interviews: Eddy Arnold, Harold Bradley, Owen Bradley, Jack Burgess, Carolina Cotton, Danny Dill, Ann Dodelin, Charles Grean, John D. Loudermilk, Brad McCuen, Gabe Tucker, Irving Waugh

Chapter 8

Bivin, Virginia. "Honest, Eddy, Virginia Doesn't Have Your Signature." *Nashville Banner.* August 19, 1955.

Upson, Dean R. v. Arnold, Richard E. 67214. Chancery Court at Nashville, Tennessee. 1949.

Author Interviews: Eddy Arnold, Johnny Hicks, Bob McCluskey, Brad McCuen, Jeff Miller, Roy Wiggins

Chapter 9

Arnold, Eddy. Interview with producers. "The Eddy Arnold Story" (radio documentary). 1973.

Arnold, Eddy. Interview with Ralph Emery. "Eddy Arnold: An Inside Look" (television show). 1991.

"Arnold, Parker Split Up Team." *Billboard*. September 5, 1953.

Asbell, Bernie. "Nashville on Rise as Hit-Making Hub." *Billboard*. February 1, 1960.

"Csida-Green Ink Arnold; Mull Pact." *Billboard*. June 12, 1954.

Eddy Arnold advertisement. *Billboard*. September 20, 1952.

"Eddy Arnold Plans Entry into TV Film." *Billboard*. September 4, 1954.

Kienzle, Rich. "The Forgotten Hank Garland." *Journal of Country Music* Vol. IX, No. 3.

Sachs, Bill. "Folk Talent and Tunes." *Billboard*. July 2, 1955.

Sachs, Bill. "Folk Talent and Tunes." *Billboard*. October 1, 1955.

Schnickel, Steve. "'Arnold Time' Packs Lore for Podunk, U.S.A." *Billboard*. December 18, 1954.

Teeter, H. B. "200 Guests from Several States Honor Folk Singer Eddy Arnold Here." *Nashville Tennessean*. June 6, 1955.

Wiggins, Roy. Interview with Douglas Green. Country Music Foundation Oral History Project. April 25, 1974, and May 9, 1974.

Author Interviews: Eddy Arnold, Jo Ann Arnold, Chick Crumpacker, Joe Csida, Bob Davie, Charles Grean, Betty Johnson, Gordon Stoker, Roy Wiggins

Chapter 10

Arnold, Eddy. Interview with Archie Campbell. "Yesteryear in Nashville" (television show). 1982.

Arnold, Eddy. *It's a Long Way from Chester County*. Old Tappan, N.J.: Hewitt House, 1969.

"Arnold to Give $5000 in Records to Orphanages." *Nashville Banner*. May 13, 1949.

Bundy, June. "Country & Western Music Holds Line on the Video Frontier." *Billboard*. March 3, 1956.

Churchill, Peg. "Eddy Arnold a 'Country Boy' Who'd Sing Pop If He Likes It." *Schenectady Gazette*. July 11, 1973.

Csida, Joe. Liner notes to *A Little on the Lonely Side*. New York: RCA Victor, 1957.

"E. Arnold for Bishop Sheen." *Billboard*. April 21, 1956.

Eddy Arnold advertisement. *Billboard*. February 4, 1956.

"Eddy Arnold Heads Troupe at Boxwell Report Banquet." *Nashville Banner*. May 13, 1959.

"Eddy Arnold Not a Candidate for Congress Seat." *Nashville Banner.* June 7, 1963.

"Eddy Arnold Time" advertisement. *Billboard.* September 3, 1955.

"Eddy Arnold, 'School Daze' Star, Sees Revival of 'Better Music.'" *Nashville Banner.* April 3, 1957.

Greene, Lee S. *Lead Me On: Frank Goad Clement and Tennessee Politics.* Knoxville: University of Tennessee Press, 1982.

Guralnick, Peter. *Last Train to Memphis: The Rise of Elvis Presley.* Boston: Little, Brown, 1994.

Sachs, Bill. "Folk Talent and Tunes." *Billboard.* June 30, 1958.

"Sholes Succeeds Carlton in Victor Pop A&R Slot." *Billboard.* August 19, 1957.

Sholes, Steve. "Preparation and Concentration Make Eddy Disk Sensation." *Billboard* (RCA Victor supplement). January 15, 1955.

Twitty, Kathryn. "Music as Written." *Billboard.* July 13, 1959.

Twitty, Pat. "Music as Written." *Billboard.* October 26, 1959.

Zhito, Lee. "Cap. Names Csida Veepee to Head All Eastern Operations." *Billboard.* February 1, 1960.

Author Interviews: Eddy Arnold, Jo Ann Arnold, Sally Arnold, Chet Atkins, Chick Crumpacker, Joe Csida, Bob Davie, Louis Grasmick, Charles Green, Betty Johnson, Gordon Stoker, Cindy Walker

Chapter 11

Arnold, Eddy. Interview with Ralph Emery. "The Ralph Emery Show" (radio show). May 26, 1980.

Arnold, Eddy. *It's a Long Way from Chester County.* Old Tappan, N.J.: Hewitt House, 1969.

Asbell, Bernie. "Nashville on Rise as Hit-Making Hub." *Billboard.* February 1, 1960.

Chase, Sam. "Bob Yorke's Success Story: Limitation, Selection, Hustle." *Billboard.* May 19, 1962.

"Csida + Nashville + Public = 1 Million." *Billboard.* February 29, 1964.

"Csida Exits RIC; Gets Album Line; Barone Quits." *Billboard.* February 20, 1965.

"Csida Expands in Many Areas." *Billboard.* May 25, 1963.

"Joe Csida Quits Capitol; 'Policy Differences' Cited." *Billboard.* September 8, 1962.

"NBC-TV to Star Arnold in New Series." *Billboard.* September 12, 1960.

Porter, Bill. Interview with John Rumble. Country Music Foundation Oral History Project. November 13, 1994.

"Vets Re-Cut Own Old Hits to R&R Beat." *Billboard.* October 28, 1958.

Author Interviews: Eddy Arnold, Jo Ann Arnold, Chet Atkins, Brenton Banks, Gordon Bossin, Joe Csida, Charles Green, Anita Kerr, Sheldon Kurland, Louis Nunley, Jerry Purcell

Chapter 12

"Arnold to Sing with Symphony." *Billboard.* December 11, 1965.

Arnold, Eddy. Interview with Ralph Emery. The Ralph Emery Show (radio show). May 30, 1980.

de Vekey, Andre. "Arnold Digs U.K., Vice Versa." *Billboard.* February 1, 1966.

"Eddy Arnold on Concerts." *Billboard.* June 18, 1966.

"Eddy Arnold Pulls Tall $74,626 in 11 C&W Dates." *Billboard.* March 16, 1966.

Escott, Colin. "Jim Reeves: Welcome to His World." *Goldmine.* November 11, 1994.

Hall, Claude. "Arnold Delivers Haymaker at His Carnegie Hall Bow." *Billboard.* June 4, 1966.

Palmer, Robert. *Deep Blues.* New York: Penguin Books, 1982.

Ruth, Jim. "Singer Eddy Arnold Still 'Crossing Over.'" *Lancaster Sun News.* October 9, 1983.

Schoenfeld, Herm. "Nashville's Eddy Arnold in Carnegie Hall to Musical $10^{1}/_{2}$G Gross." *Variety.* May 25, 1966.

Author Interviews: Eddy Arnold, Bob Ferguson, Jim Foglesong, Anita Kerr, Sheldon Kurland, Wayne Moss, Louis Nunley, Jerry Purcell, Bill Walker

Chapter 13

Buck Owens advertisement. *Music City News.* January 1967.

Burkes, M. R. Letter to Country Music Hall of Fame. January 22, 1968.

"Eddy Arnold's Style Matures, Now He's a Country Pop Singer." *Pensacola (Fla.) Journal.* January 20, 1968.

"Eddy Arnold on Concerts." *Billboard.* June 18, 1966.

Keathley, Virginia. "The Arnolds Dine at the White House." *Nashville Tennessean.* February 19, 1967.

Kennison, James. Letter to the editor. *Music City News.* November 1966.

Macera, Dom. Letter to the editor. *Music City News.* December 1966.

"RCA Engineers Vie for Awards." *Billboard.* March 12, 1966.

Simon, Marion. "Country Music Is Going to Town." *National Observer.* January 2, 1967.

Welch, Pat. "CMA Names 4 to Hall of Fame." *Nashville Tennessean.* October 22, 1966.

"Which Road Country Music?" *Music City News.* November 1966.

Williams, Bill. "Nashville Sessions Beat Out with Record Rhythm in '67." *Billboard.* December 30, 1967.

Wilson, Edward. Letter to the editor. *Music City News.* December 1966.

Author Interviews: Eddy Arnold, Jo Ann Arnold, Chet Atkins, Jerry Carrigan, John D. Loudermilk, Jim Malloy, Wayne Moss, Louis Nunley, Al Pachucki, Bill Pursell, Chuck Seitz, Henry Strzelecki, Bill Walker

Chapter 14

"Arnold to Talk It Up on NBC-TV Special on Country Music Feb. 9." *Billboard.* January 13, 1968.

Arnold, Eddy. Interview with T. Tommy Cutrer. "Music City U.S.A." (radio show). April 12, 1971.

"'Double Trouble' Poses Threat to Country Tours." *Billboard.* January 28, 1967.

Eberly, Philip K. *Music in the Air: America's Changing Tastes in Popular Music, 1920–1980.* New York: Hastings House, 1982.

Fox, Hank. "Arnold Stars in Pop and Country Grooves." *Billboard.* July 29, 1967.

Gross, Mike. "Victor's Operation Puts on Pop Steam in All Creative Areas." *Billboard.* October 15, 1966.

Hall, Claude. "Wiswell, Purcell Form Co. to Produce B'way Casters." *Billboard.* December 20, 1969.

Hawkins, Glenn. "Eddy Arnold Wins Over 'Sophisticates.'" *Los Angeles Herald-Examiner.* October 4, 1967.

Kirby, Fred. "Arnold Turns His Country Charm on NY City Slickers." *Billboard.* April 6, 1968.

NBC press release. March 11, 1968.

Newton, Dwight. "Those Giddy Music Hall Goings-On." *San Francisco Examiner.* September 14, 1968.

"RCA Disc Chief Dies at Wheel." *Nashville Tennessean.* April 23, 1968.

"Shift at RCA Nashville—Davis Exec Producer." *Billboard.* December 9, 1967.

Author Interviews: Eddy Arnold, Chet Atkins, Jerry Carrigan, Chick Crumpacker, Danny Davis, Jim Foglesong, Don DeLacy, George Hamilton IV, Don McNatt, Jerry Purcell

Chapter 15

Arnold, Eddy. Interview with producers. "The Eddy Arnold Story" (radio documentary). 1973.

Corcoran, Michael. "40 Years Later, Songs of Hank Williams Are Still in Our Hearts." *Dallas Morning News.* January 1, 1993.

Dove, Ian. "Eddy Arnold Puts Polish in Palace Songs." *New York Times.* November 27, 1974.

"Eddy Arnold's Son Critical after Accident." *Nashville Tennessean.* August 3, 1971.

"Eddy Arnold Phases Out Food Firm." *Nashville Banner.* April 20, 1971.

"Hospitalized Arnold's Son Still Critical." *Nashville Banner.* August 3, 1971.

Lesner, Sam. "Eddy Turns on Schmaltz." *Chicago Daily News.* September 2, 1971.

Lewis, Dan. "Eddie Arnold Helping His Son." *Rockford Register.* August 22, 1972.

Author Interviews: Eddy Arnold, Jo Ann Arnold, Sally Arnold, Chet Atkins, Harold Bradley, Owen Bradley, John D. Loudermilk, Jim Malloy, Jerry Purcell, Gabe Tucker

INDEX

Page numbers in *italic* type refer to illustrations.